THE ROMAN RITUAL

In Latin and English
With Rubrics and Planechant Notation

Translated and Edited
With Introduction and Notes by
THE REVEREND PHILIP T. WELLER

VOLUME III
THE BLESSINGS

Caritas Publishing

Nihil obstat: Stephen Anderl, Censor librorum
Imprimatur: ✠ Joannes P. Treacy, S.T.D.,
Coadjutor Episcopus Crossensis
Die 20 Aprilis, 1945

Republished on February 10, 2017, Feast of St. Scholastica

THE ROMAN RITUAL (RITUALE ROMANUM)
3 VOLUME SET, Year of Imprimatur: VOL 1 (1948), VOL 2 (1950), VOL 3 (1945).

ISBNs:

PAPERBACK, COLOR INTERIOR:
Vol 1: Sacraments and Processions: 978-1-945275-14-2
Vol 2: Christian Burial, Exorcisms, Reserved Blessings, Etc.: 978-1-945275-15-9
Vol 3: The Blessings: 978-1-945275-16-6

PAPERBACK, B&W INTERIOR (least expensive):
Vol 1: Sacraments and Processions: 978-1-945275-17-3
Vol 2: Christian Burial, Exorcisms, Reserved Blessings, Etc.: 978-1-945275-18-0
Vol 3: The Blessings: 978-1-945275-19-7

AUTHOR'S FOREWORD

It is my fond hope that this presentation of the Roman Ritual in Latin and English may render a service, first to my brother priests, in as much as it can be used as a manual and reference at the same time. At times it happens that a priest, when administering the sacraments or sacramentals, wishes to add the prayers in vernacular. This is one reason for the appearance of the Ritual in this form, since heretofore only a very small portion has been available in English.

I trust, moreover, that this edition of the Roman Ritual will find a welcome among the laity, and that it may create in them an interest and enthusiasm for the rites and prayers of so important a part of the liturgical books of the Church.

For the translations in verse of the hymns, Stabat Mater, Ut Queant Laxis, Veni Creator Spiritus, Vexilla Regis, I am indebted to the Reverend Matthew Britt's: "The Hymns of the Breviary and Missal," with the kind permission of the author.

I am grateful to the Very Reverend Reynold Hillenbrand and to Dom Godfrey Diekmann, O.S.B. for recommendations of decided value. And an expression of deep gratitude is due the School Sisters of St. Francis for their labor of copying the planechant notation and their painstaking correction of the manuscript.

Every constructive criticism and correction will be welcomed.

CONTENTS

INTRODUCTION

Creation Consecrated and Transformed

The Roman Martyrology on the Nativity of our Lord, Jesus Christ, reads: "The everlasting God and Son of the eternal Father, wishing to consecrate the world by His merciful coming — Jesus Christ made Man is born of the Virgin Mary in Bethlehem of Juda." The Divine Word assumes humanity, creature fashions a tabernacle for Creator, and creation receives consecration from the Anointed of God!

This, in fine, is the reason for God's appearance on earth. He assumed a material body in order that man who had become "of the earth earthly" might once more be made spiritual. "As many as received Him, He gave them power to be made the sons of God" (John I, 12). He came, in fact, to consecrate and transform all things which He had made — primarily man, made to His own image and likeness, and secondarily all irrational creation which He had made subservient to the needs of humanity.

The advent and mission of our Lord have a consecratory character and purpose. And ever since the Incarnation and Redemption, the world has been radically transformed and different from the state it had found itself in as a consequence of the first man's fall from supernatural life. Jesus Christ has consecrated and sacramentalized the world, and on Pentecost He sent His Spirit to captivate and revivify all matter. "The Spirit of the Lord hath filled the entire earth, and He Who sustaineth all things hath knowledge of all men's prayer" (Wisdom I:7: Introit of Pentecost). "Send forth thy Spirit, and the world shall arise as new. And the countenance of the earth shall be renewed" (Psalm CIII:30).

Christ has sacramentalized the world, and Christian man, therefore, is destined to live, and grow, and mature into Christian per-

fection chiefly by means of sacramental action. This is the ordinary way unto sanctification. In a sacramental act, nature and grace combine to elevate and transform the creatures of God. Here we have religion in both subjective and objective form. Here we have liturgy, wherein God is worshipped and glorified, and man is made a partaker of the light and kingdom of God. And the greatness of this type of religious act consists in this — man does not strive to ascend God-ward in isolation, but he is assisted by the totality of the Church, the Mystical Body of Christ, and what is more significant, he together with his fellow-Christians is led and directed by the God-Man, as Head of His Mystic Body. Thus a wonderful hierarchy of being unites its various elements into a most significant and efficacious kind of religious act which is called a sacramental act. The first element is Jesus Christ, the divine-human Being, Who, through the action of His Spirit, vivifies and leavens the other elements of the act; the second element is man, with his marvellous powers of reason, sentiment, emotions, and capabilities of sense, hearing, voice, singing and speaking, motion and gestures; and the third element is irrational creation, bread, wine, water, oil, lights, incense, vestments, gold, bells, organ. All these unite their forces to posit the sacramental act, whose object is in first instance the Blessed Trinity to Whom praise is directed, and in second instance creation, whose sanctification or consecration is sought, signified, and effected in the sacramental rite.

The more one is conscious of the spiritual dynamo which Christ has bequeathed to His Church in the form called the sacramental system, the better does one comprehend the pity of so great a multitude of men, groping its way to eternal life, ignorant, or unconscious, or semi-conscious of the chief means to justification and perfection! How Catholics should rejoice in the knowledge and realization that our salvation comes from God through the sacramental life, and, consequently, with what fervor and alacrity should we participate in the Eucharistic Sacrifice, the sacraments the sacramental and prayer life of the Church! What compassion

we should have for our fellow-Christians who have retained only a minimum of sacramental life, and even more for unbelievers who, entirely bereft of sacramentalism, must find their Lord and His salvation without it!

Speaking of the generality of mankind, we have been living in an age which has not been conducive to an appreciation of sacramentalism. Its opponents have been many — pride, materialism, rationalism, individualism, as well as a lack of understanding and interest in symbolism. If an age is ego-centric rather than Christo-centric, it scarcely can have a holy regard for sacramental life. Man must see again that there is no divorce between the spiritual world and the material world. As a Christian, at any rate, he must realize that for a normal and healthy supernatural life, immaterialism exclusively or materialism exclusively — each is equally ruinous. The true Christian spirit demands that man accepts the fact that supernatural life is concurrent with physical life, that spiritual contents are wed to material or external forms.

As we have said, ever since Christ's Incarnation, Passion, and Resurrection, the redeemed world belongs to a sacramental world. The effects of what the Son of God once accomplished for us in history are now transmitted by Him to His members in the way of sacramental rites. Christ has brought sacramental life into operation. The Infinite condescends to live in the finite by grace; the finite has by Him been elevated to experience living union with the Uncreated. Between the life of the Deity and the life of humanity lies the field of sacramental activity where Infinite and finite meet and are united. After man is first initiated into the sacramental system through baptism, his new life is exercised and developed by the other sacraments, but primarily by the Eucharist, the sacrament-sacrifice and the sacrament-banquet, as the Eucharist is referred to by Vonier ("Key to the Doctrine of the Eucharist"). But it is not our concern here to say anything further about the sacraments, since this volume of the Roman Ritual is devoted entirely to sacramental blessings.

If it is admitted that conditions of our age have not been conducive to a proper evaluation of sacramentalism, in so far as the sacraments are concerned, then certainly one can admit all the more readily that the sacramentals have fared even worse. If a certain measure of humility and simplicity is needed by man to recognize God at work with, and in, and for us in the greater mysteries, the Eucharist and the other sacraments, it is required even in greater measure to recognize His action in those consecratory acts which are lesser than the seven sacraments, namely, the sacramentals. Pride and sophistication are a hindrance to understanding that God, when He created the universe, consecrated all creation — not alone man, but every lower form; and that Christ removed the curse fallen on the universe, not only from man but from the lesser species. Thus for a long time, and in particular in our own time, sacramental acts such as the many consecrations and blessings of the Church have been, if not actually disdained, looked upon with apathy and indifference by her children. So much so, that many are apt to be disedified rather than edified when it is revealed to them that the Church has a mind to speak a blessing on horse, silkworm, bonfire, beer, bridal-chamber, medicine, or lard!

God's ultimate purpose in creating the world is the manifestation of His goodness and excellence, and a communication of them in part to His creatures. Consequently, creation's first reason for existence is to glorify the Creator. Humanity fulfills its obligation to glorify God by living in conformity with the laws which govern human existence, but more effectively and nobly still in those positive acts of religion — sacrifice, sacraments, social and private prayer, consecrations, and blessings. For in this latter way, man does not praise God in isolation, but he is united with the praise which his elder Brother, Jesus Christ, perpetually renders to the Most Holy Trinity. Irrational creatures fulfil their obligation too in their very existence and functions, according to the laws which govern their nature. This is their silent voice of praise. But lower creation too is destined to take part in the direct

active, and positive praise of the Creator. The psalms and canticles leave no doubt about this. The fall of man caused lower creatures to be separated from God, for they were bound to God through mankind. And they became once more consecrated in the Redemption, not purely for their own sake, but for the purposes of higher creation. The material universe is indispensable to the very existence of humanity. Irrational creation is united to man, and through him to Christ. For the Son of God, in taking and transforming our human nature, assumed the material universe to Himself. "And I, if I be lifted up from the earth, will draw all things to myself" (John XII, 32). Therefore, in union with man, and in union with the God-man, universal creation participates in the praise which without ceasing raises its voice to the Adorable Trinity, crying: "Holy, holy, holy is the Lord God of Sabaoth! Heaven and earth are full of thy glory!"

What the Church tells us by word in the Martyrology on the Nativity, she elucidates by sacramental acts in the liturgy of Holy Saturday. The blessings of the new fire, of incense, of the Paschal candle, of the baptismal font express through sacred signs and symbols as well as words that the enslavement, both of human nature and lower nature has ended. "O invisible Regenerator, do thou enkindle this nocturnal splendor; that not only the sacrifice offered this night may shine by the secret admixture of thy light, but that also the power of thy majesty may come unto whatever place anything of this mysterious blessing shall be brought, and all malicious wiles of the devil may be defeated" (Liturgy of Holy Saturday — blessing of incense). A little later, at the blessing of the font of life, before the infusion of sacred oils, the celebrant sprinkles water from the font in the four directions of the earth, in symbol of the regeneration by Christ of all life upon the world.

In the Epistle to the Romans, St. Paul records that the complete emancipation of creation will not be effected until the end of time. But ever since our Lord transfigured lower creatures by employing them in sacramental ways — consider His use of bread, wine,

water, oil, sacred signs — material things have been participating with Him and with man in divine worship. And where Christ left off, the Church continues. The consecration and transfiguration of the creatures of God is done through sacraments and sacramentals. The Passion and Resurrection of Jesus notwithstanding, the individual man is not justified until the fruit of these momentous acts is communicated to him by way of sacramental sanctification. "I saw water flowing from the right side of the temple, alleluia. And all to whom this water came were saved, and they shall say, alleluia, alleluia." Lower creatures in similar fashion are freed from their enslavement by being sacramentalized. Before the Church will use them in the service of God or of men, she wills that first they be exorcised of any allegiance to Satan, then sanctified by her consecratory hand.

Until the Council of Lyons (1274) solemnly declared that there are seven sacraments, the Church had used the term, sacrament in its broadest signification for every sacred rite which employed words, actions, and objects to dispense grace. So that not only the great seven were so designated, but the same name was used for the consecration of a church, of a monk, of a virgin, of a cemetery, of oil, of water, in fact, for quite a number of consecrations and blessings. She had always known from the first century of Christianity, of course, that there were the greater sacraments and the lesser sacraments, the big mysteries and the little mysteries, and obviously distinguished between their institution, operation, and effect. The significant fact, however, is that she showed how sacred both are, and how she treasured both, giving all the name: sacrament.

When the Church finally defined through the Council of Trent that there are seven sacraments, no more nor less, and that all seven owe their institution to Christ, this was not tantamount to declaring: the sacraments are from Christ, the sacramentals *merely* from the Church! Such misconstruction should not be placed on the definition of the Council of Trent. Certainly, there is a difference of kind and efficacy between the seven sacraments

and the lesser sacraments, or if one prefers, sacramentals! There is a difference of degree among the seven sacraments themselves. One is not so necessary or sublime as another. Furthermore, it is not true to say without qualification that one distinction between sacraments and sacramentals is that the former owe their institution to Christ, the latter to the Church. For some of the sacramentals definitely come directly from Christ, exactly how many and which ones is not clear. There is one sacramental, however, of whose divine origin there is no particle of doubt. This is the Mandatum, the washing of feet at the Last Supper, and today still listed in the liturgical books as a sacramental for Holy Thursday, and still observed, thank God, by some bishops, and abbots, and pastors, and ecclesiastical superiors. Concerning the Mandatum, St. Ambrose ("De Sacramentis") has something very interesting to say: "We are not ignorant that the Roman Church has not this custom of washing the feet. . . . There are, however, some who say and try to urge that this ought to be done, not as a sacrament, not at baptism, not at the regeneration; but only as we should wash the feet of a guest. The latter is an act of humility, the former a work of sanctification. Accordingly, learn how it is a sacrament and a means of sanctification. . . . What other places have done well to retain, we too do well to maintain." It is beside the point to speculate here whether St. Ambrose had in mind to proclaim the Mandatum as an eighth sacrament in the strict sense of the word, or whether he called it a sacrament in the then commonly accepted broader terminology. To say the least, he leaves no doubt in our minds that there is a sacramental instituted by Jesus Christ!

What requires stressing here is that we do not belittle the sacramentals, owing to the fact that they owe their institution in greatest part not to the positive will and act of Christ, but instead to the action of the Church. For in the light of the doctrine of Corpus Christi Mysticum, both have a most sacred origin — the sacraments from the personal, historical Christ, the sacramentals from the Mystic Christ — Christ living and working in His Mys-

tical Bride, the Church. The sacramentals are aptly designated as extensions and radiations of the sacraments. Both are sources of divine life; both have an identical purpose — divine life. They have, moreover, an identical Cause — the Passion and Resurrection of Jesus Christ! Albeit they differ in nature, efficacy, and intensity.

The consecrations and blessings of the Church are extensions and radiations of the sacraments. Their purpose, too, is Christ-life — building up of the Mystical Body into perfect stones to fit into the perfection of the Corner-Stone. They continue the work of the sacraments or prepare for their reception. Baptism is followed up by the sacramentals of holy water, the Sunday morning Asperges, the blessing of infants, of children. Confirmation is extended in the blessings of a school, of a library, an archive, an ambulance, or in those sacramentals which have a relation to the functioning of the Spirit's Gifts. The consecration of a monk or of a nun is patterned on holy orders. Matrimony is followed by the blessing of a bridal-chamber, the blessing of an expectant mother, the act of churching, the blessing of a home, and the profusion of blessings for material things which are used in family life. The sacrament of penance is extended in the sacramentals of the Confiteor, absolutions, the papal blessing in the hour of a Christian's departure from this world, and exorcisms. Extreme Unction has for its radiations the blessings for the sick, the blessing of sick pilgrims, blessing of wine, medicine, linens, the blessing of a corpse, of a grave. Thus the sacramentals either lead up to or continue the grace of the sacraments. The various circumstances and conditions and materials of life are consecrated, lest by their unsanctified state they prove to be obstacles in the way of sanctified humanity.

Above all in the Eucharist does matter become sacramentalized. Just as the sacraments are radiations of being from the Eucharist as their center, so also the sacramentals can be said to form an outer circle around the sacraments, all of them converging toward the Eucharist as the center. Eucharistic worship is the con-

secration of all time and all matter. A Christian's every and entire day is sanctified by it. "Go into the world, and be light-bearers," is the meaning of the dismissal at the end of the Sacrifice. "Strengthen, O God, that which thou hast wrought in us in the midst of thy holy temple which is in Jerusalem" (Ps. LXVII:29). What is begun in the morning sacrifice and banquet must be developed by the day's routine of sanctified acts. The Eucharist is the sacramental sanctification of a Christian's every day in this valley of tears, in fact, of his entire life-span. As he leaves the Eucharistic altar and banquet-table of the new Jerusalem, the Christian goes out, oftentimes into the atmosphere of a veritable Babylon. Fortified with Christ's kiss of peace, he launches the attack against Satan, using the auxiliary weapons which the Church, the worthy Spouse of Christ and our holy Mother dispenses with lavish hand to her children. May the little sacraments treated of in this volume become powerful allies to the Holy Seven, to hasten our sacramental sanctification unto the full stature of our Lord and Saviour, Jesus Christ!

THE ROMAN RITUAL

DE BENEDICTIONIBUS REGULAE GENERALES

Benedictiones impertire potest quilibet Presbyter, exceptis iis quae Romano Pontifici aut Episcopis aliisve reserventur.

Benedictio reservata quae a Presbytero detur sine necessaria licentia, illicita est, sed valida, nisi in reservatione Sedes Apostolica aliud expresserit.

Diaconi et Lectores illas tantum valide et licite benedictiones dare possunt, quae ipsis expresse a jure permittuntur.

2. Benedictiones sive constitutivae sive invocativae invalidae sunt, si adhibita non fuerit formula ab Ecclesia praescripta.

3. Benedictiones, imprimis impertiendae catholicis, dari quoque possunt catechumenis, immo, nisi obstet Ecclesiae prohibitio, etiam acatholicis ad obtinendum fidei lumen vel, una cum illo, corporis sanitatem.

4. Res benedictae constitutiva benedictione, reverenter tractentur neque ad usum profanum vel non proprium adhibeantur, etiamsi in dominio privatorum sint.

5. Benedictionem illius sacrae supellectilis quae ad normam legum liturgicarum benedici debet antequam ad usum sibi proprium adhibeatur, impertire possunt:

1°. S.R.E. Cardinales et Episcopi omnes;

2°. Locorum Ordinarii, charactere episcopali carentes, pro ecclesiis et oratoriis proprii territorii;

3°. Parochus pro ecclesiis et oratoriis in territorio suae parocciae positis, et rectores ecclesiarum pro suis ecclesiis;

GENERAL RULES CONCERNING BLESSINGS

1. Any priest may confer the blessings of the Church, except those reserved to the Pope, to bishops, or to others.

A reserved blessing which is conferred by a priest not possessing the required delegation is valid, but illicit, unless the Holy See has declared otherwise in the reservation.

Deacons and lectors may confer only those blessings which are expressly allowed them by law, in so far as both validity and liceity are concerned.

2. Both constitutive and invocative blessings are invalid if the form prescribed by the Church is not observed.

3. Blessings are designed primarily for Catholics, but may likewise be given to Catechumens. Moreover, unless the Church expressly forbids, they may be imparted to non-Catholics to assist them in obtaining the light of faith, or together with it, bodily health.

4. Objects which have received the constitutive blessing should be treated reverently, and should never be put to profane or improper use, even though they may be in private possession.

5. Blessings of the sacred appurtenances which, according to liturgical law, should be blessed before they are used, may be conferred by:

a) Cardinals and all bishops.

b) An Ordinary who is not a bishop, in the churches and oratories of his own province.

c) A pastor in the churches and oratories located within the confines of his parish, and rectors of churches in their own churches.

4°. Sacerdotes a loci Ordinario delegati, intra fines delegationis et jurisdictionis delegantis;

5°. Superiores religiosi, et Sacerdotes ejusdem religionis ab ipsis delegati, pro propriis ecclesiis et oratoriis ac pro ecclesiis monialium sibi subjectarum.

6. In omni benedictione extra Missam, Sacerdos saltem superpelliceo et stola coloris tempori convenientis utatur, nisi aliter notetur.

7. Stando semper benedicat, et aperto capite.

In principio cujusque benedictionis, nisi aliter notetur, dicat:

℣. Adjutórium nostrum in nómine Dómini.

℟. Qui fecit caelum et terram.

℣. Dóminus vobíscum.

℟. Et cum spíritu tuo.

Deinde dicat Orationem propriam, unam vel plures, prout suo loco notatum fuerit.

Postea rem aspergat aqua benedicta, et, ubi notatum fuerit, pariter incenset, nihil dicendo.

8. Cum Sacerdos aliquid benedicturus est, habeat ministrum cum vase aquae benedictae et aspersorio, et cum hoc Rituali libro, seu Missali.

9. Caveat, ne benedictionis causa ponat aliquid indecens super Altare, veluti esculenta; sed quod ejusmodi est, ponatur super mensam, commodo loco paratam.

d) Priests delegated thereto by the Ordinary of the place, subject to the extent of the delegation and the power of the one delegating.

e) Religious superiors and their priest subjects whom they delegate, in their own churches and oratories and in churches of nuns who are under their spiritual care.

6. In every blessing outside of Mass the priest should be vested in surplice and stole of the color proper to the day, unless the rubrics prescribe otherwise.

7. The one who blesses should stand with head uncovered; and at the beginning of each blessing, unless otherwise stated, he says:

℣. Our help is in the name of the Lord.

℟. Who made heaven and earth.

℣. The Lord be with you.

℟. And with thy spirit.

He then says the proper prayer or as many as are given.

Lastly he sprinkles the object with holy water, and if called for, incenses it, without saying anything.

8. When a priest blesses he should be assisted by a server who holds the holy water stoop and aspersory, and he should follow the Ritual or the Missal.

9. Care should be taken that during a blessing nothing indecorous is placed upon the altar, e.g., eatables. But things of this nature should be placed upon a table conveniently arranged.

I

BLESSINGS FOR SUNDAYS AND FEASTDAYS

1

ORDO AD FACIENDAM AQUAM BENEDICTAM

1. Diebus Dominicis, et quandocumque opus sit, praeparato sale et aqua munda benedicenda in ecclesia, vel in sacristia, Sacerdos, superpelliceo et stola violacea indutus, primo dicit:

℣. Adjutórium nostrum in nómine Dómini.

℟. Qui fecit caelum et terram.

2. Deinde absolute incipit exorcismum salis:

Exorcízo te, creatúra salis, per Deum ✠ vivum, per Deum ✠ verum, per Deum ✠ sanctum, per Deum, qui te per Eliséum Prophétam in aquam mitti jussit, ut sanarétur sterílitas aquae: ut efficiáris sal exorcizátum in salútem credéntium; et sis ómnibus suméntibus te sánitas ánimae et córporis; et effúgiat, atque discédat a loco, in quo aspérsum fúeris, omnis phantásia, et nequítia, vel versútia diabólicae fraudis, omnísque spíritus immúndus, adjurátus per eum, qui ventúrus est judicáre vivos et mórtuos, et saéculum per ignem. ℟. Amen.

Orémus.   Oratio

IMMÉNSAM cleméntiam tuam, omnípotens aetérne Deus, humíliter implorámus, ut hanc creatúram salis, quam in usum géneris humáni tribuísti, bene ✠ dícere et sancti ✠ ficáre tua pietáte dignéris: ut sit ómnibus suméntibus salus mentis et córporis; et quidquid ex eo tactum vel respérsum fúerit, cáreat omni immundítia, omníque impugnatióne spiritális nequítiae. Per Dóminum. ℟. Amen.

Translator's Note: The holy-water font is a counterpart of the baptismal font; the sacramental is related to the great sacrament. Easter is the day of Holy Baptism par excellence, and every Sunday is a little Easter. Consequently, on the Lord's day the Church blesses water to be used in the renewal of baptism, for so often as she sprinkles us with the blessed water a sign is given us of renewal

1

THE BLESSING OF HOLY WATER

1. On Sundays, or whenever water must be blessed, salt and fresh water are prepared in church or in the sacristy. The priest vested in surplice and purple stole says:

℣. Our help is in the name of the Lord.

℟. Who made heaven and earth.

2. The exorcism of salt follows:

Thou creature of salt, I purge thee of evil by the living ✠ God, by the true ✠ God, by the holy ✠ God, by the God Who ordered thee through Eliseus,* the prophet to be cast into the water to cure its unfruitfulness. Be thou a purified salt for the health of believers, giving soundness of body and soul to all who use thee. In whatever place thou art sprinkled, may phantams and wickedness, and Satan's cunning be banished. And let every unclean spirit be repulsed by Him Who shall come to judge the living and dead, and the world by fire. ℟. Amen.

Let us pray.   *Prayer*

O ALMIGHTY, everlasting God! Humbly we implore thy boundless mercy that thou wouldst deign of thy goodness to bless ✠ and sanctify ✠ this creature of salt which thou hast given for the use of mankind. May all that use it find in it a remedy for soul and body. And let everything which it touches or sprinkles be freed from uncleanness and assault from evil spirits. Through our Lord. ℟. Amen.

---

of the pristine life once bestowed by the Gift of Life — baptism. The rubrics direct that this water be blessed either in sacristy or sanctuary. For the edification of the faithful the latter place might well be chosen on occasion. Low Sunday, the octave of the Paschal Mystery would be ideal for this blessing performed in the sight of all the family of God assembled in the parish church.

* 4 Kings II, 21.

Exorcismus aquae: et dicitur absolute:

Exorcízo te, creatúra aquae, in nómine Dei ✠ Patris omnipoténtis, et in nómine Jesu ✠ Christi, Fílii ejus Dómini nostri, et in virtúte Spíritus ✠ Sancti: ut fias aqua exorcizáta ad effugándam omnem potestátem inimíci, et ipsum inimícum eradicáre et explantáre váleas cum ángelis suis apostáticis, per virtútem ejúsdem Dómini nostri Jesu Christi: qui ventúrus est judicáre vivos et mórtuos, et saéculum per ignem. ℟. Amen.

Orémus.   Oratio

D EUS, qui ad salútem humáni géneris, máxima quaeque sacraménta in aquárum substántia condidísti: adésto propítius invocatiónibus nostris, et eleménto huic multímodis purificatiónibus praeparáto, virtútem tuae bene ✠ dictiónis infúnde; ut creatúra tua, mystériis tuis sérviens, ad abigéndos daémones, morbósque pelléndos, divínae grátiae sumat efféctum; ut quidquid in dómibus, vel in locis fidélium, haec unda respérserit, cáreat omni immundítia, liberétur a noxa: non illic resídeat spíritus péstilens, non aura corrúmpens: discédant omnes insídiae laténtis inimíci; et si quid est, quod aut incolumitáti habitántium ínvidet, aut quiéti, aspersióne hujus aquae effúgiat: ut salúbritas per invocatiónem sancti tui nóminis expetíta, ab ómnibus sit impugnatiónibus defénsa. Per Dóminum. ℟. Amen.

3. Hic ter mittat sal in aquam in modum crucis, dicendo semel:

Commíxtio salis et aquae páriter fiat, in nómine Pa ✠ tris, et Fí ✠ lii, et Spíritus ✠ Sancti. ℟. Amen.

℣. Dóminus vobíscum.

℟. Et cum spíritu tuo.

Orémus.   Oratio

D EUS, invíctae virtútis auctor, et insuperábilis impérii Rex, ac semper magníficus triumphátor: qui advérsae domina-

Exorcism of water:

Thou creature of water, I purge thee of evil in the name of God ✠ the Father almighty, in the name of Jesus ✠ Christ, His Son, our Lord, and in the power of the Holy ✠ Spirit, that thou mayest be water fit to brace us against the envious foe. Mayest thou be empowered to drive him forth and exile him together with his fallen angels by the power of the selfsame Jesus Christ, our Lord Who shall come to judge the living and the dead, and the world by fire. ℟. Amen.

Let us pray.   Prayer

O GOD, Who for man's salvation dost dispense wondrous mysteries with the efficacious sign of water, hearken to our prayer — pouring forth thy benediction ✠ upon this element which we consecrate with manifold purifications. Let this creature serve thee in expelling demons and curing diseases. Whatsoever it sprinkles in the homes of the faithful, be it cleansed and delivered from harm. Let such homes enjoy a spirit of goodness and an air of tranquility, freed from baneful and hidden snares. By the sprinkling of this water may everything opposed to the safety and repose of them that dwell therein be banished, so that they may possess the well-being they seek in calling upon thy holy name, and be protected from all peril. Through our Lord. ℟. Amen.

3. Now salt is thrice put into the water in the form of a cross, saying only once:

May this salt and water be mixed together, in the name of the Father ✠ and of the Son ✠ and of the Holy ✠ Spirit. ℟. Amen

℣. The Lord be with you.
℟. And with thy spirit.

Let us pray.   Prayer

A UTHOR of invincible strength and king of an unconquerable empire, ever the gloriously Triumphant One! Who

tiónis vires réprimis: qui inimíci rugiéntis saevítiam súperas: qui hostíles nequítias poténter expúgnas: te, Dómine, treméntes et súpplices deprecámur, ac pétimus: ut hanc creatúram salis et aquae dignánter aspícias, benígnus illústres, pietátis tuae rore sanctífices; ut, ubicúmque fúerit aspérsa, per invocatiónem sancti nóminis tui, omnis infestátio immúndi spíritus abigátur: terrórque venenósi serpéntis procul pellátur: et praeséntia Sancti Spíritus nobis, misericórdiam tuam poscéntibus, ubíque adésse dignétur. Per Dóminum nostrum Jesum Christum Fílium tuum: Qui tecum vivit et regnat in unitáte ejúsdem Spíritus Sancti Deus, per ómnia saécula saeculórum. R̷. Amen.

4. Post benedictionem aquae, Sacerdos Dominicis diebus, antequam incipiat Missam, aspergit Altare, deinde se, et Ministros, ac populum, prout in Missali praescribitur, et in Appendice hujus Ritualis habetur.

5. Christifideles autem possunt de ista aqua benedicta in vasculis suis accipere, et secum deferre ad aspergendos aegros, domos, agros, vineas, et alia, et ad eam habendam in cubiculis suis, ut ea quotidie et saepius aspergi possint.

2

BENEDICTIO POPULI CUM AQUA BENEDICTA
diebus Dominicis impertienda

Sacerdos celebraturus, indutus pluviali coloris Officio convenientis, accedit ad Altare, et ibi ad gradus cum Ministris genuflexus, etiam Tempore Paschali, accipit a Diacono aspersorium, et primo ter aspergit Altare, deinde se, et erectus Ministros, incipiens Antiphonam: **Aspérges me.** Et chorus prosequitur: **Dómine, hyssópo,** etc., ut infra. Interim Celebrans aspergit clerum, deinde populum, dicens submissa voce cum Ministris Psalmum **Miserére mei, Deus.**

Translator's Note: Baptism and Eucharist have been from earliest Christian times a special work for Sundays. When we come together on the Lord's day to celebrate His praises in Eucharistic worship, we reflect that our baptism is an ever-present fact in our souls.

restrainest the force of the adversary, Who overcomest the fierceness of the devouring enemy, Who valiantly putteth down hostile influences! Prostrate and fearsome we beseech thee, Lord, consider kindly this creature of salt and water, make it honored, and sanctify it with the dew of thy sweetness. Wherever it is sprinkled in thy name, may devilish infection cease, venomous terror be driven afar. But let the presence of the Holy Spirit be ever with us as we implore thy mercy. Through our Lord, Jesus Christ, thy Son, Who liveth and reigneth with thee in unity of the same Holy Spirit, God, eternally. ℟. Amen.

4. On Sundays after water is blessed and before Mass begins, the celebrant sprinkles the altar, himself, the ministers, and the people as prescribed by the Missal and by this Ritual.

5. Christ's faithful are permitted to take holy water home with them to sprinkle the sick, their homes, vineyards, and the like. It is recommended too that they put it in fonts in the various rooms, so that daily and frequently they may use it to bless themselves.

2

THE SUNDAY BLESSING WITH HOLY WATER

The priest who will offer the Sacrifice, vested in cope of the proper color comes to the altar, and kneeling on the step with the ministrants (also in Paschaltide) receives the aspersory from the deacon. First he sprinkles the altar thrice, then himself, and standing he sprinkles the ministrants, having intoned the antiphon: Sprinkle me. The choir continues: With hyssop, O Lord, etc., as indicated below. Meanwhile the celebrant sprinkles the clergy, then the people, reciting quietly with the ministrants Psalm 50, Have mercy on me, O God.

Thus, before treading into the holy of holies of Eucharistic sacrifice and communion, we commemorate and renew that sublime mystery by which Mother Church has brought us forth out of her womb, the baptismal font, unto life within the Kingdom of God upon earth.

VII

Antiphona

Aspér- ges me, * Dómi-ne, hyssópo, et mundá-

bor: lavá- bis me, et super nívem de- albá- bor.

Ps. 50: Mi- serére mé-i, Dé-us, * se-cúndum mágnam

misericórdi-am tu- am. Gló- ri-a Pátri, et Fí-li-o, et Spi-

rítu-i Sáncto: * Sic-ut é-rat in princípi-o, et nunc, et semper,

et in saécula sae-cu- lórum. A- men.

Et repetitur Antiphona Aspérges me.

Haec Antiphona praedicto modo dicitur ad aspersionem aquae benedictae in Dominicis per totum annum: excepta Dominica de Passione, et
Dominica Palmarum, in quibus non dicitur Glória Patri; sed post Psalmum Miserére repetitur immediate Antiphona Aspérges me. Excepto
etiam Tempore Paschali, scilicet a Dominica Paschae usque ad Pente-
costen inclusive, quo tempore cantatur sequens:

VIII

Antiphona

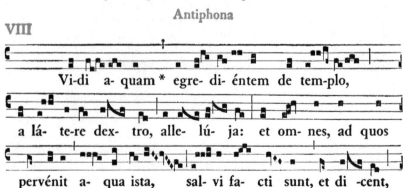

Vi-di a- quam * egre- di- éntem de tem-plo,

a lá- te-re dex- tro, alle- lú- ja: et om- nes, ad quos

pervénit a- qua ista, sal- vi fa- cti sunt, et di -cent,

Antiphon

Sprinkle me with hyssop, O Lord, and I shall be clean: wash me, and I shall be whiter than snow. Ps. 50. Be merciful to me, O God, for great is thy goodness. Glory be to the Father, and to the Son, and to the Holy Spirit: * As it was in the beginning, is now, and ever shall be world without end. Amen.

The antiphon Sprinkle me is repeated.

Thus the above is sung at the sprinkling with holy water on all Sundays of the year, except on Passion and Palm Sundays when the Glory, etc., is omitted, and after the psalm Be merciful, the antiphon Sprinkle me is repeated at once. During Paschaltide from Easter until Pentecost inclusive the following is sung:

Antiphon

I saw water flowing from the right side of the temple, alleluia: and all to whom this water came were saved, and they shall say,

alle - lú - ja, al- le-   lú- ja. **Ps. 117:** Confi - té - mini Dó-

mino quó-ni-am bonus: * quó-ni-am in saéculum mise-ri-

cór-di-a e-jus.   Glóri- a Patri, et Fí-li-o, et Spi-rí- tu- i

San-cto.* Si-cut erat in princí-pi- o, et nunc, et semper,

et in saé-cula sae-cu- ló-rum. A-men.

Repetitur Antiphona: **Vidi aquam egrediéntem.**
In Dominica vero Trinitatis resumitur Antiphona **Aspérges me,**
Dómine, etc., ut supra.
In die sancto Paschae et Pentecostes, ubi est fons baptismalis, fit
aspersio cum aqua pridie benedicta in fonte Baptismi, et ante infusio-
nem Olei et Chrismatis accepta.
Finita Antiphona supradicto modo, Sacerdos qui aspersit aquam,
reversus ad Altare, stans ante gradus Altaris junctis manibus dicat:

℣. Osténde nobis, Dómine, misericórdiam tuam(T.P. allelúia).
℞. Et salutáre tuum da nobis (T.P. allelúia).
℣. Dómine, exáudi oratiónem meam.
℞. Et clamor meus ad te véniat.
℣. Dóminus vobíscum.
℞. Et cum spíritu tuo.

Orémus.   Oratio

EXÁUDI nos, Dómine sancte, Pater omnípotens, aetérne
    Deus: et míttere dignéris sanctum Angelum tuum de caelis;
qui custódiat, fóveat, prótegat, vísitet, atque deféndat omnes habitántes in hoc habitáculo. Per Christum Dóminum nostrum.
℞. Amen.

alleluia, alleluia. **Ps. 117.** Let us give thanks to the Lord for His goodness: * for His mercy endureth forever. Glory be to the Father, and to the Son, and to the Holy Spirit. * As it was in the beginning, is now, and ever shall be world without end. Amen.

The antiphon I saw water flowing is repeated.

On Trinity Sunday the antiphon Sprinkle me, etc., is resumed.

In churches where there is a baptismal font, on Easter and Pentecost the water used for the sprinkling is that which has been blessed at the font on the day previous, before the infusion of the Sacred Oils.

The above antiphon being ended, the priest who has returned to the altar stands at the foot and with hands joined sings:

℣. Show us thy mercy, O Lord (T.P. alleluia).

℟. And grant us thy salvation (T.P. alleluia).

℣. O Lord, hear my prayer.

℟. And let my cry come unto thee.

℣. The Lord be with you.

℟. And with thy spirit.

Let us pray.   Prayer

HEAR us, holy Lord, Father almighty, eternal God! And deign to send thy holy angel from heaven to guard, cherish, protect, visit, and defend all that assemble in this dwelling. Through Christ our Lord. ℟. Amen.

3

BENEDICTIO INFANTIS

℣. Adjutórium nostrum in nómine Dómini.
℟. Qui fecit caelum et terram.
℣. Deus noster miserétur.
℟. Custódiens párvulos Dóminus.
℣. Dómine, exáudi oratiónem meam.
℟. Et clamor meus ad te véniat.
℣. Dóminus vobíscum.
℟. Et cum spíritu tuo.

Orémus. Oratio

Dómine Jesu Christe, Fili Dei vivi, qui ante ómnia saécula génitus, in témpore tamen infans esse voluisti, et hujus aetátis díligis innocéntiam: qui párvulos tibi oblátos amánter compléxus es, iísque benedixísti: infántem istum (infántes istos) práeveni in benedictiónibus dulcédinis, et praesta, ne malítia mutet intelléctum ejus (eórum): eíque (eísque) concéde, ut profíciens (proficiéntes) aetáte, sapiéntia et grátia, tibi semper placére váleat (váleant): Qui vivis et regnas cum Deo Patre in unitáte Spíritus Sancti Deus, per ómnia saécula saeculórum. ℟. Amen.

Deinde Sacerdos infantem (vel infantes) aspergat aqua benedicta, dicens:

Pax et benedíctio Dei omnipoténtis, Patris, et Fílii, ✠ et Spíritus Sancti, descéndat super te (vos), et máneat semper. ℟. Amen.

Translator's Note: Some blessings in the Ritual are designated for particular feasts or seasons of the ecclesiastical calendar. Wherefore, we place here the following blessings for children as appropriate to

3

BLESSING OF AN INFANT

℣. Our help is in the name of the Lord.
℟. Who made heaven and earth.
℣. Our God is compassionate.
℟. He is the Lord, the guardian of little ones.
℣. O Lord, hear my prayer.
℟. And let my cry come unto thee.
℣. The Lord be with you.
℟. And with thy spirit.

Let us pray.   Prayer
O Lord, Jesus Christ, Son of the living God, born before all ages, in time thou didst will to become an infant, for thou lovest the innocence of such. Thou Who when children were brought to thee didst lovingly embrace them and bless them, hasten with thy sweetest blessings to this infant (these infants) and keep its (their) mind from malice. Assist him (her, them) to advance in wisdom, age, and grace, thereby ever pleasing thee, Who livest and reignest with God the Father in the unity of the Holy Spirit, God, forever and ever. ℟. Amen.

The priest sprinkles the infant (or infants) with holy water, saying:
May the peace and blessing of almighty God, Father, Son, ✠ and Holy Spirit descend upon thee (you) and remain forever. ℟. Amen.

---

the Christmas season. The blessing of an infant is most fitting on Christ's Nativity. The other two blessings for children are well suited to Christmas and its Octave.

4

BENEDICTIO PUERI
ad obtinendam super ipsum misericordiam Dei

℣. Adjutórium nostrum in nómine Dómini.

℟. Qui fecit caelum et terram.

℣. Dóminus vobíscum.

℟. Et cum spíritu tuo.

Orémus.   Oratio

Dómine, Jesu Christe, Fili Dei vivi, qui dixísti: Sínite párvulos veníre ad me, tálium est enim regnum caelórum; super hunc púerum tuum virtútem bene✠ dictiónis tuae infúnde, ac ad Ecclésiae et paréntum illíus fidem ac devotiónem réspice; ut virtúte ac sapiéntia apud Deum et hómines profíciens, ad optátam pervéniat senectútem, et salútem consequátur aetérnam: Qui vivis et regnas in saécula saeculórum. ℟. Amen.

Psalmus 112

LAUDÁTE, púeri, Dóminum: * laudáte nomen Dómini.

Sit nomen Dómini benedíctum, * ex hoc nunc, et usque in saéculum.

A solis ortu usque ad occásum, * laudábile nomen Dómini.

Excélsus super omnes gentes Dóminus, * et super caelos glória ejus.

Quis sicut Dóminus, Deus noster, qui in altis hábitat, * et humília réspicit in caelo et in terra?

Súscitans a terra ínopem, * et de stércore érigens páuperem:

Ut cóllocet eum cum princípibus, * cum princípibus pópuli sui.

Qui habitáre facit stérilem in domo, * matrem filiórum laetántem.

Glória Patri.

Kýrie, eléison. Christe, eléison. Kýrie, eléison.

Pater noster secreto usque ad

4

BLESSING OF A CHILD

℣. Our help is in the name of the Lord.
℞. Who made heaven and earth.
℣. The Lord be with you.
℞. And with thy spirit.

Let us pray. *Prayer*

Lord, Jesus Christ, Son of the living God, Who didst say: "Suffer little children to come unto me, for the kingdom of heaven is theirs" — shower upon this thy child blessing ✠ and assistance, and consider the faith and devotion of the Church and the parents. Advancing in grace and wisdom before God and men, may he (she) reach a blessed old age and secure eternal felicity. Who livest and reignest forever. ℞. Amen.

Psalm 112

Ye children, sing praise to the Lord; praise the name of the Lord.
May the name of the Lord be blessed, now and forever.
From the rising of the sun until its setting, the Lord's name excels.
The Lord is high above all nations; His glory is above the heavens.
Who is like unto the Lord our God Who dwelleth above,
Who looketh down upon the insignificant of heaven and earth?
He lifteth the needy from the earth, and raiseth up the poor man
from the dunghill;
That He might place him with nobles, with the princes of His
people.
He causeth the barren woman of a household to be a joyful
mother of children.
Glory be to the Father.
Lord, have mercy on us. Christ, have mercy on us. Lord, have
mercy on us.
Our Father *inaudibly until*

℣. Et ne nos indúcas in tentatiónem.

℟. Sed líbera nos a malo.

Benedíctio Dei omnipoténtis, Patris, et Fílii, ✠ et Spíritus Sancti descéndat super te, et máneat semper. ℟. Amen.

5

BENEDICTIO PUERORUM
cum praesertim in ecclesia praesentantur

Die et hora constitutis, pueri conveniant in ecclesiam, quos ibi a parentibus vel magistris associari maxime deceret, ut in silentio et modestia facilius se componant. Quibus per ordinem dispositis, et pueris a puellis, si adsint, separatis, Sacerdos ad ipsos accedat, et brevissimo ac simplici sermone eos alloquatur, prout opportunum sibi visum fuerit. Deinde stans versus eos dicat:

℣. Adjutórium nostrum in nómine Dómini.

℟. Qui fecit caelum et terram.

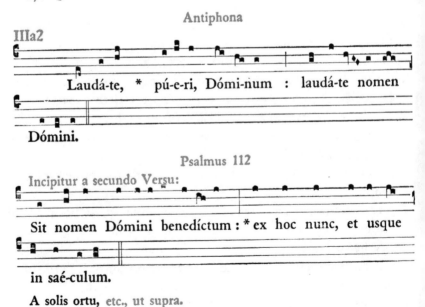

Antiphona

IIIa2

Laudá-te, * pú-e-ri, Dómi-num : laudá-te nomen

Dómini.

Psalmus 112

Incipitur a secundo Versu:

Sit nomen Dómini benedíctum : * ex hoc nunc, et usque

in saé-culum.

A solis ortu, etc., ut supra.

Et repetitur Antiphona.

℣. And lead us not into temptation.
℞. But deliver us from evil.

May the blessing of almighty God, Father, Son,✠ and Holy Spirit descend upon thee and remain forever. ℞. Amen.

5

BLESSING OF CHILDREN
when especially presented in church for a blessing

At the appointed time, the children assemble in church under the tutelage of parents or teachers to insure quiet and order. When they are properly placed, boys and girls separate, the priest approaches, and speaks to them very briefly and simply on a suitable subject.

Then standing and facing them he says:

℣. Our help is in the name of the Lord.
℞. Who made heaven and earth.

Antiphon: Ye children, sing praise to the Lord: praise the name of the Lord.

Psalm 112, beginning with the second verse: May the name of the Lord be blessed as above.

Repeat the antiphon: Ye children, sing praise to the Lord, etc.

Qui Psalmus cum sua Antiphona, si paucis tantum, aut minus solemniter .conferatur Benedictio, omitti poterit.

Finito Psalmo et repetita Antiphona, Sacerdos dicit:

℣. Sínite párvulos veníre ad me.

℟. Tálium est enim regnum caelórum.

℣. Angeli eórum.

℟. Semper vident fáciem Patris.

℣. Nihil profíciat inimícus in eis.

℟. Et fílius iniquitátis non appónat nocére eis.

℣. Dómine, exáudi oratiónem meam.

℟. Et clamor meus ad te véniat.

℣. Dóminus vobíscum.

℟. Et cum spíritu tuo.

Orémus.   Oratio

Dómine Jesu Christe, qui párvulos tibi oblátos et ad te veniéntes compléxus es, manúsque super illos impónens benedixísti eis, atque dixísti: Sínite párvulos veníre ad me, et nolíte prohibére eos, tálium est enim regnum caelórum, et Angeli eórum semper vident fáciem Patris mei; réspice, quaésumus, ad puerórum (puellárum, si solae adsint puellae) praeséntium innocéntiam, et ad eórum (eárum) paréntum devotiónem, et cleménter eos (eas) hódie per ministérium nostrum béne ✠ dic; ut in tua grátia et misericórdia semper profíciant, te sápiant, te díligant, te tímeant, et mandáta tua custódiant, et ad finem optátum felíciter pervéniant: per te, Salvátor mundi, qui cum Patre et Spíritu Sancto vivis et regnas Deus in saécula saeculórum. ℟. Amen.

Orémus.   Oratio

D EFÉNDE, quaésumus, Dómine, beáta María semper Vírgine intercedénte, istam ab omni adversitáte famíliam: et toto corde tibi prostrátam, ab hóstium propítius tuére cleménter insídiis. Per Christum, Dóminum nostrum. ℟. Amen.

Orémus.   Oratio

Deus, qui ineffábili providéntia sanctos Angelos tuos ad nostram custódiam míttere dignáris: largíre supplícibus tuis; et

This psalm and its antiphon may be omitted if the blessing is conferred less solemnly or only upon a few.

At the end of the psalm and antiphon the priest says:

℣. Suffer little children to come unto me.

℟. For theirs is the kingdom of heaven.

℣. Their angels.

℟. Ever see the face of the heavenly Father.

℣. Let the enemy be powerless against them.

℟. And the son of iniquity incapable of harming them.

℣. O Lord, hear my prayer.

℟. And let my cry come unto thee.

℣. The Lord be with you.

℟. And with thy spirit.

Let us pray.   Prayer

O Lord, Jesus Christ, Who didst embrace and lay thy hands upon the little children when they came to thee, and didst say to them: "Suffer little children to come unto me, and forbid them not, for the kingdom of heaven is theirs, and their angels always see the face of my Father," — look with a Father's eye upon the innocence of these children and their parents' devotion, and bless ✠ them this day through our ministry. In thy grace and goodness let them constantly advance, desiring thee, loving thee, fearing thee, obeying thy commandments — thus coming to their destined home, through thee, Savior of the world, Who with the Father and the Holy Spirit livest and reignest, God, forever and ever. ℟. Amen.

Let us pray.   Prayer

DEFEND, O Lord, thy children from every adversity — Mary ever Virgin blessed interceding for them. And as they humbly kneel before thee, graciously and mercifully guard them from inimical pitfalls. Through Christ our Lord. ℟. Amen.

Let us pray.   Prayer

O GOD, Who by a gracious providence didst commit thy holy angels to be our guardians, grant us thy suppliants,

eórum semper protectióne deféndi, et aetérna societáte gaudére. Per Christum, Dóminum nostrum. ℟. Amen.

Postea manu dextera producens signum crucis super pueros, benedicit eos, dicens:

Benedícat vos Deus, et custódiat corda vestra et intelligéntias vestras, Pater, et Fílius, ✠ et Spíritus Sanctus. ℟. Amen.

Deinde aspergat pueros aqua benedicta.

6

BENEDICTIO PUERORUM ET PUELLARUM
in Festis piae Unionis
a Sancta Infantia nuncupatae

Sacerdos ex Apostolico indulto delegatus dicat:

℣. Adjutórium nostrum in nómine Dómini.

℟. Qui fecit caelum et terram.

℣. Dóminus vobíscum.

℟. Et cum spíritu tuo.

Orémus.   *Oratio*

Quaésumus, omnípotens Deus, púeris istis, pro quibus tuam deprecámur cleméntiam, bene ✠ dícere dignáre: et per virtútem Sancti Spíritus corda eórum corróbora, vitam sanctífica, castimóniam prómove, sensus eórum bonis opéribus únice inténtos custódi, próspera tríbue, pacem concéde, salútem confer, caritátem largíre, et ab ómnibus diabólicis atque humánis insídiis tua protectióne et virtúte semper defénde; ut, te miseránte, paradísi réquiem tandem felíciter assequántur. Per Dóminum nostrum Jesum Christum, Fílium tuum: Qui tecum vivit et regnat in unitáte Spíritus Sancti Deus, per ómnia saécula saeculórum. ℟. Amen.

Orémus.   *Oratio*

DÓMINE Jesu Christe, qui párvulos tibi oblátos et ad te veniéntes complectebáris (hic ponat manus super capita pue-

that as we constantly enjoy their protection, we may eventually be happy with them eternally. Through Christ our Lord. ℟. Amen.

Making the sign of the cross over them, he blesses them saying:

May God bless you, and may He be the Keeper of your hearts and minds, the Father, Son, ✠ and the Holy Spirit. ℟. Amen.

He sprinkles the children with holy water.

6

BLESSING OF CHILDREN
on Feastdays of the Holy Childhood Association

The priest who enjoys the apostolic indult for this blessing says:

℣. Our help is in the name of the Lord.
℟. Who made heaven and earth.
℣. The Lord be with you.
℟. And with thy spirit.

Let us pray. Prayer

We beseech thee, almighty God, bless ✠ these children for whom we ask thy mercy and love. Strengthen their hearts by the power of the Holy Spirit, sanctify their lives, foster their innocence, keep their minds intent on good, grant them to prosper, give them peace, health, and charity, and by thy strength and protection deliver them from temptations of men or demons. Through thy mercy may they finally attain the peace of Paradise. Through our Lord, Jesus Christ, thy Son, Who liveth and reigneth with thee in the unity of the Holy Spirit, God, forever and ever. ℟. Amen.

Let us pray. Prayer

O LORD Jesus Christ, Who didst embrace little children admitted to thy presence (here the priest extends his hands

rorum), manúsque super illos impónens, eis benedicébas, dicens: Sínite párvulos veníre ad me, et nolíte prohibére eos: tálium est enim regnum caelórum, et Angeli eórum semper vident fáciem Patris mei; réspice, quaésumus, ad puerórum et puellárum praeséntium devotiónem, et benedíctio tua copiósa super illos descéndat, ut in tua grátia et caritáte profíciant, te sápiant, te díligant, te tímeant, mandáta tua custódiant, et ad exoptátum finem pervéniant, per te, Salvátor mundi, qui cum Patre et Spíritu Sancto vivis et regnas Deus in saécula saeculórum. ℟. Amen.

Benedíctio Dei omnipoténtis, Patris, et Fílii, ✠ et Spíritus Sancti, descéndat super vos, custódiat atque dírigat vos, et máneat semper vobíscum. ℟. Amen.

Et aspergantur aqua benedicta.

7

BENEDICTIO VINI
in Festo S. Joannis Apostoli et Evangelistae

In Festo sancti Joannis Ap. et Evang., expleta omnino Missa majore, hoc est post ultimum Evangelium, Sacerdos, retentis omnibus paramentis, excepto manipulo, vinum a populo oblatum, in memoriam et honorem S. Joannis, qui venenum innocue sumpsit, benedicit hoc modo:

℣. Adjutórium nostrum in nómine Dómini.
℟. Qui fecit caelum et terram.
℣. Dóminus vobíscum.
℟. Et cum spíritu tuo.

Orémus.   Oratio

Bene ✠ dícere et conse ✠ cráre dignéris, Dómine Deus, déxtera tua hunc cálicem vini, et cujúslibet potus: et praesta; ut per mérita sancti Joánnis Apóstoli et Evangelístae, omnes in te credéntes et de cálice isto bibéntes benedicántur, et protegántur. Et sicut beátus Joánnes de cálice bibens venénum, illaésus omníno permánsit, ita omnes, hac die in honórem beáti Joánnis de cálice

over them), laying thy hands in benediction upon them, saying:
"Suffer little children to come unto me, and forbid them not, for
theirs is the kingdom of heaven, and their angels always see the
face of my Father" — look kindly, we pray thee, upon the piety
of these children, and bless them in fullest measure. Help them
to advance in thy grace and love, to desire thee, love thee, fear
thee, obey thee, and finally reach the desired goal, through thee,
Savior of the world, Who livest and reignest eternally with the
Father and the Holy Spirit. ℞. Amen.

May the blessing of almighty God, Father, Son, ✠ and Holy
Spirit come upon you to guide and protect you, and remain with
you for all time. ℞. Amen.

He sprinkles them with holy water.

7

BLESSING OF WINE
on the Feast of St. John, Apostle and Evangelist

After the principal Mass on the feast of St. John, Apostle and
Evangelist, after the last gospel, the priest, retaining all vestments
except the maniple, blesses wine brought by the people. This is done in
memory and honor of St. John, who without detriment drank the
poisoned wine proffered by his enemies:

℣. Our help is in the name of the Lord.
℞. Who made heaven and earth.
℣. The Lord be with you.
℞. And with thy spirit.

    Let us pray.   Prayer

Bless ✠ and consecrate, ✠ O Lord God, this chalice of wine
(or any other beverage) through the merits of St. John, Apostle
and Evangelist. Bestow benediction and protection upon all who
drink of this cup. For as the blessed John partook of the poisoned
potion without any hurt, so may all who on this day drink of the
blessed wine to the honor of St. John, by him be freed from

isto bibéntes, méritis ipsíus ab omni aegritúdine venéni, et nóxiis quibúsvis absolvántur, et córpore ac ánima se offeréntes, ab omni culpa liberéntur. Per Christum, Dóminum nostrum. ℟. Amen.

Bene ✠ dic, Dómine, hanc creatúram potus: ut sit remédium salutáre ómnibus suméntibus: et praesta per invocatiónem sancti nóminis tui; ut, quicúmque ex eo gustáverint, tam ánimae quam córporis sanitátem, te donánte, percípiant. Per Christum, Dóminum nostrum. ℟. Amen.

Et benedíctio Dei omnipoténtis, Patris, et Fílii, ✠ et Spíritus Sancti, descéndat super hanc creatúram vini, et cujúslibet potus, et máneat semper. ℟. Amen.

Et aspergatur aqua benedicta.

Quod si benedictio illa fiat privatim extra Missam, Sacerdos, superpelliceo et stola indutus, eam conficiat modo superius tradito.

8

ALIA BENEDICTIO VINI
In Festo S. Joannis Apostoli et Evangelistae

In fine Missae post Evangelium sancti Joannis, In princípio erat Verbum, dicitur:

Psalmus 22

Dóminus regit me, et nihil mihi déerit; * in loco páscuae ibi me collocávit.

Super aquam refectiónis educávit me: * ánimam meam convértit.

Dedúxit me super sémitas justítiae, * propter nomen suum.

Nam, et si ambulávero in médio umbrae mortis, non timébo mala: * quóniam tu mecum es.

Virga tua, et báculus tuus: * ipsa me consoláta sunt.

Parásti in conspéctu meo mensam, * advérsus eos, qui tríbulant me.

Impinguásti in óleo caput meum: * et calix meus inébrians quam praeclárus est!

poisoning and similar harmful things. And as they offer themselves soul and body to thee, O Lord God, give them absolution and pardon. Through Christ our Lord. ℟. Amen.

Bless, ✝ O Lord, this draught that it be a helpful medicine to all who drink it; and grant by thy grace that all who taste thereof may enjoy bodily and spiritual health in calling upon thy holy name. Through Christ our Lord. ℟. Amen.

May the blessing of almighty God, Father, Son, ✝ and Holy Spirit come upon this wine and remain constantly. ℟. Amen.

It is sprinkled with holy water.

If the blessing is given privately outside of Mass, the priest wearing surplice and stole blesses in the manner prescribed above.

8

ANOTHER BLESSING FOR WINE
on the Feast of St. John, Apostle and Evangelist

At the end of Mass, after the last gospel the following is said:

Psalm 22

The Lord is my Shepherd and I will lack nothing; He leadeth me to encamp in green pastures.

He leadeth me to refreshing waters; He reneweth my thirsting soul.

He guideth me on straight paths for His name's sake.

Even though I walk through deadly gloom, I will fear no evil; for thou art with me.

Thy rod and thy staff, they give me security.

Thou preparest for me a banquet in sight of my oppressors.

Thou anointest my head with oil; my cup overflows, and how good it is!

Et misericórdia tua subsequétur me * ómnibus diébus vitae meae:
Et ut inhábitem in domo Dómini, * in longitúdinem diérum.
Glória Patri.
Kýrie, eléison. Christe, eléison. Kýrie, eléison.
Pater noster secreto usque ad
℣. Et ne nos indúcas in tentatiónem.
℟. Sed líbera nos a malo.
℣. Salvos fac servos tuos.
℟. Deus meus, sperántes in te.
℣. Mitte eis, Dómine, auxílium de sancto.
℟. Et de Sion tuére eos.
℣. Nihil profíciat inimícus in eis.
℟. Et fílius iniquitátis non appónat nocére eis.
℣. Et si mortíferum quid bíberint.
℟. Non eis nocébit.
℣. Dómine, exáudi oratiónem meam.
℟. Et clamor meus ad te véniat.
℣. Dóminus vobíscum.
℟. Et cum spíritu tuo.

Orémus.   Oratio

DÓMINE sancte, Pater omnípotens, aetérne Deus: qui Fílium
tuum tibi coaetérnum et consubstantiálem de caelis descén-
dere, et de sacratíssima Vírgine María in hoc témpore plenitúdinis
incarnári temporáliter voluísti, ut ovem pérditam et errántem
quaéreret, et in húmeris própriis ad ovíle reportáret; nec non
ut eum, qui in latrónes íncidit, a vúlnerum suórum dolóre, in-
fúndens ipsi vinum et óleum, curáret; béne ✠ dic et sanctí ✠
fica hoc vinum: quod de vite in potum hóminum produxísti, et
praesta: ut, quisquis in hac sacra solemnitáte de eo súmpserit vel
bíberit, salútem ánimae et córporis consequátur: et si in peregrina-
tióne fúerit, ab eódem, tua grátia mediánte, confortétur; ut via
ejus in omni prosperitáte dirigátur. Per eúndem Christum Dóminum nostrum. ℟. Amen.

Thy mercy will follow me all the days of my life.

And I will dwell in the house of the Lord to the end of my days.

Glory be to the Father.

Lord, have mercy on us. Christ, have mercy on us. Lord, have mercy on us.

Our Father inaudibly until

℣. And lead us not into temptation.

℟. But deliver us from evil.

℣. Preserve thy servants.

℟. That trust in thee, my God.

℣. Send them aid, O Lord, from heaven.

℟. And from Sion watch over them.

℣. Let the enemy be powerless against them.

℟. And the son of evil do nothing to harm them.

℣. And should they drink anything deadly.

℟. May it not hurt them.

℣. O Lord, hear my prayer.

℟. And let my cry come unto thee.

℣. The Lord be with you.

℟. And with thy spirit.

Let us pray.   Prayer

HOLY Lord, Father almighty, eternal God! Who didst will that thy Son, equal to thee in eternity and substance should descend from heaven and in the fulness of time take temporal birth of the most holy Virgin Mary, so that He could seek the lost and wayward sheep and carry it on His shoulders to the sheepfold, and could cure the man fallen among robbers of his wounds by pouring in oil and wine — do thou bless ✠ and sanctify ✠ this wine which thou hast vintaged for man's drink. Whoever partakes of it on this holy solemnity, grant him life in body and soul. By thy goodness let it be to him strength in the pilgrimage to prosper him on the way, that his journey may come to a happy termination. Through the same Christ our Lord.

℟. Amen.

Orémus. Oratio

DÓMINE Jesu Christe, qui te vitem veram, et sanctos Apóstolos tuos pálmites appellári, et de ómnibus te diligéntibus víneam eléctam plantáre voluísti; béne ✠ dic hoc vinum, et virtútem ei tuae benedictiónis infúnde: ut, quicúmque ex eo súmpserit vel bíberit, intercedénte dilécto discípulo tuo Joánne Apóstolo et Evangelísta, síngulis morbis et venénis pestíferis effugátis, sanitátem inde córporis et ánimae consequátur: Qui vivis et regnas in saécula saeculórum. ℟. Amen.

Orémus. Oratio

DEUS, qui humáno géneri panem in cibum, et vinum in potum procreásti, ut panis corpus confórtet, et vinum cor hóminis laetíficet; quique beáto Joánni praedilécto discípulo tuo tantam grátiam contulísti, ut non solum haustum venéni illaésus eváderet, sed étiam in tua virtúte venéno prostrátos a morte resuscitáret: praesta ómnibus hoc vinum bibéntibus, ut spirituálem laetítiam et vitam cónsequi mereántur aetérnam. Per Dóminum. ℟. Amen.

Et aspergatur aqua benedicta.

9

BENEDICTIO AURI, THURIS ET MYRRHAE
in Festo Epiphaniae

℣. Adjutórium nostrum in nómine Dómini.
℟. Qui fecit caelum et terram.
℣. Dóminus vobíscum.
℟. Et cum spíritu tuo.

Orémus. Oratio

Súscipe, sancte Pater, a me indígno fámulo tuo haec múnera, quae in honórem nóminis tui sancti, et in títulum omnipoténtiae tuae majestátis, humíliter tibi óffero: sicut suscepísti sacrifícium

Let us pray.   Prayer

O LORD, Jesus Christ Who didst call thyself the true vine and thy holy apostles the branches, and didst desire to plant a chosen vineyard of all who love thee, bless ✠ this wine and impart to it the power of thy benediction. And as thy beloved disciple John, Apostle and Evangelist intercedes for them that partake thereof, grant them security from all deadly and poisonous afflictions and constant good health of soul and body. Who livest and reignest forever. ℟. Amen.

Let us pray.   Prayer

O GOD, thou givest to man bread to eat and wine to drink — bread to nourish the body and wine to cheer the heart. And as thou didst confer upon blessed John, thy beloved disciple such favor that not only did he himself escape the poisoned potion, but could restore life to others so overcome; do thou grant to all that drink this wine spiritual joy and eternal life. Through our Lord. ℟. Amen.

It is sprinkled with holy water.

9

BLESSING OF GOLD, INCENSE, AND MYRRH
on Epiphany

℣. Our help is in the name of the Lord.
℟. Who made heaven and earth.
℣. The Lord be with you.
℟. And with thy spirit.

Let us pray.   Prayer

Accept, O holy Father, from me, thine unworthy servant these gifts which I offer in humility to the honor of thy holy name

Abel justi, et sicut éadem múnera a tribus Magis tibi quondam offeréntibus suscepísti.

Exorcízo te, creatúra auri, thuris et myrrhae, per Pa ✝ trem omnipoténtem, per Jesum ✝ Christum, Fílium ejus unigénitum, et per Spíritum ✝ Sanctum Paráclitum: ut a te discédat omnis fraus, dolus, et nequítia diáboli, et sis remédium salutáre humáno géneri contra insídias inimíci: et quicúmque divíno freti auxílio te in suis lóculis, dómibus, aut circa se habúerint, per virtútem et mérita Dómini et Salvatóris nostri, ac intercessiónem ejus sanctíssimae Genetrícis et Vírginis Maríae, ac eórum, qui hódie simílibus munéribus Christum Dóminum veneráti sunt, omniúmque Sanctórum, ab ómnibus perículis ánimae et córporis liberéntur, et bonis ómnibus pérfrui mereántur. ℞. Amen.

D EUS invisíbilis et interminábilis, pietátem tuam per sanctum et treméndum Fílii tui nomen, supplíciter deprecámur: ut in hanc creatúram auri, thuris, myrrhae bene ✝ dictiónem ac operatiónem tuae virtútis infúndas: ut, qui ea penes se habúerint, ab omni aegritúdinis et laesiónis incúrsu tuti sint; et omnes morbos córporis et ánimae effúgiant, nullum dominétur eis perículum, et laeti, ac incólumes tibi in Ecclésia tua desérviant: Qui in Trinitáte perfécta vivis et regnas Deus per ómnia saécula saeculórum. ℞. Amen.

Et benedíctio Dei omnipoténtis, Pa ✝ tris, et Fílii, ✝ et Spíritus ✝ Sancti, descéndat super hanc creatúram auri, thuris et myrrhae, et máneat semper. ℞. Amen.

Et aspergantur aqua benedicta.

10

BENEDICTIO CRETAE
in Festo Epiphaniae

℣. Adjutórium nostrum in nómine Dómini.
℞. Qui fecit caelum et terram.

and to thy peerless majesty; as thou didst accept the sacrifice of the just Abel and the same gifts from the hands of the Magi.

Creatures of gold, incense, and myrrh, I purge you of evil by the Father ✠ almighty, by Jesus ✠ Christ, His Sole-Begotten Son, and by the Holy ✠ Spirit, the Paraclete, that freed from all deceit, evil, and cunning of the devil, you may be a saving remedy to men against the snares of the enemy. May trustful souls who use you in their homes or about their persons be delivered from danger to soul and body, rejoicing in the possession of every good; through our Lord and Savior's power and merits, through the intercession of Mary, most holy Virgin Mother of God, of all Saints and of them who on this day venerated Christ, the Lord with similar gifts. ℟. Amen.

O GOD, thou the invisible and unending One, in the holy and awesome name of thy Son graciously bestow blessing ✠ and power upon these creatures, gold, incense, and myrrh. Protect them who will have them in their possession from illness, injury, and danger to body and soul, so they can joyously and securely serve thee with zeal in thy Church. Who in perfect Trinity livest and reignest God, forever. ℟. Amen.

And may the blessing of almighty God, Father, ✠ Son, ✠ and Holy ✠ Spirit descend upon these creatures gold, incense, and myrrh, and remain for all time. ℟. Amen.

They are sprinkled with holy water.

10

BLESSING OF CHALK
on Epiphany

℣. Our help is in the name of the Lord.
℟. Who made heaven and earth.

℣. Dóminus vobíscum.

℟. Et cum spíritu tuo.

Béne ✠dic, Dómine Deus, creatúram istam cretae: ut sit salutáris humáno géneri; et praesta per invocatiónem nóminis tui sanctíssimi, ut, quicúmque ex ea súmpserint, vel ea in domus suae portis scrípserint nómina sanctórum tuórum Gásparis, Melchióris et Baltássar, per eórum intercessiónem et mérita, córporis sanitátem, et ánimae tutélam percípiant. Per Christum Dóminum nostrum. ℟. Amen.

Et aspergatur aqua benedicta.

11

BENEDICTIO DOMORUM
in Festo Epiphaniae

In ingressu:

℣. Pax huic dómui.

℟. Et ómnibus habitántibus in ea.

Antiphona: Ab Oriénte venérunt Magi in Béthlehem, adoráre Dóminum: et apértis thesáuris suis pretiósa múnera obtulérunt, aurum Regi magno, thus Deo vero, myrrham sepultúrae ejus. Allelúia.

Canticum beatae Mariae Virginis
Luc. 1, 46–55

Magníficat * ánima mea Dóminum:

Et exsultávit spíritus meus * in Deo, salutári meo.

Quia respéxit humilitátem ancíllae suae: * ecce enim, ex hoc beátam me dicent omnes generatiónes.

Quia fecit mihi magna qui potens est: * et sanctum nomen ejus.

Et misericórdia ejus a progénie in progénies * timéntibus eum.

Fecit poténtiam in bráchio suo: * dispérsit supérbos mente cordis sui.

℣. The Lord be with you.
℟. And with thy spirit.

Bless, ✠ O Lord God, this creature chalk to render it helpful
to men. Grant that they who use it in faith and with it inscribe
upon the entrance of their homes the names of thy saints, Caspar,
Melchior, and Baltassar may through their merits and intercession enjoy health of body and protection of soul. Through Christ
our Lord. ℟. Amen.

It is sprinkled with holy water.

11

BLESSING OF HOMES
on Epiphany

Upon entering:

℣. Peace be unto this home.
℟. And unto all that dwell herein.

Antiphon: From the East came the Magi to Bethlehem to
adore the Lord; and opening their treasures, they offered costly
gifts: gold to the great King, incense to the true God, and myrrh
in symbol of His burial. Alleluia.

Canticle of the Blessed Virgin Mary
Luke I, 46–55

My soul doth magnify the Lord.
And my spirit doth rejoice in God my Savior.
For He hath regarded the low estate of His handmaid; lo, hence-
forth all generations shall call me blessed.
For He that is mighty hath done great things for me, and holy
is His name.
And His mercy is from generation to generation to them that
fear Him.
He hath shown strength with His arm; He hath scattered the
proud in the conceit of their hearts.

Depósuit poténtes de sede, * et exaltávit húmiles.

Esuriéntes implévit bonis * et dívites dimísit inánes.

Suscépit Israel, púerum suum, * recordátus misericórdiae suae.

Sicut locútus est ad patres nostros, * Abraham, et sémini ejus ir saécula.

Glória Patri.

Interea aspergitur, et incensatur domus, et in fine repetitur A·tiphona: Ab Oriénte venérunt, etc.

Pater noster secreto usque ad

℣. Et ne nos indúcas in tentatiónem.

℟. Sed líbera nos a malo.

℣. Omnes de Saba vénient.

℟. Aurum et thus deferéntes.

℣. Dómine, exáudi oratiónem meam.

℟. Et clamor meus ad te véniat.

℣. Dóminus vobíscum.

℟. Et cum spíritu tuo.

Orémus.   Oratio

DEUS, qui hodiérna die Unigénitum tuum géntibus stella duce revelásti: concéde propítius; ut, qui jam te ex fide cognóvimus, usque ad contemplándam spéciem tuae celsitúdinis perducámur. Per eúndem Dóminum nostrum Jesum Christum. Fílium tuum: Qui tecum vivit et regnat in unitáte Spíritus Sancti Deus, per ómnia saécula saeculórum. ℟. Amen.

Responsorium: Illumináre, illumináre, Jerúsalem, quia venit lux tua: et glória Dómini super te orta est, Jesus Christus ex María Vírgine.

℣. Et ambulábunt gentes in lúmine tuo: et reges in splendóre ortus tui.

℟. Et glória Dómini super te orta est.

Orémus.   Oratio

BÉNE ✠ dic, Dómine, Deus omnípotens, locum istum (vel domum istam): ut sit in eo (ea) sánitas, cástitas, victóriae

He hath put down the mighty from their seats, and exalted them
of low degree.

The hungry He hath filled with good things; the rich He hath
sent away empty.

He hath helped Israel, His servant, being mindful of His mercy.

As He hath promised our fathers, Abraham and his seed forever.

Glory be to the Father.

Meanwhile the home is sprinkled and incensed, and at the end of the
canticle repeat the antiphon: From the East, etc.

Our Father inaudibly until:

℣. And lead us not into temptation.

℞. But deliver us from evil.

℣. Many shall come from Saba.

℞. Bearing gold and incense.

℣. O Lord, hear my prayer.

℞. And let my cry come unto thee.

℣. The Lord be with you.

℞. And with thy spirit.

Let us pray. Prayer

O GOD, Who by the guidance of a star didst this day reveal
thy Sole-Begotten Son to the Gentiles, grant that we who
now know thee by faith may be brought to the contemplation of
thy heavenly majesty. Through the same Jesus Christ, our Lord,
Who liveth and reigneth with thee in unity of the Holy Spirit,
God, forever and ever. ℞. Amen.

Responsory: Be enlightened and shine forth, O Jerusalem, for
thy light is come, and upon thee is risen the glory of the Lord,
Jesus Christ born of Mary Virgin.

℣. Nations shall walk in thy light, and kings in the brilliance
of thy origin.

℞. And the glory of the Lord is risen upon thee.

Let us pray. Prayer

B LESS, ✠ O Lord, almighty God this home that it be the
shelter of health, chastity, self-conquest, humility, goodness,

virtus, humílitas, bónitas, et mansuetúdo, plenitúdo legis, et gratiárum áctio Deo Patri, et Fílio, et Spirítui Sancto; et haec benedíctio máneat super hunc locum (vel hanc domum), et super habitántes in eo (ea). Per Christum Dóminum nostrum. ℟. Amen.

12

BENEDICTIO AQUAE
in Vigilia Epiphaniae Domini

(Approbata a S. R. C. die 6 Dec. 1890)

Statuta hora Sacerdos celebrans (tenens mitram, si sit Episcopus, quam ad Preces deponit) cum Diacono et Subdiacono, ille pluviali, isti dalmatica et tunicella induti albi coloris, praecedentibus Acolythis cum cereis accensis et Cruce (quae ponuntur ad loca sua) aliisque de Clero, veniunt ad locum prope altare majus, ubi paratum est vas cum sale, et alveolus cum aqua.

Primum, omnibus genuflectentibus, dicuntur cum cantu Litaniae Sanctorum, pag. 444. Post Ut omnibus fidelibus defunctis etc., Celebrans surgit, et gradatim elevando vocem, canit:

Ut hanc Aquam bene ✠ dícere dignéris, te rogámus.

Ut hanc Aquam bene ✠ dícere et sancti ✠ ficáre dignéris, te rogámus.

Cantores prosequuntur:

Ut nos exaudíre dignéris, te rogámus usque ad psalmos.

Deinde canuntur sequentes Psalmi:

Translator's Note: Although reserved to the bishop, this blessing may be conferred by a priest who secures the faculty. The blessing of Epiphany Water is of Oriental inspiration. The Eastern Church has long emphasized in its celebration of Epiphany the Mystery of our Lord's baptism in the Jordan, and by analogy our baptism. Albeit the mind of the Western Church has not neglected this

mildness, obedience to the commandments, and thanksgiving to
God the Father, Son, and Holy Spirit. May blessing remain for
all time upon this dwelling and them that live herein. Through
Christ our Lord. ℟. Amen.

12

BLESSING OF WATER
on the Vigil of Epiphany

(Approved by the Congregation of Sacred Rites, Dec. 6, 1890)

At the appointed time, the celebrant vested in white cope (if a
bishop, the mitre is worn but removed during the prayers) with deacon
and subdeacon vested in white dalmatic and tunic respectively, preceded
by acolytes bearing the processional cross and lighted candles (these
are put in their proper place), together with the other clerics come
before the altar where a vessel of water and a container of salt are
prepared.

First the Litany of the Saints is sung (see page 445), the while all
kneel. After the invocation: "That thou wouldst grant eternal rest,
etc.," the celebrant rises, and raising his voice for each invocation, sings:

That thou wouldst bless ✠ this water—we beseech thee hear us.

That thou wouldst bless ✠ and sanctify ✠ this water—we beseech thee hear us.

The cantors continue:

That thou wouldst graciously hear us, etc., until the Pater
inclusive.

Then the following psalms are sung:

---

*aspect, as the texts of the feast demonstrate, in practice Western
Catholics have concentrated on the Mystery of the Magi. The Latin
Rite has adopted this blessing of the Orient, and officially included
it in the Roman Ritual on December 6, 1890. But for many years
previous, diocesan rituals, notably in Germany, had contained a
blessing of Epiphany Water.*

Psalmus 28

VI

Afférte Dómino, fí-li-i De-i: * afférte Dómino, fí-li-os

arí-e-tum.

Afférte Dómino glóriam et honórem, afférte Dómino glóriam nómini ejus: * adoráte Dóminum in átrio sancto ejus.

Vox Dómini super aquas, Deus majestátis intónuit: * Dóminus super aquas multas.

Vox Dómini in virtúte: * vox Dómini in magnificéntia.

Vox Dómini confringéntis cedros: * et confrínget Dóminus cedros Líbani:

Et commínuet eas tamquam vítulum Líbani: * et diléctus quemádmodum fílius unicórnium.

Vox Dómini intercidéntis flammam ignis: * vox Dómini concutiéntis desértum: et commovébit Dóminus desértum Cades.

Vox Dómini praeparántis cervos, et revelábit condénsa: * et in templo ejus omnes dicent glóriam.

Dóminus dilúvium inhabitáre facit: * et sedébit Dóminus Rex in aetérnum.

Dóminus virtútem pópulo suo dabit: * Dóminus benedícet pópulo suo in pace.

Glória Patri.

Psalmus 45

DEUS noster refúgium, et virtus: * adjútor in tribulatiónibus, quae invenérunt nos nimis.

Proptérea non timébimus dum turbábitur terra: * et transferéntur montes in cor maris.

Sonuérunt, et turbátae sunt aquae eórum: * conturbáti sunt montes in fortitúdine ejus.

Flúminis ímpetus laetíficat civitátem Dei: * sanctificávit tabernáculum suum Altíssimus.

Psalm 28

Sacrifice to the Lord, ye sons of God; bring to the Lord the offspring of rams.

Offer to the Lord praise and honor, offer glory to His name; worship the Lord in His holy court.

The voice of the Lord booms over the waters, the God of majesty hath thundered, the Lord rules over tempestuous waters.

The voice of the Lord hath power, the voice of the Lord hath splendor.

The voice of the Lord breaketh the cedars, the Lord doth shatter the cedars of Lebanon,

And scattereth them to skip like a calf, while His beloved gambol like the young of bison.

The voice of the Lord spreadeth flame into lightning; the voice of the Lord maketh the desert to tremble; and the Lord shall shake the wilderness of Cades.

The voice of the Lord frighteneth deer to calve untimely, and strippeth bare the forests, and in His heavens all sing: "Glory!"

The Lord is enthroned upon the flood, the Lord shall reign as King forever.

The Lord will give strength to His people, the Lord will bless His people with peace.

Glory be to the Father.

Psalm 45

OUR God is refuge and strength — a Helper in sorrows which often beset us.

Hence we fear not, though the earth be shaken and the mountains sink in the midst of the sea;

Though the waters thereof should roar and foam, and the mountains quake from its breakers.

Gay billows of the river gladden the city of God; the Most High hath sanctified His dwelling.

Deus in médio ejus, non commovébitur: * adjuvábit eam Deus mane dilúculo.

Conturbátae sunt gentes, et inclináta sunt regna: * dedit vocem suam, mota est terra.

Dóminus virtútum nobíscum: * suscéptor noster Deus Jacob.

Veníte, et vidéte ópera Dómini, quae pósuit prodígia super terram: * áuferens bella usque ad finem terrae.

Arcum cónteret, et confrínget arma: * et scuta combúret igni.

Vacáte, et vidéte quóniam ego sum Deus: * exaltábor in géntibus, et exaltábor in terra.

Dóminus virtútum nobíscum: * suscéptor noster Deus Jacob.

Glória Patri.

Psalmus 146

LAUDÁTE Dóminum quóniam bonus est psalmus: * Deo nostro sit jucúnda, decóraque laudátio.

Aedíficans Jerúsalem Dóminus: * dispersiónes Israélis congregábit.

Qui sanat contrítos corde: * et álligat contritiónes eórum.

Qui númerat multitúdinem stellárum: * et ómnibus eis nómina vocat.

Magnus Dóminus noster, et magna virtus ejus: * et sapiéntiae ejus non est númerus.

Suscípiens mansuétos Dóminus: * humílians autem peccatóres usque ad terram.

Praecínite Dómino in confessióne: * psállite Deo nostro in cíthara.

Qui óperit caelum núbibus: * et parat terrae plúviam.

Qui prodúcit in móntibus faenum: * et herbam servitútı hóminum.

Qui dat juméntis escam ipsórum: * et pullis corvórum invocántibus eum.

Non in fortitúdine equi voluntátem habébit: * nec in tíbiis viri beneplácitum erit ei.

God is in the midst of the city, it shall not be disturbed; God will help it at earliest dawn.

The heathen were afflicted, and kingdoms brought low; God spoke, and their land was dissolved.

The Lord of hosts is with us, the God of Jacob is our protector.

Come ye and behold the works of the Lord, what desolation He hath wrought on their land! He endeth wars through the boundaries of the earth.

He breaketh the bow and destroyeth weapons, and shields He burneth in fire.

And He spoke: "Be still, and see that I am God! I will be exalted by the heathen, I will be exalted by my own."

The Lord of hosts is with us; the God of Jacob is our protector.

Glory be to the Father.

Psalm 146

P RAISE ye the Lord, for it is good to laud Him; joyful and worthy praise becometh our God.

The Lord rebuildeth Jerusalem, and will gather the exiles of Israel.

He healeth the heart-broken, and bindeth up their wounds.

He knoweth the number of stars, and calleth all by name.

Great is our Lord and great His power, His wisdom infinite.

The Lord raiseth up the meek, but the wicked He humbleth to the dust.

Sing ye to the Lord in thanksgiving; praise our God on the harp;

Who covereth the heavens with clouds, and prepareth rain for the earth.

Who maketh grass to grow on the hills and herbs for lower creatures.

Who giveth to beasts their food, and to little ravens that cry unto Him.

He placeth no trust in the strength of a steed, nor doth man's fleetness please Him.

Beneplácitum est Dómino super timéntes eum: * et in eis, qui sperant super misericórdia ejus.

Glória Patri.

Deinde Celebrans canendo dicit:

Exorcismus

contra satanam et angelos apostaticos

Exorcizámus te, omnis immúnde spíritus, omnis satánica potéstas, omnis incúrsio infernális adversárii, omnis légio, omnis congregátio et secta diabólica, in nómine et virtúte Domini nostri Jesu ✠ Christi, eradicáre et effugáre a Dei Ecclésia, ab ómnibus ad imáginem Dei cónditis ac pretióso divíni Agni sánguine redémptis ✠. Non ultra áudeas, serpens callidíssime, decípere humánum genus, Dei Ecclésiam pérsequi, ac Dei eléctos excútere et cribráre sicut tríticum ✠. Imperat tibi Deus altíssimus ✠, cui in magna tua supérbia te símilem habéri adhuc praesúmis; qui omnes hómines vult salvos fíeri, et ad agnitiónem veritátis veníre. Imperat tibi Deus Pater ✠. Imperat tibi Deus Fílius ✠. Imperat tibi Deus Spíritus Sanctus ✠. Imperat tibi majéstas Christi, aetérnum Dei Verbum caro factum ✠, qui pro salúte géneris nostri tua invídia pérditi, humiliávit semetípsum factus oboédiens usque ad mortem; qui Ecclésiam suam aedificávit supra firmam petram, et portas ínferi advérsus eam numquam esse praevalitúras edíxit, et cum ea ipse permansúrus ómnibus diébus usque ad consummatiónem saéculi. Imperat tibi sacraméntum Crucis ✠, omniúmque christiánae fídei Mysteriórum virtus ✠. Imperat tibi excélsa Dei Génetrix Virgo Mariá ✠, quae superbíssimum caput tuum a primo instánti immaculátae suae conceptiónis in sua humilitáte contrívit. Imperat tibi fides Sanctórum Apostolórum Petri et Pauli, et ceterórum Apostolórum ✠. Imperat tibi Mártyrum sanguis, ac pia Sanctórum et Sanctárum ómnium intercéssio ✠.

Ergo, draco maledícte et omnis légio diabólica, adjurámus te per Deum ✠ vivum, per Deum ✠ verum, per Deum ✠ sanctum,

The Lord taketh pleasure in them that fear Him and in them
that trust in His mercy.
Glory be to the Father.

The celebrant then chants:

Exorcism
against Satan and the apostate angels

We cast thee out, every unclean spirit, every devilish power,
every assault of the infernal adversary, every legion, every diabolical group and sect, by the name and power of our Lord, Jesus ✠
Christ, and command thee to fly far from the Church of God and
from all who are made to the image of God and redeemed by
the Precious Blood of the Divine Lamb ✠ . Presume never again,
thou cunning serpent, to deceive the human race, to persecute the
Church of God, nor to strike the chosen of God and sift them as
wheat ✠ . For the Most High God commands thee, ✠ He to
Whom thou didst hitherto in thy great pride presume thyself
equal; He Who desireth that all men might be saved, and come
to the knowledge of truth. God the Father ✠ commandeth thee!
God the Son ✠ commandeth thee! God the Holy ✠ Spirit commandeth thee! The majesty of Christ commands thee, the Eternal
Word of God made flesh, ✠ Who for the salvation of our race,
lost through thy envy, humbled Himself and was made obedient
even unto death; Who built His Church upon a solid rock, and
proclaimed that the gates of hell should never prevail against her,
and that He would remain with her all days, even to the end of
the world! The Sacred Mystery of the Cross ✠ commands thee,
as well as the power of all Mysteries of Christian faith! ✠ The
most excellent Virgin Mary, Mother of God ✠ commands thee,
who in her lowliness crushed thy proud head from the first moment of her Immaculate Conception! The faith of the holy Apostles Peter and Paul and the other apostles ✠ commands thee!
The blood of the martyrs commands thee, as well as the pious
intercession ✠ of holy men and women!

Therefore, accursed dragon and every diabolical legion, we ad-
jure thee by the living ✠ God, by the true ✠ God, by the holy ✠

per Deum, qui sic diléxit mundum, ut Fílium suum unigénitum daret, ut omnis qui credit in eum non péreat, sed hábeat vitam aetérnam; cessa decípere humánas creatúras, eísque aetérnae perditiónis venénum propináre: désine Ecclésiae nocére, et ejus libertáti láqueos injícere. Vade, sátana, invéntor et magíster omnis falláciae, hostis humánae salútis. Da locum Christo, in quo nihil invenísti de opéribus tuis; da locum Ecclésiae, uni, sanctae, cathólicae, et apostólicae, quam Christus ipse acquisívit sánguine suo. Humiliáre sub poténti manu Dei; contremísce et éffuge, invocáto a nobis sancto et terríbili nómine Jesu, quem ínferi tremunt, cui Virtútes et Potestátes et Dominatiónes subjéctae sunt; quem Chérubim et Séraphim indeféssis vócibus laudant, dicéntes: Sanctus, Sanctus, Sanctus Dóminus, Deus Sábaoth.

Postea a Cantoribus canitur:

Antiphona

VIII

Hódi-e * cae-lésti sponso juncta est Ec-clé-si-a, quóni-am in Jordá-ne lavit Christus e- jus crími-na : currunt cum muné-ri-bus Ma-gi ad regá-les núpti-as, et ex aqua facto vi-no laetántur conví- vae, alle- lú-ja.

Canticum Zachariae
Luc. 1, 68–79

Benedíctus Dóminus, Deus Israël, * quia visi-tá-vit, et fe-cit redempti-ónem plebis suae. Et eréxit cornu salú-tis nobis: *

God, by the God Who so loved the world that He gave His Sole-Begotten Son, that whosoever believeth in Him shall not perish, but shall have life everlasting — cease thy deception of men and thy giving them to drink of the poison of eternal damnation; desist from harming the Church and fettering her freedom! Get thee gone, Satan, founder and master of all falsity, enemy of mankind! Give place to Christ in Whom thou didst find none of thy works; give place to the one, holy, catholic, and apostolic Church which Christ Himself bought with His blood! Be thou brought low under God's mighty hand; tremble and flee as we call upon the holy and awesome name of Jesus, before Whom hell trembles, and to Whom the Virtues, Powers, and Dominations are subject; Whom the Cherubim and Seraphim praise with unfailing voices, saying: Holy, Holy, Holy, the Lord God of Hosts!

The cantors sing:

Antiphon

Today the Church is espoused to the heavenly Bridegroom, for in the Jordan Christ washes her sins: the Magi hasten with gifts to the regal nuptials, and the guests are gladdened with water become wine, alleluia.

Canticle of Zachary
Luke I, 68–79

Blessed be the Lord God of Israel, for He hath visited and redeemed His people,

And hath raised up the Abundance of salvation for us in the lineage of David His servant.

in domo David, pú-e-ri su-i.

Sicut locútus est per os sanctórum, * qui a saéculo sunt, Prophetárum ejus:

Salútem ex inimícis nostris, * et de manu ómnium, qui odérunt nos:

Ad faciéndam misericórdiam cum pátribus nostris: * et memorári testaménti sui sancti.

Jusjurándum, quod jurávit ad Abraham, patrem nostrum, * datúrum se nobis:

Ut sine timóre, de manu inimicórum nostrórum liberáti, * serviámus illi.

In sanctitáte, et justítia coram ipso, * ómnibus diébus nostris.

Et tu, puer, Prophéta Altíssimi vocáberis: * praeíbis enim ante fáciem Dómini paráre vias ejus:

Ad dandam sciéntiam salútis plebi ejus: * in remissiónem peccatórum eórum:

Per víscera misericórdiae Dei nostri: * in quibus visitávit nos, óriens ex alto:

Illumináre his, qui in ténebris, et in umbra mortis sedent: * ad dirigéndos pedes nostros in viam pacis.

Glória Patri.

Vel Canticum B. Mariae Virg.
Luc. 1, 46–55

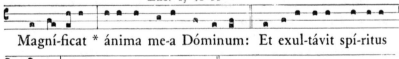

Magní-ficat * ánima me-a Dóminum: Et exul-távit spí-ritus

me-us * in De-o, salu-tári me-o.

Quia respéxit humilitátem ancíllae suae: * ecce enim, ex hoc beátam me dicent omnes generatiónes.

Quia fecit mihi magna qui potens est: * et sanctum nomen ejus.

Et misericórdia ejus a progénie in progénies * timéntibus eum.

Thus He foretold by the mouth of His holy prophets who have been from times ancient;

That we might be saved from our enemies — from the hand of all that hate us.

Now is granted the mercy promised to our fathers, remembering His holy covenant;

And the oath which He swore to Abraham our father that He would extend to us;

That we, delivered from the hand of our enemies, might serve Him without fear,

Living in holiness and righteousness before Him all our days.

And thou, child, shalt be called the prophet of the Highest, for thou shalt go before the face of the Lord to prepare His ways;

To give knowledge of salvation to His people — the remission of their sins,

Through the bounteous mercy of our God in which the Orient from on high hath visited us,

To give light to them that sit in darkness and in the shadow of death, to direct our feet into the way of peace.

Glory be to the Father.

Or instead, the following may be chosen:

Canticle of the Blessed Virgin Mary
Luke I, 46–55

My soul doth magnify the Lord.

And my spirit doth rejoice in God my Savior.

For He hath regarded the low estate of His handmaid; lo, henceforth all generations shall call me blessed.

For He that is mighty hath done great things for me, and holy is His name.

And His mercy is from generation to generation to them that fear Him.

Fecit poténtiam in bráchio suo: * dispérsit supérbos mente cordis sui.

Depósuit poténtes de sede, * et exaltávit húmiles.

Esuriéntes implévit bonis: * et dívites dimísit ináaes.

Suscépit Israel, púerum suum, * recordátus misericórdiae suae.

Sicut locútus est ad patres nostros, * Abraham, et sémini ejus in saécula.

Glória Patri.

Et repetitur Antiphona.
Deinde Celebrans canit ut sequitur:
℣. Dóminus vobíscum.
℟. Et cum spíritu tuo.

Orémus. *Oratio*

DEUS, qui hodiérna die Unigénitum tuum géntibus stella duce revelásti: concéde propítius; ut, qui jam te ex fide cognóvimus, usque ad contemplándam spéciem tuae celsitúdinis perducámur. Per eúndem Dóminum. ℟. Amen.

Postea benedicit aquam:
℣. Adjutórium nostrum in nómine Dómini.
℟. Qui fecit caelum et terram.

Exorcismus salis

Exorcízo te, creatúra salis, per Deum ✠ vivum, per Deum ✠ verum, per Deum ✠ sanctum, per Deum qui te per Eliséum prophétam in aquam mitti jussit, ut sanarétur sterílitas aquae: ut efficiáris sal exorcizátum in salútem credéntium; et sis ómnibus suméntibus te sánitas ánimae et córporis; et effúgiat, atque discédat a loco, in quo aspérsum fúeris, omnis phantásia, et nequítia, vel versútia diabólicae fraudis, omnísque spíritus immúndus, adjurátus per eum, qui ventúrus est judicáre vivos et mórtuos et saéculum per ignem. ℟. Amen.

He hath shown strength with His arm; He hath scattered the proud in the conceit of their hearts.

He hath put down the mighty from their seats, and exalted them of low degree.

The hungry He hath filled with good things; the rich He hath sent away empty.

He hath helped Israel, His servant, being mindful of His mercy.

As He hath promised our fathers, Abraham and his seed forever.

Glory be to the Father.

Repeat the antiphon.

Then the celebrant sings:

℣. The Lord be with you.

℟. And with thy spirit.

Let us pray.   Prayer

O GOD, Who by the guidance of a star didst this day reveal thy Sole-Begotten Son to the Gentiles, grant that we who now know thee by faith may be brought to the contemplation of thy heavenly majesty. Through the same Jesus Christ, our Lord, Who liveth and reigneth with thee in unity of the Holy Spirit, God, eternally. ℟. Amen.

Next he blesses the water:

℣. Our help is in the name of the Lord.

℟. Who made heaven and earth.

Exorcism of salt

Thou creature of salt, I purge thee of evil by the living ✠ God, by the true ✠ God, by the holy ✠ God, by the God Who ordered thee through Eliseus, the prophet to be cast into the water to cure its unfruitfulness. Be thou a purified salt for the health of believers, giving soundness of body and soul to all who use thee. In whatever place thou art sprinkled, may phantoms and wickedness, and Satan's cunning be banished. And let every unclean spirit be repulsed by Him Who shall come to judge the living and the dead, and the world by fire. ℟. Amen.

Orémus.   Oratio

IMMÉNSAM cleméntiam tuam, omnípotens aetérne Deus, humíliter implorámus, ut hanc creatúram salis, quam in usum géneris humáni tribuísti, bene ✠ dícere, et sancti ✠ ficáre tua pietáte dignéris: ut sit ómnibus suméntibus salus mentis et córporis; et quidquid ex eo tactum vel respérsum fúerit, cáreat omni immundítia, omníque impugnatióne spiritális nequítiae. Per Dóminum nostrum. ℞. Amen.

Exorcismus aquae

Exorcízo te, creatúra aquae, in nómine Dei ✠ Patris omnipoténtis, et in nómine Jesu ✠ Christi Fílii ejus Dómini nostri, et in virtúte Spíritus ✠ Sancti: ut fias aqua exorcizáta ad effugándam omnem potestátem inimíci, et ipsum inimícum eradicáre et explantáre váleas cum ángelis suis apostáticis, per virtútem ejúsdem Dómini nostri Jesu Christi: qui ventúrus est judicáre vivos et mórtuos et saéculum per ignem. ℞. Amen.

Orémus.   Oratio

DEUS, qui ad salútem humáni géneris, máxima quaeque sacraménta in aquárum substántia condidísti: adésto propítius invocatiónibus nostris, et eleménto huic multímodis purificatiónibus praeparáto, virtútem tuae bene ✠ dictiónis infúnde; ut creaiúra tua mystériis tuis sérviens, ad abigéndos daémones, morbósque pelléndos, divínae grátiae sumat efféctum; ut, quidquid in dómibus vel in locis fidélium haec unda respérserit, cáreat omni immundítia, liberétur a noxa: non illic resídeat spíritus péstilens, non aura corrúmpens: discédant omnes insídiae laténtis inimíci: et si quid est, quod aut incolumitáti habitántium ínvidet aut quiéti, aspersióne hujus aquae effúgiat; ut salúbritas per invocatiónem sancti tui nóminis expetíta ab ómnibus sit impugnatiónibus defénsa. Per Dóminum nostrum. ℞. Amen.

Let us pray.

O ALMIGHTY, everlasting God! Humbly we implore thy boundless mercy that thou wouldst deign of thy goodness to bless ✠ and sanctify ✠ this creature of salt which thou hast given for the use of mankind. May all that use it find in it a remedy for soul and body. And let everything which it touches or sprinkles be freed from uncleanness and assault from evil spirits. Through our Lord, Jesus Christ thy Son Who liveth and reigneth with thee in unity of the Holy Spirit, God, forever and ever. ℟. Amen.

Exorcism of water

Thou creature of water, I purge thee of evil in the name of God ✠ the Father almighty, in the name of Jesus ✠ Christ, thy Son, our Lord, and in the power of the Holy ✠ Spirit, that thou mayest be exorcized water qualified to brace us against the envious foe. Mayest thou drive him forth and exile him together with his faithless followers, by the power of the selfsame Jesus Christ, our Lord, Who shall come to judge the living and the dead and the world by fire. ℟. Amen.

Let us pray.

O GOD, Who for man's salvation dost dispense wondrous mysteries with the efficacious sign of water, hearken to our prayer — pouring forth thy benediction ✠ upon this element which we consecrate with manifold purifications. Let this creature serve thee in expelling demons and curing diseases. Whatsoever it sprinkles in the homes of the faithful, be it cleansed and delivered from harm. Let such homes enjoy a spirit of goodness and an air of tranquillity, freed from baneful and hidden snares. By the sprinkling of this water may everything opposed to the safety and repose of them that dwell therein be banished, so that they may possess the well-being they seek in calling upon thy holy name, and be protected from all peril. Through our Lord, Jesus Christ thy Son, Who liveth and reigneth with thee in the unity of the Holy Spirit, God, forever and ever. ℟. Amen.

Hic ter mittit sal in aquam in modum crucis, dicendo semel sine cantu:

Commíxtio salis et aquae páriter fiat, in nómine Pa ✠ tris, et Fí ✠ lii, et Spíritus ✠ Sancti. ℟. Amen.

Deinde canit:

℣. Dóminus vobíscum.
℟. Et cum spíritu tuo.

Orémus.   Oratio

D EUS, invíctae virtútis auctor, et insuperábilis impérii rex, ac semper magníficus triumphátor: qui advérsae dominatiónis vires réprimis: qui inimíci rugiéntis saevítiam súperas: qui hostíles nequítias poténter expúgnas: te, Dómine, treméntes et súpplices deprecámur ac pétimus: ut hanc creatúram salis et aquae dignánter aspícias, benígnus illústres, pietátis tuae rore sanctífices; ut, ubicúmque fuérit aspérsa, per invocatiónem sancti nóminis tui, omnis infestátio immúndi spíritus abigátur, terrórque venenósi serpéntis procul pellátur: et praeséntia Sancti Spíritus nobis, misericórdiam tuam poscéntibus, ubíque adésse dignétur. Per Dóminum. . . . in unitáte ejúsdem Spíritus. ℟. Amen.

Expleta benedictione, per Celebrantem aspergitur populus aqua benedicta.

Tandem sollemniter canitur Hymnus:

Te De-um laudámus: * te Dóminum confité-mur. Te aetér-

num Patrem omnis terra venerá-tur. Ti-bi omnes Ange-li,

tibi Caeli, et univérsae Po-testá- tes : Tibi Chérubim et

Séraphim inces-sábi-li voce proclá-mant : Sanctus : Sanctus:

He thrice puts salt into the water in the form of a cross, saying once without chanting it:

May this salt and water be mixed together, in the name of the Father, ✠ and of the Son, ✠ and of the Holy ✠ Spirit. ℟. Amen.

Then he sings:

℣. The Lord be with you.

℟. And with thy spirit.

Let us pray. *Prayer*

AUTHOR of invincible strength and King of an unconquerable empire, ever the gloriously Triumphant One! Who restrainest the force of the adversary, Who overcomest the fierceness of the devouring enemy, Who valiantly putteth down hostile influences! Prostrate and fearsome we beseech thee, Lord, consider kindly this creature of salt and water, make it honored, and sanctify it with the dew of thy sweetness. Wherever it is sprinkled in thy name, may devilish infection cease, venomous terror be driven afar. But let the presence of the Holy Spirit be always with us as we implore thy mercy. Through our Lord, Jesus Christ, thy Son, Who liveth and reigneth with thee in unity of the same Holy Spirit, God, eternally. ℟. Amen.

The blessing being finished, the celebrant sprinkles the people with the blessed water.

In conclusion the **Te Deum** is sung in solemn manner:

Te Deum

We praise thee, O God: we acknowledge thee to be the Lord.

All the earth doth worship thee, the Father everlasting.

To thee all angels, to thee the heavens, and all the powers therein:

To thee the Cherubim and Seraphim with unceasing voice proclaim:

'Holy, holy, holy, Lord God of Sabaoth!

Sanctus Dóminus De-us Sába-oth. Pleni sunt cae-li et terra

majestá-tis glóri-ae tu-ae. Te glori-ósus Aposto-lórum cho-rus.

Te Prophe-tárum laudábi-lis núme-rus. Te Mártyrum can-

didá-tus laudat exérci-tus. Te per orbem terrárum sancta

confité-tur Ecclé-si-a. Pa- trem imménsae ma-jestá-tis;

Venerándum tu-um verum et únicum Fíli- um; Sanctum

quoque Parácli-tum Spíri-tum. Tu Rex gló-ri-ae, Christe.

Tu Patris sempi-térnus es Fí-li-us. Tu ad libe-rándum

susceptúrus hómi-nem, non horru-ísti Vírginis úterum.

Tu devícto mortis acú- le- o, aperu- ísti credéntibus regna

caelórum. Tu ad déxteram De-i se- des, in gló-ri-a Patris

Judex créderis esse ventúrus. Te ergo quaé-sumus, tu-is

fámu-lis súbve- ni, quos pre-ti-óso sánguine redemísti.

Heaven and the earth are full of the majesty of thy glory."

Thee, the glorious choir of the apostles,

Thee, the admirable company of the prophets,

Thee, the white-robed army of martyrs praise.

Thee, the holy Church throughout the world doth acknowledge:

The Father of infinite majesty,

Thine adorable, true, and only Son,

Also the Holy Spirit, the Comforter.

Thou, O Christ, art the King of glory.

Thou art the everlasting Son of the Father.

Thou didst not abhor the Virgin's womb, when thou didst assume human nature to deliver man,

When thou hadst overcome the sting of death, thou didst open to believers the kingdom of heaven.

Thou sittest at the right hand of God, in the glory of the Father.

We believe that thou art the Judge to come.

We beseech thee, therefore, help thy servants whom thou hast redeemed with thy Precious Blood.

Aetérna fac cum Sanctis tu-is in glóri-a numerá- ri Salvum

fac pópu-lum tu-um, Dómi-ne, et bénedic heredi-tá-ti tu-ae.

Et re-ge e-os, et extólle illos usque in aetér- num. Per

síngul-os di- es bene-dícimus te. Et laudámus nomen

tu-um in sáe-cu- lum, et in saécu-lum saécu-li. Dignáre,

Dómine, di-e i- sto sine peccáto nos custódí-re. Mise-rére

nostri, Dómi- ne, mise-rére nostri. Fi-at mise-ricórdi-a tu-a,

Dómine, su-per nos, quemád-modum sperá-vimus in te.

In te, Dómine, spe-rá- vi: non confúndar in ae-tér- num.

℣. Dóminus vobiscum.
℟. Et cum spíritu tuo.

Orémus. Oratio

DEUS, cujus misericórdiae non est númerus, et bonitátis infinítus est thesáurus: piíssimae Majestáti tuae pro collátis
donis grátias ágimus, tuam semper cleméntiam exorántes; ut,
qui peténtibus postuláta concédis, eósdem non déserens, ad prae-
mia futúra dispónas. Per Christum Dóminum nostrum. ℟.
Amen.

Make them to be numbered among thy saints, in glory everlasting.
Save thy people, Lord, and bless thine inheritance.
And rule them, and exalt them forever.
Day by day, we laud thee,
And we praise thy name forever; yea, forever and ever.
Vouchsafe, O Lord, this day, to keep us without sin.
Have mercy on us, O Lord, have mercy on us.
Let thy mercy, Lord, be upon us, even as we have hoped in thee.
O Lord, in thee have I trusted: let me not be confounded forever.

℣. The Lord be with you.
℞. And with thy spirit.

Let us pray.   Prayer

O God, Whose mercy is without limits and Whose goodness is a boundless treasury! We thank thy loving Sublimity for bountiful favors, and perseveringly appeal to thy clemency. Desert us not, thou Who hearest thy suppliants, but speed us to final victory. Through Christ our Lord. ℞. Amen.

Tandem a Celebrante, si sit Episcopus, impertitur populo Benedictio: qua completa, omnes revertuntur, uti venerunt.

Aqua benedicta, uti supra, dispensatur fidelibus, ut ea devote utantur in eorum cubiculis, et etiam pro infirmis.

13

DE PUBLICATIONE FESTORUM MOBILIUM
in Epiphania Domini

In Epiphania Domini, cantato Evangelio, Archidiaconus, sive aliquis Canonicus, vel Beneficiatus, aut alius, juxta consuetudinem loci, pluviali paratus, ascendet ambonem, vel pulpitum, et ibidem vel in alio loco ubi cantari solet Evangelium, e vetusto Ecclesiae sanctae instituto publicabit Festa mobilia anni currentis juxta infrascriptam formulam, et diem Synodi dioecesanae suo loco promulgabit, licet in formula infrascripta Dominica secunda post Pascha notato sit.

VIII

No-vé-ri-tis, fratres ca-rís-si-mi, quod annuénte De-i mi-se-ri-cór-di-a, sic-ut de Na-ti-vi-tá-te Dó-mi-ni nostri Je-su Chri-sti ga-ví-si su-mus, i-ta et de Re-surre-cti-ó-ne e-júsdem Salva-tó-ris nostri gáudi-um vo-bis annunti-á-mus. Die pri-ma (vel alia, prout occurrit.) (Ja-nu-á-ri-i. vel Fe-bru-á-ri-i.) e-rit Do-mí-ni-ca in Septu-a-gé- si-ma. Vi-gé- si-ma (vel alia quae occurrit, uti et in sequentibus.) (Fe-bru-á-ri-i. Mártii, ejúsdem.) di-es Cí-ne-rum, et in-í-ti-um je-jú-ni-i sacra-

If the officiant is a bishop, he now blesses the people, and the service comes to a close.

The blessed water is given to the faithful who will use it to bless the sick and their homes.

13

THE SOLEMN ANNOUNCING OF MOVABLE FEASTDAYS
on Epiphany

On the Epiphany of our Lord, after the gospel has been sung, an archdeacon, canon, or beneficiary, or another (as local custom warrants), vested in cope, goes to the ambo or pulpit or place where the gospel usually is chanted. There, according to an ancient practice of holy Church, he announces the movable feastdays of the current year, using the rite described below. Provision is likewise made herein for the promulgation of the date for the diocesan synod:

Know ye, beloved brethren, that as by God's favor we rejoiced in the Nativity of our Lord, Jesus Christ, so, too, we announce to you the glad tidings on the Resurrection of our Savior. The Sunday of Septuagesima will fall on .... Ash Wednesday and the beginning of the most holy Lenten fast on

---

Translator's Note: This is from the Roman Pontifical. For its beauty and impressiveness and because it may be performed by one lesser than a prelate, it is included among these rites for Epiphany.

tís-si-mae Quadra-gé- -si-mae. . . . . . . $\left(\begin{smallmatrix}\text{Már-ti-i.}\\\text{A-prí-lis}\end{smallmatrix}\right)$

sanctum Pascha Dó-mi-ni nostri Je-su Chri-sti cum gáudi-o

ce-lebrá- bi-tis. Do-mí-ni-ca secúnda post Pascha di-oe-ce-

sá-na Sy-no-dus ha-bé- bi-tur. . . . . . $\left(\begin{smallmatrix}\text{Aprílis.}\\\text{Maii. Júnii.}\end{smallmatrix}\right)$

e-rit Ascén-si-o Dómi-ni nostri Je-su Chri-sti. . . . .

$\left(\begin{smallmatrix}\text{Maii. Júnii.}\\\text{ejúsdem.}\end{smallmatrix}\right)$ Festum Pente-có- stes. . . . .

$\left(\begin{smallmatrix}\text{ejúsdem.}\\\text{Júnii.}\end{smallmatrix}\right)$ Festum sacra-tís-si-mi Córpo-ris Chri- sti.

$\left(\begin{smallmatrix}\text{Novémbris.}\\\text{Decémbris.}\end{smallmatrix}\right)$ Domí-ni-ca prima Advéntus Dómi-ni nostri

Je-su Chri-sti, cu-i est honor et gló-ri-a, in saé-cu-la sae-cu-

ló- rum. A-men.

14

BENEDICTIO CANDELARUM
in Festo S. Blasii Episcopi et Martyris

℣. Adjutórium nostrum in nómine Dómini.
℟. Qui fecit caelum et terram.

.... On .... you shall celebrate with greatest joy the holy Pasch of our Lord, Jesus Christ. (On the second Sunday after Easter the diocesan synod will be held). The Ascension of our Lord, Jesus Christ will occur on .... ̇
.... The Feast of Pentecost on ....
The Feast of Corpus Christi on .... November .... (or December ....) will usher in the Advent of our Lord, Jesus Christ, to Whom be glory and honor eternally. Amen.

14

BLESSING OF CANDLES
on the Feast of St. Blase, Bishop and Martyr

℣. Our help is in the name of the Lord.
℟. Who made heaven and earth.

℣. Dóminus vobíscum.

℟. Et cum spíritu tuo.

Orémus.   Oratio

Omnípotens et mitíssime Deus, qui ómnium mundi rerum diversitátes solo Verbo creásti, et ad hóminum reformatiónem illud idem Verbum, per quod facta sunt ómnia, incarnári voluísti: qui magnus es, et imménsus, terríbilis atque laudábilis, ac fáciens mirabília: pro cujus fídei confessióne gloriósus Martyr et Póntifex Blásius, diversórum tormentórum génera non pavéscens, martýrii palmam felíciter est adéptus: quique eídem, inter céteras grátias, hanc praerogatívam contulísti, ut, quoscúmque gútturis morbos tua virtúte curáret; majestátem tuam supplíciter exorámus, ut non inspéctu reátus nostri, sed ejus placátus méritis et précibus, hanc cerae creatúram bene ✝ dícere ac sancti ✝ ficáre tua venerábili pietáte dignéris, tuam grátiam infundéndo; ut omnes, quorum colla per eam ex bona fide tacta fúerint, a quocúmque gútturis morbo ipsíus passiónis méritis liberéntur, et in Ecclésia sancta tua sani et hílares tibi gratiárum réferant actiónes, laudéntque nomen tuum gloriósum, quod est benedíctum in saécula saeculórum. Per Dóminum nostrum Jesum Christum, Fílium tuum: Qui tecum vivit et regnat in unitáte Spíritus Sancti Deus, per ómnia saécula saeculórum. ℟. Amen.

Et aspergantur aqua benedicta.

Deinde Sacerdos duos cereos in modum crucis aptatos apponit sub mento gutturi singulorum, qui benedicendi sunt, ipsis ante Altare genuflectentibus, dicens:

Per intercessiónem sancti Blásii, Epíscopi et Mártyris, líberet te Deus a malo gútturis, et a quólibet álio malo. In nómine Patris, et Fílii, ✝ et Spíritus Sancti. ℟. Amen.

℣. The Lord be with you.
℟. And with thy spirit.

Let us pray. Prayer

O God of gentleness and might, by thy Word alone thou didst create the manifold things of the world, and didst cause this same Word, Maker of all things, to take flesh in order to repurchase us. Thou art great and wonderful, awesome and praiseworthy, a doer of wonderful deeds. Wherefore, in professing his fealty to thee, the glorious martyr and bishop, Blase did not fear any manner of torment, but gladly accepted the palm of martyrdom. In virtue of which, among other gifts, thou didst bestow on him this prerogative — of healing all ailments of the throat. Thus we beg thy Majesty that overlooking our guilt, and considering only his merits and intercession thou wouldst deign to bless ✙ and sanctify ✙ and bestow thy grace on these candles. Let all Christians of good faith whose necks are touched with them be healed of every malady of the throat, and being restored in health and cheer, let them return thanks in thy holy Church, and give praise to thy wondrous name which is blessed forever. Through our Lord, Jesus Christ, thy Son, Who liveth and reigneth with thee in unity of the Holy Spirit, God, eternally. ℟. Amen.

They are sprinkled with holy water.

Then the priest, holding two crossed candles to the throat of each one to be blessed, as they kneel before the altar, says:

Through the intercession of St. Blase, Bishop and Martyr, may God deliver thee from sickness of the throat and from every other evil. In the name of the Father, and of the Son, ✙ and of the Holy Spirit. ℟. Amen.

15

BENEDICTIO PANIS, VINI, AQUAE ET FRUCTUUM
Contra Gutturis Aegritudinem
in Festo S. Blasii Episcopi et Martyris
(Approbata a S. R. C. die 25 Sept. 1883)

℣. Adjutórium nostrum in nómine Dómini.
℟. Qui fecit caelum et terram.
℣. Dóminus vobíscum.
℟. Et cum spíritu tuo.

Orémus.   Oratio

Salvátor mundi Deus, qui hodiérnam diem beatíssimi Blásii martýrio consecrásti, quique eídem inter céteras grátias, hanc praerogatívam contulísti, ut, quoscúmque gútturis morbos tua virtúte curáret: ineffábilem misericórdiam tuam supplíciter exorámus, et pétimus; ut hos panes, vinum, aquam et fructus, quae plebs fidélis tibi devóte hódie ad sanctificándum áttulit, tua pietáte bene ✠ dícere et sancti ✠ ficáre dignéris: ut, qui ex his gustáverint, ab omni gútturis plaga, et quavis ália ánimae et córporis infirmitáte, méritis et intercessióne ejúsdem beáti Blásii Mártyris tui atque Pontíficis, plenam recípiant sanitátem: Qui vivis et regnas Deus in saécula saeculórum. ℟. Amen.

Et aspergantur aqua benedicta.

16

BENEDICTIO DOMORUM
In Sabbato Sancto et reliquo Tempore Paschali

Parochus, seu alius Sacerdos de Parochi licentia, superpelliceo et stola alba indutus, cum ministro deferente vas aquae benedictae in Fonte baptismali, atque ante infusionem Olei et Chrismatis acceptae, Sabbato Sancto visitat domos suae paroeciae, aspergens eas eadem aqua benedicta.

15

BLESSING OF BREAD, WINE, WATER, AND FRUIT
for the relief of throat ailments
on the Feast of St. Blase, Bishop and Martyr

(Approved by the Congregation of Sacred Rites on Sept. 25, 1883)

℣. Our help is in the name of the Lord.
℟. Who made heaven and earth.
℣. The Lord be with you.
℟. And with thy spirit.

Let us pray. Prayer

O God, Savior of the world, Who didst consecrate this day with the martyrdom of the most venerable Blase, granting him among other gifts the power of healing all who are afflicted with throat ailments; we humbly beseech thy boundless mercy, and beg that these fruits, bread, wine, and water, which thy devoted people bring today, be blessed ✠ and sanctified ✠ by thy goodness. May they who taste thereof be fully healed of all afflictions of the throat, as well as every infirmity of soul or body, through the prayers and merits of the same Blase, Pontiff and Martyr. Thou who livest and reignest God, forevermore. ℟. Amen.

They are sprinkled with holy water.

16

BLESSING OF HOMES
on Holy Saturday and during Paschaltide

The parish priest (or a priest having his permission) vested in surplice and white stole, assisted by a server who carries a vessel containing blessed water taken from the baptismal font before the infusion of the Sacred Oils, visits the homes of his parishioners on Holy Saturday, sprinkling them with the blessed water.

Ingrediens domum dicit:

℣.Pax huic dómui.

℟.Et ómnibus habitántibus in ea.

2. Deinde aspergens loca praecipua domus, et habitantes in ea, dicit Antiphonam:

V̄idi aquam egrediéntem de templo, a látere dextro, allelúia: et omnes, ad quos pervénit aqua ista, salvi facti sunt, et dicent: allelúia, allelúia. Ps. 117, 1.Confitémini Dómino, quóniam bonus: quóniam in saéculum misericórdia ejus.

℣.Glória Patri, etc.

Repetitur Antiphona:Vidi aquam, etc.

Deinde dicit:

℣.Osténde nobis, Dómine, misericórdiam tuam, allelúia.

℟.Et salutáre tuum da nobis, allelúia.

℣.Dómine, exáudi oratiónem meam.

℟.Et clamor meus ad te véniat.

℣.Dóminus vobíscum.

℟.Et cum spíritu tuo.

Orémus.   Oratio

Exáudi nos, Dómine sancte, Pater omnípotens, aetérne Deus: et sicut domos Hebraeórum in éxitu de Aegýpto, agni sánguine linítas (quod pascha nostrum, in quo immolátus est Christus, figurábat), ab Angelo percutiénte custodísti; ita míttere dignéris sanctum Angelum tuum de caelis, qui custódiat, fóveat, prótegat, vísitet, atque deféndat omnes habitántes in hoc habitáculo. Per eúndem Christum Dóminum nostrum. ℟.Amen.

3. Ritus superius descriptus adhibetur, etiamsi benedictio domorum fiat alia die intra Tempus Paschale pro locorum consuetudine.

Entering the home he says:

℣. Peace be unto this home.

℞. And unto all that dwell herein.

2. Then he sprinkles the dwelling's main room and the occupants, saying the antiphon:

I saw water flowing from the right side of the temple, alleluia: and all to whom this water came were saved, and they shall say: alleluia, alleluia. Ps. 117, 1. Let us give thanks to the Lord for His goodness: for His mercy endureth forever.

℣. Glory be to the Father, etc.

Repeat the antiphon: I saw water, etc.

Then he says:

℣. Show us thy mercy, Lord, alleluia.

℞. And grant us thy salvation, alleluia.

℣. O Lord, hear my prayer.

℞. And let my cry come unto thee.

℣. The Lord be with you.

℞. And with thy spirit.

Let us pray.   Prayer

Hear us, holy Lord, Father almighty, eternal God! And as on their departure from Egypt thou didst guard the homes of the Israelites from the avenging angel if they were smeared with blood (prefiguring our Pasch in which Christ is slain), so likewise send thy holy angel from heaven to guard, cherish, protect, visit, and defend all who dwell in this house. Through the same Christ our Lord. ℞. Amen.

3. The blessing given above is used on any day of Paschaltide, depending upon local custom.

BENEDICTIONES ESCULENTORUM
Praesertim in Pascha

17

BENEDICTIO AGNI

℣. Adjutórium nostrum in nómine Dómini.
℟. Qui fecit caelum et terram.
℣. Dóminus vobíscum.
℟. Et cum spíritu tuo.

Orémus.   Oratio

Deus, qui per fámulum tuum Móysen, in liberatióne pópuli tui de Aegýpto, agnum occídi jussísti in similitúdinem Dómini nostri Jesu Christi, et utrósque postes domórum de sánguine ejúsdem agni perúngi praecepísti: tu bene ✠ dícere, et sancti ✠ ficáre dignéris hanc creatúram carnis, quam nos fámuli tui ad laudem tuam súmere desiderámus, per resurrectiónem ejúsdem Dómini nostri Jesu Christi; Qui tecum vivit et regnat in saécula saeculórum. ℟. Amen.

Et aspergatur aqua benedicta.

18

BENEDICTIO OVORUM

℣. Adjutórium nostrum in nómine Dómini.
℟. Qui fecit caelum et terram.
℣. Dóminus vobíscum.
℟. Et cum spíritu tuo.

Orémus.   Oratio

Subvéniat, quaésumus, Dómine, tuae bene ✠ dictiónis grátia huic ovórum creatúrae: ut cibus salúbris fiat fidélibus tuis, in

THE PASCHAL BLESSINGS OF FOOD

17

BLESSING OF LAMB

℣. Our help is in the name of the Lord.
℟. Who made heaven and earth.
℣. The Lord be with you.
℟. And with thy spirit.

Let us pray. *Prayer*

O God, Who by thy servant Moses didst command thy people in their deliverance from Egypt to kill a lamb in symbol of Jesus Christ, our Lord, and didst prescribe that its blood be used to anoint their door-posts, do thou bless ✠ and sanctify ✠ this flesh which we thy servants desire to eat in praise of thee. Through the Resurrection of the same Christ Jesus, our Lord, Who liveth and reigneth with thee in eternity. ℟. Amen.

It is sprinkled with holy water.

18

BLESSING OF EGGS

℣. Our help is in the name of the Lord.
℟. Who made heaven and earth.
℣. The Lord be with you.
℟. And with thy spirit.

Let us pray. *Prayer*

Let thy blessing, ✠ Lord, come upon these eggs that they be salutary food for the faithful who eat them in thanksgiving for

tuárum gratiárum actióne suméntibus, ob resurrectiónem Dómini nostri Jesu Christi: Qui tecum vivit et regnat in saécula saeculórum. ℞. Amen.

Et aspergantur aqua benedicta.

19

BENEDICTIO PANIS

℣. Adjutórium nostrum in nómine Dómini.
℞. Qui fecit caelum et terram.
℣. Dóminus vobíscum.
℞. Et cum spíritu tuo.

Orémus. Oratio

Dómine Jesu Christe, panis Angelórum, panis vivus aetérnae vitae, bene ✠ dícere dignáre panem istum, sicut benedixísti quinque panes in desérto: ut omnes ex eo gustántes, inde córporis et ánimae percípiant sanitátem: Qui vivis et regnas in saécula saeculórum. ℞. Amen.

Et aspergatur aqua benedicta.

20

ALIA BENEDICTIO PANIS

℣. Adjutórium nostrum in nómine Dómini.
℞. Qui fecit caelum et terram.
℣. Dóminus vobíscum.
℞. Et cum spíritu tuo.

Orémus. Oratio

Dómine sancte, Pater omnípotens, aetérne Deus, bene ✠ dícere dignéris hunc panem tua sancta spirituáli benedictióne: ut sit ómnibus suméntibus salus mentis et córporis; atque contra omnes

the Resurrection of Jesus Christ, our Lord, Who liveth and reigneth with thee forever and ever. ℟. Amen.

They are sprinkled with holy water.

19

BLESSING OF BREAD

℣. Our help is in the name of the Lord.
℟. Who made heaven and earth.
℣. The Lord be with you.
℟. And with thy spirit.

Let us pray. *Prayer*

O Lord, Jesus Christ, bread of angels, true bread of everlasting life, bless ✠ this bread as thou didst the five loaves in the wilderness; that all who eat of it may have health of body and soul. Who livest and reignest forever. ℟. Amen.

It is sprinkled with holy water.

20

ANOTHER BLESSING FOR BREAD

℣. Our help is in the name of the Lord.
℟. Who made heaven and earth.
℣. The Lord be with you.
℟. And with thy spirit.

Let us pray. *Prayer*

Holy Lord, Father almighty, everlasting God, bless ✠ this bread with thy supernatural benevolence. May it be to all partakers health for body and soul, and a safeguard against illness

morbos, et univérsas inimicórum insídias tutámen. **Per Dóminum nostrum Jesum Christum, Fílium tuum, panem vivum, qui de caelo descéndit, et dat vitam et salútem mundo: et tecum vivit et regnat in unitáte Spíritus Sancti Deus, per ómnia saécula saeculórum.** ℟. Amen.

Et aspergatur aqua benedicta.

21

BENEDICTIO NOVORUM FRUCTUUM

℣. Adjutórium nostrum in nómine Dómini.

℟. Qui fecit caelum et terram.

℣. Dóminus vobíscum.

℟. Et cum spíritu tuo.

 Orémus.   Oratio

Béne✠dic, Dómine, hos novos fructus N., et praesta: ut, qui ex eis in tuo sancto nómine vescéntur, córporis et ánimae salúte potiántur. Per Christum Dóminum nostrum. ℟. Amen.

Et aspergantur aqua benedicta.

22

BENEDICTIO AD QUODCUMQUE COMESTIBILE

℣. Adjutórium nostrum in nómine Dómini.

℟. Qui fecit caelum et terram.

℣. Dóminus vobíscum.

℟. Et cum spíritu tuo.

 Orémus.   Oratio

Béne✠dic, Dómine, creatúram istam N., ut sit remédium salutáre géneri humáno: et praesta per invocatiónem sancti nóminis tui; ut quicúmque ex ea súmpserint, córporis sanitátem, et ánimae tutélam percípiant. Per Christum Dóminum nostrum. ℟. Amen.

Et aspergatur aqua benedicta.

and all inimical assaults. Through our Lord, Jesus Christ, thy Son, the living bread which came down from heaven, Who giveth life and salvation to the world! Who liveth and reigneth with thee in unity of the Holy Spirit, God, eternally. ℟. Amen.

It is sprinkled with holy water.

21

BLESSING OF NEW PRODUCE

℣. Our help is in the name of the Lord.
℟. Who made heaven and earth.
℣. The Lord be with you.
℟. And with thy spirit.

Let us pray.   Prayer

Bless, ✠ O Lord, this new produce N., and grant that they who eat of it in praise of thee may possess health of soul and body. Through Christ our Lord. ℟. Amen.

It is sprinkled with holy water.

22

BLESSING OF ANY VICTUAL

℣. Our help is in the name of the Lord.
℟. Who made heaven and earth.
℣. The Lord be with you.
℟. And with thy spirit.

Let us pray.   Prayer

Bless, ✠ O Lord, this creature N., so it be a saving help to humanity; and grant that by calling on thy holy name all who eat of it may experience health of body and protection of soul. Through Christ our Lord. ℟. Amen.

It is sprinkled with holy water.

23

BENEDICTIO OLEI

℣. Adjutórium nostrum in nómine Dómini.
℟. Qui fecit caelum et terram.

Exorcízo te, creatúra ólei, per Deum ✠ Patrem omnipoténtem, qui fecit caelum et terram, mare, et ómnia, quae in eis sunt. Omnis virtus adversárii, omnis exércitus diáboli, et omnis incúrsus, omne phantásma sátanae eradicáre, et effugáre ab hac creatúra ólei, ut fiat ómnibus, qui eo usúri sunt, salus mentis et córporis, in nómine Dei ✠ Patris omnipoténtis, et Jesu ✠ Christi Fílii ejus Dómini nostri, et Spíritus ✠ Sancti Parácliti, et in caritáte ejúsdem Dómini nostri Jesu Christi, qui ventúrus est judicáre vivos et mórtuos, et saéculum per ignem. ℟. Amen.

℣. Dómine, exáudi oratiónem meam.
℟. Et clamor meus ad te véniat.
℣. Dóminus vobíscum.
℟. Et cum spíritu tuo.

Orémus.

DÓMINE Deus omnípotens, cui astat exércitus Angelórum cum tremóre, quorum servítium spirituále cognóscitur, dignáre respícere, bene ✠ dícere, et sancti ✠ ficáre hanc creatúram ólei, quam ex olivárum succo eduxísti, et ex eo infírmos inúngi mandásti, quátenus sanitáte percépta, tibi Deo vivo et vero grátias ágerent: praesta, quaésumus; ut hi, qui hoc óleo, quod in tuo nómine bene ✠ dícimus, usi fúerint, ab omni languóre, omníque infirmitáte, atque cunctis insídiis inimíci liberéntur, et cunctae adversitátes separéntur a plásmate tuo, quod pretióso sánguine Fílii tui redemísti, ut numquam laedátur a morsu antíqui serpéntis. Per eúndem Dóminum nostrum Jesum Christum, Fílium tuum: Qui tecum vivit et regnat in unitáte Spíritus Sancti Deus, per ómnia saécula saeculórum. ℟. Amen.

Et aspergatur aqua benedicta.

23

BLESSING OF OIL

℣. Our help is in the name of the Lord.
℟. Who made heaven and earth.

Exorcism

Thou creature of oil, I purge thee of evil, through God ✠ the Father almighty Who made heaven and earth, the sea and all contained therein! Let the adversary's power, the devil's legions, and all Satan's attacks and phantoms be dispelled and driven afar from this oil. May it be to all who use it strength for body and soul, in the name of God, ✠ the Father almighty, and of the Son, ✠ our Lord, Jesus Christ, and of the Holy ✠ Spirit, the Paraclete, and in the love of the selfsame Christ Jesus, our Lord, Who shall come to judge the living and the dead, and the world by fire. ℟. Amen.

℣. O Lord, hear my prayer.
℟. And let my cry come unto thee.
℣. The Lord be with you.
℟. And with thy spirit.

Let us pray.   Prayer

LORD God Almighty! Before thee angelic hosts stand in awe, and we acknowledge their heavenly service! Deign to regard, to bless ✠ and sanctify ✠ this creature of oil which thou hast brought forth from the sap of olives. Thou hast ordained it for anointing the sick, that being restored to health they may give thanks to thee, the living and true God. Grant we beseech thee, that they who will use this oil which we bless ✠ in thy name may be delivered from every suffering, every illness, and all snares of the enemy, and that all adversity may be averted from thy creatures. For they were redeemed by the Precious Blood of thy Son, to suffer no more the sting of the ancient serpent. Through the same Jesus Christ, our Lord, Who liveth and reigneth with thee in unity of the Holy Spirit, God, eternally. ℟. Amen.

It is sprinkled with holy water.

24

BENEDICTIO CRUCIUM
In Agris, Vineis, Etc., Plantandarum
quae fit in Festo Inventionis S. Crucis
vel Dominica proxima
(Approbata a S. R. C. die 10 Febr. 1888)

℣. Adjutórium nostrum in nómine Dómini.

℟. Qui fecit caelum et terram.

℣. Dóminus vobíscum.

℟. Et cum spíritu tuo.

Orémus.   Oratio

Omnípotens sempitérne Deus, Pater totíus consolatiónis et pietátis, per Unigéniti Fílii tui Dómini nostri Jesu Christi acerbíssimae Passiónis méritum, quam pro nobis peccatóribus in ligno Crucis sustinére dignátus est: béne ✠ dic has Cruces, quas tui fidéles in hortis, víneis, agris, aliísve locis plantándas áfferunt, ut a praédiis quibus defíxae fúerint, fragor absit grándinum, procélla túrbinum, ímpetus tempestátum, et omnis infestátio inimíci: quátenus eórum fructus ad maturitátem perdúcti, in tui nóminis honórem colligántur a sperántibus in virtúte sanctae Crucis ejúsdem Fílii tui, Dómini nostri Jesu Christi, qui tecum vivit et regnat in saécula saeculórum. ℟. Amen.

Et aspergantur aqua benedicta.

Translator's Note: Passing by the wayside in certain Catholic regions of Europe, one may spy a cross planted in field, meadow,

24

BLESSING OF CROSSES
which are to be set in vineyards, fields, etc.
This blessing is conferred on the Feast of the Finding
of the Holy Cross or on the following Sunday

(Approved by the Congregation of Sacred Rites, Feb. 10, 1888)

℣.Our help is in the name of the Lord.
℟.Who made heaven and earth.
℣.The Lord be with you.
℟.And with thy spirit.

Let us pray. Prayer

Almighty, everlasting God, Father of goodness and consolation, in virtue of the bitter suffering of thy Sole-Begotten Son, our Lord, Jesus Christ, endured for us sinners on the wood of the Cross, bless ✠these crosses which thy faithful will erect in their vineyards, fields, and gardens. Protect the land where they are placed from hail, tornado, storm, and every assault of the enemy, so that their fruits ripened to the harvest may be gathered to thy honor by those who place their hope in the holy Cross of thy Son, our Lord, Jesus Christ, Who liveth and reigneth with thee eternally. ℟.Amen.

They are sprinkled with holy water.

---

or vineyard. These are the crosses blessed by the Church on a day when the cross is the inspiration of the day's liturgy. The prayer above clarifies their purpose.

25

BENEDICTIO ROGI
quae fit a Clero extra ecclesiam
in Vigilia Nativitatis S. Joannis Baptistæ

℣. Adjutórium nostrum in nómine Dómini.

℞. Qui fecit caelum et terram.

℣. Dóminus vobíscum.

℞. Et cum spíritu tuo.

Orémus.   Oratio

Dómine Deus, Pater omnípotens, lumen indefíciens, qui es
cónditor ómnium lúminum: novum hunc ignem sanctí ✠ fica,
et praesta; ut ad te, qui es lumen indefíciens, puris méntibus post
hujus saéculi calíginem perveníre valeámus. Per Christum Dóminum nostrum. ℞. Amen.

Et aspergantur aqua benedicta. Deinde a Clero cantetur sequens:

Hymnus

Ut queant la-xis reso-ná-re fibris Mi-ra gestórum fá-mu-li

---

*Translator's Note: The blessing of a bonfire may seem somewhat
extraordinary. Nevertheless, the ceremony is one of the most
ancient blessings, just as the cult of the Baptist is very ancient in
Catholic hagiolatry. For centuries people of Christian countries
have kept a solemn vigil for the festival of John the Baptist's birth.
In the darkness of the night preceding the feast, a bonfire would
flare up before the church edifice, in the market-place, on hill, in
valley. John gave testimony of the true Light which shineth in the
darkness. He was the light-bearer before Christ, although he proclaimed in utter humility and self-abnegation: "He must increase,
but I must decrease."* But the Master also spoke in highest praise*

---

* John: III, 30.

25

BLESSING OF A BONFIRE
on the Vigil of the Birthday of St. John the Baptist
conferred by the clergy outside of church

℣. Our help is in the name of the Lord.
℟. Who made heaven and earth.
℣. The Lord be with you.
℟. And with thy spirit.

Let us pray.   Prayer

O Lord God, Father almighty, unfailing Ray and Source of all light, sanctify ✠ this new fire, and grant that after the darkness of this life we may come unsullied to thee Who art Light eternal. Through Christ our Lord. ℟. Amen.

It is sprinkled with holy water. Then the clergy sing the following hymn:

O for thy spirit, holy John, to chasten

---

of His Precursor: "I say to you, among those born of women there is not a greater prophet than John the Baptist."** Attuned to the mind of the Master, early Christians quickly cultivated with enthusiasm a special veneration of this saint — their enthusiasm and love enkindling within them a justifiable conviviality at the approach of his day. The custom of the St. John bonfires, indicative of a people with burning and childlike faith, continues in some places to this day.

** Luke: VII, 28.

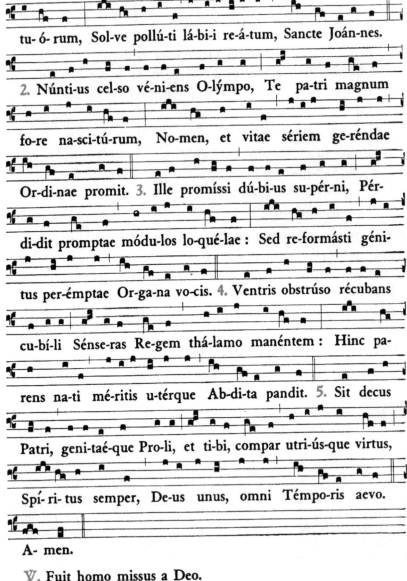

tu- ó- rum, Sol-ve pollú-ti lá-bi-i re-á-tum, Sancte Joán-nes.

2. Núnti-us cel-so vé-ni-ens O-lýmpo, Te pa-tri magnum

fo-re na-sci-tú-rum, No-men, et vitae sériem ge-réndae

Or-di-nae promit. 3. Ille promíssi dú-bi-us su-pér-ni, Pér-

di-dit promptae módu-los lo-qué-lae : Sed re-formásti géni-

tus per-émptae Or-ga-na vo-cis. 4. Ventris obstrúso récubans

cu-bí-li Sénse-ras Re-gem thá-lamo manéntem : Hinc pa-

rens na-ti mé-ritis u-térque Ab-di-ta pandit. 5. Sit decus

Patri, geni-taé-que Pro-li, et ti-bi, compar utri-ús-que virtus,

Spí- ri- tus semper, De-us unus, omni Témpo-ris aevo.

A- men.

℣. Fuit homo missus a Deo.
℟. Cui nomen erat Joánnes.

Lips sin-polluted, fettered tongues to loosen;
So by thy children might thy deeds of wonder
Meetly be chanted.

Lo! a swift herald, from the skies descending,
Bears to thy father promise of thy greatness;
How he shall name thee, what thy future story,
Duly revealing.

Scarcely believing message so transcendent,
Him for season power of speech forsaketh,
Till, at thy wondrous birth, again returneth
Voice to the voiceless.

Thou, in thy mother's womb all darkly cradled,
Knewest thy Monarch, biding in His chamber,
Whence the two parents, through their children's merits,
Mysteries uttered.

Praise to the Father, to the Son begotten,
And to the Spirit, equal power possessing,
One God whose glory, through the lapse of ages,
Ever resoundeth.

℣. There was a man sent from God.
℟. Whose name was John.

Orémus. Oratio

DEUS, qui praeséntem diem honorábilem nobis in beáti Joánnis nativitáte fecísti: da pópulis tuis spirituálium grátiam gaudiórum; et ómnium fidélium mentes dírige in viam salútis aetérnae. Per Christum Dóminum nostrum. ℟. Amen.

26

BENEDICTIO HERBARUM
in Festo Assumptionis B. Mariae V.

Absoluta aspersione, si Festum venerit in Dominica, alioquin immediate ante Missam, Sacerdos stans ante Altare, conversus ad populum tenentem herbas vel fructus, dicit voce intellegibili:

℣. Adjutórium nostrum in nómine Dómini.

℟. Qui fecit caelum et terram.

Psalmus 64

Te decet hymnus, Deus, in Sion: * et tibi reddétur votum in Jerúsalem.

Exáudi oratiónem meam: * ad te omnis caro véniet.

Verba iniquórum praevaluérunt super nos: * et impietátibus nostris tu propitiáberis.

Beátus, quem elegísti, et assumpsísti: * inhabitábit in átriis tuis.

Replébimur in bonis domus tuae: * sanctum est templum tuum, mirábile in aequitáte.

Exáudi nos, Deus, salutáris noster, * spes ómnium fínium terrae, et in mari longe.

Praéparans montes in virtúte tua, accínctus poténtia: * qui contúrbas profúndum maris sonum flúctuum ejus.

Turbabúntur gentes, et timébunt qui hábitant términos a signis tuis: * éxitus matutíni, et véspere delectábis.

Let us pray.

O GOD, Who by reason of the birth of blessed John hast made this day praiseworthy, give thy people the grace of spiritual joys, and direct the minds of the faithful along the way to eternal bliss. Through Christ our Lord. ℟. Amen.

26

BLESSING OF HERBS
on the Assumption of the Blessed Virgin Mary

After the Asperges, if it is a Sunday, otherwise immediately preceding Mass, the priest standing before the altar, and facing the people who hold the herbs and fruits, says in an audible voice:

℣. Our help is in the name of the Lord.
℟. Who made heaven and earth.

Psalm 64

Praise, O God, is due thee in Sion, and a vow must be offered thee in Jerusalem.

Hear my prayer; all flesh cometh unto thee.

Iniquities overwhelm us, but pardon thou our transgressions.

Blessed be the man whom thou dost elect and adopt, that he may dwell in thy courts.

We will be filled with the goodness of thy house; holy is thy temple and wonderful in righteousness.

Hear us, God our Savior, the Confidence of all ends of the earth and the sea afar off.

Girded with power, thou settest fast the mountains by thy strength, thou stillest the roaring of the seas and of their waves.

The nations are dismayed at thy signs; also they who dwell in uttermost parts; to the east and to the west thou givest joy.

Translator's Note: On this highest feast of the holy Virgin, the Church celebrates a harvest festival with this sacramental.

Visitásti terram, et inebriásti eam: * multiplicásti locupletáre eam.

Flumen Dei replétum est aquis, parásti cibum illórum: * quóniam ita est praeparátio ejus.

Rivos ejus inébria, multíplica genímina ejus: * in stillicídiis ejus laetábitur gérminans.

Benedíces corónae anni benignitátis tuae: * et campi tui replebúntur ubertáte.

Pinguéscent speciósa desérti: * et exsultatióne colles accingéntur.

Indúti sunt aríetes óvium, et valles abundábunt fruménto: * clamábunt, étenim hymnum dicent.

Glória Patri.

℣. Dóminus dabit benignitátem.

℟. Et terra nostra dabit fructum suum.

℣. Rigans montes de superióribus suis.

℟. De fructu óperum tuórum satiábitur terra.

℣. Prodúcens faenum juméntis.

℟. Et herbam servitúti hóminum.

℣. Ut edúcas panem de terra.

℟. Et vinum laetíficet cor hóminis.

℣. Ut exhílaret fáciem in óleo.

℟. Et panis cor hóminis confírmet.

℣. Misit verbum suum, et sanávit eos.

℟. Et erípuit eos de ómnibus interitiónibus eórum.

℣. Dómine, exáudi oratiónem meam.

℟. Et clamor meus ad te véniat.

℣. Dóminus vobíscum.

℟. Et cum spíritu tuo.

Orémus.   Oratio

OMNÍPOTENS sempitérne Deus, qui caelum, terram, mare visibília et invisibília verbo tuo ex níhilo creásti, quique herbas, arborésque ad usus hóminum animaliúmque terrae gígnere, et unumquódque juxta seméntem in semetípso fructu

Thou hast helped the land with plenteous rain; thou hast in many ways enriched it.

God's rain hath filled the earth and provided food, for then does it grow.

Fill thou the furrows, multiply their crops; gentle rain-drops gladden the buds.

Thou crownest the year with thy good things, and thy fields overflow with plenty.

The beautiful places of the wilderness grow rich, and the hill, are surrounded with joy.

The mountains are clothed with sheep, the vales abound with wheat; they shout for joy, and sing a hymn of praise.

Glory be to the Father.

℣. The Lord will be gracious.

℟. And our land bring forth its fruit.

℣. Thou waterest the mountains from the clouds.

℟. The earth is replenished from thy rains.

℣. Giving grass for cattle.

℟. And plants to the servitors of men.

℣. Thou bringest forth wheat from the earth.

℟. And wine to cheer man's heart.

℣. Oil to make his face lustrous.

℟. And bread to strengthen his heart.

℣. He sends His command, and heals their suffering.

℟. And snatches them from distressing want.

℣. O Lord, hear my prayer.

℟. And let my cry come unto thee.

℣. The Lord be with you.

℟. And with thy spirit.

Let us pray.   Prayer

ALMIGHTY, everlasting God, by thy Word alone thou hast made heaven, earth, sea, all things visible and invisible, and hast adorned the earth with plants and trees for the use of men and animals. Thou appointest each species to bring forth

habére praecepísti; atque non solum ut herbae animántibus ad victum, sed aegris étiam corpóribus prodéssent ad medicaméntum, tua ineffábili pietáte concessísti: te súpplici mente et ore deprecámur, ut has divérsi géneris herbas et fructus tua cleméntia bene ✠ dícas, et supra naturálem a te índitam virtútem, eis benedictiónis tuae novae grátiam infúndas; ut ad usum homínibus et juméntis in nómine tuo applicátae, ómnium morbórum et adversitátum efficiántur praesídium. Per Dóminum nostrum Jesum Christum, Fílium tuum: Qui tecum vivit et regnat in unitáte Spíritus Sancti Deus, per ómnia saécula saeculórum. ℟. Amen.

Orémus. Oratio

D EUS, qui per Móysen fámulum tuum mandásti fíliis Israel, ut manípulos novórum frúctuum benedicéndos deférrent ad sacerdótes, tolleréntque fructus árboris pulchérrimae, et laetaréntur coram te Dómino Deo suo: adésto propítius invocatiónibus nostris, et infúnde tuae bene ✠ dictiónis abundántiam super nos, et super manípulos novárum frugum, novárum herbárum, et frúctuum collectiónem, quae cum gratiárum actióne tibi repraesentámus, et in nómine tuo in hac sollemnitáte bene ✠ dícimus; et concéde, ut homínibus, pecóribus, pecúdibus et juméntis contra morbos, pestes, úlcera, malefícia, incantatiónes, venefícia serpéntum, et aliórum venenosórum animálium et bestiárum morsus, nec non quaecúmque venéna, remédium praestent; atque contra diabólicas illusiónes, et machinatiónes, et fraudes tutámen ferant, in quocúmque loco pósitum vel portátum aut hábitum áliquid ex eis fúerit: quátenus cum manípulis bonórum óperum, méritis beátae Maríae Vírginis, cujus Assumptiónis festum cólimus, quo ipsa assúmpta est, súscipi mereámur. Per Dóminum nostrum Jesum Christum, Fílium tuum: Qui tecum vivit et regnat in unitáte Spíritus Sancti Deus, per ómnia saécula saeculórum. ℟. Amen.

Orémus. Oratio

D EUS, qui virgam Jesse, Genetrícem Fílii tui Dómini nostri Jesu Christi, hodiérna die ad caelórum fastígia ídeo evexísti,

fruit in its kind, not only to serve as food for living creatures, but also as medicine to sick bodies. With mind and word we earnestly implore thy unspeakable goodness to bless ✠ these various herbs and fruits, and add to their natural powers the grace of thy new blessing. May they ward off disease and adversity from men and beasts who use them in thy name. Through our Lord, Jesus Christ, thy Son, Who liveth and reigneth with thee in unity of the Holy Spirit, God, forever and ever. ℟. Amen.

Let us pray.   Prayer

O GOD, by Moses, thy servant thou didst command the children of Israel to carry their sheaves of new grain to the priests for a blessing, to pluck the finest fruits of the orchards, and to make merry before thee, the Lord their God. Hear thou our supplications, and bestow blessings ✠ in abundance upon us and upon these bundles of new grain, new herbs, and this assortment of produce which we gratefully present to thee on this festival — blessing ✠ them in thy name. Grant that men, cattle, sheep, and beasts of burden find in them a remedy against sickness, pestilence, sores, injuries, spells, against the bites of serpents and other poisonous animals. May these blessed objects act as a protection against diabolical mockeries, cunnings, and deceptions wherever they are kept, carried, or other disposition made of them. And through the merits of the Blessed Virgin Mary whose Assumption we celebrate, may we likewise, laden with sheaves of good works, deserve to be lifted up to heaven. Through our Lord, Jesus Christ, thy Son, Who liveth and reigneth with thee in unity of the Holy Spirit, God, forevermore. ℟. Amen.

Let us pray.   Prayer

O GOD, Who on this day hast raised up to heavenly heights the rod of Jesse, the mother of thy Son, Jesus Christ, our

ut per ejus suffrágia et patrocínia fructum ventris illíus, eúndem Fílium tuum, mortalitáti nostrae communicáres: te súpplices exorámus; ut ejúsdem Fílii tui virtúte, ejúsque Genetrícis glorióso patrocínio, istórum terrae frúctuum praesídiis per temporálem ad aetérnam salútem disponámur. Per eúndem Dóminum nostrum Jesum Christum, Fílium tuum: Qui tecum vivit et regnat in unitáte Spíritus Sancti Deus, per ómnia saécula saeculórum. ℟. Amen.

Et benedíctio Dei omnipoténtis, Patris, et Fílii, ✠ et Spíritus Sancti, descéndat super has creatúras, et máneat semper. ℟. Amen.

Et aspergantur aqua benedicta, et thurificentur.

27

BENEDICTIO SEMINUM ET SEGETUM
in Festo Nativitatis B. Mariae Virg.

℣. Adjutórium nostrum in nómine Dómini.
℟. Qui fecit caelum et terram.
℣. Dóminus vobíscum.
℟. Et cum spíritu tuo.

Orémus.   Oratio

Dómine sancte, Pater omnípotens, sempitérne Deus: pétimus ac rogámus, ut hos fructus ségetum ac séminum tuis serénis óculis, hilaríque vultu aspícere dignéris: et sicut testátus es Móysi fámulo tuo in terra Aegypti, dicens: Dic fíliis Israel, cum ingréssi fúerint terram promissiónis, quam eis dabo, ut primítias frúctuum suórum ófferant sacerdótibus, et erunt benedícti; sic et nos rogámus te, Dómine, ut per auxílium misericórdiae tuae emíttas super hunc fructum ségetum déxterae tuae bene ✠ dictiónem, quem ad exhibéndum proférre dignéris, ut non súbruat grando, nec áëris inundátio extérminet, sed semper incólumis permáneat, propter usum animárum et córporum, et ad bene abundántem et pleníssi-

Lord, that through her prayers and patronage thou mightest communicate to our mortal nature the Fruit of her womb, thy same Son; we pray that we may use these fruits of the soil for our temporal and eternal welfare — the power of thy Son and the patronage of His glorious mother assisting us. Through the same Jesus Christ, thy Son, our Lord, Who liveth and reigneth with thee in unity of the Holy Spirit, God, forever and ever. ℟. Amen.

And may the blessing of almighty God, Father, Son, ✠ and Holy Spirit come upon these creatures, and remain for all time. ℟. Amen.

Then they are sprinkled with holy water and incensed.

27

BLESSING OF SEED AND SEEDLINGS
on the Birthday of the Blessed Virgin Mary

℣. Our help is in the name of the Lord.
℟. Who made heaven and earth.
℣. The Lord be with you.
℟. And with thy spirit.

Let us pray.   Prayer

O holy Lord, Father almighty, everlasting God, we beg thee to look with friendly countenance and benevolent eyes upon these seeds and seedlings. And as thou didst proclaim to Moses, thy servant in the land of Egypt, saying: "Tell the children of Israel that when they enter the land of promise which I shall give them, they are to offer the first-fruits to the priests, and they shall be blessed," so too at our request, O Lord, bless ✠ these seeds in thy benevolence, and let them germinate and grow. Let neither hail nor flood destroy them, but keep them unharmed unto a finest maturity and abundant harvest for the service of body and soul.

mam maturitátem perdúcere dignéris: Qui in Trinitáte perfécta vivis et regnas in saécula saeculórum. ℟. Amen.

Orémus.   Oratio

OMNÍPOTENS sempitérne Deus, caeléstis verbi seminátor et cultor, qui nostri cordis áream spiritálibus rastris exérces: adésto propítius précibus nostris, et super agros, quibus si fúerint sémina ínsita, tuam largam benedictiónem infúnde, ac ab eis omnem vim procellárum grátia tuae defensiónis avérte; ut omnis hic fructus et tua bene ✠ dictióne repleátur, et ad hórrea sine impediménto pervéniat. Per Dóminum nostrum Jesum Christum, Fílium tuum: Qui tecum vivit et regnat in unitáte Spíritus Sancti Deus, per ómnia saécula saeculórum. ℟. Amen.

Et aspergantur aqua benedicta, et, si fieri potest, thurificentur.

Thou Who livest and reignest in perfect Trinity forever. ℟.
Amen.

Let us pray.   Prayer

O MNIPOTENT, everlasting God, Sower and Tiller of the
heavenly word, Who dost cultivate the field of our hearts
with heavenly tools, hearken to our prayers, and pour forth
bountiful blessings upon the fields in which these seeds will be
sown. By thy protecting hand turn away the fury of the elements,
so that this entire fruit may be filled with thy blessing,✠ and
may be gathered without hindrance into the granary. Through
our Lord, Jesus Christ, thy Son, Who liveth and reigneth with
thee in unity of the Holy Spirit, God, forevermore. ℟. Amen.

They are sprinkled with holy water and may be incensed.

II

BLESSINGS OF PERSONS

BENEDICTIO PEREGRINORUM
AD LOCA SANCTA PRODEUNTIUM

Peregrini ad loca sancta profecturi, antequam discedant, juxta veteris Ecclesiae institutum, curent accipere patentes seu commendatitias litteras a suo Ordinario, seu Parocho. Quibus obtentis, et rebus suis dispositis, facta peccatorum suorum confessione, audiunt Missam, in qua dicitur Oratio pro peregrinantibus, ad instar Collectae pro re gravi imperatae, et Sanctissimam Eucharistiam devote suscipiunt. Expleta Missa, Sacerdos super eos genuflexos dicit sequentes Preces:

Antiphona

VIIa

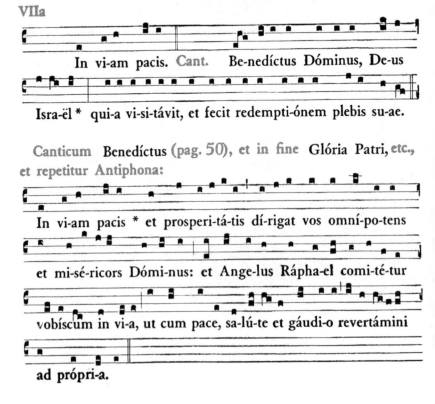

In vi-am pacis. Cant. Be-nedíctus Dóminus, De-us Isra-ël * qui-a vi-si-távit, et fecit redempti-ónem plebis su-ae.

Canticum Benedíctus (pag. 50), et in fine Glória Patri, etc., et repetitur Antiphona:

In vi-am pacis * et prosperi-tá-tis dí-rigat vos omní-po-tens et mi-sé-ricors Dómi-nus: et Ange-lus Rápha-el comi-té-tur vobíscum in vi-a, ut cum pace, sa-lú-te et gáudi-o revertámini ad própri-a.

CLESSING OF PILGRIMS
before departure

In accordance with ancient ecclesiastical discipline, pilgrims who are to visit the holy places should obtain from their Ordinary or pastor letters patent before they set out. Having set their affairs in order, they prepare themselves with sacramental confession, assist at Mass, and receive Holy Communion. In this Mass the Collect for pilgrims (pro re gravi) is said. After Mass, the priest prays as they kneel before him:

Antiphon: Along ways of peace.

Canticle: Blessed be etc. (page 51), with Glory be to the Father, etc.

Repeat the antiphon: Along ways of peace and prosperity may the almighty and merciful Lord lead you, and may the Angel Raphael accompany you on the journey. So may you in peace, health, and joy return unto your own!

Kýrie, eléison. Christe, eléison. Kýrie, eléison.

Pater noster secreto usque ad

℣. Et ne nos indúcas in tentatiónem.

℟. Sed líbera nos a malo.

℣. Salvos fac servos tuos.

℟. Deus meus, sperántes in te.

℣. Mitte eis, Dómine, auxílium de sancto.

℟. Et de Sion tuére eos.

℣. Esto eis, Dómine, turris fortitúdinis.

℟. A fácie inimíci.

℣. Nihil profíciat inimícus in eis.

℟. Et fílius iniquitátis non appónat nocére eis.

℣. Benedíctus Dóminus die cotídie.

℟. Prósperum iter fáciat nobis Deus salutárium nostrórum.

℣. Vias tuas, Dómine, demónstra nobis.

℟. Et sémitas tuas édoce nos.

℣. Utinam dirigántur viae nostrae.

℟. Ad custodiéndas justificatiónes tuas.

℣. Erunt prava in dirécta.

℟. Et áspera in vias planas.

℣. Angelis suis Deus mandávit de te.

℟. Ut custódiant te in ómnibus viis tuis.

℣. Dómine, exáudi oratiónem meam.

℟. Et clamor meus ad te véniat.

℣. Dóminus vobíscum.

℟. Et cum spíritu tuo.

Orémus.   Oratio

Deus, qui fílios Israel per maris médium sicco vestígio ire fecísti, quique tribus Magis iter ad te stella duce pandísti: tríbue eis, quaésumus, iter prósperum, tempúsque tranquíllum; ut Angelo tuo sancto cómite, ad eum, quo pergunt, locum, ac demum ad aetérnae salútis portum felíciter váleant perveníre.

Lord, have mercy on us. Christ, have mercy on us. Lord, have mercy on us.

Our Father inaudibly until

℣. And lead us not into temptation.

℟. But deliver us from evil.

℣. Preserve thy servants.

℟. Who trust in thee, my God.

℣. Send them aid, Lord, from on high.

℟. And from Sion watch over them.

℣. Be thou unto them a mighty fortress.

℟. In the face of the enemy.

℣. Let the enemy be powerless against them.

℟. And the son of iniquity do nothing to harm them.

℣. May the Lord be praised at all times.

℟. May God, our Helper grant us a successful journey.

℣. Show us thy ways, O Lord.

℟. And conduct us along thy paths.

℣. Oh, that our ways be directed!

℟. To the keeping of thy precepts.

℣. For crooked ways will be made straight.

℟. And rough ways smooth.

℣. God hath given His angels charge over you.

℟. To guard you in all undertakings.

℣. O Lord, hear my prayer.

℟. And let my cry come unto thee.

℣. The Lord be with you.

℟. And with thy spirit.

Let us pray. Prayer

O God, Who didst lead the sons of Israel through the sea over a dry path, and didst reveal the way to the three Magi by the guidance of a star; vouchsafe to grant these pilgrims a happy journey and a peaceful time, that accompanied by thy angel they may safely reach their present destination, and come finally to the haven of eternal security.

D EUS, qui Abraham púerum tuum de Ur Chaldaeórum
edúctum, per omnes suae peregrinatiónis vias illaésum
custodísti: quaésumus, ut hos fámulos tuos custodíre dignéris;
esto eis, Dómine, in procínctu suffrágium, in via solácium, in
aestu umbráculum, in plúvia et frígore teguméntum, in lassitúdine vehículum, in adversitáte praesídium, in lúbrico báculus, in
naufrágio portus: ut te duce, quo tendunt, próspere pervéniant,
et demum incólumes ad própria revertántur.

A DÉSTO, quaésumus, Dómine, supplicatiónibus nostris: et
viam famulórum tuórum in salútis tuae prosperitáte dispóne; ut inter omnes viae et vitae hujus varietátes tuo semper
protegántur auxílio.

P RAESTA, quaésumus, omnípotens Deus: ut família tua per
viam salútis incédat; et beáti Joánnis Praecursóris hortaménta
sectándo, ad eum, quem praedíxit, secúra pervéniat, Dóminum
nostrum Jesum Christum, Fílium tuum.

E XÁUDI, Dómine, preces nostras, et iter famulórum tuórum
propítius comitáre, atque misericórdiam tuam, sicut ubíque
es, ita ubíque largíre: quátenus a cunctis adversitátibus tua opitu-
latióne defénsi, gratiárum tibi réferant actiónem. Per Christum
Dóminum nostrum. ℟. Amen.

Pax et benedíctio Dei omnipoténtis, Patris, et Fílii, ✠ et Spíritus Sancti, descéndat super vos, et máneat semper. ℟. Amen.

Et aspergantur aqua benedicta.

2. Quod si unus sit peregrinaturus, Preces dicantur in numero singulari: ac si Sacerdos ipse, qui benedicit, sit socius peregrinationis, eas
dicat in persona prima numeri pluralis, quatenus congruere videbitur.

29

BENEDICTIO PEREGRINORUM
POST REDITUM

℣. Adjutórium nostrum in nómine Dómini.
℟. Qui fecit caelum et terram.

O GOD, Who didst lead thy servant, Abraham out of Ur of the Chaldeans, safeguarding him on all his wanderings — guide these thy servants, we implore thee. Be thou unto them support in battle, refuge in journeying, shade in the heat, covering in the rain, a carriage in tiredness, protection in adversity, a staff in insecurity, a harbor in shipwreck; so that under thy leadership they may successfully reach their destination, and finally return safe to their homes.

G IVE ear, we pray thee, Lord, to our entreaties! And direct the steps of thy servants on the paths of righteousness, that in all the vicissitudes of the journey and of life, they may have thee as their constant protector.

G RANT, O almighty God that thy pilgrims march forth on the way of security; and heeding the exhortations of Blessed John, the Precursor, let them come safely to Him Whom John foretold, Jesus Christ, thy Son, our Lord.

H EAR, O Lord, our prayers, and graciously accompany thy servants on the journey. And since thou art everywhere present, dispense thy mercy to them in all places; so that protected by thy help from all dangers, they will be able to offer thanksgiving to thee. Through Christ our Lord. ℟. Amen.

May the peace and blessing of almighty God, Father, Son, ✠ and Holy Spirit come upon you and remain with you for all time. ℟. Amen.

They are sprinkled with holy water.

If there is only one pilgrim, the prayers are said in the singular; but if the priest himself is the leader of the pilgrimage, they are said in the first person plural.

29

BLESSING OF PILGRIMS
upon their return

℣. Our help is in the name of the Lord.
℟. Who made heaven and earth.

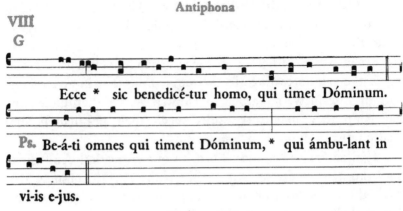

Ecce * sic benedicé-tur homo, qui timet Dóminum.

Ps. Be-á-ti omnes qui timent Dóminum, * qui ámbu-lant in

vi-is e-jus.

Psalmus 127

Beáti omnes, qui timent Dóminum, * qui ámbulant in viis ejus.
Labóres mánuum tuárum quia manducábis: * beátus es, et bene
tibi erit.
Uxor tua sicut vitis abúndans, * in latéribus domus tuae.
Fílii tui sicut novéllae olivárum, * in circúitu mensae tuae.
Ecce sic benedicétur homo, * qui timet Dóminum.
Benedícat tibi Dóminus ex Sion: * et vídeas bona Jerúsalem
ómnibus diébus vitae tuae.
Et vídeas fílios filiórum tuórum, * pacem super Israel.
Glória Patri.
Et repetitur Ant. Ecce, ut supra.
Kýrie, eléison. Christe, eléison. Kýrie, eléison.
Pater noster secreto usque ad
℣. Et ne nos indúcas in tentatiónem.
℞. Sed líbera nos a malo.
℣. Benedícti, qui véniunt in nómine Dómini.
℞. Benedícti vos a Dómino, qui fecit caelum et terram.
℣. Réspice, Dómine, in servos tuos, et in ópera tua.
℞. Et dírige eos in viam mandatórum tuórum.
℣. Dómine, exáudi oratiónem meam.
℞. Et clamor meus ad te véniat.
℣. Dóminus vobíscum.
℞. Et cum spíritu tuo.

Antiphon: Behold, thus shall he be blessed who feareth the Lord.

Psalm 127

Blessed are all that fear the Lord, that walk in His ways.

For thou shalt eat the labor of thy hands; happy art thou, and all shall be well with thee.

Thy wife shall be like the fruitful vine on the walls of thy dwelling;

Thy children like young olive plants round about thy table.

Behold, thus shall he be blessed who feareth the Lord.

May the Lord bless thee from Sion, and mayest thou see the prosperity of Jerusalem all the days of thy life.

And mayest thou see thy children's children. Peace be unto Israel!

Glory be to the Father.

Antiphon: Behold, thus shall he be blessed who feareth the Lord.

Lord, have mercy on us. Christ, have mercy on us. Lord, have mercy on us.

Our Father inaudibly until

℣. And lead us not into temptation.

℟. But deliver us from evil.

℣. Blessed are they that come in the name of the Lord.

℟. Blessed be you by the Lord, Who made heaven and earth.

℣. Regard, O Lord, thy servants and thy works.

℟. And direct them in observing thy precepts.

℣. O Lord, hear my prayer.

℟. And let my cry come unto thee.

℣. The Lord be with you.

℟. And with thy spirit.

Orémus.

L ARGÍRE, quaésumus, Dómine, fámulis tuis indulgéntiam placátus et pacem: ut páriter ab ómnibus mundéntur offensis, et secúra tibi mente desérviant.

O MNÍPOTENS sempitérne Deus, nostrórum témporum, vitaéque dispósitor, fámulis tuis contínuae tranquillitátis largíre subsídium: ut, quos incólumes própriis labóribus reddidísti, tua fácias protectióne secúros.

D EUS, humílium visitátor, qui nos fratérna dilectióne consoláris: praeténde societáti nostrae grátiam tuam; ut per eos, in quibus hábitas, tuum in nobis sentiámus advéntum. Per Dóminum. R̂. Amen.

Pax et benedíctio Dei omnipoténtis Patris, et Fílii, ✠ et Spíritus Sancti, descéndat super vos, et máneat semper. R̂. Amen.

Et aspergantur aqua benedicta.

30

BENEDICTIO PEREGRINORUM AEGROTANTIUM

Sacerdos indutus superpelliceo et stola albi coloris, ponat extremitatem stolae super caput infirmi, Evangeliumque recitet modo sequenti; si vero plures sint infirmi, stolam ipse teneat elevatam manu dextera, et benedictiones dicat in plurali.

V̂. Dóminus vobíscum.

R̂. Et cum spíritu tuo.

✠ Sequéntia sancti Evangélii secúndum Matthaéum (Cap. 13, 44–52)

R̂. Glória tibi, Dómine.

In illo témpore: Dixit Jesus discípulis suis parábolam hanc: Símile est regnum caelórum thesáuro abscóndito in agro: quem qui invénit homo, abscóndit, et prae gáudio illíus vadit, et vendit univérsa, quae habet, et emit agrum illum. Iterum símile est regnum caelórum hómini negotiatóri, quaerénti bonas margarítas.

Let us pray.   Prayer

W E BESEECH thee, Lord, be appeased, and lavish pardon on thy faithful, and peace; that they may be cleansed from all their sins, and may serve thee with tranquil hearts.

A LMIGHTY, everlasting God, Who dost dispose of our life and our destinies, grant to thy faithful people continued peace in abundance, that they whom thou dost return to their former labors may bask in the security of thy protection.

O GOD, the Support of the lowly, Who dost hearten us by thy brotherly love, bestow thy grace upon our brotherhood, that by thy indwelling we may experience thy coming. Through our Lord, Jesus Christ. ℞. Amen.

May the blessing of almighty God, Father, Son, ✝ and Holy Spirit come upon you and remain with you forever. ℞. Amen.

They are sprinkled with holy water.

30

BLESSING OF SICK PILGRIMS

The priest, vested in surplice and white stole, places the end of the stole on the head of the sick person, and reads the following passage of the Gospel. If he blesses more than one, he holds the stole aloft with his right hand, and says the blessing in the plural.

℣. **The Lord be with you.**

℞. **And with thy spirit.**

✝ Continuation of the holy Gospel according to St. Matthew (Matt. 13, 44-52)

℞. **Glory be to thee, O Lord.**

At that time, Jesus spoke this parable to His disciples: The kingdom of heaven is like unto a treasure hidden in a field. Which a man having found, hid it, and for joy thereof goeth, and selleth all that he hath, and buyeth that field. Again the kingdom of heaven is like to a merchant seeking good pearls.

Invénta autem una pretiósa margaríta, ábiit, et véndidit ómnia, quae hábuit, et emit eam. Iterum símile est regnum caelórum sagénae missae in mare, et ex omni génere píscium congregánti. Quam, cum impléta esset, educéntes, et secus litus sedéntes, elegérunt bonos in vasa, malos autem foras misérunt. Sic erit in consummatióne saéculi: exíbunt Angeli, et separábunt malos de médio justórum, et mittent eos in camínum ignis: ibi erit fletus, et stridor déntium. Intellexístis haec ómnia? Dicunt ei: Etiam. Ait illis: Ideo omnis scriba doctus in regno caelórum símilis est hómini patrifamílias, qui profert de thesáuro suo nova et vétera.

Post Evangelium benedicit infirmum dicens:

Benedíctio Dei omnipoténtis, Patris, et Fílii,✠ et Spíritus Sancti, descéndat super te (vos) et máneat semper. ℟. Amen.

Deinde porrigit extremitatem stolae deosculandam infirmo, ipsumque aspergit aqua benedicta, dicens:

Aspérgat te (vos) Deus rore grátiae suae in vitam aetérnam. ℟. Amen.

31

BENEDICTIO ADULTI AEGROTANTIS

Sacerdos cubiculum aegrotantis ingrediens dicat:

℣. Pax huic dómui.

℟. Et ómnibus habitántibus in ea.

Et continuo ad infirmum accedens subjungat:

℣. Adjutórium nostrum in nómine Dómini.

℟. Qui fecit caelum et terram.

℣. Dómine, exáudi oratiónem meam.

℟. Et clamor meus ad te véniat.

Who when he had found one pearl of great price, went his way, and sold all that he had, and bought it. Again the kingdom of heaven is like to a net cast into the sea, and gathering together of all kind of fishes. Which, when it was filled, they drew out, and sitting by the shore, they chose out the good into vessels, but the bad they cast forth. So shall it be at the end of the world. The angels shall go out, and shall separate the wicked from among the just. And shall cast them into the furnace of fire: there shall be weeping and gnashing of teeth. Have ye understood all these things? They say to him: Yes. He said unto them: Therefore every scribe instructed in the kingdom of heaven, is like to a man that is a householder, who bringeth forth out of his treasure new things and old.

After the Gospel, he blesses the sick person saying:

May the blessing of almighty God, Father, Son,✠ and Holy Spirit come upon thee (you) and remain for all time. ℟ Amen.

Then he presents the end of the stole to the sick to be kissed, and sprinkles him with holy water, saying:

May God sprinkle thee (you) with the dew of His grace unto life everlasting. ℟. Amen.

31

BLESSING OF A SICK ADULT

The priest upon entering the sick-room says:

℣. Peace be unto this home.

℟. And unto all who dwell herein.

Then approaching the sick one, he continues:

℣. Our help is in the name of the Lord.

℟. Who made heaven and earth.

℣. O Lord, hear my prayer.

℟. And let my cry come unto thee.

℣. Dóminus vobíscum.

℟. Et cum spíritu tuo.

Orémus.　　　　　　　　　　　　　Oratio

Intróeat, Dómine Jesu Christe, domum hanc ad nostrae humilitátis ingréssum pax et misericórdia tua; effúgiat ex hoc loco omnis
nequítia daémonum, adsint Angeli pacis, domúmque hanc déserat
omnis malígna discórdia. Magnífica, Dómine, super nos nomen
sanctum tuum: et bénedic nostrae conversatióni: Qui sanctus et
pius es, et pérmanes cum Patre et Spíritu Sancto in saécula saeculórum. ℟. Amen.

Orémus.　　　　　　　　　　　　　Oratio

R ÉSPICE, Dómine, fámulum tuum (fámulam tuam) in infirmitáte córporis laborántem, et ánimam réfove quam
creásti: ut castigatiónibus emendátus (-a), contínuo se séntiat
tua miseratióne salvátum (-am). Per Christum Dóminum nostrum. ℟. Amen.

Orémus.　　　　　　　　　　　　　Oratio

M ISÉRICORS, Dómine, fidélium consolátor, quaésumus imménsam pietátem tuam, ut ad intróitum humilitátis nostrae hunc fámulum tuum (hanc fámulam tuam) super lectum
dolóris sui jacéntem, visitáre dignéris, sicut socrum Simónis visitásti: propítius adésto ei, Dómine, quátenus prístina sanitáte
recépta, gratiárum tibi in Ecclésia tua réferat actiónes: Qui vivis
et regnas Deus in saécula saeculórum. ℟. Amen.

Deinde, extendens dexteram versus aegrotum, dicat:

D ÓMINUS Jesus Christus apud te sit, ut te deféndat: intra te
sit, ut te consérvet: ante te sit, ut te ducat: post te sit, ut te
custódiat: super te sit, ut te benedícat: Qui cum Patre et Spíritu
Sancto vivit et regnat in saécula saeculórum. ℟. Amen.

Benedíctio Dei omnipoténtis, Patris, et Fílii, ✠ et Spíritus
Sancti, descéndat super te, et máneat semper. ℟. Amen.

Demum aspergat infirmum aqua benedicta.

℣. The Lord be with you.

℟. And with thy spirit.

Let us pray. Prayer

O Lord, Jesus Christ, may peace and mercy enter into this home with our lowly coming, and banishing all wickedness of demons and discord, let angels of peace preside. Extol thy holy name in our esteem, and bless our visitation, Lord, thou Who art holy and loving, and everlasting with the Father and Holy Spirit, world without end. ℟. Amen.

Let us pray. Prayer

CONSIDER, O Lord, thy faithful one suffering from bodily affliction, and refresh the life which thou hast created; that being bettered by chastisement, he (she) may ever be conscious of thy merciful salvation. Through Christ our Lord. ℟. Amen.

Let us pray. Prayer

O Lord of pity, thou the Consoler of all who trust in thee, we pray that of thy boundless love thou wouldst at our humble coming visit this thy servant (handmaid) lying on his (her) bed of pain, as thou didst visit the mother-in-law of Simon Peter. Let him (her) be the recipient of thy loving consideration, so that restored to former good-health, he (she) may return thanksgiving to thee in thy Church. Thou Who livest and reignest, God, forevermore. ℟. Amen.

Then extending his right hand over the person, he says:

May the Lord, Jesus Christ be with thee to guard thee, within thee to preserve thee, before thee to lead thee, behind thee to watch thee, above thee to bless thee. Who liveth and reigneth with the Father and Holy Spirit, forever. ℟. Amen.

May the blessing of almighty God, Father, Son, ✠ and Holy Spirit descended upon thee and remain for all time. ℟. Amen.

The person is sprinkled with holy water.

32

EADEM BENEDICTIO PRO PLURIBUS INFIRMIS

Sacerdos cubiculum aegrotantium ingrediens dicat:

℣. Pax huic dómui.

℟. Et ómnibus habitántibus in ea.

Et continuo ad infirmos accedens subjungat:

℣. Adjutórium nostrum in nómine Dómini.

℟. Qui fecit caelum et terram.

℣. Dómine, exáudi oratiónem meam.

℟. Et clamor meus ad te véniat.

℣. Dóminus vobíscum.

℟. Et cum spíritu tuo.

Orémus.   Oratio

· Intróeat, Dómine Jesu Christe, domum hanc ad nostrae humi-litátis ingréssum pax et misericórdia tua; effúgiat ex hoc loco omnis nequítia daémonum, adsint Angeli pacis, domúmque hanc déserat omnis malígna discórdia. Magnífica, Dómine, super nos nomen sanctum tuum: et bénedic nostrae conversatióni: Qui sanctus et pius es, et pérmanes cum Patre et Spíritu Sancto in saécula saeculórum. ℟. Amen.

Orémus.   Oratio

R ÉSPICE, Dómine, fámulos tuos (fámulas tuas) in infirmitáte córporis laborántes, et ánimas réfove, quas creásti: ut casti-gatiónibus emendáti (–ae), contínuo se séntiant tua miseratióne salvátos (–as). Per Christum Dóminum nostrum. ℟. Amen.

Orémus.   Oratio

M ISÉRICORS, Dómine, fidélium consolátor, quaésumus im-ménsam pietátem tuam, ut ad intróitum humilitátis nostrae hos fámulos tuos (has fámulas tuas) super lectum dolóris sui jacéntes, visitáre dignéris, sicut socrum Simónis visitásti: pro-

32

THE SAME BLESSING WHEN THERE ARE SEVERAL SICK

The priest upon entering the sick-room says:

℣. Peace be unto this house.

℞. And unto all who dwell herein.

Then approaching the sick, he continues:

℣. Our help is in the name of the Lord.

℞. Who made heaven and earth.

℣. O Lord, hear my prayer.

℞. And let my cry come unto thee.

℣. The Lord be with you.

℞. And with thy spirit.

Let us pray.   Prayer

O Lord, Jesus Christ, may peace and mercy enter into this home with our lowly coming, and banishing all wickedness of demons and discord, let angels of peace preside. Extol thy holy name in our esteem, and bless our visitation, Lord, thou Who art holy and loving, and everlasting with the Father and Holy Spirit, world without end. ℞. Amen.

Let us pray.   Prayer

CONSIDER, O Lord, thy faithful ones suffering from bodily affliction, and refresh the lives which thou hast created; that being bettered by chastisement, they may ever be conscious of thy merciful salvation. Through Christ our Lord. ℞. Amen.

Let us pray.   Prayer

O LORD of pity, thou the Consoler of all who trust in thee, we pray that of thy boundless love thou wouldst at our humble coming visit these thy servants lying on their beds of pain, as thou didst visit the mother-in-law of Simon Peter. Let

pítius adésto eis, Dómine, quátenus prístina sanitáte recépta, gra
tiárum tibi in Ecclésia tua réferant actiónes: Qui vivis et regna:
Deus in saécula saeculórum. ℞. Amen.

Deinde, extendens dexteram versus aegrotos, dicat:

DÓMINUS Jesus Christus apud vos sit, ut vos deféndat: intr:
vos sit, ut vos consérvet: ante vos sit, ut vos ducat: post vo:
sit, ut vos custódiat: super vos sit, ut vos benedícat: Qui cun
Patre et Spíritu Sancto vivit et regnat in saécula saeculórum. ℞
Amen.

Benedíctio Dei omnipoténtis, Patris, et Fílii,✠ et Spíritu
Sancti, descéndat super vos, et máneat semper. ℞. Amen.

Demum aspergat infirmos aqua benedicta.

33

BENEDICTIO PUERORUM AEGROTANTIUM

Pueri infirmi, qui ad hunc usum rationis pervenerunt, ut ipsis prae
beri possit Sacramentum Extremae Unctionis, iis adjuventur exhorta
tionibus et precibus, quae describuntur in Rituali Romano, ubi agitu
de visitatione et cura infirmorum, prout feret temporis opportunitas, e
eorumdem aegrotantium status.
Verum pro ceteris junioribus pueris infirmis adhiberi possunt se
quentes preces.
Sacerdos infirmi cubiculum ingressus, primum dicit:

℣. Pax huic dómui.
℞. Et ómnibus habitántibus in ea.

Mox infirmum et lectum ejus et cubiculum aspergit, nihil dicens:
Deinde dicit Psalmum Laudáte, púeri, Dóminum: laudáte nome:
Dómini (pag. 20), cum Glória Patri, in fine.

Postea dicit:
Kýrie, eléison. Christe, eléison. Kýrie, eléison.
Pater noster secreto usque ad
℣. Et ne nos indúcas in tentatiónem.
℞. Sed líbera nos a malo.

them be the recipients of thy loving consideration, so that restored
to former good-health, they may return thanksgiving to thee in
thy Church. Thou who livest and reignest, God, forevermore.
℟. Amen.

Then extending his right hand over the persons, he says:

May the Lord, Jesus Christ be with you to guard you, within
you to preserve you, before you to lead you, behind you to watch
you, above you to bless you. Who liveth and reigneth with the
Father and the Holy Spirit in eternity. ℟. Amen.

May the blessing of almighty God, Father, Son, ✠ and Holy
Spirit descend upon you and remain for all time. ℟. Amen.

He sprinkles the sick with holy water.

33

BLESSING OF SICK CHILDREN

If children who are ill are old enough to receive the Sacrament of
Extreme Unction, the same prayers and ceremonies are used as given
in the Ritual in the chapter concerning the visitation and care of the
infirm — depending on circumstances of illness and time.

However, for younger children, the following may be used:

The priest upon entering the room where the sick child lies, says:

℣. Peace be unto this home.

℟. And unto all who dwell herein.

Next he sprinkles the sick child, the bed, and the room without
saying anything.

Then he says the Psalm Ye children, sing praise to the Lord; praise
the name of the Lord (page 21), with Glory be to the Father, at the
end.

Afterward he says:

Lord, have mercy on us. Christ, have mercy on us. Lord, have
mercy on us.

Our Father inaudibly until

℣. And lead us not into temptation.

℟. But deliver us from evil.

℣. Deus noster miserétur.

℟. Custódiens párvulos Dóminus.

℣. Sínite párvulos veníre ad me.

℟. Tálium est enim regnum caelórum.

℣. Dómine, exáudi oratiónem meam.

℟. Et clamor meus ad te véniat.

℣. Dóminus vobíscum.

℟. Et cum spíritu tuo.

Orémus.   Oratio

Deus, cui cuncta adoléscunt, et per quem adúlta firmántur: ex
ténde déxteram tuam super hunc fámulum tuum (hos, etc.)
(hanc fámulam tuam) (has, etc.), in ténera aetáte languénten
(–es): quátenus vigóre sanitátis recépto, ad annórum pervénia(n)
plenitúdinem, et tibi fidéle, gratúmque obséquium indesinénte
praeste(n)t ómnibus diébus vitae suae. Per Dóminum nostrun
Jesum Christum, Fílium tuum: Qui tecum vivit et regnat in uni
táte Spíritus Sancti Deus, per ómnia saécula saeculórum. ℟
Amen.

Orémus.   Oratio

PATER misericordiárum, et Deus totíus consolatiónis, qu
creatúrae tuae multíplici pietáte cónsulens, non solum áni
mae, sed ipsi córpori curatiónis grátiam benígnus infúndis: hun(
párvulum infírmum (has, etc.) (hanc párvulam infírmam) (has
etc.) a lecto aegritúdinis erígere, et Ecclésiae tuae sanctae, suísqu(
paréntibus incólumem (–es) restitúere dignéris; ut cunctis pro
longátae sibi vitae diébus, grátia et sapiéntia coram te et homíni
bus profíciens (–tes), in justítia et sanctitáte tibi sérvia(n)t, e
débitas misericórdiae tuae réfera(n)t gratiárum actiónes. Pe
Christum Dóminum nostrum. ℟. Amen.

Orémus.   Oratio

DEUS, qui miro órdine Angelórum ministéria, hominúmqu(
dispénsas: concéde propítius; ut, a quibus tibi ministrántibu:
in caelo semper assístitur, ab his in terra vita hujus púeri (puéllae)

℣. May our God be merciful.

℟. May the Lord watch over his children.

℣. Suffer little children to come unto me.

℟. For theirs is the kingdom of heaven.

℣. O Lord, hear my prayer.

℟. And let my cry come unto thee.

℣. The Lord be with you.

℟. And with thy spirit.

Let us pray.   *Prayer*

O God, for Whom all creatures grow in years and upon Whom all depend for continued existence, extend thy right hand upon this boy (girl) who is afflicted at this tender age; and being restored to health, may he (she) reach maturity, and ceaselessly render thee a service of gratitude and fidelity all the days of his (her) life. Through our Lord, Jesus Christ, thy Son, Who liveth and reigneth with thee in the unity of the Holy Spirit, God, forever and ever. ℟. Amen.

Let us pray.   *Prayer*

FATHER of mercy, and God of all consolation, Who having the interests of thy creatures at heart, dost graciously heal both soul and body, deign kindly to raise up this sick child from his (her) bed of suffering, and return him (her) unscathed to thy holy Church and to his (her) parents. And throughout the days of prolonged life, as he (she) advances in grace and wisdom in thy sight and man's, may he (she) serve thee in righteousness and holiness, and return thee due thanks for thy goodness. Through Christ our Lord. ℟. Amen.

Let us pray.   *Prayer*

O GOD, Who in a marvellous way dost dispense the ministries of angels and of men, mercifully grant that the life on earth

(horum puerórum) (harum puellárum) muniátur. Per Christum Dóminum nostrum. ℟. Amen.

Completa Oratione ultima, Sacerdos imponit dexteram manum super caput infirmi, et dicit:

Super aegros manus impónent, et bene habébunt. Jesus, Maríae Fílius, mundi salus et Dóminus, méritis et intercessióne sanctórum Apostolórum suórum Petri et Pauli, et ómnium Sanctórum, sit tibi (vobis) clemens et propítius. ℟. Amen.

Quod sequitur Evangelium, pro temporis opportunitate et pro aegrotantis pueri parentum desiderio, Sacerdotis arbitrio dici poterit:

℣. Dóminus vobíscum.

℟. Et cum spíritu tuo.

✠ Inítium Sancti Evangélii secúndum Joánnem.

℟. Glória tibi, Dómine.

Dum Sacerdos dicit Inítium, etc. facit signum crucis de more super se in fronte, ore et pectore; similiter super puerum infirmum, si non possit se signare.

Joann. I, 1-14

IN PRINCÍPIO erat Verbum, et Verbum erat apud Deum, et Deus erat Verbum. Hoc erat in princípio apud Deum. Omnia per ipsum facta sunt: et sine ipso factum est nihil, quod factum est: in ipso vita erat, et vita erat lux hóminum, et lux in ténebris lucet, et ténebrae eam non comprehendérunt. Fuit homo missus a Deo, cui nomen erat Joánnes. Hic venit in testimónium, ut testimónium perhibéret de lúmine, ut omnes créderent per illum. Non erat ille lux, sed ut testimónium perhibéret de lúmine. Erat lux vera, quae illúminat omnem hóminem veniéntem in hunc mundum. In mundo erat, et mundus per ipsum factus est, et mundus eum non cognóvit. In própria venit, et sui eum non recepérunt. Quotquot autem recepérunt eum, dedit eis potestátem fílios Dei fíeri, his, qui credunt in nómine ejus: qui non ex sanguínibus, neque ex voluntáte carnis, neque ex voluntáte viri, sed

of this child may be protected by those who minister to thee in heaven. Through Christ our Lord. ℟. Amen.

After this prayer, the priest puts his right hand upon the head of the child, and says:

They shall lay their hands upon the sick, and all will be well with them. May Jesus, Son of Mary, Lord and Savior of the world, through the merits and intercession of His holy Apostles Peter and Paul and all His saints, show thee favor and mercy. Amen.

If he wills, the priest may add the following gospel, depending on the child's condition and the wishes of the parents:

℣. The Lord be with you.

℟. And with thy spirit.

✠ The beginning of the holy Gospel according to St. John.

℟. Glory be to thee, O Lord.

As the priest says The beginning, *etc. he signs himself on the forehead, mouth, and breast in the usual way; and signs the sick child in the same way, if the child can not do so himself.*

John I, 1–14

IN THE beginning was the Word, and the Word was with God, and the Word was God. The same was in the beginning with God. All things were made by Him, and without Him was made nothing that was made. In Him was life, and the life was the light of men: and the light shineth in darkness, and the darkness did not comprehend it. There was a man sent from God, whose name was John. This man came for a witness, to bear witness of the light, that all men might believe through Him. He was not the light, but was to give testimony of the light. That was the true light, which enlighteneth every man that cometh into this world. He was in the world, and the world was made by Him, and the world knew Him not. He came unto His own, and His own received Him not. But as many as received Him, He gave them power to be made the sons of God, to them that believe in His name. Who are born, not of blood, nor of the will of the flesh, nor of the will of man, but of God. (Genuflect) And

ex Deo nati sunt. (Hic genuflectitur.) Et Verbum caro factum est, et habitávit in nobis: et vídimus glóriam ejus, glóriam quasi Unigéniti a Patre, plenum grátiae et veritátis. ℟. Deo grátias.

Postea benedicens puerum infirmum, subjungit, dicens:

Benedíctio Dei omnipoténtis, Patris, et Fílii, ✠ et Spíritus Sancti, descéndat super te (vos), et máneat semper. ℟. Amen.

Deinde aspergit eum (eos) aqua benedicta.

Si sint plures infirmi in eodem cubiculo vel loco, Preces et Orationes praedictae dicuntur super eos in numero plurali.

34

BENEDICTIO MULIERIS PRAEGNANTIS
in periculis partus

℣. Adjutórium nostrum in nómine Dómini.

℟. Qui fecit caelum et terram.

℣. Salvam fac ancíllam tuam.

℟. Deus meus, sperántem in te.

℣. Esto illi, Dómine, turris fortitúdinis.

℟. A fácie inimíci.

℣. Nihil profíciat inimícus in ea.

℟. Et fílius iniquitátis non appónat nocére ei.

℣. Mitte ei, Dómine, auxílium de sancto.

℟. Et de Sion tuére eam.

℣. Dómine, exáudi oratiónem meam.

℟. Et clamor meus ad te véniat.

℣. Dóminus vobíscum.

℟. Et cum spíritu tuo.

Orémus.   Oratio

Omnípotens sempitérne Deus, qui dedísti fámulis tuis in confessióne verae fídei aetérnae Trinitátis glóriam agnóscere, et in poténtia majestátis adoráre unitátem: quaésumus; ut ejúsdem fídei firmitáte haec fámula tua N. ab ómnibus semper muniátur advérsis. Per Christum Dóminum nostrum. ℟. Amen.

the Word was made flesh, and dwelt among us, and we saw His glory, the glory as it were of the only begotten of the Father, full of grace and truth. ℟. Thanks be to God.

Lastly he blesses the child saying:

May the blessing of almighty God, Father, Son, ✠ and Holy Spirit come upon thee (you) and remain for all time. ℟. Amen.

He then sprinkles him (her, or them) with holy water.

If there are several sick children in the room, these prayers are said in the plural.

34

BLESSING OF AN EXPECTANT MOTHER
at the approach of confinement

℣. Our help is in the name of the Lord.

℟. Who made heaven and earth.

℣. Preserve thy handmaid.

℟. Who places her trust in thee, my God.

℣. Be unto her a fortress of strength.

℟. In the face of the enemy.

℣. Let the enemy have no power over her.

℟. And the son of evil do nothing to harm her.

℣. Send her, Lord, aid from on high.

℟. And from Sion watch over her.

℣. O Lord, hear my prayer.

℟. And let my cry come unto thee.

℣. The Lord be with you.

℟. And with thy spirit.

Let us pray.   Prayer

O almighty, everlasting God, Who dost assist thy servants in confessing the true faith to acclaim the glory of thy eternal Trinity and to adore thy Divine Unity in its majestic power, grant thy handmaid N., by the solidity of the same faith, constant protection from all adversity. Through Christ our Lord. ℟. Amen.

Orémus.   Oratio

DÓMINE Deus, ómnium Creátor, fortis et terríbilis, justus et
miséricors, qui solus bonus et pius es; qui de omni malo
liberásti Israel, fáciens tibi patres nostros diléctos, et sanctificásti
eos manu Spíritus tui; qui gloriósae Vírginis Maríae corpus et
ánimam, ut dignum Fílii tui habitáculum éffici mererétur, Spíritu
Sancto cooperánte praeparásti; qui Joánnem Baptístam Spíritu
Sancto replésti, et in útero matris exsultáre fecísti; áccipe sacrifícium cordis contríti, ac fervens desidérium fámulae tuae N.
humíliter supplicántis pro conservatióne prolis, quam ei dedísti
concípere: custódi partem tuam, et ab omni dolo et injúria duri
hostis defénde; ut obstetricánte manu misericórdiae tuae fetus
ejus ad lucem próspere véniat, ac sanctae generatióni servétur,
tibíque in ómnibus júgiter desérviat, et vitam cónsequi mereátur
aetérnam. Per eúndem Dóminum ... in unitáte ejúsdem Spíritus.
℞. Amen.

Deinde mulier aspergatur aqua benedicta, et mox dicatur:

Psalmus 66

Deus misereátur nostri, et benedícat nobis: * illúminet vultum
suum super nos, et misereátur nostri.

Ut cognoscámus in terra viam tuam: * in ómnibus géntibus salutáre tuum.

Confiteántur tibi pópuli, Deus: * confiteántur tibi pópuli omnes.

Laeténtur et exsúltent gentes: * quóniam júdicas pópulos in aequitáte, et gentes in terra dírigis.

Confiteántur tibi pópuli, Deus, confiteántur tibi pópuli omnes: *
terra dedit fructum suum.

Benedícat nos Deus, Deus noster, benedícat nos Deus: * et métuant eum omnes fines terrae.

Glória Patri.

℣. Benedicámus Patrem, et Fílium, cum Sancto Spíritu.

℞. Laudémus et superexaltémus eum in saécula.

Let us pray.   Prayer

O LORD God, Author of the universe, strong and awesome, just and forgiving, Who alone art good and kind; Who didst deliver Israel from every evil, making our forefathers pleasing unto thee, and sanctifying them by the hand of thy Holy Spirit; Who didst by the cooperation of the Holy Spirit prepare the body and soul of the glorious Virgin Mary that she might merit to be made a worthy tabernacle for thy Son; Who didst fill John the Baptist with the Holy Spirit, and didst cause him to exult in his mother's womb — accept the offering of a contrite heart and the fervent prayer of thy handmaid N., as she humbly pleads for the life of her offspring whom she has conceived by thy Will. Guard her lying-in, and defend her from all assault and injury of the unfeeling enemy. By the obstetric hand of thy mercy may her infant happily see the light of day, and being reborn in holy baptism, forever seek thy ways and come to everlasting life. Through the same Lord, Jesus Christ, thy Son, Who liveth and reigneth with thee in unity of the Holy Spirit, God, eternally. ℟. Amen.

He then sprinkles the woman with holy water. Then he adds:

Psalm 66

May God be good to us, and bless us! May the light of His countenance shine upon us, and may He have mercy on us.

That men may know thy Providence upon earth, thy salvation among all nations.

Let people praise thee, O God, let all nations glorify thee!

Let the nations be glad and rejoice; for thou judgest the people justly, and directest the nations upon earth.

Let people praise thee, O God, let all nations glorify thee! Then shall the earth yield fruit in abundance.

God, our own God bless us! May God bless us, and let all the ends of the earth fear Him.

Glory be to the Father.

℣. Let us bless the Father, and the Son, together with the Holy Spirit.

℟. Let us praise Him and mightily exalt Him forever.

℣. Angelis suis Deus mandávit de te.

℟. Ut custódiant te in ómnibus viis tuis.

℣. Dómine, exáudi oratiónem meam.

℟. Et clamor meus ad te véniat.

℣. Dóminus vobíscum.

℟. Et cum spíritu tuo.

Orémus. Oratio

VÍSITA, quaésumus, Dómine, habitatiónem istam, et omnes insídias inimíci ab ea, et a praesénti fámula tua N. longe repélle: Angeli tui sancti hábitent in ea, qui eam et ejus prolem in pace custódiant, et bene ✠ díctio tua sit super eam semper. Salva eos, omnípotens Deus, et lucem eis tuam concéde perpétuam. Per Christum Dóminum nostrum. ℟. Amen.

Benedíctio Dei omnipoténtis, Patris, et Fílii, ✠ et Spíritus Sancti, descéndat super te, et prolem tuam, et máneat semper. ℟. Amen.

35

DE BENEDICTIONE MULIERIS POST PARTUM

Si qua puerpera post partum, juxta piam ac laudabilem consuetudinem, ad ecclesiam venire voluerit, pro incolumitate sua Deo gratias actura, petieritque a Sacerdote benedictionem, ipse superpelliceo et stola alba indutus, cum ministro aspersorium deferente, ad fores ecclesiae accedat, ubi illam foris ad limina genuflectentem et candelam accensam in manu tenentem, aqua benedicta aspergat, deinde dicat:

℣. Adjutórium nostrum in nómine Dómini.

℟. Qui fecit caelum et terram.

Ant. Haec accípiet.

Psalmus 23

Dómini est terra, et plenitúdo ejus: * orbis terrárum, et univérsi qui hábitant in eo.

℣. God appointeth His angels over thee.

℟. To guard thee along thy journeyings.

℣. O Lord, hear my prayer.

℟. And let my cry come unto thee.

℣. The Lord be with you.

℟. And with thy spirit.

Let us pray.   Prayer

VISIT, we pray thee, Lord, this dwelling, and drive forth from it and this thy handmaid N. all snares of the enemy. Let thy holy angels preside, to keep her and her offspring in peace; and let thy blessing ✠ be ever present. Save them, O almighty God, and grant them thy everlasting light. Through Christ our Lord. ℟. Amen.

May the blessing of almighty God, Father, Son, ✠ and Holy Spirit come upon thee and thy child, and remain for all time. ℟. Amen.

35

BLESSING OF A MOTHER AFTER CHILDBIRTH

After giving birth to a child, a mother may wish to render thanks to God in church for a safe delivery, and to seek the Church's blessing. This has long been a devout and praiseworthy practice. The priest vested in surplice and white stole, assisted by a server carrying the aspersory, goes to the church's threshold where the woman kneels with lighted candle. Sprinkling her with holy water, he says:

℣. Our help is in the name of the Lord.

℟. Who made heaven and earth.

Antiphon: This woman shall receive.

Psalm 23

The earth is the Lord's and the fulness thereof; the world and all that dwell therein.

Quia ipse super mária fundávit eum: * et super flúmina praeparávit eum.

Quis ascéndet in montem Dómini? * aut quis stabit in loco sancto ejus?

Innocens mánibus et mundo corde, * qui non accépit in vano ánimam suam, nec jurávit in dolo próximo suo.

Hic accípiet benedictiónem a Dómino: * et misericórdiam a Deo, salutári suo.

Haec est generátio quaeréntium eum, * quaeréntium fáciem Dei Jacob.

Attóllite portas, príncipes, vestras, et elevámini, portae aeternáles: * et introíbit Rex glóriae.

Quis est iste Rex glóriae? * Dóminus fortis et potens: Dóminus potens in proélio.

Attóllite portas, príncipes, vestras, et elevámini, portae aeternáles: * et introíbit Rex glóriae.

Quis est iste Rex glóriae? * Dóminus virtútum ipse est Rex Glóriae.

Glória Patri.

Et repetitur Antiphona:
Haec accípiet benedictiónem a Dómino, et misericórdiam a Deo salutári suo: quia haec est generátio quaeréntium Dóminum.

2. *Deinde porrigens ad manum mulieris extremam partem stolae, ex humero sinistro pendentem, eam introducit in ecclesiam, dicens:*
Ingrédere in templum Dei, adóra Fílium beátae Maríae Vírginis, qui tibi fecunditátem tríbuit prolis.

3. *Et ipsa, ingressa, genuflectit coram Altari et orat, gratias agens Deo de beneficiis sibi collatis; tunc sacerdos dicit:*
Kýrie, eléison. Christe, eléison. Kýrie, eléison.

Pater Noster *secreto usque ad*

℣. Et ne nos indúcas in tentatiónem.

℟. Sed líbera nos a malo.

For He hath founded it upon the seas, and hath established it upon the waters.

Who shall ascend the mountain of the Lord? Or who shall stand in His holy place?

He of innocent actions and pure heart, who desireth not vanity, nor hath sworn deceitfully to his neighbor.

He shall receive a blessing from the Lord and mercy from God, his Savior.

This is the people that seek Him, that seek the face of the God of Jacob.

Lift up your heads, O ye gates, open high and wide, ye everlasting doors, and the King of glory shall come in!

Who is this King of glory? The Lord strong and mighty, the Lord mighty in battle.

Lift up your heads, O ye gates, open high and wide, ye everlasting doors, and the King of glory shall come in!

Who is this King of glory? The Lord of hosts, He is the King of glory.

Glory be to the Father.

Repeat the antiphon:

This woman shall receive a blessing from the Lord and mercy from God, her Savior, for she is of the people who seek the Lord.

2. Then presenting to her the end of the stole which hangs from his left shoulder, the priest conducts her into church, saying:

Enter the temple of God, adore the Son of the Blessed Virgin Mary, Who hath given thee fruitfulness of offspring.

3. The woman kneels before the altar, and prays in gratitude to God for His benefits upon her, the while the priest says:

Lord, have mercy on us. Christ, have mercy on us. Lord, have mercy on us.

Our Father inaudibly until

℣. And lead us not into temptation.
℟. But deliver us from evil.

℣. Salvam fac ancíllam tuam, Dómine.

℞. Deus meus, sperántem in te.

℣. Mitte ei, Dómine, auxílium de sancto.

℞. Et de Sion tuére eam.

℣. Nihil profíciat inimícus in ea.

℞. Et fílius iniquitátis non appónat nocére ci.

℣. Dómine, exáudi oratiónem meam.

℞. Et clamor meus ad te véniat.

℣. Dóminus vobíscum.

℞. Et cum spíritu tuo.

    Orémus.   Oratio

O MNÍPOTENS sempitérne Deus, qui per beátae Maríae Vírginis partum fidélium pariéntium dolóres in gáudium vertísti: réspice propítius super hanc fámulam tuam, ad templum sanctum tuum pro gratiárum actióne laetam accedéntem, et praesta; ut post hanc vitam, ejúsdem beátae Maríae méritis et intercessióne, ad aetérnae beatitúdinis gáudia cum prole sua perveníre mereátur. Per Christum Dóminum nostrum. ℞. Amen.

4. Deinde illam aspergit iterum aqua benedicta, dicens:

Pax et benedíctio Dei omnipoténtis, Patris, et Fílii, ✠ et Spíritus Sancti, descéndat super te, et máneat semper. ℞. Amen.

5. Praedicta benedictio mulieris post partum fieri debet a Parocho, si expetitus ipse fuerit: potest autem fieri a quocumque Sacerdote, si expetitus pariter fuerit, in quacumque ecclesia vel oratorio publico, certiore facto Superiore ecclesiae.

℣. Preserve thy handmaid, O Lord.

℟. Who trusts in thee, my God.

℣. Send her, Lord, aid from on high.

℟. And from Sion watch over her.

℣. Let the enemy have no power over her.

℟. And the son of evil do nothing to harm her.

℣. O Lord, hear my prayer.

℟. And let my cry come unto thee.

℣. The Lord be with you.

℟. And with thy spirit.

Let us pray. *Prayer*

ALMIGHTY, everlasting God, Who through the delivery of the Blessed Virgin Mary hast turned into joy the pains of the faithful at childbirth, look kindly upon this thy handmaid who comes rejoicing into thy holy temple to make her thanksgiving. Grant that after this life she together with her offspring may merit the joys of everlasting bliss, by the merits and intercession of the same Blessed Mary. Through Christ our Lord. ℟. Amen.

4. The priest again sprinkles her with holy water saying:

May the peace and blessing of almighty God, Father, Son, ✠ and Holy Spirit come upon thee, and remain for all time. ℟. Amen.

5. The blessing of a woman after childbirth ought to be conferred by her pastor, if requested. But any priest may confer it in any church or public oratory, with the approval of the rector.

36

RITUS BENEDICTIONIS APOSTOLICAE
CUM INDULGENTIA PLENARIA
IN ARTICULO MORTIS

Benedictio Apostolica cum indulgentia plenaria in articulo mortis cum soleat impertiri post Sacramenta Paenitentiae, Eucharistiae et Extremae Unctionis illis infirmis, qui vel illam petierint, dum sana mente et integris sensibus erant, seu verisimiliter petiissent, vel dederint signa contritionis; impertienda iisdem est, etiam si postea linguae, ceterorumque sensuum usu sint destituti, aut in delirium vel amentiam inciderint. Excommunicatis vero, impaenitentibus, et qui in manifesto peccato mortali moriuntur, est omnino deneganda.

2. Parochus aliusve Sacerdos qui infirmo assistat, superpelliceo et stola violacea indutus, ingrediendo cubiculum, ubi jacet infirmus, dicat: Pax huic dómui, etc., ac deinde aegrotum, cubiculum et circumstantes aspergat aqua benedicta, dicendo Antiphonam: Aspérges me, etc.

3. Quod si aegrotus velit confiteri, audiat illum, et absolvat. Si confessionem non petat, excitet illum ad eliciendum actum contritionis; de hujus Benedictionis efficacia ac virtute, si tempus ferat, breviter admoneat; tum instruat, atque hortetur, ut sanctissimum nomen Jesu, corde saltem, invocet, morbi incommoda ac dolores in anteactae vitae expiationem libenter perferat, Deoque sese paratum offerat ad ultro acceptandum, quidquid ei placuerit, et mortem ipsam patienter obeundam in satisfactionem poenarum, quas peccando promeruit.

4. Tum piis ipsum verbis consoletur, in spem erigens, fore, ut ex divinae munificentiae largitate eam poenarum remissionem, et vitam sit consecuturus aeternam.

5. Postea dicat:

℣. Adjutórium nostrum in nómine Dómini.

℟. Qui fecit caelum et terram.

Antiphona: Ne reminiscáris, Dómine, delícta fámuli tui (fámulae tuae), neque vindíctam sumas de peccátis ejus.

Kýrie, eléison. Christe, eléison. Kýrie, eléison.

Pater noster secreto usque ad

℣. Et ne nos indúcas in tentatiónem.

℟. Sed líbera nos a malo.

℣. Salvum (–am) fac servum tuum (ancíllam tuam).

℟. Deus meus, sperántem in te.

36

THE RITE OF THE APOSTOLIC BLESSING
with Plenary Indulgence at
the Hour of Death

The Apostolic Blessing with Plenary Indulgence at the hour of death should be imparted following the reception of the Last Sacraments, to those who desire it while they are still rational and conscious. It may likewise be granted to anyone who has given any indication of such desire, or who has shown himself contrite before becoming delirious or irrational. But it absolutely must be denied the excommunicated, the impenitent, and such as patently die in mortal sin.

2. The pastor or another priest, vested in surplice and purple stole, enters the room where the sick person lies, and says: **Peace be unto this home,** etc. Next he sprinkles the sick person, the room, and the bystanders with holy water, saying the antiphon: **Asperges,** etc.

3. If the sick person wishes to confess, the priest hears his confession and absolves him. If not, he bids him make an act of contrition, and if time permits, briefly instructs him on the power and efficacy of this blessing. He then exhorts him to invoke the holy name of **Jesus,** patiently to bear his sufferings in expiation for past sins, to resign himself totally to God's holy Will, even to the extent of accepting death resignedly in satisfaction for punishment due to sin.

4. The priest consoles him, instilling confidence that by divine munificence he shall receive remission of temporal punishment and everlasting life.

5. Then he says:

℣. **Our help is in the name of the Lord.**

℟. **Who made heaven and earth.**

Antiphon: **Remember not, O Lord, the offenses of thy servant (handmaid), neither take retribution on his (her) sins.**

Lord, have mercy on us. Christ, have mercy on us. Lord, have mercy on us.

Our Father inaudibly until

℣. **And lead us not into temptation.**

℟. **But deliver us from evil.**

℣. **Preserve thy servant (handmaid).**

℟. **Who trusts in thee, my God.**

℣. Dómine, exáudi oratiónem meam.

℟. Et clamor meus ad te véniat.

℣. Dóminus vobíscum.

℟. Et cum spíritu tuo.

Orémus. Oratio

CLEMENTÍSSIME Deus, Pater misericordiárum et Deus totíus consolatiónis, qui néminem vis períre in te credéntem atque sperántem: secúndum multitúdinem miseratiónum tuárum réspice propítius fámulum tuum N. quem (fámulam tuam N. quam) tibi vera fides et spes christiána comméndant. Vísita eum (eam) in salutári tuo, et, per Unigéniti tui passiónem et mortem, ómnium ei delictórum suórum remissiónem et véniam cleménter indúlge; ut ejus ánima in hora éxitus sui te júdicem propitiátum invéniat, et, in sánguine ejúsdem Fílii tui ab omni mácula ablúta, transíre ad vitam mereátur perpétuam. Per eúndem Christum Dóminum nostrum. ℟. Amen.

6. Tunc, dicto ab uno e Clericis astantibus Confíteor, Sacerdos dicat: Misereátur et Indulgéntiam, ac deinde:

Dóminus noster Jesus Christus, Fílius Dei vivi, qui beáto Petro Apóstolo suo dedit potestátem ligándi atque solvéndi, per suam piíssimam misericórdiam recípiat confessiónem tuam, et restítuat tibi stolam primam, quam in baptísmate recepísti. Et ego, facultáte mihi ab Apostólica Sede tribúta, indulgéntiam plenáriam et remissiónem ómnium peccatórum tibi concédo. In nómine Patris, et Fílii, ✠ et Spíritus Sancti. ℟. Amen.

Per sacrosáncta humánae reparatiónis mystéria remíttat tibi omnípotens Deus omnes praeséntis et futúrae vitae poenas, paradísi portas apériat et ad gáudia sempitérna perdúcat. ℟. Amen.

Benedícat te omnípotens Deus, Pater, et Fílius, ✠ et Spíritus Sanctus. ℟. Amen.

7. Si vero infirmus sit adeo morti proximus, ut neque confessionis generalis faciendae, neque praemissarum precum recitandarum suppetat tempus, statim Sacerdos benedictionem ei impertiatur, dicendo:

℣. O Lord, hear my prayer.

℟. And let my cry come unto thee.

℣. The Lord be with you.

℟. And with thy spirit.

Let us pray.   Prayer

MOST merciful God, kind Father, our sole Comfort, Who desirest that none who believes and trusts in thee should perish; according to the multitude of thy mercy look kindly upon thy servant N. (handmaid N.) whom the true faith and Christian hope commend to thee. Visit him (her) with thy saving power, and through the suffering and death of thy Sole-Begotten Son, graciously grant him (her) pardon and remission of all sin. Let his (her) soul at the hour of its departure find in thee a merciful Judge, and cleansed from every stain in the blood of thy Son, let him (her) be worthy to pass into everlasting life. Through the same Christ our Lord. ℟. Amen.

6. The Confíteor having been said by one of the assistants, the priest says: Misereátur and Indulgéntiam. Then he continues:

May our Lord, Jesus Christ, Son of the living God, Who hath given to his blessed Apostle Peter the power of binding and loosing, mercifully receive thy confession, and restore unto thee the pristine robe of baptism. And I, by the power given to me by the Apostolic See, grant thee a Plenary Indulgence and remission of all sins. In the name of the Father, and of the Son, ✠ and of the Holy Spirit. ℟. Amen.

Through the most sacred Mysteries of mankind's restoration, may the almighty God remit unto thee the punishment of the present and of eternity, open to thee the gates of Paradise, and lead thee to everlasting happiness. ℟. Amen.

May almighty God, the Father, Son, ✠ and Holy Spirit bless thee. ℟. Amen.

7. But if the dying person is so near death that time does not permit the Confíteor nor the foregoing prayers, the priest imparts the blessing immediately, saying:

EGO, facultáte mihi ab Apostólica Sede tribúta, indulgéntiam plenáriam et remissiónem ómnium peccatórum tibi concédo. In nómine Patris, et Fílii, ✠ et Spíritus Sancti. ℞. Amen.

Per sacrosáncta, etc., ut supra.

Benedícat te, etc., ut supra.

In casu vero necessitatis sufficit dicere:

EGO, facultáte mihi ab Apostólica Sede tribúta, indulgéntiam plenáriam et remissiónem ómnium peccatórum tibi concédo, et benedíco te. In nómine Patris, et Fílii, ✠ et Spíritus Sancti. ℞. Amen.

8. Quando hujusmodi Benedictio Apostolica pluribus simul infirmis impertitur, omnia dicuntur semel ut supra, singulari tantum numero in pluralem immutato.

9. Deinde Sacerdos sequentes preces, quanta poterit majori devotione, dicat, admoneatque domesticos et circumstantes, ut simul orent pro moriente.

37

RITUS BENEDICENDI POPULOS ET AGROS
ex Apostolicae Sedis indulto

Accepto diplomate pontificio, constituatur dies Dominica, Delegato et populo commodior, pro ejusdem diplomatis publicatione, et exsecutionis inchoatione.

2. Die constituta, mane fiat contio, qua doceatur populus de contentis in diplomate pontificio, et de praeparatione ad futuram Absolutionem et Benedictionem. Deinde a Delegato celebretur Missa pro remissione peccatorum, in paramentis violaceis, sine **Glória in excélsis**, et cum **Credo**, ad instar Missae votivae sollemnis pro re gravi et publica simul causa; qua finita, Celebrans depositis casula et manipulo, induatur pluviali violaceo, et, si sit Episcopus, mitram auriphrygiatam assumat: tum, omnibus genuflexis ante Altare, cantentur Litaniae Sanctorum (pag. 444), omissis Precibus et Orationibus post eas dici solitis.

THROUGH the power given me by the Holy See, I grant thee a Plenary Indulgence and the remission of all thy sins. In the name of the Father, and of the Son, ✠ and of the Holy Spirit. ℟. Amen.

Through the most sacred Mysteries etc., as above.
May almighty God etc., as above.

In case of necessity it suffices to say:

THROUGH the power given me by the Holy See, I grant thee a Plenary Indulgence and the remission of all thy sins, and I bless thee. In the name of the Father, and of the Son, ✠ and of the Holy Spirit. ℟. Amen.

8. If this blessing is given to more than one, all is said as above, except that singular forms are converted into plural.

9. With all possible fervor, the priest should add those prayers from the rite of commending a departing soul, Title V, Chapter VII of the Roman Ritual, and should exhort the bystanders to pray for the dying person.

37

APOSTOLIC BLESSING UPON A PEOPLE AND ITS LANDS
by special Indult of the Holy See

Having received the pontifical document, a Sunday convenient for the legate and the people is selected on which to publish the document, and to begin its execution.

2. In the morning of the appointed day, the contents of the document are explained to the people, so that they can prepare themselves for the absolution and blessing. Then the legate celebrates the Mass for Remission of Sins, vested in purple (with **Credo** but omitting the Gloria). This Mass is a solemn votive for a cause both important and public. After Mass, the celebrant removes the chasuble and maniple, and puts on the purple cope (if he is a bishop he uses the gold-embroidered mitre). All kneel for the chanting of the Litany of the Saints (page 445) in which the ordinary prayers and orations at the end are omitted.

3. Sedeat Delegatus, finitis Litaniis, cooperto capite, in sede sibi parata super scabello Altaris, vel in sede episcopali, si est Episcopus, seu super faldistorio posito super dicto scabello, cum duobus Ministris paratis more diaconali et subdiaconali sine manipulis, astantibus hinc inde a lateribus omnibus de Clero: et alta voce ab aliquo legatur diploma coram populo: quo lecto, dicat Delegatus: Deo grátias.

4. Tunc nomine populi ille, qui ibi pro Diacono assistit, profunde inclinatus a sinistris Delegati facit confessionem in cantu:

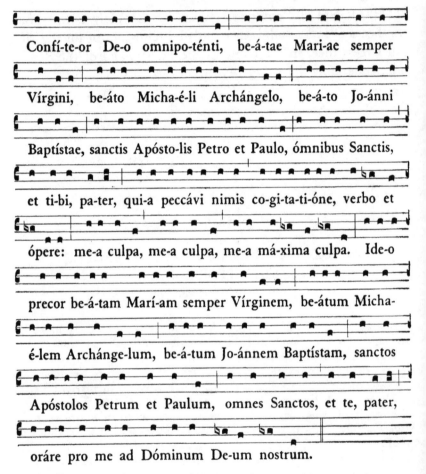

Confí-te-or De-o omnipo-ténti, be-á-tae Mari-ae semper

Vírgini, be-áto Micha-é-li Archángelo, be-á-to Jo-ánni

Baptístae, sanctis Apósto-lis Petro et Paulo, ómnibus Sanctis,

et ti-bi, pa-ter, qui-a peccávi nimis co-gi-ta-ti-óne, verbo et

ópere: me-a culpa, me-a culpa, me-a má-xima culpa. Ide-o

precor be-á-tam Marí-am semper Vírginem, be-átum Micha-

é-lem Archánge-lum, be-á-tum Jo-ánnem Baptístam, sanctos

Apóstolos Petrum et Paulum, omnes Sanctos, et te, pater,

oráre pro me ad Dóminum De-um nostrum.

5. Qua finita, Delegatus, assumpto baculo pastorali in sinistra manu, si est Episcopus, et adhuc sedens cooperto capite incipit Psalmum Miserére (pag. 436), in cujus fine dicitur Glória Patri: et deinde incipit Psalmum Deus misereátur (pag. 124).

3. After the Litany, the legate (wearing the mitre or biretta) takes the seat arranged for him on the altar foot-pace (if a bishop either the faldstool at the same place or the episcopal throne), attended by the ministers vested in dalmatic and tunic without maniples, and by the rest of the clergy. The papal document is read aloud, and at the end of the legate says: "Thanks be to God."

4. Then the deacon, standing at the legate's left, bows profoundly, and chants the **Confíteor** in the name of the people:

I confess to almighty God, to Blessed Mary ever Virgin, to Blessed Michael the Archangel, to Blessed John the Baptist, to the Holy Apostles Peter and Paul, to all the saints, and to thee, Father, that I have sinned exceedingly in thought, word, and deed. Through my fault, through my fault, through my most grievous fault. Therefore, I beseech the Blessed Mary ever Virgin, Blessed Michael the Archangel, Blessed John the Baptist, the Holy Apostles Peter and Paul, all the saints, and thee, Father, to pray to the Lord, our God for me.

5. After this, the legate — remaining in the same position (if a bishop, he takes the pastoral staff), begins the psalm **Miserére** (Page 437), concluding with the **Glória Patri.** Then he begins Psalm 66 (page 125).

6. Hi Psalmi recitantur sine cantu, alternatim a Delegato et a Clero, super universum Clerum et populum genuflexum.

7. Quibus finitis, Delegatus stans detecto capite, baculoque deposito, si est Episcopus, versus populum manibus junctis, dicit: Kýrie, eléison. Clerus prosequitur: Christe, eléison. Kýrie, eléison. Delegatus subjungit:

Pater noster secreto usque ad

℣. Et ne nos indúcas in tentatiónem.

℟. Sed líbera nos a malo.

℣. Salvos fac servos tuos.

℟. Deus meus, sperántes in te.

℣. Nihil profíciat inimícus in eis.

℟. Et fílius iniquitátis non appónat nocére eis.

℣. Esto eis, Dómine, turris fortitúdinis.

℟. A fácie inimíci.

℣. Dómine, exáudi oratiónem meam.

℟. Et clamor meus ad te véniat.

℣. Dóminus vobíscum.

℟. Et cum spíritu tuo.

Orémus.   Oratio

DEUS, cui próprium est miseréri semper et párcere: súscipe deprecatiónem nostram; ut nos et omnes fámulos tuos, quos delictórum caténa constríngit, miserátio tuae pietátis cleménter absólvat. Per Dóminum nóstrum. ℟. Amen.

8. Deinde sedens Delegatus cooperto capite, et, si est Episcopus, assumpto baculo, dicit:

MISEREÁTUR vestri omnípotens Deus, et dimíssis peccátis vestris, perdúcat vos ad vitam aetérnam. ℟. Amen.

INDULGÉNTIAM, absolutiónem, et remissiónem peccatórum vestrórum tríbuat vobis omnípotens et miséricors Dóminus. ℟. Amen.

9. Manuque dextera super populum genuflexum extensa, addit:

AUCTORITÁTE Dei omnipoténtis, et beatórum Apostolórum Petri et Pauli, a sanctíssimo Dómino nostro Papa N. mihi concéssa, absólvo vos et omnes hujus loci, ab omni vínculo excom-

6. These psalms are recited without chant, the legate and clergy alternating — during which the clergy and people kneel.

7. Afterward the legate rises (head uncovered, and giving up the staff, if he is a bishop), and facing the people prays with joined hands: **Lord, have mercy on us.** The clergy continue: **Christ, have mercy on us. Lord, have mercy on us.** The legate adds:

Our Father inaudibly until

℣. And lead us not into temptation.

℟. But deliver us from evil.

℣. Preserve thy servants.

℟. Who trust in thee, my God.

℣. Let the enemy have no power over them.

℟. And the son of iniquity do nothing to harm them.

℣. Be unto them, O Lord, a tower of strength.

℟. In the face of the enemy.

℣. O Lord, hear my prayer.

℟. And let my cry come unto thee.

℣. The Lord be with you.

℟. And with thy spirit.

Let us pray.   Prayer

O GOD, Whose nature it is ever to show mercy and to spare, receive our petition, that we and all thy servants bound by the fetters of sin may by thy sweet forgiveness be pardoned. Through our Lord. ℟. Amen.

8. The legate sits, and with head covered (if a bishop, holding the staff) says:

MAY the almighty God have mercy on you, forgive you your sins, and lead you unto everlasting life. ℟. Amen.

MAY the almighty and merciful Lord grant you pardon, absolution, and remission of your sins. ℟. Amen.

9. And with right hand extended over the kneeling congregation, he adds:

BY THE authority of God almighty and of His blessed apostles, Peter and Paul conferred upon me by our most holy lord, Pope N., I absolve you and all of this place from every bond

municatiónis, suspensiónis, interdícti, aliísque ecclesiásticis sen-
téntiis, censúris, et poenis per vos incúrsis, quas modo ignorátis,
juxta tenórem pontifícii diplómatis próxime lecti. Et restítuo vos
omnes communióni, et unitáti fidélium, et sanctis sacraméntis
Ecclésiae. In nómine Patris, et Fílii, ✠ et Spíritus Sancti. ℟.
Amen.

10. Si est Episcopus, facit ter signum crucis, dum dicit: In nómine
Pa ✠ tris, et Fí ✠ lii, et Spíritus ✠ Sancti.

11. Tunc Delegatus adhuc sedens, per se ipsum, vel alium firmioris
vocis, indicet dies tres singillatim pro jejunio; et decernat diem Domi-
nicam sequentem, vel aliam arbitrio suo, pro Communione, Benedictione agrorum et populi, et Indulgentia plenaria.

12. Die constituta, populus universus debebit communicare, et hora
competenti Delegatus cantabit Missam, quae est ad finem Missalis, sub
titulo Pro quacumque necessitate, cum paramentis violaceis, sine
Gloria, et cum **Credo,** ad instar Missae votivae sollemnis pro re gravi
et publica simul causa.

In fine Missae Celebrans benedicit de more; et, si est Episcopus, non
dat Indulgentias.

13. Finita Missa, Delegatus et duo Ministri assumunt paramenta
alba, et Delegatus, si est Episcopus, mitram pretiosam; tum, genuflexis
ante Altare cum universo Clero et populo, cantantur Litaniae Sanctorum (pag. 444), repetito ter:

℣. Ut fructus terrae dare, et conserváre dignéris.

℟. Te rogámus, audi nos.

Illisque finitis, Delegatus stans detecto capite, manibus junctis dicit.

Pater noster secreto usque ad

℣. Et ne nos indúcas in tentatiónem.

℟. Sed líbera nos a malo.

Et additur a Clero in cantu:

Psalmus 84

Benedixísti, Dómine, terram tuam: * avertísti captivitátem Jacob.

of excommunication, suspension, interdict, as well as from every ecclesiastical sentence, censure, or punishment you may have incurred, of which you are not conscious at the moment, in accordance with the purport of the pontifical document which has been read to you. And I restore you to union and communion of Christian fellowship, and to the holy Sacraments of the Church. In the name of the Father, and of the Son, ✠ and of the Holy Spirit. ℞. Amen.

10. If a bishop, he makes the cross thrice when saying the above words.

11. The legate, or someone with stronger voice, publicizes the three specific days for fasting, and indicates the Sunday following (or another day) as the day for general Communion, the Blessing, and the Plenary Indulgence.

12. All members of the parish should communicate on the day appointed. At a suitable hour the legate celebrates High Mass. This Mass will be the one found at the end of the Missal under the title: **For Any Necessity,** celebrated in purple vestments, without **Gloria** but with **Credo**—being a solemn votive for a cause both important and public.

At the end of Mass, the celebrant gives the blessing in the usual way, and if he is a bishop does not grant the customary indulgences.

13. The legate and the two ministers change to white vestments, and if the legate is a bishop, he wears the precious mitre. All kneel during the chanting of the Litany of the Saints (page 445), and the following versicle and response are sung thrice:

℣. That thou wouldst vouchsafe to give and preserve the fruits of the earth.

℞. We beseech thee, hear us.

When the Litany is concluded, the legate standing with hands folded and head uncovered, says:

Our Father inaudibly until

℣. And lead us not into temptation.

℞. But deliver us from evil.

The clergy sing the following psalm:

Psalm 84

Thou hast blessed thy land, O Lord; thou hast ended the captivity of Jacob.

Remisísti iniquitátem plebis tuae: * operuísti ómnia peccáta eórum.

Mitigásti omnem iram tuam: * avertísti ab ira indignatiónis tuae.

Convérte nos, Deus, salutáris noster: * et avérte iram tuam a nobis.

Numquid in aetérnum irascéris nobis? * aut exténdes iram tuam a generatióne in generatiónem?

Deus, tu convérsus vivificábis nos: * et plebs tua laetábitur in te.

Osténde nobis, Dómine, misericórdiam tuam: * et salutáre tuum da nobis.

Audiam quid loquátur in me Dóminus Deus: * quóniam loquétur pacem in plebem suam.

Et super sanctos suos: * et in eos, qui convertúntur ad cor.

Verúmtamen prope timéntes eum salutáre ipsíus: * ut inhábitet glória in terra nostra.

Misericórdia, et véritas obviavérunt sibi: * justítia, et pax osculátae sunt.

Véritas de terra orta est: * et justítia de caelo prospéxit.

Etenim Dóminus dabit benignitátem: * et terra nostra dabit fructum suum.

Justítia ante eum ambulábit: * et ponet in via gressus suos.

Glória Patri.

Quo finito, Delegatus dicit:

℣. Benedíces corónae anni benignitátis tuae.

℟. Et campi tui replebúntur ubertáte.

℣. Oculi ómnium in te sperant, Dómine.

℟. Et tu das illis escam in témpore opportúno.

℣. Dómine, exáudi oratiónem meam.

℟. Et clamor meus ad te véniat.

℣. Dóminus vobíscum.

℟. Et cum spíritu tuo.

Orémus.   Oratio

Deus, refúgium nostrum et virtus: adésto piis Ecclésiae tuae

Thou hast forgiven the iniquity of thy people; all their sins thou hast condoned.

Thine anger is softened; thou hast turned away from the fierceness of thy wrath.

Restore us, O God, our Savior, and turn away thy rancour from us.

Wilt thou be angry with us forever? Or wilt thou prolong thy revenge through generations?

Thou wilt grant us life again, O God, and thy people will rejoice in thee.

Show us, O Lord, thy love, and grant us thy protection.

I will listen to what the Lord God sayeth to my soul, for He shall bespeak peace for His people,

And for His saints, and for all that turn their hearts unto Him.

Surely His salvation is nigh to those that fear Him, and His glory will dwell in our land.

Mercy and truth are met together, justice and peace have kissed.

Truth is sprung out of the earth, and justice looketh down from heaven.

Indeed, the Lord shall lavish His blessings, and our land shall yield her fruit.

Justice shall be His herald, and follow in His footsteps.

Glory be to the Father.

Then the legate says:

℣. Thou crownest the year with thy good things.

℟. And the fields overflow with plenty.

℣. The eyes of thy people wait on thee, O Lord.

℟. And thou givest them food in due season.

℣. O Lord, hear my prayer.

℟. And let my cry come unto thee.

℣. The Lord be with you.

℟. And with thy spirit.

Let us pray.   Prayer

O God, our refuge and our strength, give ear to the entreaties

précibus, auctor ipse pietátis, et praesta; ut, quod fidéliter pétimus, efficáciter consequámur.

D EUS, qui in omni loco dominatiónis tuae clemens et benígnus assístis: exáudi nos, quaésumus, et concéde; ut in pósterum inviolábilis hujus loci permáneat bene✠díctio, et tui múneris benefícia, univérsitas haec fidélium, quae súpplicat, percípere mereátur.

O RÁMUS, pietátem tuam, omnípotens Deus: ut fructus terrae, quos áëris et plúviae temperaménto nutríre dignáris, benedictiónis tuae imbre perfúndas, et tríbuas huic pópulo tuo de tuis munéribus tibi semper grátias ágere: ut fertilitáte terrae, esuriéntium ánimas bonis affluéntibus répleas, et egénus et pauper laudent nomen glóriae tuae. Per Christum Dóminum nostrum. ℟. Amen.

14. Postea assumpto baculo, si est Episcopus, et cooperto capite, dicit Delegatus:

Benedíctio Dei omnipoténtis, Patris, et Fílii,✠ et Spíritus Sancti, super agros, et bona quaecúmque loci hujus, plena descéndat, et máneat semper. ℟. Amen.

15. Si est Episcopus, facit ter signum crucis, dum dicit praedicta verba.

16. Deinde accepto de manu dignioris de Clero aquae benedictae aspersorio, aspergit versus quatuor mundi partes, dicens sine cantu, et sine Psalmo Antiphonam:

Aspérges me, Dómine, hyssópo, et mundábor: lavábis me, et super nivem dealbábor.

17. Pro Benedictione populi, operto capite, manibus junctis dicit:

Pater noster secreto usque ad

℣. Et ne nos indúcas in tentatiónem.

℟. Sed líbera nos a malo.

℣. Salvos fac servos tuos.

℟. Deus meus, sperántes in te.

℣. Non secúndum peccáta nostra fácias nobis.

℟. Neque secúndum iniquitátes nostras retríbuas nobis.

of thy Church, thou Source of mercy, and grant that what we seek with faith, we may receive in fact.

O GOD, Who dost stand by merciful and good in every place under thy sway, hear us, we pray, and grant that thy blessing ✝may endure here for ages, and that this people may feel thy bounteous hand whenever it seeks thee.

WE APPEAL to thy love, O almighty God, asking thee to shower thy blessings upon the fruits of the earth which thou dost nurture with favorable rains and weather. Grant that this people enriched with thy gifts may ever be grateful to thee. And by the land's fertility, mayest thou satisfy the hungry with affluence, so that the poor and the needy may praise thy divine majesty. Through Christ our Lord. ℟. Amen.

14. If the legate is a bishop, he pronounces the following blessing with staff and mitre:

May the blessing of almighty God, Father, Son, ✝and Holy Spirit descend abundantly upon the lands and possessions of this place, and remain for all time. ℟. Amen.

15. A bishop makes the cross thrice while saying the preceding words.

16. He receives the aspersory from the highest in rank among the clergy, and sprinkles in the four directions of the earth, saying without chant:

Sprinkle me with hyssop, O Lord, and I shall be clean: wash me, and I shall be whiter than snow.

17. For the blessing of the people, he says with joined hands and head uncovered:

Our Father inaudibly until

℣. And lead us not into temptation.

℟. But deliver us from evil.

℣. Preserve thy servants.

℟. Who trust in thee, my God.

℣. Deal not with us according to our sins.

℟. Nor render unto us according to our transgressions.

℣. Mitte nobis, Dómine, auxílium de sancto.

℞. Et de Sion tuére nos.

℣. Dómine, exáudi oratiónem meam.

℞. Et clamor meus ad te véniat.

℣. Dóminus vobíscum.

℞. Et cum spíritu tuo.

Orémus. Oratio

PROTÉCTOR in te sperántium, Deus, exáudi preces pópuli tui, et praesta; ut véniat super nos sperátae a te benedictiónis ubértas, et pietátis tuae munéribus júgiter perfruámur. Per Dóminum nostrum Jesum Christum, Fílium tuum: Qui tecum vivit et regnat in unitáte Spíritus Sancti Deus, per ómnia saécula saeculórum. ℞. Amen.

18. Tunc Diaconus cantat alta voce:
Humiliáte vos ad apostólicam Benedictiónem.

Postea Delegatus stans operto capite, et, si est Episcopus, baculum sinistra tenens manu, benedicit semel, et, si est Episcopus, ter, dicens:

AUCTORITÁTE Dei omnipoténtis, et beatórum Apostolórum Petri et Pauli, et sanctíssimi Dómini nostri Papae N. benedíco vos, et omnes hujus loci: In nómine Patris, et Fílii, ✠ et Spíritus Sancti. ℞. Amen.

19. Demum cantatur Hymnus Te Deum (pag. 58), inchoatus a Delegato; quo finito, Delegatus cantat Orationem pro gratiarum actione:

Orémus. Oratio

DEUS, cujus misericórdiae non est númerus, et bonitátis infinítus est thesáurus: piíssimae majestáti tuae pro collátis donis grátias ágimus, tuam semper cleméntiam exorántes; ut, qui peténtibus postuláta concédis, eósdem non déserens, ad praémia futúra dispónas. Per Dóminum nostrum Jesum Christum, Fílium tuum: Qui tecum vivit et regnat in unitáte Spíritus Sancti Deus, per ómnia saécula saeculórum. ℞. Amen.

Cantores addunt: Benedicámus Dómino.

℞. Deo grátias.

℣. Send us, O Lord, aid from on high.

℟. And from Sion protect us.

℣. O Lord, hear my prayer.

℟. And let my cry come unto thee.

℣. The Lord be with you.

℟. And with thy spirit.

Let us pray.   Prayer

O GOD, the Protector of all who place their confidence in thee, hear the prayer of thy people, and bestow on us the plenteous blessing we expect, that we may rejoice ever in thy munificence. Through our Lord, Jesus Christ, thy Son, Who liveth and reigneth with thee in unity of the Holy Spirit, God, eternally. ℟. Amen.

18. The deacon chants with loud voice:

Humble yourselves for the Apostolic Blessing!

The legate, standing with mitre or biretta, gives the blessing (if he is a bishop he holds the pastoral staff, and makes the sign of the cross thrice), saying:

BY THE authority of almighty God, the blessed apostles, Peter and Paul, and of our most holy lord, Pope N., I bless you and all inhabitants of this place: In the name of the Father, and of the Son, ☩ and of the Holy Spirit. ℟. Amen.

19. The legate intones the Te Deum (see page 59), and when it is finished, he chants the following prayer of thanksgiving:

Let us pray.   Prayer

O GOD, Whose mercy is without limits and Whose goodness is a boundless treasury! We thank thy loving Sublimity for bountiful favors, and perserveringly appeal to thy clemency. Desert us not, thou Who hearest thy suppliants, but speed us to final victory. Through our Lord, Jesus Christ, thy Son, Who liveth and reigneth with thee in the unity of the Holy Spirit, God, forevermore. ℟. Amen.

The cantors sing: Let us bless the Lord.

℟. Thanks be to God.

38

RITUS BENEDICTIONIS PAPALIS
SUPER POPULUM ELARGIENDAE

servandus a sacerdotibus, quibus a S. Sede hujusmodi
facultas indulta est

(Juxta decretum S. C. Rituum die 12 Martii 1940)

1. Admoneatur populus de ecclesia, die et hora, qua dabitur pontificia Benedictio. Postquam populus ad ecclesiam convenerit, ad contritionis et devotionis sensus pio brevique sermone excitetur. Mox vero Sacerdos, nullis circumstantibus ministris, superpelliceo et stola alba indutus, ante altare genuflexus, sequentibus versibus Dei opem imploret.

℣. Adjutórium nostrum in nómine Dómini.

℟. Qui fecit caelum et terram.

℣. Salvum fac pópulum tuum, Dómine.

℟. Et bénedic hereditáti tuae.

℣. Dóminus vobíscum.

℟. Et cum spíritu tuo.

Deinde stans sequentem recitet Orationem:

Orémus.   Oratio

OMNÍPOTENS et miséricors Deus, da nobis auxílium de sancto, et vota pópuli hujus, in humilitáte cordis véniam peccatórum poscéntis tuámque benedictiónem praestolántis et grátiam, cleménter exáudi: déxteram tuam super eum benígnus exténde, ac plenitúdinem divínae benedictiónis effúnde, qua, bonis ómnibus cumulátus, felicitátem et vitam consequátur aetérnam. Per Christum Dóminum nostrum. ℟. Amen.

2. Postea ad cornu Epistolae accedat; ibique stans, una benedictione, unico videlicet signo crucis, benedicat, proferens alta voce haec verba:

Benedícat vos omnípotens Deus, Pater, et Fílius, ✠ et Spíritus Sanctus. ℟. Amen.

3. Sacerdotes qui facultate gaudent impertiendi Benedictionem Papalem formulam praescriptam servent; hac facultate non utantur nisi in designata ecclesia; non autem eodem die et loco quo Episcopus eam impertiat.

38

THE PAPAL BLESSING

The rite to be used by priests to whom this faculty
has been granted by the Holy See

(According to a decree of the Congregation of Sacred Rites,
dated March 12, 1940)

1. The people are to be informed about the day, the time, and the church where the papal blessing will be given. When they are assembled in church, a short and edifying instruction should be addressed to them, in order to arouse a spirit of devotion and compunction. After which the priest, vested in surplice and white stole, kneels at the altar, and implores God's help in the following words (he is not assisted by anyone):

℣. Our help is in the name of the Lord.

℟. Who made heaven and earth.

℣. O Lord, preserve thy people.

℟. And bless thine inheritance.

℣. The Lord be with you.

℟. And with thy spirit.

Then standing he continues:

Let us pray.   Prayer

AID us from on high, O almighty and merciful God, and graciously hear the prayers of these people who humbly plead for pardon from sin, and await thy blessing and grace. Extend thy right hand over them, and pour forth thy blessing in fullest measure, that filled with all good they may come to everlasting life and felicity. Through Christ our Lord. ℟. Amen.

2. He goes to the corner of the altar-steps at the Epistle side, and blesses the people with one sign of the cross, saying aloud:

May the almighty God bless you, the Father, Son, ✠ and Holy Spirit. ℟. Amen.

3. Priests who enjoy the faculty of imparting the papal blessing are obliged to observe the prescribed form, and may use this faculty only in the church designated. They may not use it on the same day nor in the same city or community on and in which a bishop imparts it.

39

RITUS ABSOLUTIONIS GENERALIS
ET BENEDICTIONIS PAPALIS
Ex Apostolicae Sedis Indulto Pro Regularibus Ordinibus Et
Tertiariis Ad Eos Pertinentibus

Pro Benedictione Apostolica cum indulgentia plenaria in articulo mortis retineatur in omnibus formula superius (pag. 132) praescripta, addito tantum ad **Confíteor** nomine Sancti proprii Fundatoris.

2. Benedictio Summi Pontificis nomine super Congregationem impertienda detur cum formula superius (pag. 150) tradita, sed nonnisi bis in anno, et sub conditione quod haec Benedictio numquam detur eodem die et loco quo Episcopus eam impertiat.

3. In Absolutione generali pro Regularibus cujuscumque Ordinis, atque in Benedictione cum indulgentia plenaria pro Tertiariis saecularibus adhibeantur omnino duae insequentes formulae:

I. Formula Absolutionis generalis
pro Regularibus cujuscumque Ordinis hoc privilegio fruentibus.

Sacerdos, superpelliceo et stola violacea indutus, dicit:

Antiphona: **Ne reminiscáris, Dómine, delícta nostra vel paréntum nostrórum, neque vindíctam sumas de peccátis nostris.**

Kýrie, eléison. Christe, eléison. Kýrie, eléison.

Pater noster secreto usque ad

℣. **Et ne nos indúcas in tentatiónem.**

℟. **Sed líbera nos a malo.**

℣. **Osténde nobis, Dómine, misericórdiam tuam.**

℟. **Et salutáre tuum da nobis.**

℣. **Dómine, exáudi oratiónem meam.**

℟. **Et clamor meus ad te véniat.**

℣. **Dóminus vobíscum.**

℟. **Et cum spíritu tuo.**

39

GENERAL ABSOLUTION AND THE PAPAL BLESSING
By Indult of the Holy See for Religious Orders and
Their Affiliate Tertiaries

When giving the papal blessing with plenary indulgence at the hour of death, the form prescribed on page 133 is followed, except that in the **Confíteor** the name of the Saint-Founder of the respective order is inserted.

2. When imparting the papal blessing, the form given on page 151 is followed. This blessing can be used only twice a year and never on the same day nor in the same city or community on and in which the bishop imparts it.

3. In imparting the general absolution to any religious order or the papal blessing with plenary indulgence to secular tertiaries, the two following forms must be used:

I. General Absolution
for every religious order which enjoys this privilege

The priest vested in surplice and purple stole says:

Antiphon: **Be not mindful, O Lord, of our transgressions or those of our parents, nor take vengeance on our sins.**

Lord, have mercy on us. Christ, have mercy on us. Lord, have mercy on us.

Our Father inaudibly until

℣. **And lead us not into temptation.**

℟. **But deliver us from evil.**

℣. **Show us thy mercy, O Lord.**

℟. **And grant us thy salvation.**

℣. **O Lord, hear my prayer.**

℟. **And let my cry come unto thee.**

℣. **The Lord be with you.**

℟. **And with thy spirit.**

Orémus. Oratio

Deus, cui próprium est miseréri semper et párcere, súscipe deprecatiónem nostram, ut nos, et omnes fámulos tuos, quos delictórum caténa constríngit, miserátio tuae pietátis cleménter absólvat.

EXÁUDI, quaésumus, Dómine, súpplicum preces, et confiténtium tibi parce peccátis, ut páriter nobis indulgéntiam tríbuas benígnus et pacem.

INEFFÁBILEM nobis, Dómine, misericórdiam tuam cleménter osténde: ut simul nos et a peccátis ómnibus éxuas, et a poenis, quas pro his merémur, erípias.

DEUS, qui culpa offénderis, poeniténtia placáris: preces pópuli tui supplicántis propítius réspice; et flagélla tuae iracúndiae, quae pro peccátis nostris merémur, avérte. Per Christum Dóminum nostrum. ℟. Amen.

Completis precibus, ab uno ex astantibus dicitur Confíteor, addito nomine Sancti proprii Fundatoris.

Deinde Sacerdos dicit: Misereátur vestri, *etc.,* Indulgéntiam, absolutiónem, *etc.*

Postea subjungit:

DÓMINUS noster Jesus Christus per mérita suae sacratíssimae passiónis vos absólvat, et grátiam suam vobis infúndat. Et ego auctoritáte ipsiús, et beatórum Apostolórum Petri et Pauli, et Summórum Pontíficum Ordini nostro ac vobis concéssa, et mihi in hac parte commíssa, absólvo vos ab omni vínculo excommunicatiónis, suspensiónis et interdícti, si quod forte incurrístis, et restítuo vos unióni, et participatióni fidélium, necnon sacrosánctis Ecclésiae sacraméntis. Item eádem auctoritáte absólvo vos ab omni transgressióne votórum et régulae, constitutiónum, ordinatiónum et admonitiónum majórum nostrórum, ab ómnibus poeniténtiis oblítis, seu étiam negléctis, concédens vobis remissiónem et indulgéntiam ómnium peccatórum, quibus contra Deum et próximum fragilitáte humána, ignorántia, vel malítia deliquístis, ac de quibus jam conféssi estis: In nómine Patris, et Fílii, ✠ et Spíritus Sancti. Amen.

Let us pray.   Prayer

O God, Whose nature it is ever to show mercy and to spare, receive our petition, that we and all thy servants bound by the fetters of sin may by thy sweet forgiveness be pardoned.

WE BESEECH thee, O Lord, hear the plea of thy suppliants, and pardon the sins of thy penitents; and deign to grant us thy tender forgiveness together with thy peace.

SHOW us, O Lord, thine unutterable mercy, that blotting out our transgressions, thou wouldst vouchsafe to snatch us from the condemnation they deserve.

O GOD, our sins offend thee, but our penance placates thine anger! Regard graciously the entreaties of thy people, and turn away the stripes which our transgressions justly deserve. Through Christ our Lord. R⁄. Amen.

After these prayers, the **Confíteor** is said by the people or by one representing them, inserting in its proper place the name of the Saint-Founder of the order.

Then the priest says: **Misereátur**, etc., **Indulgéntiam, absolutiónem,** etc.

Lastly he adds:

MAY our Lord, Jesus Christ absolve you by the merits of His sacred passion, and shower upon you His grace. And I — by His authority and that of the blessed apostles, Peter and Paul, and by the authority which the holy pontiffs have granted to you and our Order and committed to me in this instance — absolve you from every bond of excommunication, suspension, and interdict which you may have incurred, and I restore you to the unity and communion of the faithful and to the holy Sacraments of the Church. Likewise, I absolve you, by the same authority, from every violation of vows, the rule, constitutions, admonitions, and orders of our superior, from all penances which you have neglected or forgotten. And lastly I grant you remission and indulgence of all sins which by human frailty, ignorance, or malice you have committed against God and neighbor, and which you have already confessed: In the name of the Father, and of the Son, ✠ and of the Holy Spirit. Amen

II. Formula Benedictionis
cum indulgentia plenaria
pro Tertiariis saecularibus
ceterisque omnibus communicationem privilegiorum
et gratiarum cum iisdem, vel cum Regularibus cujuscumque
Ordinis habentibus.

Sacerdos, superpelliceo et stola violacea indutus, dicit:

Antiphona: Intret orátio mea in conspéctu tuo, Dómine; inclína aurem tuam ad preces nostras; parce, Dómine, parce pópulo tuo, quem redemísti sánguine tuo pretióso, ne in aetérnum irascáris nobis.

Kýrie, eléison. Christe, eléison. Kýrie, eléison.

Pater noster secreto usque ad

℣. Et ne nos indúcas in tentatiónem.

℟. Sed líbera nos a malo.

℣. Salvos fac servos tuos.

℟. Deus meus, sperántes in te.

℣. Mitte eis, Dómine, auxílium de sancto.

℟. Et de Sion tuére eos.

℣. Esto eis, Dómine, turris fortitúdinis.

℟. A fácie inimíci.

℣. Nihil profíciat inimícus in nobis.

℟. Et fílius iniquitátis non appónat nocére nobis.

℣. Dómine, exáudi oratiónem meam.

℟. Et clamor meus ad te véniat.

℣. Dóminus vobíscum.

℟. Et cum spíritu tuo.

Orémus.   Oratio

Deus, cui próprium est miseréri semper et párcere, súscipe deprecatiónem nostram, ut nos, et omnes fámulos tuos, quos delictórum caténa constríngit, miserátio tuae pietátis cleménter absólvat.

EXÁUDI, quaésumus, Dómine, súpplicum preces, et confiténtium tibi parce peccátis: ut páriter nobis indulgéntiam tríbuas benígnus et pacem.

II. Papal Blessing With Plenary Indulgence
for Secular Tertiaries and for all others who
share with them or with religious of any order
these same privileges and graces.

The Priest vested in surplice and purple stole says:

Antiphon: Let my prayer, O Lord, have entrance to the throne
of thy Majesty. Bend thine ear to our entreaties. Spare, Lord, spare
thy people whom thou hast redeemed with thy Precious Blood,
and be not angry with us forever.

Lord, have mercy on us. Christ, have mercy on us. Lord, have
mercy on us.

Our Father inaudibly until

℣. And lead us not into temptation.
℟. But deliver us from evil.
℣. Preserve thy servants.
℟. Who trust in thee, my God.
℣. Send them aid, O Lord, from on high.
℟. And from Sion protect them.
℣. Be unto them, O Lord, a tower of strength.
℟. In the face of the enemy.
℣. Let the enemy have no power over them.
℟. And the son of iniquity do nothing to harm them.
℣. O Lord, hear my prayer.
℟. And let my cry come unto thee.
℣. The Lord be with you.
℟. And with thy spirit.

Let us pray.   Prayer

O God, Whose nature it is ever to show mercy and to spare,
receive our petition, that we and all thy servants bound by the
fetters of sin may by thy sweet forgiveness be pardoned.

WE BESEECH thee, O Lord, hear the plea of thy suppliants,
and pardon the sins of thy penitents; and deign to grant
us thy tender forgiveness together with thy peace.

INEFFÁBILEM nobis, Dómine, misericórdiam tuam cleménter osténde: ut simul nos et a peccátis ómnibus éxuas, et a poenis, quas pro his merémur, erípias.

DEUS, qui culpa offénderis, poeniténtia placáris: preces pópuli tui supplicántis propítius réspice; et flagélla tuae iracúndiae, quae pro peccátis nostris merémur, avérte. Per Christum Dóminum nostrum. ℞. Amen.

Dicto deinde **Confíteor**, etc., **Misereátur**, etc., **Indulgéntiam**, etc., Sacerdos prosequitur:

DÓMINUS noster Jesus Christus, qui beáto Petro Apóstolo dedit potestátem ligándi atque solvéndi, ille vos absólvat ab omni vínculo delictórum, ut habeátis vitam aetérnam et vivátis in saécula saeculórum. Amen.

PER sacratíssimam passiónem et mortem Dómini nostri Jesu Christi, précibus et méritis beatíssimae semper Vírginis Maríae, beatórum Apostolórum Petri et Pauli, beáti Patris nostri N. et ómnium Sanctórum, auctoritáte a Summis Pontifícibus mihi commíssa, plenáriam indulgéntiam ómnium peccatórum vestrórum vóbis impértior. In nómine Patris, et Fílii, ✠ et Spíritus Sancti. Amen.

Si haec indulgentia immediate post sacramentalem absolutionem impertiatur, reliquis omissis, Sacerdos absolute incipiat a verbis: **Dóminus noster Jesus Christus,** etc., et ita prosequatur usque ad finem, plurali tantum numero in singularem immutato.

40

**FORMULA BREVIOR BENEDICTIONIS PAPALIS
CUM INDULGENTIA PLENARIA**
pro Tertiariis saecularibus
speciale indultum habentibus

Si haec indulgentia immediate post sacramentalem absolutionem impertiatur, et adjuncta vetent integram adhibere formulam in hoc Rituali Romano (pag. 156) praescriptam, Sacerdos, reliquis omissis, dicere poterit:

S HOW us, O Lord, thine unutterable mercy, that blotting out
our transgressions, thou wouldst vouchsafe to snatch us from
the condemnation they deserve.

O GOD, our sins offend thee, but our penance placates thine
anger! Regard graciously the entreaties of thy people, and
turn away the stripes which our transgressions justly deserve.
Through Christ our Lord. ℞. Amen.

After the **Confíteor** etc., the priest continues:

M AY our Lord, Jesus Christ, Who gave to the blessed apostle,
Peter the power of binding and loosing, absolve you from
every bond of sin, that you may have everlasting life. Amen.

T HROUGH the sacred passion and death of our Lord, Jesus
Christ, through the prayers and merits of Blessed Mary ever
Virgin, of the blessed apostles, Peter and Paul, of our blessed
father N. and all saints, and by the authority committed to me
by the holy pontiffs, I impart unto you a plenary indulgence for
all your sins. In the name of the Father, and of the Son, ✠ and
of the Holy Spirit. Amen.

If the indulgence is imparted immediately after the absolution of the
sacrament of penance, the priest begins at the words: **May our Lord,
Jesus Christ,** etc., continuing through to the end, but changing plural
forms to the singular.

40

THE SHORT FORM FOR THE PAPAL BLESSING
with Plenary Indulgence
for secular tertiaries who enjoy this special indult

When the indulgence is imparted immediately after the absolution
of the sacrament of penance, this shorter form may be substituted by
the priest if circumstances prevent using the longer form given above:

AUCTORITÁTE a Summis Pontifícibus mihi concéssa, plenáriam ómnium peccatórum tuórum indulgéntiam tibi impértior. In nómine Patris, et Fílii, ✠ et Spíritus Sancti. ℟. Amen.

41

FORMULA BENEDICTIONIS PAPALIS
CUM INDULGENTIA PLENARIA
in fine contionum
(Approbata a S. R. C. die 11 Maji 1911)

Si in Brevi edicitur, ut Benedictio cum indulgentia plenaria in fine
contionum a Sacerdote populo impertiatur cum Crucifixo, juxta ritum
formulamque praescriptam, fiat unicum signum crucis cum Crucifixo,
adhibita formula:

BENEDÍCTIO Dei omnipoténtis, Patris, et Fílii, ✠ et Spíritus
Sancti, descéndat super vos, et máneat semper. ℟. Amen.

42

BENEDICTIO
CONTRA INUNDATIONES AQUARUM
(Approbata a S. R. C. die 1 Dec. 1886)

Sacerdos indutus superpelliceo et stola, populo concomitante, portet
ad rivum vel flumen benedicendum Reliquiam sanctae Crucis, ibique
in quatuor partibus legat devote initia quatuor Evangeliorum, et post
singula Evangelia subjungat sequentes Versiculos et Orationem:

℣. Adjuva nos, Deus salutáris noster.

℟. Et propter glóriam nóminis tui líbera nos.

℣. Salvos fac servos tuos.

℟. Deus meus, sperántes in te.

℣. Dómine, non secúndum peccáta nostra fácias nobis.

℟. Neque secúndum iniquitátes nostras retríbuas nobis.

B Y THE authority given to me by the holy pontiffs, I impart unto thee a plenary indulgence for all thy sins. In the name of the Father, and of the Son, ✠ and of the Holy Spirit. ℟. Amen.

41

THE PAPAL BLESSING

With Plenary Indulgence at the end of a Sermon, Mission, or Retreat
(Approved by the Congregation of Sacred Rites, May 11, 1911)

If the Brief states that the papal blessing with plenary indulgence at the end of a sermon is to be given with a crucifix — i.e., according to the rite prescribed here — a single sign of the cross is made with a crucifix, using the form:

M AY the blessing of almighty God, Father, Son, ✠ and Holy Spirit descend upon you and remain for all time. ℟. Amen.

42

BLESSING OF A COMMUNITY AGAINST FLOODS
(Approved by the Congregation of Sacred Rites, Dec. 1, 1886)

The priest, vested in surplice and stole, accompanied by the people, carries the relic of the True Cross to the river or stream, and there devoutly reads at each of four different spots one of the introductions to the four Gospels. After each Gospel he adds the following verses and prayers:

℣. Stand by us, O God, our Helper.
℟. And for thy name's sake deliver us.
℣. Preserve thy servants.
℟. Who trust in thee, my God.
℣. Deal not with us, Lord, according to our sins.
℟. And take not vengeance on us because of our misdeeds.

℣. Mitte nobis, Dómine, auxílium de sancto.

℟. Et de Sion tuére nos.

℣. Dómine, exáudi oratiónem meam.

℟. Et clamor meus ad te véniat.

℣. Dóminus vobíscum.

℟. Et cum spíritu tuo.

Orémus. Oratio

Deus, qui justíficas ímpium, et non vis mortem peccatóris: majestátem tuam supplíciter deprecámur; ut fámulos tuos de tua misericórdia confidéntes, ab aquárum perículis, caelésti prótegas benígnus auxílio, et assídua protectióne consérves: ut tibi júgiter famuléntur, nullísque tentatiónibus a te separéntur. Per Christum Dóminum nostrum. ℟. Amen.

Et benedíctio Dei omnipoténtis, Patris, et Fílii,✠ et Spíritus Sancti, descéndat super has aquas, eásque coérceat. ℟. Amen.

43

BENEDICTIO DEPRECATORIA
contra mures, locustas, bruchos, vermes et alia animalia nociva

Sacerdos delegatus, indutus superpelliceo et stola coloris violacei, veniat ad agros, a locustis, bruchis vel aliis animalibus noxiis vexatos, et dicat:

Antiphona: Exsúrge, Dómine, ádjuva nos: et líbera nos propter nomen tuum.

Ps. 43: Deus, áuribus nostris audívimus: patres nostri annuntiavérunt nobis.

℣. Glória Patri. Sicut erat.

Repetitur Antiphona: Exsúrge, etc.

℣. Adjutórium nostrum in nómine Dómini.

℟. Qui fecit caelum et terram.

℣. Dómine, exáudi oratiónem meam.

℟. Et clamor meus ad te véniat.

℣. Send us help, O Lord, from thy holy place.

℟. And from Sion watch over us.

℣. O Lord, hear my prayer.

℟. And let my cry come unto thee.

℣. The Lord be with you.

℟. And with thy spirit.

Let us pray.   Prayer

O God, Who dealest justly with the wicked, and dost not will the death of sinners, humbly we entreat thy Majesty! Protect with heavenly aid thy trusting servants from perils of flood, and keep them constantly under thy heavenly protection. May they at all times serve thee, and never through any temptation be separated from thee. Through Christ our Lord. ℟. Amen.

And may the blessing of God almighty, Father, Son, ☩ and Holy Spirit descend upon these waters, and keep them under control. ℟. Amen.

43

BLESSING OF A COMMUNITY TO WARD OFF PESTS
such as mice and rats, locusts, worms, etc.

The priest who has faculties, vested in surplice and purple stole comes to the field or place which is infested with these creatures, and says:

Antiphon: Bestir thee, O Lord, and help us! Deliver us for thy name's sake!

Psalm 43: With our own ears we heard, O God, the things which our forefathers told us.

℣. Glory be to the Father. As it was in the beginning.

Repeat the antiphon: Bestir thee, O Lord, and help us! Deliver us for thy name's sake!

℣. Our help is in the name of the Lord.

℟. Who made heaven and earth.

℣. O Lord, hear my prayer.

℟. And let my cry come unto thee.

℣. Dóminus vobíscum.
℟. Et cum spíritu tuo.

Orémus. Oratio

Preces nostras, quaésumus, Dómine, cleménter exáudi: ut, qui juste pro peccátis nostris afflígimur, et hanc múrium (vel locustárum, vel bruchórum, vel vérmium, sive aliorum animalium) persecutiónem pátimur, pro tui nóminis glória ab ea misericórditer liberémur; ut tua poténtia procul expúlsi (-ae) nulli nóceant, et campos, agrósque nostros in tranquillitáte, et quiéte dimíttant, quátenus ex eis surgéntia et orta tuae majestáti desérviant, et nostrae necessitáti subvéniant. Per Christum Dóminum nostrum. ℟. Amen.

Orémus. Oratio

O MNÍPOTENS, sempitérne Deus, ómnium bonórum remunerátor, et peccatórum máximus miserátor, in cujus nómine ómnia genuflectúntur, caeléstia, terréstria, et infernália: tua poténtia nobis peccatóribus concéde; ut, quod de tua misericórdia confísi ágimus, per tuam grátiam efficácem ejus consequámur efféctum; quátenus hos (has) pestíferos (-as) mures (vel locústas, vel bruchos, vel vermes, vel alia animalia) per nos servos tuos maledicéndo maledícas, segregándo ségreges, exterminándo extérmines; ut per tuam cleméntiam ab hac peste liberáti, gratiárum actiónes majestáti tuae líbere referámus. Per Christum Dóminum nostrum. ℟. Amen.

Exorcismus

Exorcízo vos pestíferos (-as) mures (vel locústas, vel bruchos, vel vermes, vel alia animalia), per Deum ✠ Patrem omnipoténtem, per Jesum ✠ Christum, Fílium ejus únicum, per Spíritum ✠ Sanctum ab utróque procedéntem, ut conféstim recedátis a campis et agris nostris, nec ámplius in eis habitétis, sed ad ea loca transeátis, in quibus némini nocére possítis: pro parte omnipoténtis Dei, et totíus cúriae caeléstis, et Ecclésiae sanctae Dei vos maledícens, ut, quocúmque iéritis, sitis maledícti (-ae), deficiéntes de die in diem in vos ipsos (ipsas), et decrescéntes; quá-

℣. The Lord be with you.

℟. And with thy spirit.

Let us pray.   Prayer

Graciously hear, O Lord, our request! And though because of our sins we justly deserve this plague of mice (or locusts, worms, etc.), mercifully deliver us for thy glory's sake. By thy might let this plague be expelled, and our land and fields be left in peace, that all it produces redound to thy greatness and serve our necessities. Through Christ our Lord. ℟. Amen.

Let us pray.   Prayer

ALMIGHTY, everlasting God! Thou rewardest our every good deed, and dealest most kindly with our transgressions. Before thee all bow the knee, in heaven, on earth, and below the earth. Preserve also us sinners by thy might, that whatever we undertake with confidence in thy protection may be brought to completion by thy grace. And by our blessing, curse these noxious vermin, destroy and exterminate them, that spared from this plague we may render generous thanksgiving to thee. Through Christ our Lord. ℟. Amen.

Exorcism

By God, ✠ the Father Almighty, by Jesus ✠ Christ, His Sole-Begotten Son, by the Holy ✠ Spirit Who proceedeth from the Father and the Son, I purge you noxious vermin of evil, that speedily you be banished from our land and fields, never returning, but departing into places where you can do no harm. In the name of the almighty God and of all the heavenly legion, as well as in the name of the holy Church of God, we pronounce a curse on you, that wherever you go, you be cursed, decreasing from day to day unto your extermination. Let no remnant of you remain

tenus relíquiae de vobis nullo in loco inveniántur, nisi necessáriae ad salútem et usum humánum. Quod praestáre dignétur, qui ventúrus est judicáre vivos et mórtuos, et saéculum per ignem. ℞. Amen.

Postremo loca infecta aspergantur aqua benedicta.

44

BENEDICTIO NUPTIALIS EXTRA MISSAM
danda ex Apostolico indulto quando Missa non dicitur
(Approbata a S. R. C. d. 11 Martii 1914)

Expleto ritu celebrandi Matrimonii sacramentum (Ritual. Rom., tit. VII, cap. II), post Orationem **Réspice, etc.,** si permittatur benedictio nuptialis, sed non dicatur Missa, Sacerdos qui speciale indultum a Sancta Sede obtinuerit, ad neo-conjugatos conversus, dicit Psalmum sequentem:

Psalmus 127

Beáti omnes, qui timent Dóminum, * qui ámbulant in viis ejus.

Labóres mánuum tuárum quia manducábis: * beátus es, et bene tibi erit.

Uxor tua sicut vitis abúndans, * in latéribus domus tuae.

Fílii tui sicut novéllae olivárum, * in circúitu mensae tuae.

Ecce, sic benedicétur homo, * qui timet Dóminum.

Benedícat tibi Dóminus ex Sion: * et vídeas bona Jerúsalem ómnibus diébus vitae tuae.

Et vídeas fílios filiórum tuórum, * pacem super Israel.

Glória Patri, et Fílio, * et Spirítui Sancto.

Sicut erat in princípio, et nunc, et semper, * et in saécula saeculórum. Amen.

Kýrie, eléison. Christe, eléison. Kýrie, eléison.

Pater noster secreto usque ad

℣. Et ne nos indúcas in tentatiónem.

℞. Sed líbera nos a malo.

except that which might be necessary for the welfare and use of mankind. This grant, thou Who shalt come to judge the living and the dead, and the world by fire. ℟.Amen.

The places infested are sprinkled with holy water.

44

THE NUPTIAL BLESSING OUTSIDE OF MASS
Permitted by Apostolic Indult when Mass is not celebrated
(Approved by the Congregation of Sacred Rites, March 11, 1914)

After the administration of the sacrament of matrimony (Roman Ritual, T. VII, C. II), when Mass does not follow, this nuptial blessing may be given by a priest having special indult from the Holy See. The priest facing the bridal pair says the following psalm:

Psalm 127
Blessed are all that fear the Lord, that walk in His ways.

For thou shalt eat the labor of thy hands; happy art thou, and all shall be well with thee.

Thy wife shall be like the fruitful vine on the walls of thy dwelling;

Thy children like young olive plants round about thy table.

Behold, thus shall he be blessed who feareth the Lord.

May the Lord bless thee from Sion, and mayest thou see the prosperity of Jerusalem all the days of thy life.

And mayest thou see thy children's children. Peace be unto Israel!

Glory be to the Father.

Lord, have mercy on us. Christ, have mercy on us. Lord, have mercy on us.

Our Father   inaudibly until

℣.And lead us not into temptation.

℟.But deliver us from evil.

℣. Dómine, exáudi oratiónem meam.

℟. Et clamor meus ad te véniat.

℣. Dóminus vobíscum.

℟. Et cum spíritu tuo.

Orémus. Oratio

B ÉNE ✠ DIC, Dómine, et réspice de caelis super hanc con-junctiónem: et sicut misísti sanctum Angelum tuum Raphaélem pacíficum ad Tobíam et Saram, fíliam Raguélis; ita dignéris, Dómine, míttere benedictiónem tuam super hos cón-juges, ut in tua benedictióne permáneant, in tua voluntáte persís-tant, et in tuo amóre vivant. Per Christum Dóminum nostrum.

℟. Amen.

Deinde elevatis manibus et extensis super capita eorum, ministro librum tenente, dicit:

Dóminus Deus omnípotens benedícat vos, impleátque benedic-tiónem in vobis, et videátis fílios filiórum vestrórum usque in tértiam et quartam generatiónem et progéniem, et ad optátam perveniátis senectútem. Per Christum Dóminum nostrum. ℟ Amen.

II.

Preces Recitandae extra Missam super Conjuges
ex Apostolicae Sedis indulto
quando benedictio nuptialis non permittitur

(Approbatae a S. R. C. d. 11 Martii 1914)

Si sponsa sit vidua jam in primis nuptiis benedicta, vel etiam si prima vice nubat, sed tempore clauso, expleto ritu celebrandi Matri-monii sacramentum (Ritual. Rom., tit. VII, cap. II), post Orationem Réspice, etc., Sacerdos, qui speciale indultum a S. Sede obtinuerit, ad neo-conjugatos conversus, dicit Psalmum sequentem:

Psalmus 127

Beáti omnes, qui timent Dóminum, * qui ámbulant in viis ejus.

Labóres mánuum tuárum quia manducábis: * beátus es, et bene tibi erit.

Uxor tua sicut vitis abúndans, * in latéribus domus tuae.

Fílii tui sicut novéllae olivárum, * in circúitu mensae tuae.

℣. O Lord, hear my prayer.

℟. And let my cry come unto thee.

℣. The Lord be with you.

℟. And with thy spirit.

Let us pray.   *Prayer*

LOOK down from heaven with favor, Lord, upon this union, and bestow thy ✠ blessing. And as thou didst send thy Angel Raphael as a harbinger of peace to Tobias and Sara, the daughter of Raguel, so, too, graciously bless, O Lord, this husband and wife, that they may abide in thy blessing, persist in thy will, and live in thy love. Through Christ our Lord. ℟. Amen.

He then extends his hands over their heads, while the assistant holds the ritual, and says:

May the Lord God Almighty bless you most abundantly, and may you see your children's children unto the third and fourth generation, and may you reach a longed-for old age. Through Christ our Lord. ℟. Amen.

II. Prayers at a Marriage Which Takes Place Outside of Mass
permitted by Apostolic Indult
when the nuptial blessing is prohibited

(Approved by the Congregation of Sacred Rites, March 11, 1914)

If the bride is a widow who has previously received the nuptial blessing, or if the marriage takes place during the forbidden time (See Roman Ritual, Tit. VII, Ch. II), a priest having the special indult from the Holy See may add the following prayers after the administration of the sacrament:

Psalm 127

Blessed are all that fear the Lord, that walk in His ways.

For thou shalt eat the labor of thy hands; happy art thou, and all shall be well with thee.

Thy wife shall be like the fruitful vine on the walls of thy dwelling;

Thy children like young olive plants round about thy table.

Ecce, sic benedicétur homo, * qui timet Dóminum.

Benedícat tibi Dóminus ex Sion: * et vídeas bona Jerúsalem ómnibus diébus vitae tuae.

Et vídeas fílios filiórum tuórum, * pacem super Israel.

Glória Patri, et Fílio, * et Spirítui Sancto.

Sicut erat in princípio, et nunc, et semper, * et in saécula saeculórum. Amen.

Kýrie, eléison. Christe, eléison. Kýrie, eléison.

Pater noster secreto usque ad

℣. Et ne nos indúcas in tentatiónem.

℟. Sed líbera nos a malo.

℣. Dómine, exáudi oratiónem meam.

℟. Et clamor meus ad te véniat.

℣. Dóminus vobíscum.

℟. Et cum spíritu tuo.

Orémus.   Oratio

PRAETÉNDE, quaésumus, Dómine, fidélibus tuis déxteram caeléstis auxílii, ut te toto corde perquírant, et quae digne póstulant, assequántur. Per Christum Dóminum nostrum. ℟ Amen.

45

BENEDICTIO ANULI NUPTIALIS

℣. Adjutórium nostrum in nómine Dómini.

℟. Qui fecit caelum et terram.

℣. Dómine, exáudi oratiónem meam.

℟. Et clamor meus ad te véniat.

℣. Dóminus vobíscum.

℟. Et cum spíritu tuo.

Orémus.   Oratio

Béne ✠ dic, Dómine, ánulum hunc, quem nos in tuo nómine

Behold, thus shall he be blessed who feareth the Lord.

May the Lord bless thee from Sion, and mayest thou see the prosperity of Jerusalem all the days of thy life.

And mayest thou see thy children's children. Peace be unto Israel!

Glory be to the Father.

Lord, have mercy on us. Christ, have mercy on us. Lord, have mercy on us.

Our Father inaudibly until

℣. And lead us not into temptation.

℟. But deliver us from evil.

℣. O Lord, hear my prayer.

℟. And let my cry come unto thee.

℣. The Lord be with you.

℟. And with thy spirit.

    Let us pray.   Prayer

E XTEND over thy servants, we beseech thee, Lord, thy protecting hand, that they may seek thee wholeheartedly, and obtain whatever they rightfully ask for. Through Christ our Lord. ℟. Amen.

45

BLESSING OF A WEDDING RING

℣. Our Help is in the name of the Lord.

℟. Who made heaven and earth.

℣. O Lord, hear my prayer.

℟. And let my cry come unto thee.

℣. The Lord be with you.

℟. And with thy spirit.

    Let us pray.   Prayer

Bless ✠ thou, O Lord, this ring which we bless ✠ in thy name,

bene ✠ dícimus, ut, quae eum gestáverit, fidelitátem íntegram suo sponso tenens, in pace, et voluntáte tua permáneat atque in mútua caritáte semper vivat. Per Christum Dóminum nostrum. ℟. Amen

Et aspergatur aqua benedicta.

that she who is to wear it may render to her husband unbroken fidelity. Let her abide in thy peace, and be obedient to thy will, and may they live together in constant mutual love. Through Christ our Lord. ℟. Amen.

The ring is sprinkled with holy water.

III

BLESSINGS OF PLACES DESTINED TO SACRED PURPOSE

RITUS BENEDICENDI NOVAM ECCLESIAM
SEU ORATORIUM PUBLICUM

Sacerdos novam ecclesiam seu oratorium publicum de licentia Ordinarii benedicturus, ut ibi divinum Missae sacrificium rite celebretur, amictu, alba, cingulo, stola ac pluviali albi coloris indutus, aliquot Clericis adhibitis, praelata Cruce media inter duos Clericos deferentes cereos accensos, mane procedit ad primariam ecclesiae, vel oratorii januam: ubi stans capite aperto, conversus ad eam dicat absolute Orationem:

ACTIÓNES nostras, quaésumus, Dómine, aspirándo praéveni, et adjuvándo proséquere: ut cuncta nostra orátio et operátio a te semper incípiat, et per te coepta finiátur. Per Christum Dóminum nostrum. ℟. Amen.

2. Deinde inchoat, Clero prosequente, Antiphonam:

Aspérges me, * Dómine, hyssópo, et mundábor: lavábis me, et super nivem dealbábor.

Et Clerus alternatim dicit Psalmum Miserére (pag. 436): in fine Glória Patri.

3. Interim circumdant exterius ecclesiam (quae intus debet esse vacua et nuda, et pariter Altaria nuda excluso populo, donec absoluta sit benedictio), et Sacerdos accepto aspergillo ex herba hyssopi, ad ejus dexteram se convertens, parietes ecclesiae in superiori parte, et in fundamentis aqua benedicta aspergit, dicens: Aspérges me, etc.

Translator's Note: For all realization of the solemnity, dignity, power, and beauty of consecrating a church to God's service, one must have recourse to the Roman Pontifical: the rite of consecration of a church. Nevertheless, even in the Ritual's less solemn blessing of a church edifice, one does grasp something of the Church's mind, when she sets herself to the task of removing from profane purpose her places of worship, and constituting them·to sacred purpose. Every Catholic church is a model of the City of God, the heavenly

BLESSING OF A NEW CHURCH OR PUBLIC ORATORY

A priest — to bless a new church or public oratory where the Holy Sacrifice of the Mass will be celebrated — must have the permission of the Ordinary. Vested in amice, alb, cincture, and white stole and cope, in the morning he goes with the assisting clergy to the main entrance of the church or oratory, being led by the processional cross carried between two acolytes with lighted candles. Standing before the door (head uncovered), he says:

WE BESEECH thee, Lord, inspire and guide our works in their beginning, and accompany them unto fruition, that our every prayer and work may ever begin with thee, and through thee be accomplished. Through Christ our Lord. ℟. Amen.

2. He then intones and the clergy continue the antiphon:

Sprinkle me with hyssop, O Lord, and I shall be clean: wash me, and I shall be whiter than snow.

The clergy alternate in reciting the psalm Miserére (page 437), with Glory be to the Father at the end.

3. Meanwhile, the procession goes around the exterior of the church (everyone should remain outside the edifice until these ceremonies are completed; the interior should be empty and unadorned, and the altars bare). The priest, having received the aspersory, sprinkles the upper walls and the foundations, beginning on his right and encircling the building, the while he says: Aspérges etc.

Jerusalem. Within its walls are effected the sacramental praises of God, the song of Christ, the sanctifying of His Mystic Bride, the yearning for the Parousia — His final coming and the permanent establishment of His eternal Kingdom. And for so sublime an office, the building must first receive at least a blessing. Later, as the rubrics here direct, it should receive the plenitude of unction — the episcopal consecration.

4. Reversi ad locum, unde Processio initium habuit, repetita Antiphona a Clero, Sacerdos stans ut prius versus ad ecclesiam, dicit: Orémus.
Ministri: Flectámus génua. ℞. Leváte.

Sacerdos: Oratio

DÓMINE Deus, qui licet caelo et terra non capiáris, domum tamen dignáris habére in terris, ubi nomen tuum júgiter invocétur: locum hunc, quaésumus, beátae Maríae semper Vírginis, et beáti N. (nominando Sanctum vel Sanctam, in cujus honorem ac nomen benedicitur ecclesia), omniúmque Sanctórum intercedéntibus méritis, seréno pietátis tuae intúitu vísita, et per infusiónem grátiae tuae ab omni inquinaménto purífica, purificatúmque consérva; et qui dilécti tui David devotiónem in fílii sui Salomónis ópere complevísti, in hoc ópere desidéria nostra perfícere dignéris, effugiántque omnes hinc nequítiae spirituáles. Per Dóminum. ℞. Amen.

5. Qua finita Oratione, omnes bini in ecclesiam intrant, et ad altare majus procedunt, Litanias ordinarias (pag. 444) decantantes.

6. Sacerdos coram altari genuflectit: cumque dictum fuerit: Ut ómnibus fidélibus defúnctis réquiem aetérnam donáre dignéris. ℞. Te rogámus, audi nos, surgit Sacerdos, et intellegibili voce dicit:

Ut hanc ecclésiam, et altáre hoc, ad honórem tuum, et nomen Sancti tui N., purgáre, et bene ✠ dícere dignéris. ℞. Te rogámus, audi nos.

Cum dicit **benedícere**, manu dextera benedicit ecclesiam et altare; deinde, ut prius, genuflectit donec perficiantur Litaniae, et cantores prosequuntur:
Ut nos exaudíre dignéris, etc.

7. Dicto ultimo Kýrie, eléison, Sacerdos stans dicit: Orémus.
Ministri: Flectámus génua. ℞. Leváte.

Sacerdos: Oratio

PRAEVÉNIAT nos, quaésumus, Dómine, misericórdia tua: et, intercedéntibus ómnibus Sanctis tuis, voces nostras cleméntia tuae propitiatiónis antícipet. Per Christum Dóminum nostrum. ℞. Amen.

4. Returning to the place where the procession began, the antiphon is repeated, and the priest standing in his former place says: **Let us pray.**

Assistants: **Let us bend the knee.** ℞. **Arise!**

The priest: Prayer

O LORD GOD, Whom the heavens and the earth cannot contain, but Who dost condescend to have a dwelling on earth where thy name can be continually invoked; we beseech thee, through the merits and intercession of Blessed Mary ever Virgin, of Blessed N. (insert here the name of the saint in whose name and honor the church is blessed), and of all the saints, visit this edifice with thy kindly countenance, and purge it of all evil by the infusion of thy grace. And as thou didst cause the vow of thy beloved David to be fulfilled in the work of Solomon, his son, grant us in this work the realization of our desires, and banish hence all wicked spirits. **Through our Lord.** ℞. **Amen.**

5. After this prayer, all go into church, two by two, and the ministrants proceed to the altar. During this procession the Litany (page 445) is chanted.

6. The priest kneels at the altar until the words: **That thou mayest grant eternal rest to all the faithful departed.** ℞. **We beseech thee, hear us,** when he rises, and sings in a loud voice:

That thou wouldst purify and bless ✠ this church and this altar to thy honor and the name of Saint N. ℞. **We beseech thee, hear us.**

As he says: **bless,** he blesses the church and the altar with his right hand. Then he kneels again until the Litany is concluded, and the chanters continue: **That thou wouldst vouchsafe to hear us,** etc.

7. After the last **Kyrie,** the priest stands, and says: **Let us pray.**

Assistants:

Let us bend the knee. ℞. **Arise!**

The priest: Prayer

LET thy mercy, we pray thee, Lord, be upon us, and through the intercession of thy saints, may thy goodness and forgiveness anticipate our requests. **Through Christ our Lord.** ℞. **Amen.**

8. Tum distans ab altari congruenti spatio genuflexus, et se signans, dicit: Deus, in adjutórium meum inténde; et statim surgit, Clero respondente: Dómine, ad adjuvándum me festína; ipse vero stans dicit: Glória Patri, et Fílio, et Spirítui Sancto. Chorus respondet: Sicut erat in princípio, et nunc, et semper, et in sáecula saeculórum. Amen.

9. Postea Sacerdos dicit: Orémus.

Ministri: Flectámus génua. ℟. Leváte.

Sacerdos: Oratio

OMNÍPOTENS et miséricors Deus, qui Sacerdótibus tuis tantam prae céteris grátiam contulísti, ut quidquid in tuo nómine digne, perfectéque ab eis ágitur, a te fíeri credátur: quaésumus imménsam cleméntiam tuam; ut quidquid modo visitatúri sumus, vísites, et quidquid benedictúri sumus, bene ✠ dícas: sitque ad nostrae humilitátis intróitum, Sanctórum tuórum méritis, fuga daémonum, Angeli pacis ingréssus. Per Dóminum. ℟. Amen.

10. His dictis, inchoat, Clero prosequente, Antiphonam:

IIIa

Bénedic, Dómine, * domum istam, nómini tu-o ae-di-fi - cá-tam. Ps. Ad Dóminum cum tribu-lárer clamá-vi * : et ex-audívit me.

Et dicuntur tres Psalmi sequentes, videlicet:

Psalmus 119

Ad Dóminum cum tribulárer clamávi: * et exaudívit me.

Dómine, líbera ánimam meam a lábiis iníquis, * et a lingua dolósa.

Quid detur tibi, aut quid apponátur tibi * ad linguam dolósam?

Sagíttae poténtis acútae, * cum carbónibus desolatóriis.

Heu mihi, quia incolátus meus prolongátus est: habitávi cum habitántibus Cedar: * multum íncola fuit ánima mea.

8. The priest kneels at some distance from the altar, and signing himself with the cross, says: **Attend, O God, to my defense;** and immediately he rises, and the clergy respond: **Make haste, O Lord, to help me.** Standing he continues: **Glory be to the Father, and to the Son, and to the Holy Spirit.** The choir responds: **As it was in the beginning, is now, and ever shall be, world without end. Amen.**

9. Priest: **Let us pray.** Assistants: **Let us bend the knee.** ℟. **Arise!**

The priest: Prayer

G OD of mercy and of strength, Who didst confer on thy priests above all others so great a grace, that whatever they do worthily and perfectly in thy name, is, as it were, done by thee, we beseech thy boundless goodness, that whatever we presume to visit, may be visited by thee, and whatever we presume to bless, may be blessed ✠ by thee. And at our lowly coming, through the merits of thy saints, may demons flee, and angels of peace enter in. Through our Lord. ℟. Amen.

10. The priest intones and the clergy continue the antiphon:

Bless, O Lord, * this dwelling erected to Thy name.

The following three psalms are said:

Psalm 119

In my distress I cry to the Lord, and He heareth me.

Deliver me, O Lord, from lying lips, and from treacherous tongues.

What shall become of thee, or punishment meted to thee, thou deceitful tongue?

Sharp arrows will pierce thee, and burning coals destroy thee.

Woe is me that I must continue among strangers, that I must abide with tribes of Cedar! Too long have I been a sojourner.

Cum his, qui odérunt pacem, eram pacíficus: * cum loquébar illis, impugnábant me gratis.
Glória Patri.

LEVÁVI óculos meos in montes, * unde véniet auxílium mihi.

Auxílium meum a Dómino, * qui fecit caelum et terram.

Non det in commotiónem pedem tuum: * neque dormítet qui custódit te.

Ecce, non dormitábit neque dórmiet, * qui custódit Israel.

Dóminus custódit te, Dóminus protéctio tua, * super manum déxteram tuam.

Per diem sol non uret te: * neque luna per noctem.

Dóminus custódit te ab omni malo: * custódiat ánimam tuam Dóminus.

Dóminus custódiat intróitum tuum, et éxitum tuum: * ex hoc nunc, et usque in saéculum.
Glória Patri.

LAETÁTUS sum in his, quae dicta sunt mihi: * In domum Dómini íbimus.

Stantes erant pedes nostri, * in átriis tuis, Jerúsalem.

Jerúsalem, quae aedificátur ut cívitas: * cujus participátio ejus in idípsum.

Illuc enim ascendérunt tribus, tribus Dómini: * testimónium Israel ad confiténdum nómini Dómini.

Quia illic sedérunt sedes in judício, * sedes super domum David.

Rogáte quae ad pacem sunt Jerúsalem: * et abundántia diligén- tibus te:

Fiat pax in virtúte tua: * et abundántia in túrribus tuis.

Propter fratres meos, et próximos meos, * loquébar pacem de te:

Propter domum Dómini, Dei nostri, * quaesívi bona tibi.
Glória Patri.

With them that hate peace, I lived in peace, yet when I speak friendly, they attack me without cause.

Glory be to the Father.

Psalm 120

I LIFT mine eyes to the hills; whence shall help come to me? My help is from the Lord Who made heaven and earth.

He will not suffer thy foot to stumble, He will not slumber Who keepeth thee.

He slumbereth not nor sleepeth — the Keeper of Israel!

The Lord guardeth thee; He is thy protection at thy right hand.

The sun shall not burn thee by day, nor the moon smite thee by night.

The Lord keepeth thee from all evil, the Lord shall protect thy life.

May the Lord guard thy coming and going, henceforth and forever.

Glory be to the Father.

Psalm 121

I REJOICED when 'twas said unto me: "Let us go to the house of the Lord."

Our feet have taken their stand in thy courts, O Jerusalem.

Jerusalem — thou city well built, as a fortress compact!

Thither go up the tribes, the tribes of the Lord. Israel fulfils its law to praise the Lord.

For there are set the tribunals of judgment, the judges of David's lineage.

Pray for the welfare of Jerusalem! And let prosperity be theirs that love her.

Peace be within thy walls, and abundance in thy towers.

In my brethren and neighbor's behalf, I pray: "Peace be unto thee!"

Because of the house of the Lord, our God, I seek thy good.

Glory be to the Father.

Antiphona

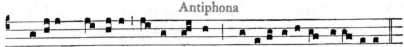

Bénedic, Dómine, domum istam, nómini tu-o ae-di-fi-cátam.

11. Interim aspergit interius parietes in parte superiori et inferiori, inchoans aspersionem a parte Evangelii, dicens:Aspérges me, etc., tum ad altare reversus, dicit:Orémus.
Ministri:Flectámus génua. ℟. Leváte.

Sacerdos: Oratio

DEUS, qui loca nómini tuo dicánda sanctíficas, effúnde super hanc oratiónis domum grátiam tuam: ut ab ómnibus hic nomen tuum invocántibus auxílium tuae misericórdiae sentiátur. Per Dóminum nostrum, etc. ℟. Amen.

12. His peractis, dicitur Missa de Mysterio vel Sancto, in cujus honorem ecclesia est benedicta; sed, si occurrat Officium Missas votivas sollemnes pro re gravi excludens, dicitur Missa de die occurrenti, cum Commemoratione Titularis, juxta Missalis rubricas.
13. Ecclesiae vero cathedrales, et, quantum fieri potest, ecclesiae collegiatae, conventuales et paroeciales, quamvis a simplici Sacerdote, ut supra, sint benedictae, sollemniter tamen consecrandae sunt.
14. Oratoria privata seu domestica nec consecrari nec benedici possunt more ecclesiarum.

47

RITUS RECONCILIANDI ECCLESIAM VIOLATAM
quae fuerit tantummodo benedicta

Violata ecclesia, non ideo coemeterium, etsi contiguum, violatum censetur, et viceversa. Si vero coemeterium ecclesiae pollutae contiguum violatum fuerit, illud una cum ecclesia reconciliatur.
Ecclesiae benedictae ac violatae reconciliatio per Rectorem ejusdem, vel quemlibet Sacerdotem de consensu saltem praesumpto Rectoris, fiat hoc modo. Altare ecclesiae omnino nudetur, provideaturque, ut ecclesia possit libere circumiri tam exterius, quam interius, si fieri potest. Paretur vasculum cum aqua benedicta, et aspergillum de herba hyssopi factum. Sacerdos, indutus amictu, alba, cingulo, stola et pluviali albi coloris, adhibitis aliquot Clericis, procedit ad primariam ecclesiae portam, ubi stans, incipit, Clero prosequente, Antiphonam:

Antiphon: **Bless, O Lord, this dwelling erected to thy name.**

11. Meanwhile the priest sprinkles the interior walls at the top and bottom, beginning on the gospel side, saying: **Aspérges, etc.**
Returning to the altar, he says: **Let us pray.**
Assistants: **Let us bend the knee.** ℟. **Arise!**

The priest: Prayer

O GOD, Who dost sanctify the places dedicated to thy name, pour forth thy grace upon this house of prayer, so that all who here invoke thee, may experience thy assistance. Through our Lord. ℟. **Amen.**

12. Following the blessing, Mass is celebrated of the Mystery or saint in whose honor the church has been blessed. But if the day's liturgy does not permit a solemn votive Mass pro re gravi, the Mass of the day is celebrated with a commemoration of the Titular Mass, in accordance with the rubrics of the Missal.

13. Cathedral churches, and if possible also collegiate, conventual, and parish churches should be solemnly consecrated later, even though blessed by a priest in the manner prescribed above.

14. Private or domestic oratories may neither be consecrated nor blessed in the same manner as churches.

47

RECONCILIATION OF A PROFANED CHURCH
which previously was only blessed

If a church is profaned, a cemetery which is contiguous is not thereby to be considered profaned, or vice versa. But if both are profaned, their reconciliation is simultaneous.

A church which was blessed, if profaned, may be reconciled by the pastor or by any priest who has his permission, expressed or presumed. The altar should be entirely bare. It should be prearranged that the officiants can conveniently go around the building, both outside and inside. The sacristan should have ready the stoop of holy water and aspersory of hyssop. The priest, vested in amice, alb, cincture, white stole and cope, goes with his assistants to the main entrance of the church, and standing outside facing the door, he intones and the clergy continue the antiphon:

Aspérges me, * Dómine, hyssópo, et mundábor: lavábis me, et super nivem dealbábor.

Et dicitur totus Psalmus **Miserére** (pag. 436), cum **Glória Patri.** Quo finito, Antiphona repetitur. Interim dum Antiphona et Psalmus dicuntur, Sacerdos aqua benedicta aspergit in circuitu extrinsecus ecclesiam, et coemeterium, simul aspergendo alternatim ad parietes ecclesiae, ac ad terram coemeterii, praesertim ad loca contaminata. Si vero coemeterium violatum non fuerit, ejus aspersio omittitur.

Quo facto, redit ad locum, ubi incepit aspergere, et stans dicit:

Orémus.   Oratio

O MNÍPOTENS et miséricors Deus, qui Sacerdótibus tuis tantam prae céteris grátiam contulísti, ut quidquid in tuo nómine digne, perfectéque ab eis ágitur, a te fíeri credátur: quaésumus imménsam cleméntiam tuam; ut, quidquid modo visitatúri sumus, vísites, et quidquid benedictúri sumus, bene ✠ dícas; sitque ad nostrae humilitátis intróitum, Sanctórum tuórum méritis, fuga daémonum, Angeli pacis ingréssus. Per Christum Dóminum nostrum. R̡. Amen.

2. Deinde omnes bini in ecclesiam ingrediuntur, et ad altare majus accedunt, Litanias ordinarias (pag. 444) decantantes. Sacerdos coram altari genuflectit: cumque dictum fuerit:

Ut ómnibus fidélibus defúnctis réquiem aetérnam donáre dignéris. R̡. Te rogámus, audi nos.

Sacerdos surgit, et clara voce dicit:

Ut hanc ecclésiam, et altáre hoc (ac coemetérium) purgáre, et reconci ✠ liáre dignéris. R̡. Te rogámus, audi nos.

3. Si vero coemeterium violatum non fuerit, omittuntur verba ad coemetérium.

Deinde rursus genuflectit, et Litaniae perficiuntur. Quibus finitis, Sacerdos versus ad dictum altare dicit: **Orémus.**

Ministri: **Flectámus génua.** R̡. **Leváte.**

Sacerdos: Oratio

P RAEVÉNIAT nos, quaésumus, Dómine, misericórdia tua: et intercedéntibus ómnibus Sanctis tuis, voces nostras cleménti tuae propitiatiónis antícipet. Per Christum Dóminum nostrum R̡. Amen.

Sprinkle me with hyssop, O Lord, and I shall be clean: wash me, and I shall be whiter than snow.

Then the entire Miserere (page 437) is said, adding Glory be to the Father, and repeating the antiphon. Meantime the priest goes around the exterior of the church, alternately sprinkling the walls of the edifice and the cemetery grounds. However, the cemetery is not sprinkled if it has not been desecrated.

Returning to the same place, he says:

Let us pray. Prayer

God of mercy and of strength, Who didst confer on thy priests above all others so great a grace, that whatever they do worthily and perfectly in thy name, is, as it were, done by thee, we beseech thy boundless goodness, that whatever we presume to visit, may be visited by thee, and whatever we presume to bless, may be blessed ✠ by thee. And at our lowly coming, through the merits of thy saints, may demons flee, and angels of peace enter in. Through Christ our Lord. ℟. Amen.

2. After this prayer, all go into church, two by two, and the ministrants proceed to the altar. During this procession the Litany (page 445) is chanted. The priest kneels at the altar until the words:

That thou wouldst grant eternal rest to all the faithful departed. ℟. We beseech thee, hear us.

Then he rises, and sings with a loud voice:

That thou wouldst purify and reconcile ✠ this church and this altar (and cemetery). ℟. We beseech thee, hear us.

3. However, if the cemetery has not been profaned, omit the words and cemetery.

Then he kneels again until the Litany is concluded. After this he stands, and facing the aforesaid altar, he says: Let us pray.

Assistants: Let us bend the knee. ℟. Arise!

The priest: Prayer

LET thy mercy, we pray thee, Lord, be upon us, and through the intercession of thy saints, may thy goodness and forgiveness anticipate our requests. Through Christ our Lord. ℟. Amen.

4. Deinde Sacerdos genuflectit ante altare, et se signo crucis muniens, clara voce dicit: **Deus, in adjutórium meum inténde:** tum surgit, et Chorus, seu astantes Clerici respondent: **Dómine, ad adjuvándum me festína;** et Sacerdos stans, dicit:

Glória Patri, et Fílio, et Spirítui Sancto.

℟. Sicut erat in princípio, et nunc, et semper, et in saécula saeculórum. Amen.

5. Quo dicto, Sacerdos inchoat, Clero prosequente, Antiphonam:

Antiphona

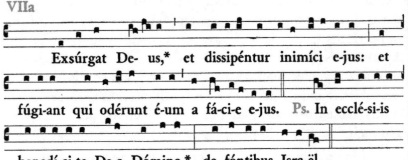

VIIa

Exsúrgat De- us,* et dissipéntur inimíci e-jus: et fúgi-ant qui odérunt é-um a fá-ci-e e-jus. Ps. In ecclé-si-is benedí-ci-te De-o Dómino,* de fóntibus Isra-ël.

Psalmus 67

IN ECCLÉSIIS benedícite Deo Dómino, * de fóntibus Israel.

Repetitur Antiphona.

Ibi Bénjamin adolescéntulus, * in mentis excéssu.

Repetitur Antiphona.

Príncipes Juda, duces eórum: * príncipes Zábulon, príncipes Néphtali.

Repetitur Antiphona.

Manda, Deus, virtúti tuae: * confírma hoc, Deus, quod operátus es in nobis.

Repetitur Antiphona.

A templo sancto tuo in Jerúsalem, * tibi ófferent reges múnera.

Repetitur Antiphona.

Increpa feras arúndinis, congregátio taurórum in vaccis populórum: * ut exclúdant eos, qui probáti sunt argénto.

Repetitur Antiphona.

4. The priest kneels at the altar, and signing himself with the cross. says with loud voice: **Attend, O God, to my defense:** and immediately he rises, and the clergy or choir respond: **Make haste, O Lord, to help me.** Standing he continues:

Glory be to the Father, and to the Son, and to the Holy Spirit.

℞. **As it was in the beginning, is now, and ever shall be, world without end. Amen.**

5. He intones and the clergy continue the antiphon:

Antiphon: **May God rise up, * and His enemies be scattered, and let them that hate Him flee from His sight!**

Psalm 67

BLESS ye God in the assemblies, ye offspring of Israel praise the Lord!

Repeat the antiphon.
There is Benjamin, the youth, in ecstasy of mind.

Repeat the antiphon.
The princes of Juda are their leaders, the princes of Zabulon, the princes of Nephtali.

Repeat the antiphon.
Renew thy strength, O God; confirm, O God, what thou hast wrought in us.

Repeat the antiphon.
At thy sanctuary in Jerusalem kings shall offer thee presents.

Repeat the antiphon.
Rebuke the wild crocodiles of the reeds [the Egyptians], the horde of bulls [Egyptian princes] with the calves [Egyptian people] of the people, who seek to reject them [Israelites] that try peace with gifts of silver.

Repeat the antiphon.

Díssipa Gentes, quae bella volunt: vénient legáti ex Aegýpto: *
Aethiópia praevéniet manus ejus Deo.

Repetitur Antiphona.

Regna terrae, cantáte Deo: * psállite Dómino.

Repetitur Antiphona.

Psállite Deo, qui ascéndit super caelum caeli, * ad Oriéntem.

Repetitur Antiphona.

Ecce dabit voci suae vocem virtútis, date glóriam Deo super Israel,
* magnificéntia ejus, et virtus ejus in núbibus.

Repetitur Antiphona.

Mirábilis Deus in sanctis suis, Deus Israel ipse dabit virtútem,
et fortitúdinem plebi suae, * benedíctus Deus.

Et non dicitur Glória Patri, sed Antiphona repetitur.

6. Interim dum Antiphona et Psalmus praedicti dicuntur, Sacerdos
circuit ecclesiam intrinsecus aspergendo: aspergit etiam specialiter loca
contaminata. Quo facto, stans in presbyterio versus ad altare, dicit:

D EUS, qui in omni loco dominatiónis tuae clemens et benígnus purificátor assístis: exáudi nos, quaésumus, et concéde;
ut in pósterum inviolábilis hujus loci permáneat benedíctio, et tui
múneris benefícia univérsitas fidélium, quae súpplicat, percípere
mereátur. Per Christum Dóminum nostrum. ℟. Amen.

7. Deinde dicitur Missa de die occurrenti.

8. Simplex Sacerdos tantum de licentia Ordinarii potest ecclesiam
consecratam reconciliare, et tunc utatur ritu in Pontificali praescripto:
procedatque indutus amictu, alba, cingulo, stola et pluviali albi coloris,
adhibitis secum aliquot Clericis superpelliceis indutis.

In casu tamen gravis et urgentis necessitatis, si Ordinarius adiri
nequeat, Rectori ecclesiae consecratae eamdem reconciliare fas est, certiore facto postea Ordinario.

Scatter the nations that delight in war! For legates shall come
out of Egypt; Ethiopia shall hasten with gifts of homage to
God.

Repeat the antiphon.

Ye kingdoms of earth, sing unto God, sing hymns to the Lord!

Repeat the antiphon.

Sing unto God Who rideth the heavenly heights which are of old.

Repeat the antiphon.

Lo, He will send out His voice, a voice of power! Give glory to
God; over Israel is manifest His majesty, and His strength is in
the clouds.

Repeat the antiphon.

God is wonderful in His temple; the God of Israel shall give
strength and might to His people. Blessed be God!

Repeat the antiphon, but omit Glory be to the Father.

6. While the foregoing antiphon and psalm are said, the priest goes
around the interior of the church sprinkling it, particularly the place
where defilement took place. Then he returns to the middle of the
sanctuary, faces the altar, and says:

O GOD, Who dost look graciously to the purity of every place
under thy sway, kindly hear us, and grant in future that
this spot may remain inviolably sanctified, and that the body of
faithful who invoke thee may be the recipients of thy liberality.
Through Christ our Lord. ℟. Amen.

7. Now the Mass of the day is celebrated.

8. A priest may reconcile a consecrated church only if he has the
permission of the Ordinary, in which case he uses the rite given in the
Roman Pontifical. He vests in the manner noted above, and is assisted
by some clerics vested in surplices.

In real and urgent necessity, if the Ordinary cannot be reached, the
pastor of a church which had been consecrated may reconcile it without
delay, and later inform his superior of the fact.

48

DE CONSECRATIONE ALTARIUM EXSECRATORUM

I

Ritus seu formula brevior consecrationis altaris immobilis quod amisit consecrationem ob separationem, etsi momentaneam, tabulae seu mensae a stipite: uti in casu de quo agit Codex Juris Canonici in can. 1200, 1.

Instaurato altari immobili, et mensa, integrum Reliquiarum sepulcrum habente, cum stipite conjuncta, Pontifex, indutus rochetto et stola alba, vel Presbyter ab Ordinario delegatus, indutus superpelliceo et stola alba, accedit versus altare, et pollice dexterae manus Chrismate intincto inungat, ad modum crucis, conjunctiones mensae cum stipite in quatuor angulis, quasi illas conjungens, ad singulas cruces dicens:

In nómine Pa ✠ tris, et Fí ✠ lii, et spíritus ✠ Sancti.

Deinde recitet sequentes Orationes:

Orémus.   Oratio

Majestátem tuam, Dómine, humíliter implorámus, ut altáre hoc sacrae unctiónis libámine ad suscipénda pópuli tui múnera inúnctum poténter bene ✠ dícere et sancti ✠ ficáre dignéris; ut quod nunc a nobis indígnis, sub tui nóminis invocatióne, in honórem beatíssimae Vírginis Maríae, et ómnium Sanctórum, atque in memóriam sancti tui N. sacrosáncti Chrísmatis unctióne delibútum est, pláceat tibi, atque altáre máneat perpétuum; ut quidquid deínceps super illud oblátum sacratúmve fúerit, dignum tibi fiat holocáustum; atque ómnium hic offeréntium sacrifícia a te pio Dómino benígne suscipiántur, et per ea víncula peccatórum nostrórum absolvántur; máculae deleántur; véniae impetréntur; et grátiae acquirántur: quátenus una cum Sanctis et Eléctis tuis vitam percípere mereámur aetérnam. Per Christum Dóminum nostrum. ℞. Amen.

Orémus.   Oratio

S UPPLICES te deprecámur, omnípotens aetérne Deus, per unigénitum Fílium tuum Dóminum nostrum Jesum Chris-

48

THE CONSECRATION OF ALTARS WHICH HAVE BEEN DESECRATED

I

The Short Form for Consecrating a Fixed Altar
which has lost its consecration if the table or mensa was removed from its support, even if only for a moment. See the Code of Canon Law, 1200, 1.

After the altar has been repaired, the pontiff vested in rochette and white stole (or a delegated priest vested in surplice and white stole) goes to the altar, and anoints with Chrism in the form of a cross the four points of contact between table and base. At each anointing he says:

In the name of the Father, ✠ and of the Son, ✠ and of the Holy ✠ Spirit.

Then he says the following prayers:

Let us pray.   Prayer

In humility, Lord, we implore thy sovereignty, that this altar, anointed with a libation of holy unction for receiving the offerings of thy people, may be wondrously blessed ✠ and sanctified ✠ by thee. For now by our unworthy hands, invoking thy name, it is anointed with sacred and holy Chrism to the honor of the Blessed Virgin Mary and all saints, and to the memory of Saint N. May it remain a permanent altar, and may it please thee. Let whatever henceforth be offered or consecrated upon it become for thee a worthy holocaust. O sweet Lord, accept the sacrifices of all who offer here, and thereby absolve us from our sins, wash away our stains, bestow pardon, give grace. And with thy saints and thy elect may we attain life everlasting. Through Christ our Lord. ℟. Amen.

Let us pray.   Prayer

O GOD, eternal and omnipotent, we thy suppliants pray that through thy Sole-Begotten Son, our Lord, Jesus Christ, thou

tum, ut altáre hoc sanctis úsibus praeparátum, caelésti bene ✠ dictióne sanctífices; et, sicut Melchísedech sacerdótis praecípui oblatiónem dignatióne mirábili suscepísti, ita impósita huic novo altári múnera, semper accépta ferre dignéris; ut pópulus, qui in hanc Ecclésiae domum sanctam convéniet, per haec libámina caelésti sanctificatióne salvátus, animárum quoque suárum salútem perpétuam consequátur. Per eúndem Christum Dóminum nostrum. ℞. Amen.

Subinde scripto declaret ac testetur praefatum altare a se, ordinaria vel delegata auctoritate, rite consecratum, uti tale habendum esse et sub eodem titulo quo ipsum ante exsecrationem gaudebat.

II

Ritus seu formula brevior consecrationis altaris
quod amisit consecrationem: uti in casu de quo agit
Codex Juris Can. in canone 1200, 2, nn. 1 et 2.

Pontifex, indutus rochetto et stola alba, vel Presbyter ab Ordinario delegatus, indutus superpelliceo et stola alba, accedit versus altare, et loco congruenti stans, benedicit aquam cum sale, cinere, et vino, incipiens absolute exorcismum salis:

Exorcízo te, creatúra salis, in nómine Dómini nostri Jesu Christi, qui Apóstolis suis ait: Vos estis sal terrae, et per Apóstolum dicit: Sermo vester semper in grátia sale sit condítus; ut sancti ✠ ficéris ad consecratiónem hujus altáris, ad expelléndas omnes daémonum tentatiónes; et ómnibus, qui ex te súmpserint, sis ánimae et córporis tutaméntum, sánitas, protéctio et confirmátio salútis. Per eúndem Dóminum nostrum Jesum Christum, Fílium tuum, qui ventúrus est judicáre vivos et mórtuos, et saéculum per ignem. ℞. Amen.

Deinde dicit:
℣. Dóminus vobíscum.
℞. Et cum spíritu tuo.

wouldst sanctify with celestial benediction ✠ this altar built for sacred purpose. And as thou didst with wondrous favor accept the offering of the priest, Melchisedech, so too, receive at all times the gifts which will be placed upon this new altar. May the people who assemble in this holy dwelling of the Church be sanctified for heaven by these sacrifices, and their souls be rewarded with life everlasting. Through the same Christ our Lord. ℞. Amen.

Immediately thereupon the officiant should declare in writing, testifying to the fact that this altar has been duly consecrated by him with ordinary or delegated authority, and that it is to be used as such, and under the same title it enjoyed before it was desecrated.

II

The Short Form for Consecrating an Altar

which has lost consecration by serious breakage or by the reliquary tomb having been broken or opened: Code of Canon Law, 1200, 2, n. 1–2.

The pontiff, vested in rochette and white stole (or a delegated priest vested in surplice and white stole), goes to the altar, and at some distance from it blesses water, salt, ashes, and wine, beginning with the exorcism of salt:

Thou creature of salt, I purge thee of evil in the name of our Lord, Jesus Christ Who said to His apostles: "You are the salt of the earth," and through the Apostle says: "Let your speech be at all times pleasing, seasoned with salt." Be thou sanctified ✠ for the consecration of this altar, to drive off every diabolical assault. And mayest thou be protection to body and soul, health, safeguard, and assurance of salvation to them that use thee. Through the same Lord, Jesus Christ, thy Son, Who shall come to judge the living and the dead and the world by fire. ℞. Amen.

Then he says:

℣. The Lord be with you.

℞. And with thy spirit.

Orémus.

DÓMINE Deus, Pater omnípotens, qui hanc grátiam caélitus sali tribúere dignátus es, ut ex illo possint univérsa condíri, quae homínibus ad escam procreásti, béne ✠ dic hanc creatúram salis, ad effugándum inimícum; et ei salúbrem medicínam immítte, ut profíciat suméntibus ad ánimae et córporis sanitátem. Per Christum Dóminum nostrum. ℟. Amen.

Tum procedit absolute ad exorcismum aquae:

Exorcízo te, creatúra aquae, in nómine Dei Pa ✠ tris, et Fí ✠ lii, et Spíritus ✠ Sancti, ut repéllas diábolum a término justórum, ne sit in umbráculis hujus ecclésiae et altáris. Et tu, Dómine Jesu Christe, infúnde Spíritum Sanctum in hanc ecclésiam tuam et altáre; ut profíciat ad sanitátem córporum animarúmque adorántium te, et magnificétur nomen tuum in géntibus: et incréduli corde convertántur ad te, et non hábeant álium Deum, praeter te, Dóminum solum, qui ventúrus es judicáre vivos et mórtuos, et saéculum per ignem. ℟. Amen.

Deinde dicit:

℣. Dómine, exáudi oratiónem meam.
℟. Et clamor meus ad te véniat.
℣. Dóminus vobíscum.
℟. Et cum spíritu tuo.

Orémus.

DÓMINE Deus, Pater omnípotens, statútor ómnium elementórum, qui per Jesum Christum, Fílium tuum Dóminum nostrum, eleméntum hoc aquae in salútem humáni géneris esse voluísti, te súpplices deprecámur, ut, exaudítis oratiónibus nostris, eam tuae pietátis aspéctu sanctí ✠ fices; atque ita ómnium spirítuum immundórum ab ea recédat incúrsio, ut ubicúmque fúerit in nómine tuo aspérsa, grátia tuae benedictiónis advéniat, et mala ómnia, te propitiánte, procul recédant. Per eúndem Dóminum nostrum Jesum Christum, Fílium tuum: Qui tecum vivit et regnat Deus, per ómnia saécula saeculórum. ℟. Amen.

Let us pray.   Prayer

O LORD GOD, almighty Father Who hast endowed salt
with the heavenly power to season whatever thou hast
made as food for men, bless✠ this creature salt to banish the foe,
and endow it with medicinal character for healing the bodies
and souls of them that use it. Through Christ our Lord. ℟.
Amen.

He now exorcises the water:

Thou creature, water, I purge thee of evil in the name of God,
the Father,✠ and of the Son,✠ and of the Holy✠ Spirit, that
thou canst repulse Satan from the realms of the just, lest ever he
linger within the shadow of this church and altar. And thou,
Lord Jesus Christ, pour out thy Holy Spirit upon this thy church
and altar that thy worshippers be rewarded in body and soul,
that thy name be glorified among all nations, and that the in-
credulous of heart be converted to thee, and have no other God
except thee, the only Lord, Who shalt come to judge the living
and the dead and the world by fire. ℟. Amen.

Next he says:

℣. O Lord, hear my prayer.
℟. And let my cry come unto thee.
℣. The Lord be with you.
℟. And with thy spirit.

Let us pray.   Prayer

O LORD GOD, the Father Omnipotent, Founder of the elements, Who through Jesus Christ, thy Son, our Lord didst
will that this element of water serve in the redemption of mankind, we humbly beseech thee that by our prayers thou wouldst
sanctify✠ it. By its use may every assault of unclean spirits be
warded off, that wheresoever it is sprinkled in thy name, thy
blessing come, and evil depart afar. Through the same Jesus
Christ, thy Son, our Lord, Who liveth and reigneth with thee,
God, forever and ever. ℟. Amen.

Tum dicit super cineres:

Benedictio cinerum

℣. Dómine, exáudi oratiónem meam.

℟. Et clamor meus ad te véniat.

℣. Dóminus vobíscum.

℟. Et cum spíritu tuo.

Orémus.   Oratio

OMNÍPOTENS sempitérne Deus, parce poeniténtibus, propitiáre supplicántibus, et míttere dignéris sanctum Angelum tuum de caelis, qui bene ✠ dícat et sanctí ✠ ficet hos cíneres, ut sint remédium salúbre ómnibus, nomen sanctum tuum humíliter implorántibus, ac semetípsos pro consciéntia delictórum suórum accusántibus, ante conspéctum divínae cleméntiae tuae facínora sua deplorántibus, vel sereníssimam pietátem tuam supplíciter obnixéque flagitántibus; et praesta, per invocatiónem sanctíssimi nóminis tui, ut quicúmque eos super se aspérserint, pro redemptióne peccatórum suórum, córporis sanitátem et ánimae tutélam percípiant. Per Christum Dóminum nostrum. ℟. Amen.

Tum accipit sal, et miscet cineri in modum crucis, dicens:

COMMÍXTIO salis et cíneris páriter fiat. In nómine Pa ✠ tris, et Fí ✠ lii, et Spíritus ✠ Sancti. ℟. Amen.

Deinde, accipiens pugillum de mixtura salis et cinerum, mittit in aquam in modum crucis, dicens:

COMMÍXTIO salis, cíneris et aquae páriter fiat. In nómine Pa ✠ tris, et Fí ✠ lii, et Spíritus ✠ Sancti. ℟. Amen.

Deinde dicit super vinum:

Benedictio vini

℣. Dómine, exáudi oratiónem meam.

℟. Et clamor meus ad te véniat.

℣. Dóminus vobíscum.

℟. Et cum spíritu tuo.

Blessing of ashes:

℣. O Lord, hear my prayer.

℟. And let my cry come unto thee.

℣. The Lord be with you.

℟. And with thy spirit.

Let us pray. **Prayer**

ALMIGHTY, everlasting God, spare thy penitents, be merciful to thy suppliants, and deign to send thy holy angel from on high to bless ✠ and sanctify ✠ these ashes. Let them be a saving remedy for all who humbly implore thy holy name, for those who accuse themselves of their transgressions, for all who bewail their crimes in the sight of thy clemency, or earnestly entreat thy loving pardon. Grant that by invoking thy holy name they who sprinkle these ashes on themselves in token of redemption from their sins, may experience corporal health and spiritual protection. Through Christ our Lord. ℟. Amen.

He takes salt and mixes it with the ashes in the form of a cross, saying:

MAY the salt and ashes be mixed together! In the name of the Father, ✠ and of the Son, ✠ and of the Holy ✠ Spirit. ℟. Amen.

Taking a handful of this mixture, he casts it into the water in the form of a cross, saying:

MAY this salt, ashes, and water be mixed together! In the name of the Father, ✠ and of the Son, ✠ and of the Holy ✠ Spirit. ℟. Amen.

Blessing of the wine:

℣. O Lord, hear my prayer.

℟. And let my cry come unto thee.

℣. The Lord be with you.

℟. And with thy spirit.

Orémus.　　　　　　　　　　　　　　　　Oratio

DÓMINE Jesu Christe, qui in Cana Galilaéae ex aqua vinum fecísti, quique es vitis vera, multíplica super nos misericórdiam tuam; et bene✠ dícere et sancti✠ ficáre dignéris hanc creatúram vini, ut ubicúmque fusum fúerit, vel aspérsum, divínae id benedictiónis tuae opuléntia repleátur, et sanctificétur: Qui cum Patre, et Spíritu Sancto, vivis et regnas Deus, per ómnia saécula saeculórum. ℟. Amen.

Deinde mittit in modum crucis vinum in aquam ipsam, dicens:

COMMÍXTIO vini, salis, cíneris et aquae páriter fiat. In nómine Pa✠ tris, et Fí✠ lii, et Spíritus✠ Sancti. ℟. Amen.

℣. Dómine, exáudi oratiónem meam.

℟. Et clamor meus ad te véniat.

℣. Dóminus vobíscum.

℟. Et cum spíritu tuo.

Orémus.　　　　　　　　　　　　　　　　Oratio

OMNÍPOTENS sempitérne Deus, creátor et conservátor humáni géneris, et dator grátiae spirituális, ac largítor aetérnae salútis, emítte Spíritum Sanctum tuum super hoc vinum cum aqua, sale et cínere mixtum; ut armátum caeléstis defensióne virtútis, ad consecratiónem hujus altáris tui profíciat. Per Dóminum nostrum Jesum Christum, Fílium tuum: Qui tecum vivit et regnat in unitáte ejúsdem Spíritus Sancti Deus, per ómnia saécula saeculórum. ℟. Amen.

Postea cum praemissa aqua benedicta facit maltam, seu caementum, quod benedicit, dicens:

℣. Dóminus vobíscum.

℟. Et cum spíritu tuo.

Orémus.　　　　　　　　　　　　　　　　Oratio

SUMME Deus, qui summa et média ímaque custódis, qui omnem creatúram intrínsecus ambiéndo conclúdis, sancti✠ fica et béne✠ dic has creatúras calcis et sábuli. Per Christum Dóminum nostrum. ℟. Amen.

Let us pray.   Prayer

O LORD, Jesus Christ, thou Who art the true Vine, Who in
Cana of Galilee didst change water into wine, multiply thy
mercy upon us, and bless ✠ and sanctify ✠ this creature, wine.
Whatever it sprinkles or is poured out on, let it be sanctified and
filled with benediction. Who with the Father and the Holy Spirit
livest and reignest, God, eternally. ℟. Amen.

He then pours the wine into the water in the form of a cross, saying:

M AY this wine, salt, ashes, and water be mixed together! In
the name of the Father, ✠ and of the Son, ✠ and of the
Holy ✠ Spirit. ℟. Amen.

℣. O Lord, hear my prayer.

℟. And let my cry come unto thee.

℣. The Lord be with you.

℟. And with thy spirit.

Let us pray.   Prayer

O GOD, almighty and everlasting, Creator and Preserver of
mankind, Giver of supernatural grace, Dispenser of eternal
salvation; send down thy Holy Spirit upon this mixture of wine,
water, salt, and ashes, that fortified with heavenly power it may
avail unto the consecration of this altar. Through our Lord, Jesus
Christ, thy Son, Who liveth and reigneth with thee in unity of
the same Holy Spirit, God, forevermore. ℟. Amen.

*Finally with this blessed water he makes a plaster or cement which
he blesses, saying:*

℣. The Lord be with you.

℟. And with thy spirit.

Let us pray.   Prayer

M OST High God, Who keepeth all things from the highest
to the lowest, Whose solicitude embraces every creature,
sanctify ✠ and bless ✠ these creatures of sand and cement.
Through Christ our Lord. ℟. Amen.

Caementum benedictum reservatur, et residuum aquae benedictae funditur in sacrarium.

Deinde consecrator, accedens ad altare, signat pollice dexterae manus ex Chrismate confessionem, id est sepulcrum altaris, a quo ablatae sunt Reliquiae, in quatuor angulis, faciens in singulis signum crucis, et dicens, dum unamquamque crucem facit:

CONSE ✠ CRÉTUR, et sancti ✠ ficétur hoc sepúlcrum. In nómine Pa ✠ tris, et Fí ✠ lii, et Spíritus ✠ Sancti. Pax huic dómui.

Deinde recondit ibi vasculum cum Reliquiis et aliis in eo inclusis veneranter, atque accipiens lapidem seu tabulam, qua debet claudi sepulcrum, facit pollice crucem ex Chrismate subtus in medio ejus, dicens:

CONSE ✠ CRÉTUR et sancti ✠ ficétur haec tábula (vel hic lapis), per istam unctiónem et Dei benedictiónem. In nómine Pa ✠ tris, et Fí ✠ lii, et Spíritus ✠ Sancti. Pax tibi.

Et mox, caemento benedicto adhibito, adjuvante, si opus sit, caementario, ponit et coaptat tabulam, seu lapidem, super sepulcrum, claudens illud, et dicit:

Orémus.   Oratio

DEUS, qui ex ómnium cohabitatióne Sanctórum, aetérnum majestáti tuae condis habitáculum, da aedificatióni tuae increménta caeléstia: et praesta; ut quorum hic Relíquias pio amóre compléctimur, eórum semper méritis adjuvémur. Per Christum Dóminum nostrum. ℟. Amen.

Tunc, caementario adjuvante, cum eodem caemento firmat ipsam tabulam, seu lapidem, super sepulcrum: deinde ipse facit crucem desuper ex Chrismate pollice dexterae manus, dicens:

SIGNÉ ✠ TUR et sancti ✠ ficétur hoc altáre. In nómine Pa ✠ tris, et Fí ✠ lii, et Spíritus ✠ Sancti. Pax tibi.

This blessed cement is reserved, whereas the remaining water is poured into the sacrarium.

Then the consecrator goes to the altar, and anoints with Chrism the sepulchre from which the relics have been removed. He anoints each of the four corners of the opening with the sign of the cross, saying for each cross:

M AY this sepulchre be consecrated ✠ and sanctified ✠. In the name of the Father, ✠ and of the Son, ✠ and of the Holy ✠ Spirit. Peace be unto this place.

He reverently buries therein the box containing the relics and other contents; and receiving the stone or cover, he anoints its lower part in the middle with Chrism, saying:

M AY this cover (or this stone) be consecrated ✠ and sanctified ✠ by this anointing and God's blessing. In the name of the Father, ✠ and of the Son, ✠ and of the Holy ✠ Spirit. Peace be unto thee.

Using the blessed cement, he fits the cover to the sepulchre (being assisted if required by a mason); then says:

Let us pray.   Prayer

O GOD, Who in the assembly of the saints hast prepared an everlasting dwelling unto thy Sublimity, give also to this thy construction heavenly increase, and grant that we who lovingly venerate the saints whose relics lie here, may continually be assisted by their merits. Through Christ our Lord. ℟. Amen.

Then he seals the cover with the cement, and signs the top with Chrism, saying:

M AY this altar be signed ✠ and sanctified ✠. In the name of the Father, ✠ and of the Son, ✠ and of the Holy ✠ Spirit. Peace be unto thee.

49

RITUS BENEDICENDI ET IMPONENDI PRIMARIUM LAPIDEM PRO ECCLESIA AEDIFICANDA

Nulla ecclesia aedificetur sine expresso Ordinarii loci consensu scriptis dato, quem tamen Vicarius Generalis praestare nequit sine mandato speciali.

Si Sacerdos, ejus aedificationis primarium lapidem benedicendi potestatem habens ab Ordinario, ejusmodi functionem peragat, hunc ritum servabit.

2. Pridie quam primarius lapis benedicatur, ligneam Crucem in loco, ubi debet esse Altare, figat ipse, vel alius Sacerdos. Sequenti vero die lapis in ecclesiae fundatione ponendus, qui debet esse quadratus, et angularis, benedicatur hoc modo.

3. Sacerdos indutus amictu, alba, cingulo, stola et pluviali albi coloris, adhibitis aliquot Clericis, sal et aquam benedicit, nisi prius in promptu habeat aquam jam benedictam, ordinaria benedictione, ut supra (pag. 9), et interim, dum cantatur a Clericis Antiphona cum Psalmo sequenti, aspergit locum, ubi Crux posita est, aqua benedicta.

Antiphona

VIII
G

Signum sa-lú-tis * po-ne, Dómi-ne Jesu Chris-te, in loco isto: et non permíttas in-tro-í- re Ange-lum percu-ti-éntem. Ps. Quam dilécta tabernácu-la tu-a, Dómine virtú-tum: * concupíscit, et dé-fi-cit ánima me-a in átri-a Dómi-ni.

Translator's Note: The consecration of church and altar signify so perfectly the mystical indwelling of Jesus Christ, Who is the Altar and Temple of redemption and sanctification, and Whose constant

49

BLESSING AND LAYING THE CORNER-STONE
OF A CHURCH   .

No church should be erected without the express consent in writing of the Ordinary. The Vicar General may not give this permission without a special mandate.

A priest who has the faculty from the Ordinary for blessing the corner-stone must use the following form:

2. The day before the blessing, he or another priest erects a wooden cross on the spot where the future altar will be. The corner-stone must be quadrangular, and is blessed as follows.

3. The celebrant, vested in amice, alb, cincture, and white stole and cope, assisted by clerics, blesses salt and water with the ordinary blessing, unless he will use water previously blessed. During the singing of the following antiphon and psalm, he sprinkles with holy water the spot where the cross is placed.

Antiphon: **Erect, O Lord Jesus Christ, the sign of salvation in this place: and forbid entrance to the angel of death.**

---

office is to form us into fitting stones for the Kingdom of God. But Christ's Bride, the Church is not content to wait until her edifices are complete for an anointing from her Spouse. So soon as the foundations are laid and the walls ready to receive the corner-stone, God must bless the stone, manifesting to His holy people that the work must begin with Him, and must be built upon His Son: "Christ, the corner-stone was sent to be the foundation, bound in both joints of the walls." (Vesper Hymn: "Urbs Jerusalem," the ancient version, from the Office of Dedication of Churches.)

Psalmus 83

Quam dilécta tabernácula tua, Dómine virtútum: * concupíscit, et déficit ánima mea in átria Dómini.

Cor meum, et caro mea * exsultavérunt in Deum vivum.

Etenim passer invénit sibi domum: * et turtur nidum sibi, ubi ponat pullos suos.

Altária tua, Dómine virtútum: * Rex meus, et Deus meus.

Beáti, qui hábitant in domo tua, Dómine: * in saécula saeculórum laudábunt te.

Beátus vir, cujus est auxílium abs te: * ascensiónes in corde suo dispósuit, in valle lacrimárum in loco, quem pósuit.

Etenim benedictiónem dabit legislátor, ibunt de virtúte in virtútem: * vidébitur Deus deórum in Sion.

Dómine, Deus virtútum, exáudi oratiónem meam: * áuribus pércipe, Deus Jacob.

Protéctor noster, áspice, Deus: * et réspice in fáciem Christi tui:

Quia mélior est dies una in átriis tuis, * super míllia.

Elégi abjéctus esse in domo Dei mei: * magis quam habitáre in tabernáculis peccatórum.

Quia misericórdiam, et veritátem díligit Deus: * grátiam et glóriam dabit Dóminus.

Non privábit bonis eos, qui ámbulant in innocéntia: * Dómine virtútum, beátus homo, qui sperat in te.

Glória Patri.

4. Finito Psalmo, Sacerdos, versus ad locum a se aspersum, dicit:

Orémus.   Oratio

DÓMINE Deus, qui licet caelo et terra non capiáris, domum tamen dignáris habére in terris, ubi nomen tuum júgiter invocétur: locum hunc quaésumus, beátae Maríae semper Vírginis, et beáti N. (nominando Sanctum vel Sanctam, in cujus honorem ac nomen fundabitur ecclesia), omniúmque Sanctórum intercedéntibus méritis, seréno pietátis tuae intúitu vísita, et per

Psalm 83

How delightful are thy tabernacles, O Lord of hosts! My soul
    pineth and fainteth for the courts of the Lord.
My soul and my body exult in the living God;
Even as the sparrow that hath found herself a home, and the
    turtledove a nest where she may lay her young.
So are thine altars, O Lord of Hosts! My King and my God!
Happy are they who dwell in thy house, O Lord; they praise thee
    eternally.
Happy the man whose strength is from thee; he longeth for thy
    highways through the valley of tears, to thy place of pilgrimage.
For the Lawgiver will give a blessing, and they shall gain in
    strength, until on Sion they behold the God of gods.
Lord, God of hosts, hear thou my prayer, give ear, O God of
    Jacob!
Thou our Protector look upon us, and behold the face of thine
    Anointed.
For better is one day in thy courts than thousands elsewhere.
I choose to be the lowest in the house of my God, rather than
    abide in the tents of evil-doers.
For God loveth mercy and truth; the Lord will give grace and
    glory.
To the upright He denieth no good thing. O Lord of hosts,
    happy is the man that trusteth in thee!
Glory be to the Father.

4. After the psalm, the priest, facing the spot which he has blessed,
says:

Let us pray.   *Prayer*

O LORD GOD, Whom the heavens and the earth cannot
    contain, but Who dost condescend to have a dwelling on
earth where thy name can constantly be invoked; we beseech
thee, through the merits and intercession of blessed Mary ever
Virgin, of blessed N. (he names the saint in whose name and
honor the church will be built), and of all thy saints, visit this
place with thy goodness and love, and by the infusion of thy

infusiónem grátiae tuae ab omni inquinaménto puríficá, purificatúmque consérva; et qui dilécti tui David devotiónem in fílii sui Salomónis ópere complevísti, in hoc ópere desidéria nostra perfícere dignéris, effugiántque omnes hinc nequítiae spirituáles. Per Dóminum. ℟. Amen.

5. Postea stans benedicit primarium lapidem, dicens:

℣. Adjutórium nostrum in nómine Dómini.

℟. Qui fecit caelum et terram.

℣. Sit nomen Dómini benedíctum.

℟. Ex hoc nunc et usque in saéculum.

℣. Lápidem, quem reprobavérunt aedificántes.

℟. Hic factus est in caput ánguli.

℣. Tu es Petrus.

℟. Et super hanc petram aedificábo Ecclésiam meam.

℣. Glória Patri, et Fílio, et Spirítui Sancto.

℟. Sicut erat in princípio, et nunc, et semper, et in saécula saeculórum. Amen.

Orémus.   Oratio

DÓMINE Jesu Christe, Fili Dei vivi, qui es verus omnípotens Deus, splendor, et imágo aetérni Patris, et vita aetérna: qui es lapis anguláris de monte sine mánibus abscíssus, et immutábile fundaméntum: hunc lápidem collocándum in tuo nómine confírma; et tu, qui es princípium et finis, in quo princípio Deus Pater ab inítio cuncta creávit, sis, quaésumus, princípium, et increméntum, et consummátio ipsíus óperis, quod debet ad laudem et glóriam tui nóminis inchoári: Qui cum Patre et Spíritu Sancto vivis et regnas Deus, per ómnia saécula saeculórum. ℟. Amen.

6. Tunc aspergit lapidem ipsum aqua benedicta, et, accepto cultro, per singulas partes sculpit in eo signum crucis, dicens:

In nómine Pa ✠ tris, et Fí ✠ lii, et Spíritus ✠ Sancti. ℟. Amen.

grace, purify it of all uncleanness, and keep it undefiled. And as thou didst fulfil the vow of David, thy beloved, in the work of Solomon, his son, deign in this work to fulfil our desires, and banish hence all wicked spirits. Through our Lord. ℟. Amen.

5. Then he blesses the corner-stone, saying:

℣. Our help is in the name of the Lord.

℟. Who made heaven and earth.

℣. May the name of the Lord be blessed.

℟. Henceforth and forever.

℣. The stone which the builders rejected.

℟. The same is become the corner-stone.

℣. Thou art Peter.

℟. And upon this rock I will build my Church.

℣. Glory be to the Father, and to the Son, and to the Holy Spirit.

℟. As it was in the beginning, is now, and ever shall be, world without end. Amen.

Let us pray.   Prayer

LORD Jesus Christ, Son of the living God, thou Who art true God and omnipotent, the splendor and image of the eternal Father, and everlasting life; thou Who art the corner-stone hewn from the mountain not by the hand of man; thou Who art a foundation which cannot be moved — do thou make firm this stone which is laid in thy name. And thou, the Beginning and the End, in Whom from the first instant God the Father created all things, be likewise, we pray, the beginning, and the increase, and the consummation of this work which is begun for thy fame and glory. Who with the Father and the Holy Spirit livest and reignest, God, forevermore. ℟. Amen.

6. He sprinkles the stone with holy water, and receiving the trowel makes with it three crosses on each of the six sides of the stone, saying as he forms the crosses:

In the name of the Father, ✠ and of the Son, ✠ and of the Holy ✠ spirit. ℟. Amen.

Quo facto dicit:

Orémus. Oratio

BENE ✛ DIC, Dómine, creatúram istam lápidis, et praesta per invocatiónem sancti tui nóminis: ut, quicúmque ad hanc ecclésiam aedificándam pura mente auxílium déderint, córporis sanitátem, et ánimae medélam percípiant. Per Christum Dóminum nostrum. ℟. Amen.

7. Postea dicantur Litaniae ordinariae (pag. 444) sine Orationibus in fine positis: quibus dictis, parato caemento, et caementario assistente, Sacerdos inchoat, Clericis prosequentibus, Antiphonam:

Antiphona

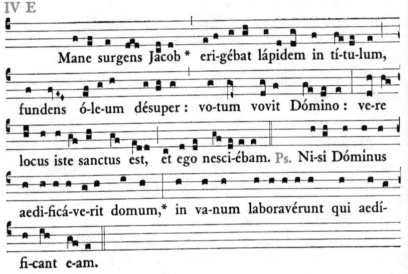

IV E

Mane surgens Jacob * eri-gébat lápidem in tí-tu-lum, fundens ó-le-um désuper: vo-tum vovit Dómino: ve-re locus iste sanctus est, et ego nesci-ébam. Ps. Ni-si Dóminus aedi-ficá-ve-rit domum,* in va-num laboravérunt qui aedí-fi-cant e-am.

Psalmus 126

Nisi Dóminus aedificáverit domum, * in vanum laboravérunt qui aedíficant eam.

Nisi Dóminus custodíerit civitátem, * frustra vígilat qui custódit eam.

Vanum est vobis ante lucem súrgere: * súrgite postquam sedéritis, qui manducátis panem dolóris.

Cum déderit diléctis suis somnum: * ecce heréditas Dómini fílii: merces, fructus ventris.

Let us pray.

B LESS, ✛ O Lord, this creature of stone, and grant by our
   prayer that all who devotedly assist in the building of this
church may enjoy health in body and healing in soul. Through
Christ our Lord. ℟. Amen.

7. The Litany of the Saints (page 445) is sung, omitting the orations,
i.e., inclusive of the second **Kyrie.** Then the priest intones the next
antiphon, and the clergy continue it. Meanwhile the cement, etc., are
made ready for the laying of the stone.

Antiphon: Jacob arising in the morning, set up a stone as a
sign: and pouring oil thereon, made a vow to the Lord: Indeed
this place is holy, and I knew it not.

Psalm 126

Except the Lord build the house, they toil in vain that build it.
Except the Lord guard the city, in vain does the keeper watch.
It is futile for you to rise before dawn. Rise ye after you have
    rested, ye that eat the bread of sorrow.
For He giveth to His beloved in sleep. Behold, sons are the in-
    heritance of the Lord, the fruit of the womb is His reward.

Sicut sagíttae in manu poténtis: * ita fílii excussórum.

Beátus vir qui implévit desidérium suum ex ipsis: * non confundétur cum loquétur inimícis suis in porta.

Glória Patri.

8. Quo dicto, Sacerdos stans ponit ipsum primarium lapidem in fundamento, vel saltem illum tangit, dicens:

In fide Jesu Christi collocámus lápidem istum primárium in hoc fundaménto, in nómine Pa ✠ tris, et Fí ✠ lii, et Spíritus ✠ Sancti: ut vígeat vera fides hic, et timor Dei, fratérnaque diléctio; et sit hic locus destinátus oratióni, et ad invocándum, et laudándum nomen ejúsdem Dómini nostri Jesu Christi, qui cum Patre et Spíritu Sancto vivit et regnat Deus, per ómnia saécula saeculórum. ℟. Amen.

9. Interim caementarius aptat ipsum lapidem cum caemento: postea Sacerdos spargit super lapidem aquam benedictam, dicens:

Aspérges me, Dómine, hyssópo, et mundábor: lavábis me, et super nivem dealbábor.

Deinde dicitur totus Psalmus **Miserére mei, Deus** (pag. 436), cum Glória Patri.

Quo dicto, Sacerdos spargit aquam benedictam per omnia fundamenta, si sunt aperta: si vero non sunt aperta, circuit aspergendo fundamenta ecclesiae designata, hoc modo. Incipiens aspergere, inchoat, Clero prosequente, Antiphonam:

Antiphona

VI F

O quam me-tu-éndus est * locus iste! Ve- re non est hic á-li- ud, ni-si domus De- i, et por- ta cae-li.

Ps. Fundaménta e-jus in móntibus sanctis: * dí-li-git Dómi-

nus portas Si-on super ómni-a taber-nácu-la Jacob.

As arrows in the hands of a hero, so are the children of the
vigorous.

Happy is the man that hath fulfilled his desire for sons; he shall
not be ashamed when he reckons with his rival at the gate.

Glory be to the Father.

8. The celebrant places his hand upon the corner-stone as it is low-
ered into place, saying:

In the faith of Jesus Christ, we lay this corner-stone on this
foundation, in the name of the Father,✠ and of the Son,✠ and
of the Holy✠ Spirit. May the true faith wax strong here, and the
fear of God, and the love of the brethren, that this place be truly
destined for prayer, to invoke and praise the name of the same
Jesus Christ, thy Son, our Lord, Who with the Father and the
Holy Spirit liveth and reigneth, God, eternally. ℞. Amen.

9. The assisting mason fastens the stone with cement; then the priest
sprinkles it with holy water, saying:

Sprinkle me with hyssop, O Lord, and I shall be clean: wash
me, and I shall be whiter than snow.

The entire psalm Miserére (page 437) is said, with Glory be to the
Father.

Then the priest intones the next antiphon, and sprinkles holy water
on the foundations. But if the foundations are not yet built up, he goes
around the church sprinkling the designated lines thereof.

Antiphon: O how awesome is this place! * Truly it is none
other than the house of God and the gate of Heaven.

Psalm 86

His temple is on the holy hill. For the Lord loveth the gates of
Sion above all the tabernacles of Jacob.

Psalmus 86

Fundaménta ejus in móntibus sanctis: * díligit Dóminus portas Sion super ómnia tabernácula Jacob.

Gloriósa dicta sunt de te, * cívitas Dei.

Memor ero Rahab, et Babylónis * sciéntium me.

Ecce alienígenae, et Tyrus, et pópulus Aethíopum * hi fuérunt illic.

Numquid Sion dicet: Homo, et homo natus est in ea: * et ipse fundávit eam Altíssimus?

Dóminus narrábit in scriptúris populórum, et príncipum: * horum, qui fuérunt in ea.

Sicut laetántium ómnium * habitátio est in te.

Glória Patri.

Antiphona

O quam me-tu-éndus est locus iste! Ve- re non est hic áli- ud, ni-si domus De- i, et por- ta cae-li.

10. Interim aspergendo procedit usque ad fundamenta aperta, seu designata, et repetita Antiphona a Clero, Sacerdos stans dicit: Orémus. Ministri: Flectámus génua. ℞. Leváte.

Sacerdos: Oratio

O MNÍPOTENS et miséricors Deus, qui Sacerdótibus tuis tantam prae céteris grátiam contulísti, ut quidquid in tuo nómine digne, perfectéque ab eis ágitur, a te fíeri credátur: quaésumus imménsam cleméntiam tuam; ut quidquid modo visitatúri sumus, vísites, et quidquid benedictúri sumus, bene ✠ dícas: sitque ad nostrae humilitátis intróitum, Sanctórum tuórum méritis, fuga daémonum, Angeli pacis ingréssus. Per Christum Dóminum nostrum. ℞. Amen.

D EUS, qui ex ómnium cohabitatióne Sanctórum aetérnum majestáti tuae condis habitáculum: da aedificatióni tuae increménta caeléstia; ut, quod te jubénte fundátur, te largiénte perficiátur. Per Christum Dóminum nostrum. ℞. Amen.

Glorious things are said of thee, O city of God!

"I will reckon Rahab [Egypt] and Babylon as among them that know Me.

Behold, the foreigners of Tyre and Ethiopia are at home here."

Of Sion shall it not be said: "This man and that man was born in her, and the Most High Himself hath founded her?"

The Lord shall tell in His writings of people and princes that know her as home.

And all will exult: "Our dwelling is in thee!"

Glory be to the Father.

Antiphon: O how awesome is this place! Truly it is none other than the house of God and the gate of Heaven.

10. When the sprinkling is done, and the antiphon repeated, the priest says: Let us pray.

Assistants: Let us bend the knee. ℟. Arise!

The Priest: Prayer

GOD of mercy and of strength, Who didst confer on thy priests above all others so great a grace, that whatever they do worthily and perfectly in thy name, is, as it were, done by thee, we beseech thy boundless goodness, that whatever we presume to visit, may be visited by thee, and whatever we presume to bless, may be blessed ✠ by thee. And at our lowly coming, through the merits of thy saints, may demons flee, and angels of peace draw near. Through Christ our Lord. ℟. Amen.

O GOD, Who in the assembly of the saints hast prepared an everlasting dwelling unto thy Sublimity, give also to this thy construction heavenly increase, that what has been started with thy blessing, may be completed through thy generosity. Through Christ our Lord. ℟. Amen.

50

BENEDICTIO PRIMARII LAPIDIS AEDIFICII

℣. Adjutórium nostrum in nómine Dómini.

℟. Qui fecit caelum et terram.

℣. Dóminus vobíscum.

℟. Et cum spíritu tuo.

Orémus. Oratio

Deus, a quo omne bonum sumit inítium, et semper ad potióra progrédiens pércipit increméntum: concéde, quaésumus, supplicántibus nobis; ut, quod ad laudem nóminis tui inchoáre aggrédimur, aetérno tuae patérnae sapiéntiae múnere perducátur ad términum. Per Christum Dóminum nostrum. ℟. Amen.

Et aspergatur aqua benedicta.

51

RITUS BENEDICENDI NOVUM COEMETERIUM

Pridie quam fiat benedictio, ponitur in medio coemeterii benedicendi lignea Crux, alta ad staturam hominis, et ante ipsam Crucem in terra figitur paxillus tridens ligneus, altus ad cubitum unum, aptus ad affigendum illi tres candelas.

2. Sequenti die mane Sacerdos, ab Ordinario delegatus, in sacristia paratur amictu, alba, cingulo, stola ac pluviali albi coloris, et, adhibitis aliquot Clericis indutis superpelliceis, qui deferant vasculum aquae benedictae, aspergillum, thuribulum cum incensi navicula, hunc Ritualem librum et tres candelas cereas, procedit ad coemeterium benedicendum ante Crucem in medio positam, et affiguntur, et accenduntur tres candelae super ligneum paxillum: tunc Sacerdos ante Crucem e candelas stans, discooperto capite, dicit:

Orémus. Oratio

OMNÍPOTENS Deus, qui es custos animárum, et tutéla salútis, fides credéntium: réspice propítius ad nostrae servitút officium, et ad intróitum nostrum purgétur, bene ✠ dicátur, sancti ✠ ficétur hoc coemetérium; ut humána córpora hic po

50

BLESSING OF A CORNER-STONE FOR ANY BUILDING

℣. Our help is in the name of the Lord.

℞. Who made heaven and earth.

℣. The Lord be with you.

℞. And with thy spirit.

Let us pray. Prayer

O God, from Whom every good thing takes its beginning, and receives its increase as it advances unto perfection, grant, we earnestly pray, that what we undertake for thy holy praise, may by the eternal gift of thy fatherly wisdom be brought to completion. Through Christ our Lord. ℞. Amen.

It is sprinkled with holy water.

51

BLESSING OF A NEW CEMETERY

On the day preceding the blessing, a wooden cross about six feet in height is placed in the middle of the cemetery. In front of the cross a stake about twenty inches long with a cross-piece to form the letter T is fixed in the ground, having three sconces sufficiently large for candles to be inserted.

2. Next morning, the priest delegated by the Ordinary vests in alb, cincture, stole, and white cope, and assisted by others wearing surplices, and carrying the holy-water stoop, aspersory, thurible, incense-boat, Ritual, and three candles, goes to the cemetery to the place where the cross is erected. The three candles are fixed upon the stake and lighted. The priest standing with uncovered head before the cross and candles, says:

Let us pray. Prayer

ALMIGHTY GOD, Who art the Keeper of souls, the Guardian of salvation, the Confidence of believers, graciously consider this act of our servitude, and by our coming may this cemetery be purified, blessed, ✠ and sanctified ✠ ; that on the

vitae cursum quiescéntia, in magno judícii die simul cum felíci-
bus animábus mereántur adipísci vitae perénnis gáudia. Pei
Christum Dóminum nostrum. Ɽ. Amen.

3. Mox ante ipsam Crucem omnes genibus flexis dicunt Litanias
ordinarias (pag. 444), incipiente cantore, ceteris respondentibus; et cum
dictum fuerit: Ut ómnibus fidélibus defúnctis, etc. Ɽ. Te rogámus
audi nos, Sacerdos surgit, et clara voce dicit, producens manu signum
crucis:

Ut hoc coemetérium purgáre, et bene ✠ dícere dignéris. Ɽ.
Te rogámus, audi nos.

4. Deinde Sacerdos, ut prius, genuflectit, et Litaniae perficiuntur.

5. Quibus finitis, surgunt omnes, et Sacerdos Crucem aspergit aqua
benedicta, dicens Antiphonam:

Aspérges me, Dómine, hyssópo, et mundábor: lavábis me, et
super nivem dealbábor.

6. Deinde dicitur ab astantibus totus Psalmus **Miserére** (pag. 436),
cum **Glória Patri.** Quo dicto repetitur Antiphona. Dum dicitur
Psalmus, Sacerdos circuit, et perambulat totum coemeterium, incipiens
ad ejus dexteram, aspergens ubique aqua benedicta: quo facto, redit
ante Crucem, et ad ipsam respiciens, dicit:

Orémus. Oratio

DEUS, qui es totíus orbis cónditor, et humáni géneris redémptor, cunctarúmque creaturárum visibílium et invisibílium
perféctus dispósitor: te súpplici voce, ac puro corde expóscimus:
ut hoc coemetérium, in quo famulórum, famularúmque tuárum
córpora quiéscere debent, post currícula hujus vitae labéntia
pur ✠ gáre, bene ✠ dícere, et sancti ✠ ficáre dignéris: quique
remissiónem ómnium peccatórum per tuam magnam misericórdiam in te confidéntibus praestitísti, corpóribus quoque eórum
in hoc coemetério quiescéntibus, et tubam primi Archángeli exspectántibus, consolatiónem perpétuam lárgiter impertíre. Pei
Christum Dóminum nostrum. Ɽ. Amen.

7. Tunc figit in summitate Crucis unam ex tribus candelis ardenti-
bus, et alias duas similiter ardentes in duobus brachiis ejusdem Crucis.
Deinde incensat ipsam Crucem, et aspergens coemeterium aqua benedicta, redit cum Ministris in sacristiam.

great Judgment Day the bodies resting here after life's span, in union with their fortunate souls, may delight in the joys of life without ceasing. Through Christ our Lord. ℟. Amen.

3. Now all kneel before the cross, and pray the Litany of the Saints (page 445) in the usual manner. At the words: **That thou wouldst grant to all faithful departed, etc.** ℟. **We beseech thee, hear us,** the celebrant rises, and making the sign of the cross, says:

That thou wouldst deign to purify and bless ✠ this cemetery. ℟. We beseech thee, hear us.

4. Then he kneels again, and the Litany is resumed to the end.

5. At its conclusion, all rise, and the priest sprinkles the cross with holy water, saying the antiphon:

Sprinkle me with hyssop, O Lord, and I shall be clean: wash me and I shall be whiter than snow.

6. The bystanders say the entire psalm **Miserére** (page 437), concluding with **Glory be to the Father,** and repeating the antiphon. Meanwhile, the priest, starting at his right, walks around the entire cemetery, sprinkling it with holy water. Returning to the cross, and facing it, he says:

Let us pray.   Prayer

O GOD, Designer of the universe, Redeemer of mankind, and Disposer of all creatures visible and invisible! Thee we entreat with pleading voice and unstained heart that thou wouldst purify, ✠ bless, ✠ and sanctify ✠ this cemetery where will repose the bodies of thy servants and thy handmaids after the fatiguing contest of life. Mercifully pardon the sins of them who trust in thee; and to their bodies awaiting here the clarion of the angelic herald, graciously grant perpetual consolation. Through Christ our Lord. ℟. Amen.

7. The celebrant fixes one of the lighted candles at the top of the cross and one on each arm of the cross. Lastly he incenses the cross and the cemetery, and sprinkles them with holy water. Then he and his assistants return to the sacristy.

52

RITUS RECONCILIANDI COEMETERIUM VIOLATUM

Si coemeterium ecclesiae pollutae contiguum violatum fuerit, illud una cum ecclesia reconciliatur, ut supra (pag. 184) dictum est. Secus coemeterii reconciliatio fit hoc modo.

Mane diei, qua facienda est reconciliatio, Rector coemeterii vel quilibet Sacerdos, de consensu saltem praesumpto Rectoris, adhibitis aliquot Clericis indutis superpelliceis, in sacristia, aut alio decenti loco, vestitus amictu, alba, cingulo, stola et pluviali albi coloris, accedit ad medium coemeterii, Clerico vasculum aquae benedictae et aspergillum deferente: et ibi super tapete genuflectit una cum Ministris; et cantores, aliique omnes genibus flexis, dicunt Litanias ordinarias (pag. 444). In quibus cum dictum fuerit:

Ut ómnibus fidélibus defúnctis, etc. ℞. Te rogámus, audi nos.

Sacerdos surgit et manu dextera producens signum crucis super coemeterium, clara voce dicit:

Ut hoc coemetérium recon✠ ciliáre et sancti✠ ficáre dignéris. ℞. Te rogámus, audi nos.

2. Deinde Sacerdos, ut prius, genuflectit, cantoribus Litanias perficientibus.

3. Quibus finitis, surgunt omnes, et Sacerdos, accepto aspergillo cum aqua benedicta, inchoat, Clero prosequente, Antiphonam:

Aspérges me, * Dómine, hyssópo, et mundábor: lavábis me, et super nivem dealbábor.

Et dicitur totus Psalmus Miserére (pag. 436), sine Glória Patri. Quo finito, Antiphona repetitur.

4. Dum haec dicuntur, Sacerdos circuit totum coemeterium, incipiens ad ejus dexteram, aspergens ubique aqua benedicta, praesertim in loco, ubi violatio commissa est. Quo peracto, redit ad locum ubi Litaniae dictae fuerunt, et ibi stans dicit: Oremus.

Ministri: Flectámus génua. ℞. Leváte.

Sacerdos: Oratio

DÓMINE pie, qui agrum fíguli prétio sánguinis tui in sepultúram peregrinórum comparári voluísti: quaésumus, dignánter reminíscere clementíssimi hujus mystérii tui. Tu es enim, Dómine, fígulus noster: tu quiétis nostrae ager: tu agri hujus

52

RECONCILIATION OF A CEMETERY
Which Has Been Profaned

If a cemetery contiguous to a profaned church has likewise been profaned, it is reconciled together with the church (See: Reconciliation of a Church). Otherwise, the reconciling of a cemetery takes place as follows:

In the morning, the rector of the cemetery, or another priest who has at least the presumed permission of the former, vested as above, comes with his assistants to the middle of the cemetery. There he and the other ministrants kneel upon a carpet; and all others kneeling, the Litany of the Saints is chanted in the usual way (page 445). At the words: **That thou wouldst grant eternal rest, etc.** ℟. **We beseech thee, hear us,** the celebrant rises, and making the sign of the cross over the cemetery, says:

That thou wouldst deign to reconcile ✝ and sanctify ✝ this cemetery. ℟. **We beseech thee, hear us.**

2. He kneels again, and the Litany is resumed to its conclusion.

3. Then all rise, and the celebrant receiving the aspersory, intones and the assistants continue the antiphon and the psalm:

Sprinkle me, * with hyssop, O Lord, and I shall be clean: wash me, and I shall be whiter than snow.

The entire psalm **Miserére** (page 437) is said without **Glory be to the Father,** and the antiphon is repeated.

4. During the psalmody, the celebrant beginning at the right goes about the entire cemetery, sprinkling it with holy water, especially the spot where the profanation took place. When he returns, he says: **Let us pray.**

Assistants: **Let us bend the knee.** ℟. **Arise!**

The priest: Prayer

O GRACIOUS Lord, Whose will it was that the potter's field priced with thy blood should become a burial place for strangers, kindly remember, we pray thee, this mystery of thy goodness. For thou, Lord, art also our potter, the field of our

prétium. Tu dedísti étiam, et suscepísti. Tu de prétio tui vivífici sánguinis nos requiéscere donásti. Tu ergo, Dómine, qui es offensiónis nostrae clementíssimus indúltor, exspectantíssimus judicátor, judícii tui superabundantíssimus miserátor: judícium tuae justíssimae severitátis abscóndens, post miseratiónem tuae piae redemptiónis, adésto exaudítor et efféctor nostrae reconciliatiónis: hocque coemetérium peregrinórum tuórum, caeléstis pátriae incolátum exspectántium, benígnus puríﬁca, et reconcília; et hic tumulatórum et tumulandórum córpora, de poténtia et pietáte tuae resurrectiónis ad glóriam incorruptiónis, non damnans, sed gloríﬁcans resúscita: Qui ventúrus es judicáre vivos, et mórtuos, et saéculum per ignem. ℟. Amen.

53

BENEDICTIO ORATORII PRIVATI SEU DOMESTICI

℣. Adjutórium nostrum in nómine Dómini.
℟. Qui fecit caelum et terram.
℣. Dóminus vobíscum.
℟. Et cum spíritu tuo.

Orémus.   Oratio

Deus, qui loca nómini tuo dicánda sanctíﬁcas, effúnde super hanc oratiónis domum grátiam tuam: ut ab ómnibus hic nomen tuum invocántibus auxílium tuae misericórdiae sentiátur. Per Dóminum. ℟. Amen.

Et aspergatur aqua benedicta.

rest, the price of this field. Thou didst give the prize even as thou didst accept it, and hast bequeathed us peaceful rest at the price of thy life-renewing blood. Wherefore, Lord, thou Who art the most merciful pardoner of our guilt, the most considerate judge, the most lavish dispenser of clement judgment, we beg thee to forget the judgment of severity and justice which we deserve, and remembering only the mercies of thy holy Redemption, be unto us an advocate and reconciler. Graciously purify and reconcile this resting place of thy wanderers who await a place of dwelling in the heavenly fatherland. And mayest thou finally awaken the bodies of them who are or who will be here interred, by the power and goodness of thine own Resurrection, to incorruptible glory, calling them forth not to condemnation but to beatification. Thou Who shalt come to judge the living and the dead and the world by fire. ℟. Amen.

53

BLESSING OF A PRIVATE OR DOMESTIC ORATORY

℣. Our help is in the name of the Lord.
℟. Who made heaven and earth.
℣. The Lord be with you.
℟. And with thy spirit.

    Let us pray.   Prayer

O God, Who dost sanctify the dwellings dedicated to thy name, pour down thy grace upon this house of prayer, that all who here will worship thee may experience thy gracious assistance. Through our Lord. ℟. Amen.

It is sprinkled with holy water.

54

BENEDICTIO DOMUS SCHOLARIS

Sacerdos ingrediens aspergat cubicula aqua benedicta, dicens:

℣. Pax huic dómui.

℟. Et ómnibus habitántibus in ea.

℣. Adjutórium nostrum in nómine Dómini.

℟. Qui fecit caelum et terram.

℣. Dóminus vobíscum.

℟. Et cum spíritu tuo.

Orémus.   Oratio

Dómine Jesu Christe, qui Apóstolis tuis praecepísti, ut, in quamcúmque domum intrárent, pacem illi adprecaréntur, sanctí ✠fica, quaésumus, per ministérium nostrum hanc domum púeris (vel puéllis) educándis destinátam; effúnde super eam tuae bene ✠dictiónis et pacis abundántiam, fiat eis salus, sicut dómui Zacháei, te intránte, facta est; manda Angelis tuis, ut eam custódiant, et ab ea omnem inimíci repéllant potestátem; reple docéntes in ea spíritu sciéntiae, sapiéntiae et timóris tui; discéntes caelésti grátia fove, ut, quae salutáriter edocéntur, intelléctu cápiant, corde retíneant, ópere exsequántur; atque omnes habitatóres ejus virtútum ómnium opéribus tibi pláceant, ut in aetérnam domum in caelis aliquándo récipi mereántur. Per te, Jesu Christe, Salvátor mundi, qui vivis et regnas Deus in saécula saeculórum. ℟. Amen.

55

ALIA BENEDICTIO DOMUS SCHOLARIS

Die Dominicali vel festiva, a Parocho et Patrono constituta et rite promulgata, Officians et qui adsunt Sacerdotes et Ministri, in domc paroeciali, vel, si in loco, ubi schola benedicenda sit, domus paroecialis

54

BLESSING OF A SCHOOL

The priest upon entering sprinkles the rooms with holy water saying:

℣. Peace be unto this place.

℟. And unto all who assemble here.

℣. Our help is in the name of the Lord.

℟. Who made heaven and earth.

℣. The Lord be with you.

℟. And with thy spirit.

Let us pray.   Prayer

Lord Jesus Christ, Who didst charge thine apostles to entreat peace upon every home which they might enter, sanctify ✠ by our ministry this school. Bestow on it peace and blessing ✠ in abundance to sanctify it, as thou didst bless the house of Zacheus upon entering there. Command thy angels to guard it, and to drive out all power of the evil one. Fill them who teach herein with the spirit of knowledge, wisdom, and fear of thee. Support the pupils with heavenly assistance, so that they may grasp, retain, and practice wholesome doctrine. Let teachers and scholars please thee by virtuous works, receiving finally an everlasting home in heaven as their reward. Through thee, Jesus Christ, Savior of the world, who livest and reignest, God, forever and ever. ℟. Amen.

55

ANOTHER BLESSING FOR A SCHOOL

On a Sunday or feastday chosen by the pastor and the patron and duly announced, the officiant and the clergy and other assistants assemble in the rectory or other suitable place, where they vest in white

non adsit, in aliqua alia decenti domo, paramentis coloris albi induti, omnibus bene paratis, hora statuta, praecedente scholari juventute cum vexillo suo, choro et Subdiacono cum Cruce, et sequente Patrono vel ejus commissario, cum reliquis fidelibus ad hanc sollemnitatem invitatis, bono ordine in sollemni processione, sub pulsu campanarum et cantu Litaniarum ad omnes Sanctos vel piorum Hymnorum, ex domo paroeciali in ecclesiam se conferunt, ubi Officians ad aram majorem in infimo gradu genuflexus, tono consueto intonat sequentem Hymnum, quem chorus prosequitur. Quod si nulla ecclesia sit in loco, sequentia dicantur in domo, e qua egrediuntur.

Hymnus

VIII

Veni, Cre-á-tor Spí-ri-tus, Mentes tu-ó-rum ví-si-ta:

Imple su-pér-na grá-ti-a Quae tu creá- sti péc-tora. 2. Qui

dí- ce- ris Pa-rácli-tus, Altíssimi do-num De-i, Fons vivus,

ignis, cári-tas, Et spi-ri- tá-lis úncti-o. 3. Tu septi- fórmis

múnere, Dí-gi-tus pa-térnae déxterae, Tu ri- te promíssum

Patris, Sermóne di-tans gúttura. 4. Accénde lumen sénsibus,

Infúnde amórem córdibus, Infírma nostri córpo-ris Virtú-te

firmans pérpe-ti. 5. Hostem re-péllas lóngi-us, Pacémque

dones pró-tinus: Ductóre sic te praévi-o, Vi-témus omne

vestments. Everything being ready, at the time appointed all march in solemn procession to the church midst ringing of church-bells, singing the Litany of the Saints or sacred hymns. The procession proceeds in the following order: school-children preceded by their banner, choir, subdeacon with cross, followed by the patron or his representative, the faithful, and the clergy. Having come into the church, the officiant kneeling on the lowest step of the altar, intones the following hymn, which is continued to the end by the chanters. If there is no church, what follows is sung in the place of assembly and vesting.

Hymn

Creator-Spirit, all-Divine,
Come, visit every soul of Thine,
And fill with Thy celestial flame
The hearts which Thou Thyself didst frame.

O gift of God, Thine is the sweet
Consoling name of Paraclete —
And spring of life and fire and love
And unction flowing from above.

The mystic sevenfold gifts are Thine,
Finger of God's right hand divine;
The Father's promise sent to teach
The tongue a rich and heavenly speech.

Kindle with fire brought from above
Each sense, and fill our hearts with love;
And grant our flesh, so weak and frail,
The strength of Thine which cannot fail.

Drive far away our deadly foe,
And grant us Thy true peace to know;
So we, led by Thy guidance still,
May safely pass through every ill.

nóxi-um. 6. Per te sciámus da Pa-trem, Noscámus atque

Fí-li-um, Teque utri- ús-que Spí-ri-tum Credámus omni

témpore. 7. De-o Patri sit gló-ri-a, Et Fí-li-o, qui a mórtu-is

Surré-xit, ac Par-á-cli-to, In sae-cu-lórum saécu-la. A- men.

Hoc finito, cantatur:

Kýrie, eléison. ℟. Christe, eléison. ℣. Kýrie, eléison.

Pater noster secreto usque ad

℣. Et ne nos indúcas in tentatiónem.

℟. Sed líbera nos a malo.

℣. Dómine, exáudi oratiónem meam.

℟. Et clamor meus ad te véniat.

℣. Dóminus vobíscum.

℟. Et cum spíritu tuo.

Orémus.   *Oratio*

D EUS, qui corda fidélium Sancti Spíritus illustratióne docuísti, da nobis in eódem Spíritu recta sápere, et de ejus semper consolatióne gaudére.

D EUS, cui omne cor patet, et omnis volúntas lóquitur, et quem nullum latet secrétum: purífica per infusiónem Sancti Spíritus cogitatiónes cordis nostri; ut hanc nostram benedictiónem digne perfícere, et tuis fidélibus perínde optátam salútem procuráre valeámus.

A CTIÓNES nostras, quaésumus, Dómine, aspirándo praéveni, et adjuvándo proséquere: ut cuncta nostra orátio et operátio a te semper incípiat, et per te coepta finiátur. Per Dóminum nostrum Jesum Christum, Fílium tuum: Qui tecum vivit et

To us, through Thee, the grace be shown
To know the Father and the Son;
And Spirit of Them both, may we
Forever rest our faith in Thee.

To Sire and Son be praises meet,
And to the Holy Paraclete;
And may Christ send us from above
That Holy Spirit's gift of love.

After the hymn, the following prayers are sung:

℣. Lord, have mercy on us.
℟. Christ, have mercy on us.
℣. Lord, have mercy on us.
Our Father inaudibly until
℣. And lead us not into temptation.
℟. But deliver us from evil.
℣. O Lord, hear my prayer.
℟. And let my cry come unto thee.
℣. The Lord be with you.
℟. And with thy spirit.

Let us pray.   Prayer

O GOD, Who didst teach the hearts of the faithful by the enlightening of the Holy Spirit, grant us by the same Spirit ever to choose wisely and to rejoice in His comfort.

O GOD, to Whom every heart openeth, every mind speaketh, and nothing remaineth hidden, chasten our innermost thoughts by the infusion of the Holy Spirit, that worthily and well we perform this blessing, and thereby obtain for thy servants the welfare they seek.

WE BESEECH thee, Lord, inspire and guide our works in their beginning, and accompany them unto fruition, that our every prayer and work may ever begin with thee, and through thee be accomplished. Through our Lord, Jesus Christ,

regnat in unitáte Spíritus Sancti Deus, per ómnia saécula saeculórum. ℟. Amen.

℣. Sínite párvulos veníre ad me.

℟. Tálium est enim regnum caelórum.

Orémus.   Oratio

OMNÍPOTENS sempitérne Deus, te supplíciter deprecámur, ut respícere dignéris super infántulos tuos: infúnde in corda eórum grátiam Spíritus Sancti; ut per eúndem illumináti et edócti sciant, quid accéptum sit coram te omni témpore, et profíciant sapiéntia, aetáte et grátia. Per Christum Dóminum nostrum. ℟. Amen.

℣. Adjutórium nostrum in nómine Dómini.

℟. Qui fecit caelum et terram.

Diaconus: ℣. Procedámus in pace. ℟. In nómine Christi. Amen.

Nunc Officians in processione sollemni, sub cantu scholaris juventutis et pulsu campanarum, vadit ad scholam benedicendam. Quo cum pervenerit, stans ante januam exteriorem, cantat solus:

℣. Pax huic dómui.

℟. Et ómnibus habitántibus in ea.

Tunc intonat Antiphona: **Aspérges me.** Et chorus prosequitur tono Psalmi:

Dómine, hyssópo, et mundábor: lavábis me, et super nivem dealbábor.

Miserére mei, Deus, secúndum magnam misericórdiam tuam.

Glória Patri, et Fílio, et Spirítui Sancto.

Sicut erat in princípio, et nunc, et semper: et in saécula saeculórum. ℟. Amen.

Deinde repetitur Antiphona: **Aspérges me, Dómine, hyssópo,** et mundábor: lavábis me, et super nivem dealbábor.

Interim dum haec cantantur, Officians aspergit parietes exteriores, saltem in anteriori parte, aqua benedicta. His finitis cantat:

℣. Dóminus vobíscum.

℟. Et cum spíritu tuo.

thy Son, Who liveth and reigneth with thee in unity of the Holy
Spirit, God, eternally. ℟. Amen.

℣. Suffer the little children to come unto Me.
℟. For theirs is the kingdom of Heaven.

Let us pray. *Prayer*

ALMIGHTY, everlasting God, fervent in spirit we pray thee
to regard with tenderness these thy little ones. Pour into
their souls the grace of the Holy Spirit, that through Him they
be enlightened and instructed to know for all time that which
is pleasing to thee, and thus make progress in wisdom, age, and
grace. Through Christ our Lord. ℟. Amen.

℣. Our help is in the name of the Lord.
℟. Who made heaven and earth.

Deacon: Let us go in peace. ℟. In the name of Christ. Amen.

Now the celebrant goes in solemn procession to the school, midst
ringing of church-bells and the singing of the children. Arriving there,
he stands outside before the door, and chants:

℣. Peace be unto this edifice.
℟. And to all who assemble here.

He then intones the antiphon: Sprinkle me. And the choir continues
the chant: with hyssop, O Lord, and I shall be clean: wash me, and I
shall be whiter than snow.

Be merciful to me, O God, for great is thy goodness.

Glory be to the Father, and to the Son, and to the Holy Spirit.

As it was in the beginning, is now, and ever shall be, world
without end. ℟. Amen. And the antiphon is repeated.

While this is being sung, he sprinkles the outer walls with holy
water, at least at the front. Then he sings:

℣. The Lord be with you.
℟. And with thy spirit.

Orémus.   Oratio

O MNÍPOTENS et miséricors Deus, qui sacerdótibus tuis tantam prae céteris grátiam contulísti, ut, quidquid in tuo
nómine digne, perfectéque ab iis ágitur, a te fíeri credátur: quaésumus imménsam cleméntiam tuam; ut, quidquid modo visitatúri sumus, vísites, et, quidquid benedictúri sumus, bene ✠ dícas,
sitque ad nostrae humilitátis intróitum, Sanctórum tuórum méritis, fuga inimíci, Angeli pacis ingréssus.

D ÓMINE sancte, Pater omnípotens, per intercessiónem sanctórum Ignátii et Aloísii béne ✠ dic domum istam, béne ✠
dic intróitum nostrum, béne ✠ dic ingréssum pedum nostrórum:
sicut dignátus es domum Patriarchárum Abraham, Isaac, et Jacob
benedícere. Per Christum Dóminum nostrum. ℟. Amen.

Nunc sequitur ingressus. Officians intrando amplius scholae cubiculum, cantat:

℣. Pax huic dómui.

Chorus respondet:

℟. Et ómnibus habitántibus in ea.

Progrediens cum Clero et choro ad mensam linteo albo tectam, in
qua inter duos cereos accensos Crucifixi imago est posita, cantat:

℣. Dómine, exáudi oratiónem meam.
℟. Et clamor meus ad te véniat.
℣. Dóminus vobíscum.
℟. Et cum spíritu tuo.

Orémus.   Oratio

E XÁUDI nos, Dómine sancte, Pater omnípotens, aetérne
Deus: et míttere dignéris sanctum Angelum tuum de
caelis, qui custódiat, fóveat, prótegat, vísitet, atque deféndat
omnes habitántes, docéntes et discéntes in hoc habitáculo. Per
Christum Dóminum nostrum. ℟. Amen.

Orémus.   Oratio

D ÓMINE Jesu Christe, qui discípulis tuis dixísti: In quamcúmque domum intravéritis, salutáte eam, dicéntes: Pax
huic dómui; véniat, quaésumus, pax illa super hanc domum,

Let us pray.

G OD of mercy and of strength, Who didst confer on thy priests above all others so great a grace, that whatever they do worthily and perfectly in thy name, is, as it were, done by thee, we beseech thy boundless goodness, that whatever we presume to visit, may be visited by thee, and whatever we presume to bless, may be blessed ✠ by thee. And at our lowly coming, through the merits of thy saints, may demons flee, and angels of peace draw near.

O HOLY LORD, almighty Father, through the intercession of St. Ignatius and St. Aloysius, bless ✠ this building, bless ✠ our entering, bless ✠ the threshold over which we pass, as thou didst vouchsafe to bless the home of thy Patriarchs Abraham, Isaac, and Jacob. Through Christ our Lord. ℟. Amen.

Now all enter, and the celebrant, going into the main room, sings:
℣. Peace be unto this place.
The choir responds: ℟. And unto all who assemble here.
The celebrant, with the clergy and choir, goes to the linen-covered table on which stands a crucifix between two burning candles. And he sings:
℣. O Lord, hear my prayer.
℟. And let my cry come unto thee.
℣. The Lord be with you.
℟. And with thy spirit.

Let us pray.

H EAR us, O holy Lord, Father almighty, eternal God, and send thy holy angel from heaven to guard, cherish, protect, visit, and defend all who assemble, teach, and study in this building. Through Christ our Lord. ℟. Amen.

Let us pray.

O LORD Jesus Christ, Who didst say to thine apostles: "In whatever home you enter, salute it, saying: 'Peace be unto this house,'" let this same peace, we pray, come upon this school,

instituéndae juventúti destinátam, et super omnes habitántes, docéntes et discéntes in ea; et eos, Dómine, ab omni infirmitáte erípere, et liberáre dignéris: reple docéntes in ea spíritu sciéntiae, sapiéntiae, et timóris tui; reple discéntes in ea grátia tua, ut, quae salutáriter et utíliter edocéntur, intelléctu cápiant, corde retíneant, ópere exsequántur, et in ómnibus nomen tuum honorificétur. Ad intróitum ergo nostrum bene ✝ dícere, et sancti ✝ ficáre dignéris hanc scholam, et intra paríetes domus istíus Angeli tuae lucis hábitent, eámque et in ea habitántes, docéntes et discéntes custódiant: Qui vivis et regnas in saécula saeculórum. ℟. Amen.

Postea Officians intonat Antiphonam: **Aspérges me** et chorus prosequitur, ut supra, pag. 230. Interim fit aspersio cubiculi aqua benedicta. Reversus ad mensam, Officians imponit thus in thuribulum, et benedicit illud, dicens:

Per intercessiónem sancti Michaélis Archángeli, stantis a dextris altáris incensi, et ómnium sanctórum Angelórum, incénsum istud dignéris, Dómine, bene ✝ dícere, et in odórem suavitátis accípere. Per Christum Dóminum nostrum. ℟. Amen.

Hoc dicto, sumit Officians thuribulum, et incensat cubiculum, choro cantante:

Antiphona

VIId

Incénsum istud, * a te bene-díctum, a-scéndat ad te, Dómi-ne : et descéndat super nos mi-se-ri-cór- di-a tu-a.

Ps. Di-rigá-tur, Dómine, orá-ti-o me-a, sicut in-cénsum in conspéctu tu-o: * ele-vá-ti-o mánu-um me-árum sacri-fí-ci-um vespertínum.

as well as upon all who enter here. Protect them, O Lord, from all sickness. Fill them who teach here with the spirit of knowledge, wisdom, and fear of the Lord. Support the pupils with heavenly assistance, so that they may grasp, retain, and practice all useful and wholesome lessons, and in everything give honor to thy name. Wherefore, at our coming mayest thou bless ✠ and sanctify ✠ this school, and let the angels of light dwell within its walls, and may they stand guard over teachers and scholars. Thou Who livest and reignest eternally. ℟. Amen.

The officiant again intones the antiphon: **Aspérges** as above. While the choir continues the chant, he sprinkles the room with holy water, then returns to the table, where he puts incense into the thurible, saying as he blesses it:

Through the intercession of St. Michael the Archangel, standing to the right of the altar of incense, and of all holy angels, mayest thou deign, O Lord, to bless ✠ this incense, and to accept it as an odour of sweetness. Through Christ our Lord. ℟. Amen.

Receiving the censer, he incenses the room while the choir sings the following:

Antiphon: This incense blessed by thee, O Lord, may it ascend unto thee: and may thy mercy descend upon us.

Psalmus 140, 2-4

DIRIGÁTUR, Dómine, orátio mea, sicut incénsum in conspéctu tuo: * elevátio mánuum meárum sacrifícium vespertínum.

Pone, Dómine, custódiam ori meo: * et óstium circumstántiae lábiis meis.

Non declínet cor meum in verba malítiae, * ad excusándas excusatiónes in peccátis.

Glória Patri.

Incensatione peracta, Officians stans coram imagine Crucifixi, cantat:

℣. Dóminus vobíscum.

℟. Et cum spíritu tuo.

Orémus. *Oratio*

VÍSITA, quaésumus, Dómine, habitatiónem istam, et omnes insídias inimíci ab ea longe repélle: Angeli tui sancti hábitent in ea, qui omnes hic habitántes, docéntes et discéntes in pace custódiant, et benedíctio tua super illos sit semper.

BÉNE ✠ DIC, Dómine, domum istam, et sit ibi sánitas, sánctitas, virtus et glória, humílitas, bónitas, mansuetúdo, lénitas, docílitas, et plenitúdo legis, oboediéntia et gratiárum áctio Deo Patri, et Fílio, et Spirítui Sancto. Et haec benedíctio sit super hanc domum et locum istum: atque super omnes habitántes, docéntes et discéntes in eo descéndat septifórmis grátia Spíritus Sancti. Per eúndem Christum Dóminum nostrum. ℟. Amen.

Officians nunc affigit sanctam Crucem in loco apto cubiculi, dicendo:

Signum salútis impóne, Dómine, super hanc domum: et non permíttas introíre in eam ángelum percutiéntem. In nómine Patris, et Fílii, ✠ et Spíritus Sancti. ℟. Amen.

Versus Crucem:

Orémus. *Oratio*

OMNÍPOTENS, sempitérne Deus, qui in omni loco dominatiónis tuae totus assístis, solus operáris: adésto supplicatióni-

LET my prayer, O Lord, ascend as incense in thy sight, and the lifting up of my hands be as an evening sacrifice.

Set a watch, O Lord, before my mouth and a guard round about my lips.

Let my heart not stoop to wickedness, to defend the perpetrators of sin.

Glory be to the Father.

After the incensing, the celebrant stands before the crucifix, and sings:

℣. The Lord be with you.

℟. And with thy spirit.

Let us pray. *Prayer*

VISIT, we pray thee, Lord, this building, and drive afar every assault of the enemy. Let thy holy angels dwell here to guard in peace all who here assemble, teach, and study, and may thy blessing be always upon them.

BLESS,✠ O Lord, this edifice, and let there be here health and holiness, virtue and glory, humility, goodness, mildness, gentleness, docility and fidelity to the law, obedience, and thanksgiving to God the Father, Son, and Holy Spirit. May this blessing be upon this place, and may the seven-fold gifts of the Holy Spirit descend upon teachers and pupils. Through the selfsame Christ our Lord. ℟. Amen.

The officiant hangs the cross in a prominent place in the room, saying:

Bestow, O Lord, the sign of salvation upon this building, and forbid entrance to the avenging angel. In the name of the Father, and of the Son,✠ and of the Holy Spirit. ℟. Amen.

Turning to the cross, he prays:

Let us pray. *Prayer*

ALMIGHTY, everlasting God, Who standest by mightily in every place under thy sway, and Who alone dost act, hear

bus nostris, ut hujus domus sis protéctor, et nulla hic nequítia contráriae potestátis obsístat; sed in virtúte sanctae Crucis et operatióne Spíritus Sancti fiat tibi hic purum servítium, et devóta libértas exsístat. Per Christum Dóminum nostrum. ℟. Amen.

Orémus.   Oratio

A DÉSTO nobis, Dómine, Deus noster: et eos, qui in sanctae Crucis praesídio confídunt, perpétuis defénde auxíliis. Per Christum Dóminum nostrum. ℟. Amen.

Tandem benedicit Officians cubiculo et omnibus praesentibus manu dextera, formans signum crucis, et dicens:

Benedíctio Dei omnipoténtis, Patris, et Fílii, ✝ et Spíritus Sancti, descéndat super hanc domum, super omnes habitántes, docéntes et discéntes in ea, super nos omnes, et máneat semper. ℟. Amen.

His finitis, sub cantu juventutis et pulsu campanarum processionaliter fit reditus in ecclesiam statuto ordine, ubi celebratur Missa conveniens Officio diei.

56

BENEDICTIO DOMORUM
extra Tempus Paschale

Parochus, seu alius Sacerdos, volens aliquam particularem domum, vel generaliter domos fidelium, extra Tempus Paschale aspergere aqua benedicta, ingrediens domum dicit:

℣. Pax huic dómui.

℟. Et ómnibus habitántibus in ea.

Translator's Note: After the blessings of places destined for sacred purpose in the canonical sense, the blessing of the Christian home follows rightfully as a sacred place in the broader sense. It also is a place of liturgical worship, and therefore, very sacred. Frequently it witnesses the celebration of great Mysteries, the sacraments of penance, Eucharist, last anointing, the perfection of matrimony. In a home worthy of the dignified name of Christian is continued the

our humble entreaties. Be thou the protector of this habitation, and let no evil power be opposed to it. But in virtue of the holy Cross and the working of the Holy Spirit, let a worthy service be rendered to thee in this spot, and devoted freedom abide. Through Christ our Lord. ℟. Amen.

Let us pray.   Prayer

ABIDE with us, O Lord our God, and succour constantly them that place their trust and refuge in the holy Cross. Through Christ our Lord. ℟. Amen.

Lastly, he blesses the room and all present, saying:

May the blessing of almighty God, Father, Son, ✠ and Holy Spirit descend upon this school, upon all who come here, teachers and pupils, and upon us all, and may it remain for all time. ℟. Amen.

To the accompaniment of church-bells ringing and the singing of the school-children, the procession returns to the church, where the Mass proper to the day is celebrated.

56

BLESSING OF HOMES
outside of Paschaltide

A pastor or any priest, when he blesses a home outside of Paschaltide, says upon entering it:

℣. Peace be unto this home.
℟. And unto all who dwell herein.

---

communal praise of God, begun in the church edifice in first instance, and continued in the home through family prayer. Here a soul falling asleep in Christ is commended to the merciful hands of its Author, and here begins the service of committing the body to the earth. And to the Christian dwelling, the Church reaches out with her consecratory hand, and dispenses the sacramentals.

2.Deinde loca praecipua domus aspergendo, dicit Antiphonam:

Aspérges me, Dómine, hyssópo, et mundábor: lavábis me, et super nivem dealbábor.

Ps. 50, 3. Miserére mei, Deus, secúndum magnam misericórdiam tuam. ℣. Glória Patri, etc.

Et repetitur Antiphona: Aspérges me, etc.

℣. Dómine, exáudi oratiónem meam.

℟. Et clamor meus ad te véniat.

℣. Dóminus vobíscum.

℟. Et cum spíritu tuo.

Orémus. Oratio

Exáudi nos, Dómine sancte, Pater omnípotens, aetérne, Deus: et míttere dignéris sanctum Angelum tuum de caelis, qui custódiat, fóveat, prótegat, vísitet, atque deféndat omnes habitántes ın hoc habitáculo. Per Christum Dóminum nostrum. ℟. Amen.

57

ALIA BENEDICTIO DOMUS

℣. Adjutórium nostrum in nómine Dómini.

℟. Qui fecit caelum et terram.

℣. Dóminus vobíscum.

℟. Et cum spíritu tuo.

Orémus. Oratio

Te Deum Patrem omnipoténtem supplíciter exorámus pro hac domo, et habitatóribus ejus, ac rebus: ut eam bene ✠ dícere, et sancti ✠ ficáre, ac bonis ómnibus ampliáre dignéris: tríbue eis, Dómine, de rore caeli abundántiam, et de pinguédine terrae vitae substántiam, et desidéria voti eórum ad efféctum tuae miseratiónis perdúcas. Ad intróitum ergo nostrum bene ✠ dícere, et sancti ✠ ficáre dignéris hanc domum, sicut benedícere dignátus

2. As he sprinkles the principal room, he prays:

Sprinkle me with hyssop, O Lord, and I shall be clean: wash me, and I shall be whiter than snow. Ps. 50, 3. Be merciful to me, O God, for great is thy goodness. ℣. Glory be to the Father, etc. And repeat the antiphon.

℣. O Lord, hear my prayer.

℟. And let my cry come unto thee.

℣. The Lord be with you.

℟. And with thy spirit.

Let us pray.   Prayer

Hear us, holy Lord, almighty Father, eternal God! And deign to send thy holy angel from heaven to guard, cherish, protect, visit, and defend all who dwell in this home. Through Christ our Lord. ℟. Amen.

57

ANOTHER BLESSING OF A HOME

℣. Our help is in the name of the Lord.

℟. Who made heaven and earth.

℟. And with thy spirit.

℣. The Lord be with you.

Let us pray.   Prayer

Thee, God the Father Almighty, we fervently implore for the sake of this home, and its occupants and possessions, that thou wouldst bless ✠ and sanctify ✠ it, enriching it with every good. Pour out on them, O Lord, heavenly dew in good measure, as well as the fatness of earthly needs. Mercifully hear and grant the fulfilment of their prayers. And at our lowly coming, deign to bless ✠ and sanctify ✠ this home, as thou didst bless the homes

es domum Abraham, Isaac, et Jacob: et intra pariétes domus istíus Angeli tuae lucis inhábitent, eámque, et ejus habitatóres custódiant. Per Christum Dóminum nostrum. ℟. Amen.

Et aspergatur aqua benedicta.

58

BENEDICTIO LOCI VEL DOMUS

℣. Adjutórium nostrum in nómine Dómini.
℟. Qui fecit caelum et terram.
℣. Dóminus vobíscum.
℟. Et cum spíritu tuo.

Orémus.   Oratio

Béne ✠ dic, Dómine, Deus omnípotens, locum istum (vel domum istam): ut sit in eo (ea) sánitas, cástitas, victória, virtus, humílitas, bónitas, et mansuetúdo, plenitúdo legis, et gratiárum áctio Deo Patri, et Fílio, et Spirítui Sancto; et haec benedíctio máneat super hunc locum (vel super hanc domum) et super habitántes in eo (ea) nunc et in ómnia saécula saeculórum. ℟. Amen.

Et aspergatur aqua benedicta.

59

BENEDICTIO THALAMI

℣. Adjutórium nostrum in nómine Dómini.
℟. Qui fecit caelum et terram.
℣. Dóminus vobíscum.
℟. Et cum spíritu tuo.

of Abraham, Isaac, and Jacob. Within these walls let thine angels of light preside and stand watch over them that dwell here. Through Christ our Lord. ℟. Amen.

It is sprinkled with holy water.

58

BLESSING OF A ROOM OR APARTMENT
or any Territory or District

℣. Our help is in the name of the Lord.
℟. Who made heaven and earth.
℣. The Lord be with you.
℟. And with thy spirit.

Let us pray.   Prayer

Bless, ✠ O Lord, almighty God this place (or dwelling) that it be the shelter of health, chastity, self-conquest, humility, goodness, mildness, obedience to the commandments, and thanksgiving to God the Father, Son, and Holy Spirit. May blessing remain for all time on this place (or on this dwelling) and them that live here. ℟. Amen.

It is sprinkled with holy water.

59

BLESSING OF A BRIDAL CHAMBER

℣. Our help is in the name of the Lord.
℟. Who made heaven and earth.
℣. The Lord be with you.
℟. And with thy spirit.

Orémus.

Béne ✠ dic, Dómine, thálamum hunc: ut omnes habitántes in eo, in tua pace consístant, et in tua voluntáte permáneant, et senéscant, et multiplicéntur in longitúdinem diérum, et ad regna caelórum pervéniant. Per Christum Dóminum nostrum. ℟. Amen.

Et aspergatur aqua benedicta.

Let us pray.

Bless, ✠ O Lord, this bridal chamber, that they who share it establish themselves in thy peace, conform themselves to thy will. And as their years increase, may they be enriched with fulness of life, and come finally into thy heavenly kingdom. Through Christ our Lord. ℟. Amen.

It is sprinkled with holy water.

IV

BLESSINGS OF OBJECTS DESTINED TO SACRED PURPOSE

BENEDICTIO FONTIS SEU AQUAE BAPTISMALIS
Extra Pervigilium Paschae et Pentecostes
cum Aqua Consecrata non Habetur

Primum lavatur, et mundatur vas Baptisterii, deinde limpida aqua
repletur. Tum Sacerdos cum suis Clericis, vel etiam aliis Presbyteris,
cruce et duobus cereis praecedentibus, ac thuribulo et incenso, et cum
vasculis Chrismatis, et Olei Catechumenorum accedit ad Fontem, et
ibi, vel ante Altare Baptisterii, dicit Litanias ordinarias, prout habentur
infra (pag. 444), post septem Psalmos Poenitentiales.

2. Potest etiam dicere Litanias breviores, ut in Missali in Sabbato
Sancto.

3. Sed ante ℣. **Ut nos exaudíre dignéris,** dicat et secundo repetat
sequentem versum:

**Ut fontem istum ad regenerándam tibi novam prolem bene ✠
dícere, et conse ✠ cráre dignéris. ℟. Te rogámus, audi nos.**

4. Dicto autem ultimo **Kýrie, eléison,** Sacerdos dicit: **Pater noster** et
Credo in Deum, etc., omnia clara voce: quibus finitis dicit:

℣. **Apud te, Dómine, est fons vitae.**

℟. **Et in lúmine tuo vidébimus lumen.**

℣. **Dómine, exáudi oratiónem meam.**

℟. **Et clamor meus ad te véniat.**

℣. **Dóminus vobíscum.**

℟. **Et cum spíritu tuo.**

Orémus. Oratio

OMNÍPOTENS sempitérne Deus, adésto magnae pietátis tuae
mystériis, adésto sacraméntis: et ad recreándos novos pópulos, quos tibi fons Baptísmatis párturit, spíritum adoptiónis emítte;
ut, quod nostrae humilitátis geréndum est ministério, virtútis
tuae impleátur efféctu. Per Dóminum nostrum Jesum Christum,
Fílium tuum, qui tecum vivit, et regnat in unitáte Spíritus Sancti
Deus, per ómnia saécula saeculórum. ℟. Amen.

BLESSING OF THE BAPTISMAL FONT
Outside of the Vigils of Easter and Pentecost
if There is No Baptismal Water at Hand

The font should be thoroughly cleansed, then filled with fresh water. The priest goes to the font preceded by the crucifer and acolytes, the thurifer, the bearers of the Sacred Oils of Chrism and Catechumens, and accompanied by other assistants or priests. Arriving there, the Litany of the Saints is said as given on page 445, after the seven Penitential Psalms.

2. Or the shorter Litany as given in the Missal for Holy Saturday may be used.

3. Before the verse: **That thou wouldst graciously hear us,** following verse is said twice:

That thou wouldst bless ✠ and sanctify ✠ this font unto the rebirth of new children for thee. ℟. **We beseech thee, hear us.**

4. After the Litany, the Lord's Prayer and Apostle's Creed are prayed aloud. Then:

℣. **Thou, O Lord, art the fountain of life.**

℟. **And by thy splendor we will see the light.**

℣. **O Lord, hear my prayer.**

℟. **And let my cry come unto thee.**

℣. **The Lord be with you.**

℟. **And with thy spirit.**

Let us pray. Prayer

ALMIGHTY and everlasting God, assist at these mysteries of thy great mercy, assist at these sacraments, and send forth the spirit of adoption to beget new life in them that are born unto thee in this font of baptism; that what we do by our humble ministry, thou mayest effect by thy power. Through Jesus Christ, thy Son, our Lord, who liveth and reigneth with thee in unity of the Holy Spirit, God, eternally. ℟. **Amen.**

Exorcismus aquae

Exorcízo te, creatúra aquae, per Deum ✠ vivum, per Deum ✠ verum, per Deum ✠ sanctum, per Deum, qui te in princípio verbo separávit ab árida: cujus Spíritus super te ferebátur, qui te de paradíso manáre jussit.

5. Hic manu aquam dividit, et deinde effundit eam extra marginem Fontis, versus quatuor mundi partes, prosequens:

Et in quátuor flumínibus totam terram rigáre praecépit: qui te in desérto amáram per lignum, dulcem fecit atque potábilem; qui te de petra prodúxit, ut pópulum, quem ex Aegýpto liberáverat, siti fatigátum recreáret. Exorcízo te per Jesum Christum, Fílium ejus únicum, Dóminum nostrum: qui te in Cana Galilaéae signo admirábili sua poténtia convértit in vinum: qui super te pédibus ambulávit, et a Joánne in Jordáne in te baptizátus est. Qui te una cum sánguine de látere suo prodúxit: et discípulis suis jussit, ut credéntes baptizárent in te, dicens: Ite, docéte omnes gentes, baptizántes eos in nómine Patris, et Fílii, et Spíritus Sancti; ut efficiáris aqua sancta, aqua benedícta, aqua, quae lavat sordes, et mundat peccáta. Tibi ígitur praecípio, omnis spíritus immúnde, omne phantásma, omne mendácium, eradicáre, et effúgare ab hac creatúra aquae, ut qui in ipsa baptizándi erunt, fiat eis fons aquae saliéntis in vitam aetérnam, regénerans eos Deo Patri, et Fílio, et Spirítui Sancto, in nómine ejúsdem Dómini nostri Jesu Christi, qui ventúrus est judicáre vivos et mórtuos, et saéculum per ignem. ℞. Amen.

Orémus.   Oratio

DÓMINE sancte, Pater omnípotens, aetérne Deus, aquárum spirituálium sanctificátor, te supplíciter deprecámur: ut ad hoc ministérium humilitátis nostrae respícere dignéris, et super has aquas, abluéndis et purificándis homínibus praeparátas,

Exorcism of water

Thou creature of water, I purge thee of evil by the living ☩ God, by the true ☩ God, by the holy ☩ God, by the God Who in the beginning separated thee by His word from the dry land, Whose Spirit moved over thee, Who made thee flow from Paradise.

5. He divides the water with his hand, and sprinkles it outside of the font toward the four quarters of the earth, and continues:

And He commanded thee to water the whole earth with thy four rivers; Who by the wood cast into thee did change thy bitterness in the desert, making thee sweet and fit to drink; Who produced thee out of a rock to quench the thirst of the languishing people whom He had delivered out of Egypt. I purge thee by Jesus Christ, His Sole-Begotten Son, our Lord, Who in Cana of Galilee changed thee into wine by a wondrous miracle, Who walked upon the waves, and was baptized in thee by John in the Jordan. Who let thee flow out of His side together with His blood, and commanded His disciples to baptize with thee them that believe, saying: "Go teach all nations, baptizing them in the name of the Father, and of the Son, and of the Holy Spirit." Mayest thou become a water which is holy, a water which is blessed, a water which washes away filth and cleanses from sin. Wherefore, I command thee — every unclean spirit, every phantam, every falsehood, leave, and vanish from this creature of water, that it may be unto all that will be baptized with it a fountain of water gushing forth unto life everlasting, regenerating them in God the Father, and in the Son, and in the Holy Spirit; in the name of the selfsame Jesus Christ, our Lord, Who shall come to judge the living, and the dead, and the world by fire. ℟. Amen.

Let us pray. *Prayer*

HOLY Lord, almighty Father, eternal God, we earnestly beseech thee, thou Sanctifier of spiritual waters, look with favor upon our lowly ministry, and send thy messenger of holi-

Angelum sanctitátis emíttas, quo, peccátis vitae prióris ablútis, reatúque detérso, purum Sancto Spirítui habitáculum regeneráti éffici mereántur. Per Dóminum. ℞. Amen.

6. Tunc sufflat ter in aquam versus tres partes secundum hanc figuram ✠; deinde imponit incensum in thuribulo, et Fontem incensat. Postea infundens de Oleo Catechumenorum in aquam in modum crucis, clara voce dicit:

Sanctificétur, et foecundétur fons iste óleo salútis renascéntibus ex eo in vitam aetérnam, in nómine Pa ✠ tris, et Fí ✠ lii, et Spíritus ✠ Sancti. ℞. Amen.

7. Deinde infundit de Chrismate, modo quo supra, dicens:

Infúsio Chrísmatis Dómini nostri Jesu Christi, et Spíritus Sancti Parácliti, fiat in nómine sanctae Trinitátis. ℞. Amen.

8. Postea accipit ambas ampullas dicti Olei sancti et Chrismatis, et de utroque simul in modum crucis infundendo, dicit:

Commíxtio Chrísmatis sanctificatiónis, et Olei unctiónis, et aquae Baptísmatis páriter fiat in nómine Pa ✠ tris, et Fí ✠ lii, et Spíritus ✠ Sancti. ℞. Amen.

9. Tum, depositis ampullis, dextera manu Oleum sanctum, et Chrisma infusum miscet cum aqua et spargit per totum Fontem. Deinde medulla panis manum tergit; et si quis baptizandus sit, eum baptizat, ut supra. Quod si neminem baptizet, statim manus abluat, et ablutio effundatur in sacrarium.

61

BENEDICTIO FONTIS SEU AQUAE BAPTISMALIS

Haec formula brevior pro benedictione Fontis seu aquae baptismalis, a Paulo Papa III Missionariis Peruanis apud Indos olim concessa, nonnisi in iis locis adhiberi potest, ad quae speciali Apostolicae Sedis indulto extensa fuit.

ness upon these waters which we make ready to cleanse and purify mankind. Wash them from the sins of their former state, so that their guilt being blotted out, they may be reborn unto a pure dwelling for thy Holy Spirit. Through Christ our Lord. ℟. Amen.

6. He breathes thrice upon the water in the form of the Greek letter ψ; then incenses the font. After this he pours the Oil of Catechumens into the water in the form of a cross, saying:

May this font be sanctified and made fruitful by the oil of salvation for them that are born anew herein unto life everlasting, in the name of the Father, ✠ and of the Son, ✠ and of the Holy ✠ Spirit. ℟. Amen.

7. Then he pours in Chrism in the same manner, saying:

May this infusion of the chrism of our Lord Jesus Christ and of the Holy Spirit, the Comforter be made in the name of the Holy Trinity. ℟. Amen.

8. After this he takes the two phials of holy oils, and pours both together into the water in the form of a cross, saying:

May this mingling of the chrism of salvation with the oil of anointing and the water of Baptism be made in the name of the Father, ✠ and of the Son, ✠ and of the Holy ✠ Spirit. ℟. Amen.

9. He mixes the oils and water with his hand, and sprinkles it over the font. Then he cleanses the oil from his hand with a piece of bread. If there are any to be baptized, he baptizes in the ordinary way. Otherwise he washes his hands, and the ablution is poured into the sacrarium.

61

THE SHORT FORM FOR BLESSING THE BAPTISMAL FONT

This shorter blessing which Pope Paul III allowed by concession to the missionaries among the Indians of Peru may be used only where the indult has been extended by the Holy See.

Exorcismus aquae

Exorcízo te, creatúra aquae, in nómine Dei ✠ Patris omnipoténtis, et in nómine Jesu ✠ Christi, Fílii ejus, Dómini nostri, et in virtúte Spíritus ✠ Sancti. Exorcízo te, omnis virtus adversárii diáboli: ut omnis phantásia eradicétur, ac effugétur ab hac creatúra aquae, et fiat fons aquae saliéntis in vitam aetérnam: ut, qui ex ea baptizáti fúerint, fiant templum Dei vivi, et Spíritus Sanctus hábitet in eis, in remissiónem peccatórum: in nómine Dómini nostri Jesu Christi, qui ventúrus est judicáre vivos et mórtuos, et saéculum per ignem. ℞. Amen.

Orémus.   Oratio

DÓMINE sancte, Pater omnípotens, aetérne Deus, aquárum spirituálium sanctificátor, te supplíciter deprecámur: ut hoc ministérium humilitátis nostrae respícere dignéris, et super has aquas, abluéndis et vivificándis homínibus praeparátas, Angelum sanctitátis emíttas; ut peccátis prióris vitae ablútis, reatúque detérso, purum sacráto Spirítui habitáculum regeneratiónibus procúret. Per Christum Dóminum nostrum. ℞. Amen.

Sacerdos deinceps infundat Oleum Catechumenorum in aquam, in modum crucis, dicens:

Conjúnctio Olei unctiónis, et aquae Baptísmatis sanctificétur, et foecundétur. In nómine Pa ✠ tris, et Fí ✠ lii, et Spíritus ✠ Sancti. ℞. Amen.

Deinde infundat Chrisma in aquam, in modum crucis, dicens:

Conjúnctio Chrísmatis sanctificatiónis et Olei unctiónis et aquae Baptísmatis sanctificétur, et foecundétur. In nómine Pa ✠ tris, et Fí ✠ lii, et Spíritus ✠ Sancti. ℞. Amen.

Thou creature of water, I purge thee of evil in the name of God, ✠ the Father almighty, in the name of Jesus ✠ Christ, His Son, our Lord, and in the power of the Holy ✠ Spirit. I cast thee forth, thou power of diabolical enmity, that every wicked phantom may be dispelled and put to flight from this creature of water, that it be a fountain springing forth unto life everlasting. May they who will be baptized herein become temples of the living God, and may the Holy Spirit dwell in them unto the forgiveness of sins, in the name of our Lord Jesus Christ, Who shall come to judge the living and the dead, and the world by fire. ℟. Amen.

Let us pray.   Prayer

HOLY Lord, almighty Father, eternal God, we earnestly beseech thee, thou Sanctifier of spiritual waters, look with favor upon our lowly ministry, and send thy messenger of holiness upon these waters which we make ready to cleanse and purify mankind. Wash them from the sins of their former state, so that their guilt being blotted out, they may be reborn unto a pure dwelling for thy Holy Spirit. Through Christ our Lord. ℟. Amen.

The priest pours the Oil of Catechumens into the water in the form of a cross, saying:

May this union of the oil of anointing with the water of baptism be sanctified and made fruitful. In the name of the Father, ✠ and of the Son, ✠ and of the Holy ✠ Spirit. ℟. Amen.

Then he pours in Chrism in the same manner, saying:

May this union of the chrism of salvation and the oil of anointing with the water of baptism be sanctified and made fruitful. In the name of the Father, ✠ and of the Son, ✠ and of the Holy ✠ Spirit. ℟. Amen.

62

BENEDICTIO TABERNACULI SEU VASCULI
Pro Sacrosancta Eucharistia Conservanda

℣. Adjutórium nostrum in nómine Dómini.
℞. Qui fecit caelum et terram.
℣. Dóminus vobíscum.
℞. Et cum spíritu tuo.

Orémus. Oratio

Omnípotens sempitérne Deus, majestátem tuam súpplices deprecámur: ut tabernáculum (seu vásculum) hoc pro Córpore Fílii tui, Dómini nostri Jesu Christi, in eo condéndo fabricátum, bene ✠ dictiónis tuae grátia dicáre dignéris. Per eúndem Dóminum nostrum Jesum Christum, Fílium tuum: Qui tecum vivit et regnat in unitáte Spíritus Sancti Deus, per ómnia saécula saeculórum. ℞. Amen.

Et aspergatur aqua benedicta.

63

BENEDICTIO TABERNACULI SEU OSTENSORII
Pro Sanctissimo Sacramento
Fidelium Venerationi Exponendo

℣. Adjutórium nostrum in nómine Dómini.
℞. Qui fecit caelum et terram.
℣. Dóminus vobíscum.
℞. Et cum spíritu tuo.

Translator's Note: The Furnishings of Divine Worship
The sacred furnishings (sacra supellex) required in divine worship — vessels, utensils, vestments, linens, ornaments may be blessed or consecrated before they are put to sacred use. Liturgical law determines which must be consecrated, which must be blessed, which may be blessed, and which must not be blessed. Although

62

BLESSING OF A TABERNACLE, PYX, CIBORIUM
or similar receptacle for reserving the Holy Eucharist

℣. Our help is in the name of the Lord.
℟. Who made heaven and earth.
℣. The Lord be with you.
℟. And with thy spirit.

Let us pray.   Prayer

O almighty and everlasting God, humbly we entreat thy Majesty to dedicate with thy blessing ✠ this tabernacle (or pyx, etc.) made to contain the Body of thy Son, our Lord Jesus Christ. Through the selfsame Jesus Christ, thy Son, our Lord, Who liveth and reigneth with thee in unity of the Holy Spirit, God, eternally. ℟. Amen.

It is sprinkled with holy water.

63

BLESSING OF A MONSTRANCE OR OSTENSORIUM
for Exposition of the Blessed Sacrament

℣. Our help is in the name of the Lord.
℟. Who made heaven and earth.
℣. The Lord be with you.
℟. And with thy spirit.

these blessings are reserved to bishops, in most dioceses the faculties given to priests at ordination include that of blessing the sacra supellex. Consequently, all blessings listed in this category are as a rule permitted to priests by general delegation. Canon 1304 of the Code permits pastors to bless the sacred furnishings within their own churches, but the Congregation of Sacred Rites interprets this to apply only to blessings in which no sacred anointing is required.

Orémus.

Omnípotens sempitérne Deus, vásculum istud, pro Fílii tui Dómini nostri Jesu Christi Córpore fidélium veneratióni exponéndo fabrefáctum, bene ✠ dícere, et sancti ✠ ficáre dignáre: ut omnes, qui eúndem Unigénitum in hoc saéculo pio afféctu venerántur, et in futúro perpétuam pietátis suae mercédem accípiant. Per eúndem Christum Dóminum nostrum. ℟. Amen.

Et aspergatur aqua benedicta.

64

BENEDICTIO CAPSARUM
Pro Reliquiis Sanctorum Includendis

℣. Adjutórium nostrum in nómine Dómini.
℟. Qui fecit caelum et terram.
℣. Dóminus vobíscum.
℟. Et cum spíritu tuo.

Orémus.

Béne ✠ dic, Dómine, cápsulam hanc Sanctórum tuórum Relíquiis condéndis praeparátam; et praesta; ut, quicúmque eas pro mentis afféctu veneráti fúerint, ipsis Sanctis tuis intercedéntibus, ómnium delictórum suórum véniam obtíneant, et contra omnes adversitátes tuo semper muniántur auxílio. Per Christum Dóminum nostrum. ℟. Amen.

Et aspergatur aqua benedicta.

65

BENEDICTIO VASORUM
Pro Sacris Oleis Includendis

℣. Adjutórium nostrum in nómine Dómini.
℟. Qui fecit caelum et terram.
℣. Dóminus vobíscum.
℟. Et cum spíritu tuo.

Let us pray.

O almighty and everlasting God, deign to bless ✛ and sanctify ✛ this vessel made to expose before faithful worshippers the Body of thy Son, our Lord, Jesus Christ, that all who in this life piously adore thy Sole-Begotten One may hereafter possess Him as their eternal recompense. Through the selfsame Christ our Lord. ℞. Amen.

It is sprinkled with holy water.

64

BLESSING OF A RELIQUARY

℣. Our help is in the name of the Lord.
℞. Who made heaven and earth.
℣. The Lord be with you.
℞. And with thy spirit.

Let us pray.

Bless, ✛ O Lord, this reliquary made to contain the sacred remains of thy holy ones, and grant through the intercession of the saints that all who devoutly venerate their relics may obtain pardon for sin and protection from every adversity. Through Christ our Lord. ℞. Amen.

It is sprinkled with holy water.

65

BLESSING OF OIL-STOCKS

℣. Our help is in the name of the Lord.
℞. Who made heaven and earth.
℣. The Lord be with you.
℞. And with thy spirit.

Orémus. Oratio

Exáudi, Dómine, Pater clementíssime, preces nostras: et haec purificánda vasa, Ecclésiae tuae sacri ministérii úsui praeparáta, bene ✠ dícere, et sancti ✠ ficáre dignéris. Per Christum Dóminum nostrum. ℟. Amen.

Orémus. Oratio

OMNÍPOTENS sempitérne Deus, a quo ómnia immúnda purgántur, et in quo ómnia purgáta claréscunt: súpplices omnipoténtiam tuam invocámus; ut ab his vasis, quae tibi ófferunt fámuli tui, omnis spíritus immúndus confúsus longe discédat, et per tuam bene ✠ dictiónem ad usum et ministérium Ecclésiae tuae sanctificáta permáneant. Per Christum Dóminum nostrum. ℟. Amen.

Et aspergantur aqua benedicta.

66

BENEDICTIO SACRORUM VASORUM

Aliorumque Ornamentorum in Genere

℣. Adjutórium nostrum in nómine Dómini.
℟. Qui fecit caelum et terram.
℣. Dóminus vobíscum.
℟. Et cum spíritu tuo.

Orémus. Oratio

Exáudi, Dómine, Pater clementíssime, preces nostras: et haec purificánda vasa et ornaménta sacri Altáris, atque Ecclésiae tuae sacri ministérii úsui praeparáta, bene ✠ dícere, et sancti ✠ ficáre dignéris. Per Christum Dóminum nostrum. ℟. Amen.

Orémus. Oratio

OMNIPOTENS sempitérne Deus, a quo ómnia immúnda purgántur, et in quo ómnia purgáta claréscunt: súpplices omnipoténtiam tuam invocámus; ut ab his vasis et ornaméntis,

Let us pray. Prayer

Most gracious Father and Lord, hear our prayer, and bless ✠ and sanctify ✠ these vessels prepared for the sacred ministry of thy Church. Through Christ our Lord. ℟. Amen.

Let us pray. Prayer

ALMIGHTY and eternal God, by Whom all things defiled are purified, and in Whom all things purified retain their lustre, humbly we ask thy Omnipotence that these vessels which thy servants offer unto thee, be freed from the contaminating influence of evil spirits, and that by thy blessing ✠ they remain sanctified for holy purpose. Through Christ our Lord. ℟. Amen.

They are sprinkled with holy water.

66

BLESSING OF SACRED VESSELS
or Ornaments in General

℣. Our help is in the name of the Lord.
℟. Who made heaven and earth.
℣. The Lord be with you.
℟. And with thy spirit.

Let us pray. Prayer

Most gracious Father and Lord, hear our prayers, and bless ✠ and sanctify ✠ these vessels and ornaments of the altar prepared for the sacred ministry of thy Church. Through Christ our Lord. ℟. Amen.

Let us pray. Prayer

ALMIGHTY and eternal God, by Whom all things defiled are purified, and in Whom all things purified retain their lustre, humbly we ask thy Omnipotence that the vessels and orna-

quae tibi ófferunt fámuli tui, omnis spíritus immúndus confúsus longe discédat, et per tuam bene ✠ dictiónem ad usum et ministérium sancti Altáris et Ecclésiae tuae sanctificáta permáneant. Per Christum Dóminum nostrum. ℟. Amen.

Et aspergantur aqua benedicta.

67

BENEDICTIO SACERDOTALIUM INDUMENTORUM

℣. Adjutórium nostrum in nómine Dómini.
℟. Qui fecit caelum et terram.
℣. Dóminus vobíscum.
℟. Et cum spíritu tuo.

Orémus.   *Oratio*

Omnípotens, sempitérne Deus, qui per Móysen fámulum tuum pontificália, et sacerdotália, seu levítica vestiménta, ad expléndum in conspéctu tuo ministérium eórum, ad honórem et decórem nóminis tui fíeri decrevísti: adésto propítius invocatiónibus nostris: ut haec induménta sacerdotália (hoc induméntum sacerdótale), désuper irrigánte grátia tua, ingénti benedictióne per nostrae humilitátis servítium puri ✠ ficáre, bene ✠ dícere, et conse ✠ cráre dignéris: ut divínis cúltibus et sacris mystériis apta et benedícta exsístant (aptum et benedíctum exsístat): his quoque sacris véstibus (hac quoque sacra veste) Pontífices, et Sacerdótes, seu Levítae tui indúti, ab ómnibus impulsiónibus, seu tentatiónibus malignórum spirítuum muníti et defénsi esse mereántur: tuísque mystériis apte et condígne servíre et inhaerére, atque in his tibi plácite et devóte perseveráre tríbue. Per Christum Dóminum nostrum. ℟. Amen.

Orémus.   *Oratio*

DEUS, invíctae virtútis triumphátor, et ómnium rérum creátor ac sanctificátor: inténde propítius preces nostras; et haec

ments which thy servants offer unto thee, be freed from the contaminating influence of evil spirits, and that by thy blessing ✠ they remain sanctified for divine worship. Through Christ our Lord. ℞. Amen.

They are sprinkled with holy water.

67

BLESSING OF VESTMENTS

℣. Our help is in the name of the Lord.
℞. Who made heaven and earth.
℣. The Lord be with you.
℞. And with thy spirit.

Let us pray.   Prayer

O almighty, everlasting God, thou didst ordain of old through Moses, thy servant that the sacred vesture of high-priest, priest, and levite be worn to dignify and beautify the worship of thee. Wherefore, mercifully give heed to our supplications, and through our lowly ministry deign to purify, ✠ bless, ✠ and consecrate ✠ these priestly vestments (this priestly vestment), bestowing thereon thy consecration, that they (it) be made fitting for the service of thy holy mysteries. Let every bishop, priest, or deacon vested with them (it) be guarded and defended from all assault or temptation of wicked spirits, and help them to celebrate thy mysteries reverently and well, thus ever rendering unto thee a service pleasing and devout. Through Christ our Lord. ℞. Amen.

Let us pray.   Prayer

O GOD, Author and Sanctifier of every creature, triumphant and unconquerable, graciously bow down to hear us, and

induménta (hoc induméntum) levíticae, sacerdotális, et pontificális glóriae, minístris tuis fruénda (–éndum), tuo ore próprio bene ✠ dícere, sancti ✠ ficáre, et conse ✠ cráre dignéris: omnésque eis (eo) uténtes, tuis mystériis aptos, et tibi in eis devóte ac laudabíliter serviéntes, gratos effícere dignéris. Per Christum Dóminum nostrum. ℞. Amen.

Orémus. Oratio

Dómine Deus omnípotens, qui vestiménta Pontifícibus, Sacerdótibus, et Levítis in usum tabernáculi foéderis necessária, Móysen fámulum tuum ágere jussísti, eúmque spíritu sapiéntiae ad id peragéndum replevísti: haec vestiménta (hoc vestiméntum) in usum et cultum mystérii tui bene ✠ dícere, sancti ✠ ficáre, et conse ✠ cráre dignéris: atque minístros altáris tui, qui ea (id) indúerint, septifórmis Spíritus grátia dignánter repléri, atque castitátis stola, beáta fácias cum bonórum fructu óperum ministérii congruéntis immortalitáte vestíri. Per Dóminum . . . in unitáte ejúsdem Spíritus. ℞. Amen.

Et aspergantur (aspergatur) aqua benedicta.

68

BENEDICTIO MAPPARUM SEU TOBALEARUM ALTARIS

℣. Adjutórium nostrum in nómine Dómini.
℞. Qui fecit caelum et terram.
℣. Dóminus vobíscum.
℞. Et cum spíritu tuo.

Orémus. Oratio

Exáudi, Dómine, preces nostras: et haec lineámina (hoc linteámen), sacri Altáris úsui praeparáta (–um), bene ✠ dícere, et sancti ✠ ficáre dignéris. Per Christum Dóminum nostrum. ℞. Amen.

with thine own lips bless, ✠ sanctify, ✠ and consecrate ✠ these vestments (this vestment) destined to be worn by thine anointed ones. Clothed with them, may they celebrate thy mysteries devoutly and praiseworthily, and thus become beloved of thee. Through Christ our Lord. ℟. Amen.

Let us pray. *Prayer*

O LORD God Omnipotent, Who didst command Moses, thy servant to see to the making of sacerdotal vesture for the worship of the former covenant, and didst inspire him with wisdom to perfect thy wish; vouchsafe to bless, ✠ sanctify, ✠ and consecrate ✠ these vestments (this vestment) to thy holy service. Clothed with them, may the ministrants of thine altar be filled with the sevenfold grace of the Holy Spirit and endowed with the stole of chastity, that serving thee faithfully they may be rewarded finally with a blessed immortality. Through Jesus Christ, thy Son, our Lord, Who liveth and reigneth with thee in the unity of the same Holy Spirit, God, eternally. ℟. Amen.

They (it is) are sprinkled with holy water.

68

BLESSING OF ALTAR LINENS

℣. Our help is in the name of the Lord.
℟. Who made heaven and earth.
℣. The Lord be with you.
℟. And with thy spirit.

Let us pray. *Prayer*

Hear, O Lord, our prayers, and bless ✠ and sanctify ✠ these linens (this linen) made for the vesting of thy holy altar. Through Christ our Lord. ℟. Amen.

Orémus.   Oratio

DÓMINE Deus omnípotens, qui Móysen fámulum tuum ornaménta et linteámina fácere per quadragínta dies do cuísti, quae étiam María téxuit, et fecit in usum ministérii tabernáculi foéderis; bene ✠ dícere, sancti ✠ ficáre, et conse ✠ cráre dignéris haec linteámina (hoc linteámen) ad tegéndum involvendúmque altáre gloriosíssimi Fílii tui, Dómini nostri Jesu Christi: Qui tecum vivit et regnat in unitáte Spíritus Sancti Deus, per ómnia saécula saeculórum. ℟. Amen.

Et aspergantur (aspergatur) aquae benedicta.

69

BENEDICTIO PALLAE ET CORPORALIS

℣. Adjutórium nostrum in nómine Dómini.
℟. Qui fecit caelum et terram.
℣. Dóminus vobíscum.
℟. Et cum spíritu tuo.

Orémus.   Oratio

Clementíssime Dómine, cujus inenarrábilis est virtus, cujus mystéria arcánis mirabílibus celebrántur: tríbue, quaésumus; ut hoc linteámen tuae propitiatiónis bene ✠ dictióne sanctificétur ad consecrándum super illud Corpus et Sánguinem Dei et Dómini nostri Jesu Christi, Fílii tui: Qui tecum vivit et regnat in unitáte Spíritus Sancti Deus, per ómnia saécula saeculórum. ℟. Amen.

Orémus.   Oratio

OMNÍPOTENS sempitérne Deus, bene ✠ dícere, sancti ✠ ficáre, et conse ✠ cráre dignéris linteámen istud ad tegéndum involvendúmque Corpus et Sánguinem Dómini nostri Jesu Christi, Fílii tui: Qui tecum vivit et regnat in unitáte Spíritus Sancti Deus, per ómnia saécula saeculórum. ℟. Amen.

Translator's Note: The pall and corporal should be blessed together, with the blessing given here.

Let us pray. *Prayer*

O LORD God Omnipotent, Who for forty days didst instruct Moses, thy servant in the making of linens and sacred appointments, and didst cause Mary to weave linens for the service of the old covenant; deign to bless, ✠ sanctify, ✠ and consecrate ✠ these linens (this linen), that they (it) may fittingly vest the altar of thy most glorious Son, Jesus Christ, our Lord, Who liveth and reigneth with thee in unity of the Holy Spirit, God, eternally. ℞. Amen.

They (it is) are sprinkled with holy water.

69

BLESSING OF A PALL AND CORPORAL

℣. Our help is in the name of the Lord.
℞. Who made heaven and earth.
℣. The Lord be with you.
℞. And with thy spirit.

Let us pray. *Prayer*

Most gracious and merciful Lord, Whose strength is indescribable and Whose mysteries are solemnized with wondrous symbols! Grant, we pray, that this linen be sanctified by thy blessing, ✠ for upon it will be consecrated the Body and Blood of our Lord and God, Jesus Christ, thy Son, Who liveth and reigneth with thee in unity of the Holy Spirit, God, forevermore. ℞. Amen.

Let us pray. *Prayer*

A LMIGHTY and everlasting God, bless, ✠ sanctify, ✠ and consecrate ✠ this linen, that it may protect and enshroud the Body and Blood of Jesus Christ, thy Son, our Lord, Who liveth and reigneth with thee in unity of the Holy Spirit, God, forever and ever. ℞. Amen.

Orémus.   Oratio

O MNÍPOTENS Deus, mánibus nostris opem tuae benedictiónis infúnde: ut per nostram bene ✠dictiónem hoc linteámen sanctificétur, et Córporis ac Sánguinis Redemptóris nostri novum sudárium, Spíritus Sancti grátia efficiátur. Per eúndem Dóminum nostrum Jesum Christum, Fílium tuum: Qui tecum vivit et regnat in unitáte ejúsdem Spíritus Sancti Deus, per ómnia saécula saeculórum. ℞. Amen.

Et aspergatur aqua benedicta.

70

RITUS ERIGENDI STATIONES VIAE CRUCIS
Proprius Ordinis Minorum

Sacerdos, superpelliceo et stola violacei coloris indutus, uno saltem Clerico adhibito, qui ei opportuno tempore porrigere possit vasculum aquae benedictae cum aspersorio, et thuribulum cum incensi navicula, ascendit Altare, ibique stans brevi sermone super praestantia et utilitate pii exercitii Viae Crucis populum alloquitur. Deinde genuflexus in infimo gradu intonat Hymnum: **Veni, Creátor Spíritus,** (pag. 226), quem chorus prosequitur.

Hymno finito, Sacerdos dicit:

℣. Emítte Spiritum tuum, et creabúntur.

℞. Et renovábis fáciem terrae.

Orémus.   Oratio

D EUS, qui corda fidélium Sancti Spíritus illustratióne docuísti: da nobis in eódem Spíritu recta sápere, et de ejus semper consolatióne gaudére.

D EFÉNDE, quaésumus, Dómine, beata María semper Vírgine intercedénte, istum (–am) ab omni adversitáte pópulum (vel famíliam): et toto corde tibi prostrátum (–am), ab hóstium propítius tuére cleménter insídiis.

A CTIÓNES nostras, quaésumus, Dómine, aspirándo praéveni, et adjuvándo prósequere: ut cuncta nostra orátio et operátio

Let us pray.

O ALMIGHTY God, bestow on us thy power of benediction, that by our blessing ✠ this linen be sanctified, and by the grace of the Holy Spirit it become a new napkin for the Body and Blood of our Redeemer. Through the same Jesus Christ, thy Son, our Lord, Who liveth and reigneth with thee in unity of the Holy Spirit, God, eternally. ℟. Amen.

It is sprinkled with holy water.

70

BLESSING AND ERECTING STATIONS OF THE CROSS
Reserved to the Order of Friars Minor

The priest who has this faculty vests in surplice and purple stole. He should be assisted by at least one cleric who at the times designated hands him the aspersory and thurible. From the altar-predella he addresses the people briefly on the excellence and value of the devotion of the Way of the Cross. Then kneeling on the lowest step, he intones the **Veni Creator** (See page 227) which is continued by the choir.

Following the hymn, he sings:

℣. Send forth thy Spirit, and the world shall arise as new.

℟. And the countenance of the earth shall be renewed.

Let us pray.

O GOD, Who didst teach the hearts of the faithful by the enlightening of the Holy Spirit, grant us by the same Spirit ever to choose wisely and to rejoice in His comfort.

P ROTECT thy people, we beseech thee, O Lord, from every adversity, Mary ever Virgin interceding on their behalf; and as they fervently prostrate themselves before thee, mercifully guard them from Satan's cunning.

W E BESEECH thee, Lord, inspire and guide our works in their beginning, and accompany them unto fruition, that

a te semper incípiat, et per te coepta finiátur. Per Dóminum nostrum Jesum Christum, Fílium tuum: Qui tecum vivit et regnat in unitáte Spíritus Sancti Deus, per ómnia saécula saeculórum. ℞. Amen.

Deinde fit benedictio tabularum pictarum seu imaginum Stationum, si adsint.

℣. Adjutórium nostrum in nómine Dómini.
℞. Qui fecit caelum et terram.
℣. Dóminus vobíscum.
℞. Et cum spíritu tuo.

Orémus.   Oratio

OMNÍPOTENS sempitérne Deus, qui Sanctórum tuórum imágines sculpi aut pingi non réprobas, ut, quóties illas óculis córporis intuémur, tóties eórum actus et sanctitátem ad imitándum memóriae óculis meditémur: has, quaésumus, imágines, in honórem et memóriam unigéniti Fílii tui Dómini nostri Jesu Christi adaptátas, bene ✝ dícere, et sancti ✝ ficáre dignéris; et praesta; ut, quicúmque coram illis unigénitum Fílium tuum supplíciter cólere et honoráre studúerit, illíus méritis et obténtu, a te grátiam in praesénti, et aetérnam glóriam obtíneat in futúrum. Per eúndem Christum Dóminum nostrum. ℞. Amen.

Tunc Sacerdos eas aspergit aqua benedicta, et incensat. In Oratorio privato omitti potest incensatio.

Postea Sacerdos benedicit quatuordecim Cruces, quae ex ligno esse debent.

℣. Adjutórium nostrum in nómine Dómini.
℞. Qui fecit caelum et terram.
℣. Dóminus vobíscum.
℞. Et cum spíritu tuo.

Orémus.   Oratio

ROGÁMUS te, Dómine sancte, Pater omnípotens, aetérne Deus: ut dignéris bene ✝ dícere haec signa Crucis, ut sint remédia salutária géneri humáno; sint solíditas fídei, proféctus

our every prayer and work may ever begin with thee, and
through thee be accomplished. Through Jesus Christ, thy Son,
our Lord, Who liveth and reigneth with thee in unity of the
Holy Spirit, God, in eternity. Ry. Amen.

Then follows the blessings of the images or paintings which are a
part of the stations:

Vy. Our help is in the name of the Lord.

Ry. Who made heaven and earth.

Vy. The Lord be with you.

Ry. And with thy spirit.

Let us pray.   Prayer

ALMIGHTY, everlasting God! Thou dost approve of the
sculptured or painted images of thy saints, so that when
we behold them, we may be led to contemplate and imitate their
lives and holiness. Wherefore, we thy suppliants pray that thou
wouldst bless ✠ and sanctify ✠ these likenesses wrought to the
memory and honor of thy Sole-Begotten Son, our Lord Jesus
Christ. And grant that whosoever, through the inspiration of
these images, strives to honor and worship Him, may by His
merits obtain grace in this life and eternal glory in the next.
Through the selfsame Christ our Lord. Ry. Amen.

The Priest sprinkles them with holy water, and incenses them. In a
private oratory the incensation may be omitted.

Then the fourteen wood crosses are blessed:

Vy. Our help is in the name of the Lord.

Ry. Who made heaven and earth.

Vy. The Lord be with you.

Ry. And with thy spirit.

Let us pray.   Prayer

WE BESEECH thee, holy Lord, almighty Father, eternal
God to bless ✠ these crosses, that they be salutary to mankind. Let them be a strengthening of faith, a motive for good

bonórum óperum, redémptio animárum; sint solámen, et protéctio, ac tutéla contra saeva jácula inimicórum. Per Christum
Dóminum nostrum. ℟. Amen.

Orémus.   Oratio

B ÉNE✠ DIC, Dómine Jesu Christe, has Cruces, quia per
   Crucem sanctam tuam eripuísti mundum a potestáte daémonum, et superásti passióne tua suggestórem peccáti, qui
gaudébat in praevaricatióne primi hóminis per ligni vétiti
sumptiónem.

Tunc Sacerdos eas aspergens aqua benedicta, dicit:

S ANCTIFICÉNTUR haec signa Crucis in nómine Pa✠ tris,
  et Fí✠ lii, et Spíritus✠ Sancti: ut orántes, inclinantésque
se propter Dóminum ante istas Cruces, invéniant córporis et
ánimae sanitátem. Per eúndem Christum Dóminum nostrum.
℟. Amen.

Deinde, ubi fit processio, cantantur sequentes Hymni:

Hymnus

Vexíl- la Re- gis próde-unt : Fulget Crucis my-sté-ri-um,

Qua vi-ta mortem pértu-lit, Et mor- te vi - tam pró-tu-lit.

2. Quae vulne-rá- ta lánce-ae Mucróne di-ro críminum

Ut nos lavá- ret sórdibus, Ma-ná- vit unda et sánguine.

3. Implé- ta sunt quae cón-cinit David fidé- li cármine,

Dicéndo na-ti-ó- nibus : Regná- vit a ligno De-us.

works, and salvation to souls. May they be comfort, protection, and a safeguard against the cruel darts of the enemy. Through Christ our Lord. ℞. Amen.

Let us pray. Prayer

BLESS, ✠ O Lord, these crosses, for by thy holy Cross thou hast snatched the world from Satan's grasp, and hast conquered by thy passion the tempter who rejoiced in Adam's partaking of the forbidden tree.

He sprinkles them with holy water, saying:

MAY these crosses be blessed, in the name of the Father, ✠ and of the Son, ✠ and of the Holy ✠ Spirit; and may they who kneel in prayer before them in honor of our Lord, experience health of soul and body. Through the selfsame Christ our Lord. ℞. Amen.

If there will be a procession, the following hymns are sung:

Hymn

Abroad the Regal Banners fly,
Now shines the Cross's mystery;
Upon it Life did death endure,
And yet by death did life procure.

Who, wounded with a direful spear,
Did, purposely to wash us clear
From stain of sin, pour out a flood
Of precious Water mixed with Blood.

That which the Prophet-King of old
Hath in mysterious verse foretold,
Is now accomplished, whilst we see
God ruling nations from a Tree.

4. Arbor decó-ra et fúl- gi-da, Ornáta Re-gis púrpura,

Elécta digno sti-pi-te Tam sanc- ta membra tángere.

5. Be-á- ta, cu- jus brá-chi- is Pré-ti-um pepéndit saécu-li :

Staté-ra fac-ta córpo-ris, Tu- lít- que praedam tárta-ri.

6. O Crux ave, spes ú- ni-ca, In hac tri-úmphi gló-ri-a :[1]

Pi-is adáuge gráti-am, Re- ís- que, de-le crímina. 7. Te,

fons sa-lú- tis Trí - ni-tás, Colláu-det om-nis spí-ritus :

Quibus Crucis victó- ri-am Lar- gí- ris, adde praémi-um.

A- men.

[1] Tempore Passionis dicitur: Hoc passiónis témpore. Tempore Paschali dicitur: Paschále quae fers gáudium.

Hymnus

VI

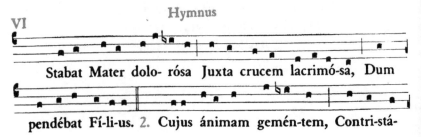

Stabat Mater dolo- rósa Juxta crucem lacrimó-sa, Dum

pendébat Fí-li-us. 2. Cujus ánimam gemén-tem, Contri-stá-

O lovely and refulgent Tree,
Adorned with purpled majesty;
Culled from a worthy stock, to bear
Those Limbs which sanctified were.

Blest Tree, whose happy branches bore
The wealth that did the world restore;
The beam that did that Body weigh
Which raised up hell's expected prey.

Hail, Cross, of hopes the most sublime!
Now in this mournful Passion time, *
Improve religious souls in grace,
The sins of criminals efface.

Blest Trinity, salvation's spring,
May every soul Thy praises sing:
To those Thou grantest conquest by
The holy Cross, rewards apply.

Hymn

At the Cross her station keeping,
Stood the mournful Mother weeping,
Close to Jesus to the last:
Through her heart, His sorrows sharing,
All His bitter anguish bearing,
Now at length the sword had passed.

---

* Outside of Passiontide this line reads: In this the glory of thy conquest.
In Paschaltide it reads: Which beareth joys of Paschaltide.

tam et do-léntem Pertransí-vit glá-di-us. 3. O quam tristis

et afflícta Fu-it illa benedícta Mater Uni-géni-ti! 4. Quae

maerébat et do-lébat, Pi-a Ma-ter, dum vidébat Nati poenas

íncly-ti. 5. Quis est homo qui non fleret, Matrem Christi si

vidéret In tanto supplí-ci-o? 6. Quis non posset contristá-ri,

Christi Matrem contemplári Doléntem cum Fí-li-o? 7. Pro

peccá-tis su-ae gentis, Vidit Jesum in tor-méntis, Et flagéllis

súbditum. 8. Vidit su-um dul-cem natum Mori-éndo deso-

látum, Dum emísit spíri-tum. 9. E-ja Ma-ter, fons amóris,

Me sentíre vim doló-ris Fac, ut tecum lúge-am. 10. Fac, ut

ár-de-at cor me-um In amándo Christum De-um, Ut si-bi

compláce-am.   A- men.

℣. Adorámus te, Christe, et benedícimus tibi.
℟. Quia per sanctam Crucem tuam redemísti mundum.

Oh, how sad and sore distressed
Was that Mother highly blest
of the sole-begotten One!
Christ above in torment hangs;
She beneath beholds the pangs
Of her dying glorious Son.

Is there one who would not weep,
Whelmed in miseries so deep
Christ's dear Mother to behold?
Can the human heart refrain
From partaking in her pain,
In that Mother's pain untold?

Bruised, derided, cursed, defiled,
She beheld her tender Child
All with bloody scourges rent;
For the sins of His own nation,
Saw Him hang in desolation,
Till His Spirit forth He sent.

O thou Mother! fount of love!
Touch my spirit from above,
Make my heart with thine accord:
Make me feel as thou hast felt;
Make my soul to glow and melt
With the love of Christ my Lord.

℣. We adore thee, O Christ, and we bless thee.
℟. For by thy holy Cross thou hast redeemed the world.

Orémus.   Oratio

D EUS, qui nos ínclyta passióne Fílii tui per viam Crucis ad
aetérnam glóriam perveníre docuísti: concéde propítius; ut
quem piis ad Calváriae locum sociámus afféctibus, in suis étiam
triúmphis pérpetim subsequámur: Qui tecum vivit et regnat in
saécula saeculórum. ℟. Amen.

Sacerdos accedens ad locum primae Stationis, osculatur Crucem et
tabulam, easque, vel per se, vel per laicum decenti habitu indutum,
collocat in loco ad id praeparato; deinde legit meditationem et preces
huic Stationi respondentes: quod et fiet in ceteris Stationibus. Quibus
finitis cantatur Hymnus: **Te Deum laudámus** (pag. 58).

℣. **Benedicámus Patrem, et Fílium, cum Sancto Spíritu.**

℟. **Laudémus, et superexaltémus eum in saécula.**

Orémus.   Oratio

D EUS, cujus misericórdiae non est númerus, et bonitátis infinítus est thesáurus, piíssimae majestáti tuae pro collátis
donis grátias ágimus: tuam semper cleméntiam exorántes; ut,
qui peténtibus postuláta concédis, eósdem non déserens, ad praémia futura dispónas. Per Christum Dóminum nostrum. ℟.
Amen.

Tunc Sacerdos benedicit populum cum Cruce.
Affixio autem Crucium et tabularum Stationum fieri potest a quocumque privatim sine caeremoniis, etiam alio tempore sive post sive
ante ipsarum benedictionem faciendam a Sacerdote in loco, in quo
Stationes sunt erigendae.

Formula ad fidem faciendam de erectione
Viae Crucis

V IGORE facultatis mihi commissae ego N. N. Viam Crucis
cum adnexis Indulgentiis erexi in loco ut supra in precibus,
juxta regulas a S. Indulgentiarum Congregatione die 10 Maji
1742 praescriptas. In quorum fidem testimonium hoc mea manu
exaravi hac die, etc.   N. N.

Let us pray.   Prayer

O GOD, Who in the glorious passion of thy Son hast taught us to gain heaven by the royal road of the cross, mercifully grant us who devoutly associate ourselves with Him on Calvary, to reign in triumph with Him in glory. Who liveth and reigneth with thee eternally. R̷. Amen.

The priest, coming to the place of the first station, kisses the cross, and then hangs it in place with his own hands or with the aid of a layman who is properly dressed for the service. He then reads the meditation and prayers proper to this station. The same is done in the case of each station. At the conclusion the **Te Deum** is sung (page 59).

V̷. **Let us worship the Father, and the Son, with the Holy Spirit.**

R̷. **Let us praise and exalt Him forever.**

Let us pray.   Prayer

O GOD, Whose mercy is without limits and Whose goodness is a boundless treasury! We thank thy loving Sublimity for bountiful favors, and perseveringly appeal to thy clemency. Desert us not, thou Who hearest thy suppliants, but speed us to final victory. Through Christ our Lord. R̷. Amen.

The priest blesses the people with a crucifix.

The fastening of the stations to the walls may be done privately by anyone and without ceremony, whether before or after their blessing by the priest.

Following is the form for the document in testimony of the formal erecting of the stations:

I N VIRTUE of the faculty granted me, I N.N. erected the Way of the Cross with its annexed indulgences at the place named above in the delegation, in accordance with the rules prescribed by the Congregation of Sacred Indulgences on May 10, 1742. In testimony of which I add my signature on this day, etc.   (Signed):

71

SOLEMNIS BENEDICTIO CRUCIS

Si Cruces, publicae venerationi expositae, solemniter benedicantur, haec benedictio Ordinario reservatur, qui tamen potest eam cuilibet Sacerdoti committere.

Privatim autem haec benedictio a quolibet Sacerdote fieri potest sine ulla Ordinarii licentia.

℣. Adjutórium nostrum in nómine Dómini.

℟. Qui fecit caelum et terram.

℣. Dóminus vobíscum.

℟. Et cum spíritu tuo.

Orémus.   Oratio

Rogámus te, Dómine sancte, Pater omnípotens, aetérne, Deus: ut dignéris bene ✠ dícere hoc signum Crucis, ut sit remédium salutáre genéri humáno; sit solíditas fídei, proféctus bonórum óperum, redémptio animárum; sit solámen, et protéctio, ac tutéla contra saeva jácula inimicórum. Per Christum Dóminum nostrum. ℟. Amen.

Orémus.   Oratio

BÉNE ✠ DIC, Dómine Jesu Christe, hanc Crucem, per quam eripuísti mundum a potestáte daémonum, et superásti passióne tua suggestórem peccáti, qui gaudébat in praevaricatióne primi hóminis per ligni vétiti sumptiónem. Hic aspergatur aqua benedicta. Sanctificétur hoc signum Crucis in nómine Pa ✠ tris, et Fí ✠ lii, et Spíritus ✠ Sancti; ut orántes, inclinantésque se propter Dóminum ante istam Crucem, invéniant córporis et ánimae sanitátem. Per eúndem Christum Dóminum nostrum. ℟. Amen.

2. Postea Sacerdos ante Crucem genuflexus ipsam devote adorat, et osculatur, et idem faciunt quicumque voluerint.

71

SOLEMN BLESSING OF A CROSS

If a cross is to be exposed for public veneration, it should be solemnly blessed. This blessing is reserved to the Ordinary who may delegate any priest to perform it.

If the cross is for private use, it may be blessed by any priest without the Ordinary's permission:

℣. Our help is in the name of the Lord.

℟. Who made heaven and earth.

℣. The Lord be with you.

℟. And with thy spirit.

Let us pray. Prayer

O HOLY Lord, almighty Father, eternal God, bless ✠ this cross that it be a saving help to mankind. Let it be a bulwark of faith, an encouragement to good works, the redemption of souls; and may it be consolation, protection, and a shield against the cruel darts of the enemy. Through Christ our Lord. ℟. Amen.

Let us pray. Prayer

BLESS, ✠ O Lord Jesus Christ, this cross by which thou hast snatched the world from Satan's grasp and upon which thou hast overcome by thy suffering him, who is the prompter of sin, who rejoiced in Adam's deception at the accursed tree of Paradise. Here it is sprinkled with holy water. May this symbol of salvation be sanctified in the name of the Father, ✠ and of the Son, ✠ and of the Holy ✠ Spirit, and may all who kneel and pray before this cross for our Lord's honor receive health of body and soul. Through the selfsame Christ our Lord. ℟. Amen.

2. After this the priest, kneeling before the crucifix, devoutly venerates and kisses it, and others may do likewise.

72

BENEDICTIO SOLEMNIOR CRUCIS

Paratis thure thuribuloque cum igne, et aqua benedicta, Sacerdos delegatus, superpelliceo, stola et pluviali rubri coloris indutus, stans dicit:

℣. Adjutórium nostrum in nómine Dómini.

℞. Qui fecit caelum et terram.

℣. Dóminus vobíscum.

℞. Et cum spíritu tuo.

Orémus.   Oratio

Béne ✠ dic, Dómine Jesu Christe, hanc Crucem, per quam eripuísti mundum a potestáte daémonum, et superásti passióne tua suggestórem peccáti, qui gaudébat in praevaricatióne primi hóminis per ligni vétiti sumptiónem: Qui cum Deo Patre et Spíritu Sancto vivis et regnas in saécula saeculórum. ℞. Amen.

Orémus.   Oratio

ROGÁMUS te, Dómine sancte, Pater omnípotens, sempitérne Deus: ut dignéris bene ✠ dícere hoc signum Crucis, ut sit remédium salutáre géneri humáno: sit solíditas fídei, proféctus bonórum óperum, redémptio animárum: sit solámen et protéctio ac tutéla contra saeva jácula inimicórum. Per Dóminum nostrum Jesum Christum, Fílium tuum: Qui tecum vivit et regnat in unitáte Spíritus Sancti Deus.

Deinde dicit voce mediocri, extensis manibus ante pectus, Praefationem.

℣. Per ómnia saécula saeculórum.

℞. Amen.

℣. Dóminus vobíscum.

℞. Et cum spíritu tuo.

℣. Sursum corda.

℞. Habémus ad Dóminum.

72

THE MORE SOLEMN BLESSING OF A CROSS

Having at hand the censer and holy water, the priest delegated for this blessing, vested in surplice, red stole, and cope, says:

℣. Our help is in the name of the Lord.
℟. Who made heaven and earth.
℣. The Lord be with you.
℟. And with thy spirit.

Let us pray.   Prayer

Bless, ✠ O Lord Jesus Christ, this cross by which thou hast snatched the world from Satan's grasp, and upon which thou hast overcome by thy suffering him, who is the prompter of sin, who rejoiced in Adam's deception at the accursed tree of Paradise. Thou Who livest and reignest with the Father and the Holy Spirit in eternity. ℟. Amen.

Let us pray.   Prayer

O HOLY Lord, almighty Father, eternal God, bless ✠ this cross that it be a saving help to mankind. Let it be a bulwark of faith, an encouragement to good works, the redemption of souls; and may it be consolation, protection, and a shield against the cruel darts of the enemy. Through Jesus Christ, thy Son, our Lord, Who liveth and reigneth with thee in unity of the Holy Spirit, God,

Then with hands extended he prays the following preface in a moderately loud voice:

℣. World without end.
℟. Amen.
℣. The Lord be with you.
℟. And with thy spirit.
℣. Lift up your hearts.
℟. We have lifted them up to the Lord.

℣. Grátias agámus Dómino, Deo nostro.

℞. Dignum et justum est.

VERE dignum et justum est, aequum et salutáre, nos tibi semper et ubíque grátias ágere, Dómine sancte, Pater omnípotens, aetérne Deus: cujus sanctum ac terríbile Nomen, inter céteras visíbiles creatúras, ligna quoque fructífera laudáre ac benedícere non cessant: qui in figúram unigénitae Sapiéntiae tuae ligno vitae a princípio paradísum voluptátis ornásti, ut ejúsdem fructu, sacro mystério, Protoparéntes nostri géneris mortem cavére, et vitam admonéres obtinére perpétuam: quique nos vétitae árboris attáctu justae morti addíctos, ejúsdem coaetérnae tibi Sapiéntiae, Dei et Dómini nostri Jesu Christi, innóxia morte ad vitam misericórditer revocáre dignátus es: Te súpplices exorámus, ut hoc singuláre signum, quod ad exémplum primi illíus sacratíssimi vexílli, quo pretióso Fílii tui sánguine triumphásti, fidélium tuórum devotióne compáctum, erectúmque est, caelésti tua bene ✠ dictióne sanctificáre dignéris; ut ómnibus hic génua flecténtibus, ac tuae Majestáti supplicántibus, lárgior et cordis compúnctio, et admissórum indulgéntia concedátur, atque intercedénte ipsa victoriosíssima unigéniti Fílii tui passióne, et tibi plácita postuláre, et cítius váleant postuláta percípere. Da, quaésumus, clementíssime Pater, in quo vívimus, movémur et sumus: ut, quóties triúmphum divínae humilitátis, quae supérbiam nostri hostis dejécit, óculis intuémur quotiésque mente recólimus, et contra hostem ipsum fidúciam fortitúdinis, et majórem tibi devótae humilitátis grátiam consequámur: quátenus in illo treméndo tuae Majestátis exámine, cum pavéntibus eleméntis, caelorúmque commótis virtútibus, signum istud gloríficum redemptiónis nostrae apparúerit in caelo, ipsi de morte ad vitam transíre, ac perpétua beátae resurrectiónis vidére gáudia mereámur. Quod sequitur, dicitur submissa voce legendo, ita tamen, ut a circumstantibus audiri possit: Per eúndem Dóminum nostrum Jesum Christum, Fílium tuum: Qui tecum vivit et regnat in unitáte Spíritus Sancti Deus, per ómnia saécula saeculórum. ℞. Amen.

℣. Let us give thanks to the Lord, our God.

℞. It is meet and just.

IT IS truly meet and just, right and salutary that ever and everywhere we give thanks to thee, holy Lord, almighty Father, eternal God. For among thy visible creatures, fruitful trees do praise and worship unceasingly thy awesome majesty. In figure of thy Sole-Begotten Wisdom, thou didst in the beginning beautify the Garden of Eden with the tree of life, and by its fruit, as by a holy symbol, thou didst admonish our First Parents to beware of death and seek perpetual life. We too condemned to a just death by the contamination of the forbidden tree, were mercifully recalled from death to life by the selfsame coeternal Wisdom, Jesus Christ, our God and Lord. Wherefore, we thy suppliants implore that thou wouldst sanctify with thy celestial blessing ✠ this singular symbol wrought and raised up for the faithful's devotion, as a remembrance of that first sacred standard on which thou didst triumph by the precious blood of thy Son. May all who kneel before it as thy petitioners win heartfelt sorrow for crimes and forgiveness, and in merit of the victorious suffering and death of thy Sole-Begotten Son, may they seek what pleases thee, and speedily obtain what they ask for. Grant, we pray, O most loving Father in Whom we live, and move, and have our being, that as often as we behold and call to mind the triumphant sign of thy divine humility which crushed the pride of our foe, we may obtain strong confidence against the enemy and greater humility before thee. And on that dreadful day of Judgment, when the elements shall quake, and the powers of heaven be moved, and this glorified sign of our redemption shall appear in the skies, may we pass from death to life, and see the perpetual joys of a blessed resurrection. What follows is said in a subdued tone, loud enough, however, to be heard by the bystanders: Through the same Jesus Christ, thy Son, our Lord, Who liveth and reigneth with thee in unity of the Holy Spirit, God, forevermore. ℞. Amen.

Orémus.   Oratio

DEUS, qui beátae Crucis patíbulum, quod prius erat sceléstis ad poenam, convertísti redémptis ad vitam: concéde plebi tuae, ejus vallári praesídio, cujus est armáta vexíllo. Sit ei Crux fídei fundaméntum, spei suffrágium, in advérsis defénsio, in prósperis adjuvámen: sit ei in hostes victória, in civitáte custódia, in campis protéctio, in domo fultúra: ut per eam Pastor in futúro gregem consérvet incólumem, quae nobis, Agno ✠ vincénte, convérsa est in salútem. Per eúndem Dóminum nostrum Jesum Christum, Fílium tuum: Qui tecum vivit et regnat in unitáte Spíritus Sancti Deus, per ómnia saécula saeculórum. ℟. Amen.

Orémus.   Oratio

SANCTÍ ✠ FICA, Dómine Jesu Christe, signáculum istud passiónis tuae: ut sit inimícis tuis obstáculum, et credéntibus in te perpétuum efficiátur victóriae vexíllum: Qui cum Deo Patre vivis et regnas in unitáte Spíritus Sancti Deus, per ómnia saécula saeculórum. ℟. Amen.

Tum offertur Sacerdoti thus in navicula, quod stans benedicit, dicens:

Orémus.   Oratio

DÓMINE Deus omnípotens, cui assístit exércitus Angelórum cum tremóre, quorum servítium spirituále, et ígneum esse cognóscitur: dignáre respícere, bene ✠ dícere, et sancti ✠ ficáre hanc creatúram incénsi, ut omnes languóres, omnésque infirmitátes, atque insídiae inimíci, odórem ejus sentiéntes, effúgiant, et separéntur a plásmate tuo; ut numquam laedátur a morsu antíqui serpéntis, quod pretióso Fílii tui sánguine redemísti. Per eúndem Christum Dóminum nostrum. ℟. Amen.

Quo facto, Sacerdos imponit thus in thuribulum. Deinde aspergit Crucem aqua benedicta, et mox eam incensat. Tunc dicit adhuc stans:

Let us pray.   Prayer

O GOD, Who by the instrument of the blessed cross, a one-time instrument of punishment for criminals, hast brought back life to thy redeemed, grant thy faithful to find in it a fortress of support, who see in it their standard of battle. Let the cross be unto them a foundation of faith, a pillar of hope, a defense in adversity, a service in prosperity, a victory amid enemies, a guard in cities, a protection in the country, a prop in their homes. By it may the Good Shepherd preserve His flock unscathed, for on it did the conquering Lamb ✠ win our salvation. Through the same Jesus Christ, thy Son, our Lord, Who liveth and reigneth with thee in unity of the Holy Spirit, God, for all eternity. ℟. Amen.

Let us pray.   Prayer

SANCTIFY, ✠ O Lord Jesus Christ, this seal of thy passion, that it be a stumbling-block to thine enemies, but unto thy beloved a perpetual banner of victory. Who livest and reignest with God the Father in the unity of the Holy Spirit, God, forever and ever. ℟. Amen.

The priest blesses the incense, saying:

Let us pray.   Prayer

O LORD God Almighty, before Whom the host of angelic spirits stands in awe, and renders thee a spiritual service glowing with love, deign to look with favor upon this creature of incense, and bless ✠ it and sanctify ✠ it. May every weakness, every infirmity, and every inimical assault, sensing its fragrance, fly and be separated from thy creature, man, that he whom thou hast redeemed by the precious blood of thy Son, may never suffer from the bite of the ancient serpent. Through the same Christ our Lord. ℟. Amen.

Then the priest puts incense into the thurible, sprinkles the cross with holy water, and incenses it.

If the cross is made of wood, he adds the prayer indicated by 1; if of metal or stone, the prayer indicated by 2:

1. Si Crux sit ex ligno:

SANCTIFICÉTUR lignum istud in nómine Pa ✠ tris, et Fí ✠ lii, et Spíritus ✠ Sancti: et benedíctio illíus ligni, in quo membra sancta Salvatóris suspénsa sunt, sit in isto ligno; ut orántes inclinantésque se propter Deum ante istam Crucem, invéniant córporis et ánimae sanitátem. Per eúndem Dóminum nostrum Jesum Christum, Fílium tuum: Qui tecum vivit et regnat in unitáte ejúsdem Spíritus Sancti Deus, per ómnia saécula saeculórum. ℞. Amen.

Tum Sacerdos, flexis ante Crucem genibus, ipsam devote adorat, et osculatur. Idem faciunt quicumque voluerint.

2. Si vero Crux sit ex metallo vel lapide:

DEUS glóriae, Deus excélse Sábaoth, fortíssime Emmánuel, Deus Pater veritátis, Pater sapiéntiae, Pater beatitúdinis, Pater illuminatiónis ac vigilatiónis nostrae; qui mundum regis, qui cuncta regna dispónis, qui es bonórum collátor múnerum, et bonórum ómnium attribútor; cui omnes gentes, pópuli, tribus et linguae sérviunt; cui assístit omnis Angelórum légio; qui largíris fámulis tuis fidem et laudem tui nóminis, ut débita tibi obláta persólvant: cui prius fides offeréntium cómplacet, deínde sacrificátur oblátio: quaésumus exorábilem misericórdiae tuae pietátem, ut sanctí ✠ fices tibi hoc signum Crucis, et cónse ✠ cres, quod tota mentis devotióne famulórum tuórum religiósa fides constrúxit, trophaéum scílicet victóriae tuae ac redemptiónis nostrae, quod in amórem Christi triumphális glória consecrávit. Aspice hoc signum Crucis insuperábile, per quod diáboli exinaníta est potéstas, mortálium restitúta libértas: quae licet fúerit aliquándo in poenam, sed nunc versa est in honórem per grátiam, et quae reos quondam puniébat supplício, nunc et nóxios absólvit a débito. Et tibi quid per hoc placére pótuit, nisi id, per quod tibi plácuit nos redímere? Et nullum tibi débitum ámplius munus est, quam quod tibi tunc córporis dedicávit affíxio: nec tibi est magis familiáris oblátio, quam quae familiári mánuum tuárum extensióne sacráta est. Illis ergo mánibus hanc Crucem áccipe, quibus illam ampléxus es, et de sanctitáte illíus hanc sanctí ✠ fica:

(1.):

MAY this wood be sanctified, in the name of the Father, ✝ and of the Son, ✝ and of the Holy ✝ Spirit; and may this blessing be in the wood on which the sacred members of the Savior were hung, so that all who adore God as they kneel in prayer before this cross may have health of soul and body. Through the same Jesus Christ, thy Son, our Lord, Who liveth and reigneth with thee in unity of the Holy Spirit, God, eternally. ℟. Amen.

After this the priest, kneeling before the cross, devoutly venerates and kisses it, and others who wish may do likewise.

(2.):

O GOD of beauty, God of Sabaoth, Emmanuel the Strong One, God the Father of truth, Father of Wisdom, Father of holiness, Father of light and vigilance! Thou rulest the world, thou reignest over kingdoms, thou art the dispenser of gifts and disposer of all goods. Thee, nations, peoples, tribes, and tongues serve; before thee all angelic legions assist. Thou givest thy servants the powers of faith and worship, to render due offerings unto thee; for it is thy will that faith must precede sacrifice. Wherefore, we beseech thy tender mercy that thou wouldst sanctify ✝ and consecrate ✝ this emblem of the cross which Christian devotion and faith have fashioned — a memorial of thy victory and our redemption, the victorious and glorious sign of Christ's love. Behold this unconquerable sign of the cross by which devilish power is destroyed and human liberty restored! Once it stood for shame, but by grace it now is held in honor. That which once punished the condemned with death, now absolves criminals from debt. And why doth it please thee, except that by it thou wast pleased to redeem us? And now no gift becometh thee more than that in which thy body onetime was nailed to the hallowed wood, nor can any offering please thee more than that made holy formerly by thine outstretched hands. Wherefore, receive this cross with those hands which once embraced the true cross, and by the holiness of the true cross, sanctify ✝ this one. As by the

et sícuti per illam mundus expiátus est a reátu, ita offeréntium famulórum tuórum ánimae, devotíssimae hujus crucis mérito, omni cáreant perpetráto peccáto, et tuae verae Crucis obtéctu enitéscant succéssibus assíduis triumphatóres. Rádiet hic unigéniti Fílii tui, Dómini nostri, splendor divinitátis in auro, émicet glória passiónis ejus in ligno: in Cruce rútilet nostrae mortis redémptio; in crystálli splendóre vitae nostrae purificátio. Sit suórum pro-téctio, spei certa fidúcia; eos simul cum gente et plebe fide con-fírmet, spe et pace consóciet: áugeat triúmphis, amplíficet in secúndis, profíciat eis ad perpetuitátem témporis, ad vitam aeter-nitátis, ut eos temporáli floréntes glória múniat, et ad perpétuam redémptos corónam, ad regna caeléstia poténti virtúte perdúcat. Praesta per propitiatiónem sánguinis ejus, per ipsum datórem qui seípsum dedit redemptiónem pro multis, qui se hóstiam pro delíctis offérre dignátus est, qui exaltátus in ligno Crucis suae principátus et potestátes humiliávit, qui tecum sidéreo cónsidet throno, indissolúbili connexióne Spíritus Sancti, per infiníta sae-culórum saécula. ℞. Amen.

Tum Sacerdos flexis ante Crucem genibus ipsam devote adorat, et osculatur. Idem faciunt quicumque voluerint.

73

SOLEMNIS BENEDICTIO IMAGINIS
Jesu Christi Domini Nostri
Vel B. Mariae Virginis Vel Alius Sancti

Si imagines, publicae venerationi expositae, solemniter benedicantur, haec benedictio Ordinario reservatur, qui tamen potest eam cuilibet Sacerdoti committere.

Privatim autem haec benedictio a quolibet Sacerdote fieri potest sine ulla Ordinarii licentia.

true cross the world's guilt was expiated, so by this cross may thy servants merit deliverance from sin. And fighting the battle of life under the standard of thy cross, may they advance step by step to a triumphant eternity. Here on the cross let the divine splendor of thy Sole-Begotten Son, our Lord, sparkle like gold — the glory of His suffering and death upon the tree become increasingly brilliant. By the cross of Jesus Christ, may our redemption from death shine with golden lustre, and our purification unto life reflect its resplendent crystal. Unto its followers, be it protection and assurance; may it strengthen in faith the mighty and the low, may it bring them together in peace and in hope. Through their victories, may its followers be led to greater heights; may it increase their prosperity! May it prosper them in time and in eternity! This grant by the appeasing blood of thy Son — through Him, the Bestower, Who gave Himself unto the redemption of many, Who offered Himself as a holocaust for sin, Who being exalted upon the wood of the cross, humbled the principalities and powers, Who with thee, in the indissoluble bond of the Holy Spirit, sitteth upon the celestial throne for all eternity. ℟. Amen.

The priest, kneeling before the cross, devoutly venerates and kisses it, and others may do likewise.

73

SOLEMN BLESSING OF AN IMAGE
of our Lord, Jesus Christ, the Blessed
Virgin Mary, or any Saint

If such images are exposed for public veneration, they should be solemnly blessed. This blessing is reserved to the Ordinary who may delegate it to any priest.

If they are for private use, any priest may bless them without the Ordinary's permission.

℣. Adjutórium nostrum in nómine Dómini.

℞. Qui fecit caelum et terram.

℣. Dóminus vobíscum.

℞. Et cum spíritu tuo.

Orémus. Oratio

Omnípotens sempitérne Deus, qui Sanctórum tuórum imágines (sive effígies) sculpi, aut pingi non réprobas, ut quóties illas óculis córporis intuémur, tóties eórum actus et sanctitátem ad imitándum memóriae óculis meditémur: hanc, quaésumus, imáginem (seu sculptúram) in honórem et memóriam Unigéniti Fílii tui Dómini nostri Jesu Christi vel beatíssimae Vírginis Maríae, matris Dómini nostri Jesu Christi, vel beáti N. (Apóstoli) tui, (vel Mártyris), (vel Pontíficis), (vel Confessóris), vel beatae N. (Vírginis), (vel Mártyris) adaptátam bene ✠ dícere, et sancti ✠ ficáre dignéris: et praesta; ut quicúmque coram illa Unigénitum Fílium tuum vel beatíssimam Vírginem, vel gloriósum (Apóstolum), (vel Mártyrem), (vel Pontíficem), (vel Confessórem), vel gloriosam (Vírginem), (vel Mártyrem) supplíciter cólere et honoráre studúerit, illíus méritis et obténtu a te grátiam in praesénti, et aetérnam glóriam obtíneat in futúrum. Per (eúndem) Christum Dóminum nostrum. ℞. Amen.

Et aspergatur aqua benedicta.

74

BENEDICTIO HABITUS CLERICALIS

Si quis militiae clericalis candidatus, impetrata facultate induendi ejusdem ordinis habitum, ipsum petierit a Sacerdote benedici, Sacerdos delegatus habitum clericalem, quem induendus genuflexus brachiis sustentat, hac forma benedicat:

℣. Adjutórium nostrum in nómine Dómini.

℞. Qui fecit caelum et terram.

℣. Our help is in the name of the Lord.
℟. Who made heaven and earth.
℣. The Lord be with you.
℟. And with thy spirit.

Let us pray.   Prayer

O almighty, everlasting God! Thou dost approve of the sculptured or painted images (or likenesses) of thy saints, in order that when we behold them, we may be led to contemplate and imitate their lives and holiness. Wherefore, we beseech thee to bless ✠ and sanctify ✠ this image (or statue) wrought to the memory and honor of thy Sole-Begotten Son, our Lord Jesus Christ or the Blessed Virgin Mary, Mother of our Lord Jesus Christ, or Blessed N. thine Apostle, (or Martyr), (or Pontiff), (or Confessor), (or Virgin). And grant that whosoever through the inspiration of this image earnestly strives to honor and worship Him (or the Blessed Virgin, or the glorious Apostle, or Martyr, or Pontiff, or Confessor, or Virgin), may by His (his or her) merits obtain grace in this life and eternal glory in the next. Through (the same) Christ our Lord. ℟. Amen.

The image is sprinkled with holy water.

74

BLESSING OF THE CLERICAL CASSOCK

A candidate for sacred orders who has obtained the permission to wear the clerical cassock, may desire to have this garment blessed. The clerical aspirant, holding the cassock folded over outstretched arms, kneels before the priest delegated for this blessing:

℣. Our help is in the name of the Lord.
℟. Who made heaven and earth.

℣. Dóminus vobíscum.
℟. Et cum spíritu tuo.

    Orémus.   Oratio

Dómine Jesu Christe, qui tégumen nostrae mortalitátis indúere dignátus es, obsecrámus imménsam tuae largitátis abundántiam: ut hoc genus vestiménti, quod sancti patres ad innocéntiae vel humilitátis indícium, deponéntes ignomíniam saeculáris hábitus, ferre sanxérunt, tu ita bene ✠ dícere dignéris, ut hi fámuli tui, qui hoc indúti fúerint (vel hic fámulus tuus, qui hoc indútus fúerit) vestiménto, te quoque indúere mereántur (–átur), et tibi agnoscántur (–átur) esse dicáti (–us): Qui vivis et regnas Deus in saécula saeculórum. ℟. Amen.

Et aspergatur aqua benedicta.

75

BENEDICTIO CINGULI
in honorem Domini nostri Jesu Christi

℣. Adjutórium nostrum in nómine Dómini.
℟. Qui fecit caelum et terram.
℣. Dóminus vobíscum.
℟. Et cum spíritu tuo.

    Orémus.   Oratio

Deus, qui, ut servum redímeres, Fílium tuum per manus impiórum ligári voluísti: béne ✠ dic, quaésumus, cíngulum istud et praesta, ut fámulus tuus, qui (fámula tua, quae) eo véluti sui córporis poenitentiáli ligámine cingétur, vinculórum ejúsdem Dómini nostri Jesu Christi perpétuus exsístat amátor (perpétua exsístat amátrix), tuísque semper obséquiis se alligátum (–am) esse cognóscat. Per eúndem Dóminum nostrum Jesum Christum Fílium tuum: Qui vivit et regnat in unitáte Spíritus Sancti Deus per ómnia saécula saeculórum. ℟. Amen.

Et aspergatur aqua benedicta.

℣. The Lord be with you.

℟. And with thy spirit.

Let us pray.   Prayer

O Lord Jesus Christ, Who hast condescended to clothe thyself with our wounded nature, we beg thee of thine immeasurable goodness to bless ✠ this garment which ecclesiastical superiors have sanctioned for clerics, as a token of the innocence and humility which should be theirs. Laying aside the vanity of secular garb, may these thy servants (or this thy servant) wear the cassock, and in so doing may they (he) likewise put on thee, and be recognized as men (a man) dedicated to thy ministry. Who livest and reignest, God, in eternity. ℟. Amen.

The cassock is sprinkled with holy water.

75

BLESSING OF A CINCTURE
to be worn in honor of our Lord Jesus Christ

℣. Our help is in the name of the Lord.

℟. Who made heaven and earth.

℣. The Lord be with you.

℟. And with thy spirit.

Let us pray.   Prayer

O God, thou didst will, in redeeming mankind, that thy Son should be bound by impious hands. Bless, ✠ we pray thee, this cincture, that thy servant (handmaid) who wears it as a reminder of bodily mortification, may respect the fetters of our Lord Jesus Christ, and may ever recognize that he (she) is bound to thee by obedience to thy commandments. Through the selfsame Jesus Christ, thy Son, our Lord, Who liveth and reigneth with thee in unity of the Holy Spirit, God, forever and ever. ℟. Amen.

It is sprinkled with holy water.

76

BENEDICTIO CINGULI
in honorem beatae Mariae Virginis
vel alicujus Sancti canonizati

℣. Adjutórium nostrum in nómine Dómini.
℞. Qui fecit caelum et terram.
℣. Dóminus vobíscum.
℞. Et cum spíritu tuo.

Orémus.   Oratio

Dómine Jesu Christe, béne ✠ dic, quaésumus, hoc cíngulum, et praesta: ut, qui (quae) illud gestáverit, beatíssimae Vírginis Maríae Matris tuae (vel Sancti N. vel Sanctae N.) protectióne munítus (–a), ab ómnibus perículis deféndi, atque ánimae et córporis sanitátem percípere mereátur: Qui vivis et regnas in saécula saeculórum. ℞. Amen.

Et aspergatur aqua benedicta.

77

BENEDICTIO VESTIS
in honorem beatae Mariae Virginis

℣. Adjutórium nostrum in nómine Dómini.
℞. Qui fecit caelum et terram.
℣. Dóminus vobíscum.
℞. Et cum spíritu tuo.

Orémus.   Oratio

Béne ✠ dic, Dómine, vestem istam, in honórem et sub protectióne beatíssimae Vírginis Maríae suméndam: et praesta per invocatiónem sancti tui nóminis; ut qui (quae) eam indúerit, córporis sanitátem et ánimae tutélam percípiat. Per Christum Dóminum nostrum. ℞. Amen.

Et aspergatur aqua benedicta.

76

BLESSING OF A CINCTURE
to be worn in honor of the Blessed Virgin Mary
or a canonized Saint

℣. Our help is in the name of the Lord.
℟. Who made heaven and earth.
℣. The Lord be with you.
℟. And with thy spirit.

Let us pray. Prayer

Bless, ✠ O Lord Jesus Christ, this cincture that he (she) who wears it may by the protection of the Blessed Virgin Mary, thy mother (or of St. N.) be shielded from every danger, and obtain health of soul and body. Who livest and reignest forever. ℟. Amen.

It is sprinkled with holy water.

77

BLESSING OF A HABIT
to be worn in honor of the Virgin Mary

℣. Our help is in the name of the Lord.
℟. Who made heaven and earth.
℣. The Lord be with you.
℟. And with thy spirit.

Let us pray. Prayer

Bless, ✠ O Lord, this habit which will be worn in honor of the Blessed Virgin Mary and to obtain her patronage. Grant that he (she) who wears it may enjoy health of body and protection of soul. Through Christ our Lord. ℟. Amen.

It is sprinkled with holy water.

78

BENEDICTIO VESTIS
in honorem beatae Mariae Virginis
vel alicujus Sancti canonizati

℣. Adjutórium nostrum in nómine Dómini.
℟. Qui fecit caelum et terram.
℣. Dóminus vobíscum.
℟. Et cum spíritu tuo.

Orémus.   Oratio

Dómine Jesu Christe, qui pro nostra salúte suscípiens humánam
natúram, te vestiménto carnis indúere dignátus es, benedictióne
sancta béne ✠ dic istud vestiméntum, quod pro grátiis tibi ex-
solvéndis cum omni devotióne sanctóque voto, ac veneratióne
beatíssimae Vírginis Maríae (vel Sancti N. vel Sanctae N.), fámulus tuus (fámula tua) super se susceptúrus (–a) est: infúnde
in eum (eam), quaésumus, tuam sanctam bene ✠ dictiónem; ut,
cum primum indúerit hoc religiónis símile vestiméntum, intercedénte beatíssima Vírgine María (vel Sancto N. vel Sancta N.)
descéndat super eum (eam) grátia tua, et prótegat eum (eam) ab
omni malo mentis et córporis: Qui vivis et regnas in saécula
saeculórum. ℟. Amen.

Et aspergatur aqua benedicta.

79

BENEDICTIO CINGULORUM
in honorem sancti Joseph Sponsi B. M. V.
(Approbata a S. R. C. die 19 Sept. 1859)

Sacerdos qui ab Apostolica Sede privilegium obtinuerit benedicendi
cingula in honorem S. Joseph Sponsi B. M. V., superpelliceo et stola
alba indutus, dicit:

℣. Adjutórium nostrum in nómine Dómini.
℟. Qui fecit caelum et terram.

78

BLESSING OF A HABIT
to be worn in honor of the Virgin Mary
or a canonized Saint

℣. Our help is in the name of the Lord.
℟. Who made heaven and earth.
℣. The Lord be with you.
℟. And with thy spirit.

Let us Pray. *Prayer*

O Lord Jesus Christ, Who for our salvation didst clothe thyself in the habit of mortals, bless ✠ this habit with a holy benediction. For thy servant (handmaid) will wear it in devout thanksgiving to thee and in veneration of the Blessed Virgin Mary (or of St. N.). Pour forth on him (her) thy sacred blessings, ✠ that when he (she) puts on this garb, like unto the habit of a religious, he (she) may receive thy grace, and through the intercession of the Blessed Virgin Mary (or of St. N.) be protected from every ill of soul or body. Who livest and reignest eternally. ℟. Amen.

It is sprinkled with holy water.

79

BLESSING OF A CINCTURE OF ST. JOSEPH
by a priest who has the Apostolic Indult
(Approved by the Congregation of Sacred Rites on Sept. 19, 1859)

The priest who has this privilege from the Holy See, vested in surplice and white stole, says:

℣. Our help is in the name of the Lord.
℟. Who made heaven and earth.

℣. Dóminus vobíscum.

℟. Et cum spíritu tuo.

Orémus. Oratio

Dómine Jesu Christe, qui virginitátis consílium et amórem íngeris atque castitátem praécipis: orámus cleméntiam tuam, ut haec cíngula castitátis tésseram bene ✠ dícere, et sancti ✠ ficáre dignéris, ut, quicúmque pro castitáte servánda illis praecíncti fúerint, intercedénte beáto Joseph, sanctíssimae Genitrícis tuae sponso, gratam tibi continéntiam, mandatorúmque tuórum obediéntiam servent, atque véniam peccatórum suórum obtíneant, et sanitátem mentis et córporis percípiant, vitámque consequántur aetérnam: Qui vivis et regnas cum Deo Patre in unitáte Spíritus Sancti Deus, per ómnia saécula saeculórum. ℟. Amen.

Orémus. Oratio

DA, quaésumus, omnípotens aetérne Deus: ut puríssimae Vírginis Maríae, ejúsque sponsi Joseph, integérrimam virginitátem venerántes, eórum intercessiónibus puritátem mentis et córporis consequámur. Per Christum Dóminum nostrum. ℟. Amen.

Orémus. Oratio

OMNÍPOTENS sempitérne Deus, qui castíssimo viro Joseph puríssimam Maríam semper Vírginem, et púerum Jesum commisísti: te súpplices exorámus; ut fidéles tui, qui his cíngulis in honórem et sub protectióne ejúsdem sancti Joseph praecíncti fúerint, te largiénte, et ipso intercedénte, in castitáte semper devóte persístant. Per eúndem Dóminum nostrum Jesum Christum, Fílium tuum: Qui tecum vivit et regnat in unitáte Spíritus Sancti Deus, per ómnia saécula saeculórum. ℟. Amen.

Orémus. Oratio

DEUS, innocéntiae restitútor et amátor: quaésumus, ut fidéles tui, qui haec cíngula adhibúerint, intercedénte beáto Joseph, sanctíssimae Genitrícis tuae sponso, in lumbis suis sint semper

℣. The Lord be with you.
℟. And with thy spirit.

Let us Pray.   Prayer

O Lord Jesus Christ, Who didst inculcate the counsel of virginity and precept of chastity, we beseech thy goodness that thou
wouldst vouchsafe to bless ✠ and sanctify ✠ this cincture as a
symbol of purity. Let all who gird themselves therewith to preserve their chastity, through the intercession of St. Joseph, spouse
of thy holy mother, preserve this desired virtue in obedience to
thy law. May they obtain pardon of their sins, bodily and spiritual
health, and eternal life. Thou Who livest and reignest with God
the Father in unity of the Holy Spirit, God, for all eternity. ℟.
Amen.

Let us Pray.   Prayer

GRANT, we beseech thee, almighty and eternal God, that
they who revere the inviolate chastity of the Holy Virgin
Mary and Joseph, her spouse, may through their intercession attain purity of body and soul. Through Christ our Lord. ℟.
Amen.

Let us pray.   Prayer

ALMIGHTY and everlasting God, Who didst commit the
Christ-Child and His sinless mother to the care of the
chaste Joseph, we humbly pray that they who are girded with
this cincture in honor of St. Joseph and under his protection, may
by thy goodness and his intercession persevere in chastity for all
time. Through the same Jesus Christ, thy Son, our Lord, Who
livest and reignest with thee in unity of the Holy Spirit, God,
forevermore. ℟. Amen.

Let us pray.   Prayer

O GOD, the restorer and lover of innocence, we beseech thee
through the intercession of Blessed Joseph, spouse of thy
fairest mother, that all who wear this cincture may be girt in

praecíncti, et lucérnas ardéntes gestent in mánibus suis; ac símiles sint homínibus exspectántibus dóminum suum, quando revertátur a núptiis, ut, cum vénerit et pulsáverit, conféstim apériant ei, et in aetérna gáudia récipi mereántur: Qui vivis et regnas in saécula saeculórum. ℞. Amen.

Deinde Sacerdos, imposito thure in thuribulo, aqua benedicta aspergit cingula, dicens: Aspérges me, Dómine, hyssópo et mundábor: lavábis me, et super nivem dealbábor; postea incensat, et tandem dicit:

℣. Salvos fac servos tuos.

℞. Deus meus, sperántes in te.

℣. Mitte eis, Dómine, auxílium de sancto.

℞. Et de Sion tuére eos.

℣. Dómine, exáudi oratiónem meam.

℞. Et clamor meus ad te véniat.

℣. Dóminus vobíscum.

℞. Et cum spíritu tuo.

    Orémus.   Oratio

DEUS miséricors, Deus clemens, cui bona cuncta placent, sine quo nihil boni inchoátur, nihílque boni perfícitur: adsint nostris humíllimis précibus tuae pietátis aures, et fidéles tuos, qui in tuo sancto nómine cíngulo benedícto in honórem et sub protectióne sancti Joseph praecíncti fúerint, a mundi impediménto, vel saeculári desidério defénde; et concéde eis, ut in hoc sancto propósito devóti persístere, et remissióne percépta ad electórum tuórum váleant pervveníre consórtium. Per Dóminum nostrum Jesum Christum, Fílium tuum: Qui tecum vivit et regnat in unitáte Spíritus Sancti Deus, per ómnia saécula saeculórum. ℞. Amen.

their loins, and hold burning lamps in their hands; and be like to men who wait for their lord when he shall return from the wedding, that when he cometh and knocketh, they may open unto him, and be found worthy to be taken into everlasting joys. Who liveth and reigneth eternally. R̷. Amen.

Then the priest puts incense into the thurible, sprinkles the cincture with holy water saying: **Sprinkle me with hyssop, O Lord, and I shall be clean: wash me, and I shall be whiter than snow;** after which he incenses it, and then continues:

V̷. **Preserve thy servants.**

R̷. **Who trust in thee, my God.**

V̷. **Send them aid, Lord, from on high.**

R̷. **And from Sion watch over them.**

V̷. **O Lord, hear my prayer.**

R̷. **And let my cry come unto thee.**

V̷. **The Lord be with you.**

R̷. **And with thy spirit.**

Let us pray.   Prayer

O GOD of mercy, God of goodness! Thee all good things please, and without thee no good is finished or begun. Hear thou our lowly entreaties, and guard thy faithful, who wear this blessed cincture in honor of St. Joseph, from contagion of the world and its desires. Grant them, moreover, to persist in their holy resolution, and to be freed from sin, that they may merit to be numbered among thy elect. Through Jesus Christ, thy Son, our Lord, Who liveth and reigneth with thee in unity of the Holy Spirit, God, eternally. R̷. Amen.

80

BENEDICTIO LILIORUM
in Festo S. Ántonii Patavini Conf.
(Approbata a S. R. C. die 26 Febr. 1901)

Sacerdos facultatem habens ab Apostolica Sede concessam, super-pelliceo et stola coloris albi indutus, lilia benedicturus dicit:

℣. Adjutórium nostrum in nómine Dómini.
℞. Qui fecit caelum et terram.
℣. Dóminus vobíscum.
℞. Et cum spíritu tuo.

Orémus.   Oratio

Deus, Creátor et Conservátor géneris humáni, sanctae puritátis amator, dator grátiae spirituális, et largítor aetérnae salútis, benedictióne tua sancta béne✠dic haec lília, quae pro grátiis exsólvéndis, in honórem sancti Antónii Confessóris tui súpplices hódie tibi praesentámus, et pétimus benedíci. Infúnde illis salutári signáculo sanctíssimae Cru✠cis rorem caeléstem. Tu benigníssime, qui ea ad odóris suavitátem depellendásque infirmitátes humáno úsui tribuísti, tali virtúte reple et confírma; ut, quibuscúmque morbis adhíbita, seu in dómibus locísque pósita, vel cum devotióne portáta fúerint, intercedénte eódem fámulo tuo António, fugent daémones, continéntiam salutárem indúcant, languóres avértant, tibíque serviéntibus pacem et grátiam concílient. Per Christum Dóminum nostrum. ℞. Amen.

Deinde aspergit lilia aqua benedicta, interim dicens:

Aspérges me, Dómine, hyssópo et mundábor: lavábis me, et super nivem dealbábor, ac postea subdit:

℣. Ora pro nobis, beáte Antóni.
℞. Ut digni efficiámur promissiónibus Christi.

Orémus.   Oratio

SUBVÉNIAT plebi tuae, quaésumus, Dómine, praeclári Confessóris tui beáti Antónii devóta et jugis deprecátio: quae in

80

BLESSING OF LILIES
on the Feast of St. Anthony of Padua
(Approved by the Congregation of Sacred Rites on Feb. 26, 1901)
by Apostolic Indult

The priest who has this privilege from the Holy See, vested in surplice and white stole says:

℣. Our help is in the name of the Lord.

℟. Who made heaven and earth.

℣. The Lord be with you.

℟. And with thy spirit.

Let us pray.   Prayer

O God, the Creator and Preserver of mankind, thou Who art the lover of holy purity, the giver of spiritual grace, the dispenser of eternal salvation, bless ✠ these lilies we bring on this day in thanksgiving to thee and in honor of St. Anthony, thy Confessor. Pour out on them heavenly dew by the saving sign ✠ of the most holy cross. O God of love! Thou hast endowed these lilies with delicious fragrance to be a comfort and help to those on their sickbeds. Wherefore, imbue them with so great strength that whether they are used in a home, in a sickroom, or carried about one's person, they may have power, through the intercession of St. Anthony, to drive out evil spirits, to safeguard chastity, to turn away illness, and to bestow on thy servants peace and grace. Through Christ our Lord. ℟. Amen.

Then he sprinkles the lilies with holy water, saying: Sprinkle me with hyssop, O Lord, and I shall be clean: wash me, and I shall be whiter than snow, and continues:

℣. Pray for us, St. Anthony.

℟. That we may be made worthy of the promises of Christ.

Let us Pray.   Prayer

MAY the devout and constant intercession of Blessed Anthony, thy Confessor come to our aid, we beseech thee,

praesénti nos tua grátia dignos effíciat, et in futúro gáudia donet aetérna. Per Christum Dóminum nostrum. R̷. Amen.

His dictis, lilia distribuit.

81

BENEDICTIO VEXILLI PROCESSIONALIS
cujuslibet Societatis

V̷. Adjutórium nostrum in nómine Dómini.
R̷. Qui fecit caelum et terram.
V̷. Dóminus vobíscum.
R̷. Et cum spíritu tuo.

Orémus.   Oratio

Dómine Jesu Christe, cujus Ecclésia est véluti castrórum ácies ordináta: béne ☩ dic hoc vexíllum; ut omnes sub eo tibi Dómino Deo exercítuum militántes, per intercessiónem beáti N. (vel beátae N.) inimícos suos visíbiles et invisíbiles in hoc saéculo superáre, et post victóriam in caelis triumpháre mereántur. Per te, Jesu Christe: Qui vivis et regnas cum Deo Patre et Spíritu Sancto, in saécula saeculórum. R̷. Amen.

Et aspergatur aqua benedicta.

82

BENEDICTIO CANDELARUM

V̷. Adjutórium nostrum in nómine Dómini.
R̷. Qui fecit caelum et terram.
V̷. Dóminus vobíscum.
R̷. Et cum spíritu tuo.

O Lord, that we become worthy of thy grace in this life, and merit everlasting joys in the next. Through Christ our Lord. ℞. Amen.

The lilies are distributed to the people.

81

BLESSING OF THE PROCESSIONAL BANNER
of a Society

℣. Our help is in the name of the Lord.
℞. Who made heaven and earth.
℣. The Lord be with you.
℞. And with thy spirit.

Let us Pray.   Prayer

O Lord Jesus Christ, Whose Church is like unto a fortress of armies, bless ✠ this banner, so that all who fight under this standard for thy sake, O Lord God, may through the intercession of blessed N. overcome their visible and invisible enemies in this life, and after the victory reign triumphantly in heaven. Through thee, Jesus Christ, Who livest and reignest with God the Father and the Holy Spirit, for all eternity. ℞. Amen.

It is sprinkled with holy water.

82

BLESSING OF CANDLES

℣. Our help is in the name of the Lord.
℞. Who made heaven and earth.
℣. The Lord be with you.
℞. And with thy spirit.

Orémus.

Dómine Jesu Christe, Fili Dei vivi, béne ✠ dic candélas istas supplicatiónibus nostris: infúnde eis, Dómine, per virtútem sanctae Cru ✠ cis, benedictiónem caeléstem, qui eas ad repelléndas ténebras humáno géneri tribuísti; talémque benedictiónem signáculo sanctae Cru ✠ cis accípiant, ut, quibuscúmque locis accénsae, sive pósitae fúerint, discédant príncipes tenebrárum, et contremíscant, et fugiant pávidi cum ómnibus minístris suis ab habitatiónibus illis, nec praesúmant ámplius inquietáre, aut molestáre serviéntes tibi omnipoténti Deo: Qui vivis et regnas in saécula saeculórum. ℞. Amen.

Et aspergantur aqua benedicta.

83

BENEDICTIO INSTRUMENTORUM ORGANI
in Ecclesia

℣. Adjutórium nostrum in nómine Dómini.
℞. Qui fecit caelum et terram.

Psalmus 150

Laudáte Dóminum in sanctis ejus: * laudáte eum in firmaménto virtútis ejus.

Laudáte eum in virtútibus ejus: * laudáte eum secúndum multitúdinem magnitúdinis ejus.

Laudáte eum in sono tubae: * laudáte eum in psaltério, et cíthara.

Laudáte eum in tympano, et choro: * laudáte eum in chordis, et órgano.

Laudáte eum in cýmbalis benesonántibus: laudáte eum in cýmbalis jubilatiónis: * omnis spíritus laudet Dóminum.

Glória Patri.

℣. Laudáte Dóminum in týmpano et choro.
℞. Laudáte eum in chordis et órgano.
℣. Dóminus vobíscum.
℞. Et cum spíritu tuo.

Let us Pray.

O Lord Jesus Christ, Son of the living God, bless ✠ these candles at our request. By the power of the holy cross, ✠ bestow a heavenly blessing on them, O Lord, Who didst give them to mankind to dispel the gloom. Empowered with the seal of thy holy cross, ✠ let the spirits of darkness depart trembling and fly in fear from all places where their light shines, and never more disturb nor molest those who serve thee, the almighty God, Who livest and reignest forevermore. ℞. Amen.

They are sprinkled with holy water.

83

BLESSING OF A CHURCH ORGAN

℣. Our help is in the name of the Lord.
℞. Who made heaven and earth.

Psalm 150

Praise the Lord in His sanctuary; praise Him in the surety of His heavenly fortress.

Praise Him because of His mighty deeds; praise Him because of His wonderful greatness.

Praise Him with the sound of trumpet; praise Him on harp and zither.

Praise Him with cymbal and dance; praise Him with strings and organ.

Praise Him with sweet-sounding cymbals; praise Him with cymbal of jubilation. Let every living being praise the Lord.

Glory be to the Father.

℣. Praise the Lord with drums and dance.
℞. Praise Him with strings and organ.
℣. The Lord be with you.
℞. And with thy spirit.

Orémus.　　　　　　　　　　　　　　　　Oratio

DEUS, qui per Móysen fámulum tuum tubas ad canéndum super sacrifíciis, nómini tuo offeréndis, fácere praecepísti, quique per fílios Israel in tubis et cýmbalis laudem tui nóminis decantári voluísti: béne ✠ dic, quaésumus, hoc instruméntum órgani, cúltui tuo dedicátum; et praesta, ut fidéles tui in cánticis spirituálibus jubilántes in terris, ad gáudia aetérna perveníre mereántur in caelis. Per Dóminum nostrum Jesum Christum, Fílium tuum: Qui tecum vivit et regnat in unitáte Spíritus Sancti Deus, per ómnia saécula saeculórum. ℟. Amen.

Et aspergatur aqua benedicta.

84

BENEDICTIO CAMPANAE
quae ad usum ecclesiae benedictae vel
oratorii inserviat
(Approbata a S. R. C. die 22 Jan. 1908)

℣. Adjutórium nostrum in nómine Dómini.
℟. Qui fecit caelum et terram.

Psalmus 50
Miserére mei, Deus, * secúndum magnam misericórdiam tuam.
Et secúndum multitúdinem miseratiónum tuárum, * dele iniquitátem meam.
Amplius lava me ab iniquitáte mea: * et a peccáto meo munda me.
Quóniam iniquitátem meam ego cognósco: * et peccátum meum contra me est semper.
Tibi soli peccávi, et malum coram te feci: * ut justificéris in sermónibus tuis, et vincas cum judicáris.
Ecce enim in iniquitátibus concéptus sum: * et in peccátis concépit me mater mea.

Let us Pray. Prayer

O GOD, Who by Moses, thy servant didst order the sounding of trumpets to accompany the sacrifices offered to thee, and didst will that the Israelites sing praise to thy name with trumpets and cymbals, bless ✠ this organ which we dedicate to thy service. And grant that thy faithful who rejoice in spiritual canticles upon earth, may attain everlasting joys in heaven. Through Jesus Christ, thy Son, our Lord, Who liveth and reigneth with thee in unity of the Holy Spirit, God, forever and ever. ℟. Amen.

It is sprinkled with holy water.

84

BLESSING OF A CHURCH BELL
destined to use in a church which is
merely blessed
or in an oratory*
(Approved by the Congregation of Sacred Rites, Jan. 22, 1908)

℣. Our help is in the name of the Lord.
℟. Who made heaven and earth.

Psalm 50

Be merciful to me, O God, for great is thy goodness.
And with the fulness of thy mercy blot out my transgressions.
Wash me thoroughly from my guilt, and cleanse me from my sin.
For I am conscious of transgressions, and my sin is ever before me.
Against thee alone have I sinned, and done what is evil in thy sight. My guilt I confess that thou mayest appear just and above reproach when thou judgest me.
Lo, iniquity was born with me! And in sin did my mother conceive me.

---

* Reserved to the Ordinary or to one delegated by him.

Ecce enim veritátem dilexísti: * incérta et occúlta sapiéntiae tuae manifestásti mihi.

Aspérges me hyssópo, et mundábor: * lavábis me, et super nivem dealbábor.

Audítui meo dabis gáudium et laetítiam: * et exsultábunt ossa humiliáta.

Avérte fáciem tuam a peccátis meis: * et omnes iniquitátes meas dele.

Cor mundum crea in me, Deus: * et spíritum rectum ínnova in viscéribus meis.

Ne projícias me a fácie tua: * et spíritum sanctum tuum ne áuferas a me.

Redde mihi laetítiam salutáris tui: * et spíritu principáli confírma me.

Docébo iníquos vias tuas: * et ímpii ad te converténtur.

Líbera me de sanguínibus, Deus, Deus salútis meae: * et exsultábit lingua mea justítiam tuam.

Dómine, lábia mea apéries: * et os meum annuntiábit laudem tuam.

Quóniam si voluísses sacrifícium, dedíssem útique: * holocáustis non delectáberis.

Sacrifícium Deo spíritus contribulátus: * cor contrítum, et humiliátum, Deus, non despícies.

Benígne fac, Dómine, in bona voluntáte tua Sion: *ut aedificéntur muri Jerúsalem.

Tunc acceptábis sacrifícium justítiae, oblatiónes, et holocáusta: * tunc impónent super altáre tuum vítulos.

Glória Patri.

Psalmus 53

D EUS, in nómine tuo salvum me fac: * et in virtúte tua júdica me.

Deus, exáudi oratiónem meam: * áuribus pércipe verba oris mei

Surely thou lovest my sincerity; therefore, givest thou me insight to thy wisdom.

Sprinkle me with hyssop, and I shall be clean; wash me, and I shall be whiter than snow.

Let me hear joy and gladness, that the bones which thou hast humbled may rejoice.

Turn away thy face from my sins, and blot out all my wrong-doing.

Create a clean heart in me, O God, and renew a right spirit within me.

Drive me not from thy presence, and take not from me the power of thy holy spirit.

Give me again the delight of thy grace, and uphold me with thy leading spirit.

Then will I show the godless thy ways, and sinners shall be converted to thee.

Save me from bloody violence, my Helper and my God, and my tongue shall praise thy righteousness.

O Lord, open thou my lips, and my mouth shall declare thy praise.

For hadst thou requested sacrifice, surely would I have given it. But in burnt-offerings thou hast no pleasure.

A sacrifice pleasing God is a spirit which is penitent; my heart sorrowing and humbled, O Lord, do not despise!

Deal kindly, O Lord, and graciously with Sion, and let Jerusalem arise anew.

Then shalt thou be honored with true oblations; then shall they lay young bullocks upon thine altar.

Glory be to the Father.

Psalm 53

SAVE me, O God, for thy name's sake, and win me justice by thy power.

O God, hear my prayer; give ear to the words of my mouth.

Quóniam aliéni insurrexérunt advérsum me, et fortes quaesiérunt
ánimam meam: * et non proposuérunt Deum ante conspéctum
suum.

Ecce enim Deus ádjuvat me: * et Dóminus suscéptor est ánimae
meae.

Avérte mala inimícis meis: * et in veritáte tua dispérde illos.

Voluntárie sacrificábo tibi, * et confitébor nómini tuo, Dómine:
quóniam bonum est:

Quóniam ex omni tribulatióne eripuísti me: * et super inimícos
meos despéxit óculus meus.

Glória Patri.

Psalmus 56

M ISERÉRE mei, Deus, miserére mei: * quóniam in te con-
fídit ánima mea.

Et in umbra alárum tuárum sperábo, * donec tránseat iníquitas.

Clamábo ad Deum altíssimum: * Deum qui benefécit mihi.

Misit de caelo, et liberávit me: * dedit in oppróbrium concul-
cántes me.

Misit Deus misericórdiam suam, et veritátem suam, * et erípuit
ánimam meam de médio catulórum leónum: dormívi contur-
bátus.

Fílii hóminum dentes eórum arma et sagíttae: * et lingua eórum
gládius acútus.

Exaltáre super caelos, Deus: * et in omnem terram glória tua.

Láqueum paravérunt pédibus meis: * et incurvavérunt ánimam
meam.

Fodérunt ante fáciem meam fóveam: * et incidérunt in eam.

Parátum cor meum, Deus, parátum cor meum: * cantábo, et
psalmum dicam.

Exsúrge, glória mea, exsúrge, psaltérium et cíthara: * exsúrgam
dilúculo.

Confitébor tibi in pópulis, Dómine: * et psalmum dicam tibi in
géntibus:

Quóniam magnificáta est usque ad caelos misericórdia tua, * et
usque ad nubes véritas tua.

For enemies have risen up against me; the mighty seek after my soul, their eyes are not on God.

But I know that God is my helper, and the Lord supporteth my life.

He shall turn evil upon my enemies, and cut them off as He threatened.

Gladly will I sacrifice unto thee. I will praise thy name, O Lord, for thou art good.

In every need thou rescuest me, and I can scoff at my foes.

Glory be to the Father.

Psalm 56

BE MERCIFUL to me, O God, be merciful; my soul trusteth in thee.

In the shadow of thy wings I find security, until this affliction passeth.

I will cry unto God in the highest, unto God Who renders good to me.

He reacheth from heaven to help me; He shameth my foes.

He is merciful to me and loyal, and rescueth my soul; while I lie overcome with fear in the midst of young lions.

There are sons of men whose teeth are weapons and arrows, whose tongues are a sharp sword.

Be thou exalted, O God, above the heavens, and thy glory be above all the earth.

The snare they set for me endangered my life;

But the pit they dug for me becomes their own grave.

My heart is unshakable, O God, my heart is ready; I will sing praise to thee.

Awake, my soul, awake lyre and harp! I will arise with the dawn.

I will praise thee, O Lord, among the peoples, and sing thy glory among the heathen.

For thy mercy and kindness rise to the heavens, and thy truth unto the clouds.

Exaltáre super caelos, Deus: * et super omnem terram glória tua.
Glória Patri.

Psalmus 66

DEUS misereátur nostri, et benedícat nobis: * illúminet vultum suum super nos, et misereátur nostri.

Ut cognoscámus in terra viam tuam: * in ómnibus géntibus salutáre tuum.

Confiteántur tibi pópuli, Deus: * confiteántur tibi pópuli omnes.

Laeténtur et exsúltent gentes: * quóniam júdicas pópulos in aequitáte, et gentes in terra dírigis.

Confiteántur tibi pópuli, Deus, confiteántur tibi pópuli omnes: * terra dedit fructum suum.

Benedícat nos Deus, Deus noster, benedícat nos Deus: *et métuant eum omnes fines terrae.

Glória Patri.

Psalmus 69

DEUS, in adjutórium meum inténde: * Dómine, ad adjuvándum me festína.

Confundántur et revereántur, * qui quaerunt ánimam meam.

Avertántur retrórsum, et erubéscant, * qui volunt mihi mala.

Avertántur statim erubescéntes, * qui dicunt mihi: Euge, euge.

Exsúltent et laeténtur in te omnes qui quaerunt te, * et dicant semper: Magnificétur Dóminus: qui díligunt salutáre tuum.

Ego vero egénus, et pauper sum: * Deus, ádjuva me.

Adjútor meus, et liberátor meus es tu: * Dómine, ne moréris.

Glória Patri.

Psalmus 85

INCLÍNA, Dómine, aurem tuam, et exáudi me: * quóniam inops, et pauper sum ego.

Custódi ánimam meam, quóniam sanctus sum: * salvum fac servum tuum, Deus meus, sperántem in te.

Miserére mei, Dómine, quóniam ad te clamávi tota die: * laetífica ánimam servi tui, quóniam ad te, Dómine, ánimam meam levávi.

Be thou exalted, O God, above the heavens, and thy glory over all the earth.

Glory be to the Father.

Psalm 66

MAY God be good to us, and bless us! May the light of His countenance shine upon us, and may He have mercy on us.

That men may know thy Providence upon earth, thy salvation among all nations.

Let people praise thee, O God, let all nations glorify thee!

Let the nations be glad and rejoice; for thou judgest the people justly, and directest the nations upon earth.

Let people praise thee, O God, let all nations glorify thee! The earth did yield fruit in abundance.

God, our own God bless us! May God bless us, and let all the ends of the earth fear Him.

Glory be to the Father.

Psalm 69

ATTEND, O God, to my defense; make haste, O Lord, to help me.

Let them be ashamed and tremble, that seek after my life.

Let them be turned back blushing, that desire my ruin.

May confusion be their reward that say to me: " 'Tis so, 'tis so!"

But let them rejoice and be glad that seek after thee; may they that love thy grace say without ceasing: "Magnify the Lord!"

But I am poor and miserable. Help me, O God!

My helper art thou and my savior; tarry not, O Lord!

Glory be to the Father.

Psalm 85

BEND down thine ear, O Lord, and hear me, for I am poor and wretched.

Protect me because of my devotion; save thy servant that trusts in thee, my God.

Pity me, O Lord, for I cry to thee at all times. Gladden the soul of thy servant, for my longing is directed toward thee.

Quóniam tu, Dómine, suávis, et mitis: * et multae misericórdiae ómnibus invocántibus te.

Auribus pércipe, Dómine, oratiónem meam: * et inténde voci deprecatiónis meae.

In die tribulatiónis meae clamávi ad te: * quia exaudísti me.

Non est símilis tui in diis, Dómine: * et non est secúndum ópera tua.

Omnes gentes quascúmque fecísti, vénient, et adorábunt coram te, Dómine: * et glorificábunt nomen tuum.

Quóniam magnus es tu, et fáciens mirabília: * tu es Deus solus.

Deduc me, Dómine, in via tua, et ingrédiar in veritáte tua: * laetétur cor meum ut tímeat nomen tuum.

Confitébor tibi, Dómine, Deus meus, in toto corde meo, * et glorificábo nomen tuum in aetérnum:

Quia misericórdia tua magna est super me: * et eruísti ánimam meam ex inférno inferióri.

Deus, iníqui insurrexérunt super me, et synagóga poténtium quaesiérunt ánimam meam: * et non proposuérunt te in conspéctu suo.

Et tu, Dómine, Deus miserátor et miséricors, * pátiens, et multae misericórdiae, et verax.

Réspice in me, et miserére mei, * da impérium tuum púero tuo: et salvum fac fílium ancíllae tuae.

Fac mecum signum in bonum, ut vídeant qui odérunt me, et confundántur: * quóniam tu, Dómine, adjuvísti me, et consolátus es me.

Glória Patri.

Psalmus 129

DE PROFÚNDIS clamávi ad te, Dómine: * Dómine, exáudi vocem meam:

Fiant aures tuae intendéntes, * in vocem deprecatiónis meae.

Si iniquitátes observáveris, Dómine: * Dómine, quis sustinébit?

Thou, O Lord, art kind and loving, and quick to forgive thy suppliants.

Let my prayer pierce thy hearing, O Lord, and attend to my entreaty.

In the day of misfortune I call upon thee, for thou hearest me.

There is none among the gods like thee, O Lord, and nothing comparable to thy works.

All peoples thou hast made shall come, O Lord, to worship and to praise thee.

Truly thou art great, a doer of wonderful deeds. Thou alone art God!

Lead me, O Lord, on thy way, and I will walk aright; dispose my heart to reverence thy name.

I will praise thee, O Lord, my God with my whole heart; I will glorify thee forevermore.

For great is thy graciousness toward me; thou hast delivered my soul from deepest hell.

Evil men have risen against me, O God; an assembly of mighty ones seek after my life; and none thinks of thee.

But thou, O Lord, art gracious and merciful, patient, true, and compassionate.

Look on me, and be merciful; give strength to thy servant, and help thy slave.

Show me a token of thy goodness, so they that hate me may stare in confusion; because thou, O Lord, hast helped and consoled me.

Glory be to the Father.

Psalm 129

O UT of the depths, I cry, O Lord, to thee; Lord, hearken to my plea!

Let thine ears be attentive to my suppliant sigh.

If thou shouldst retain man's iniquity, O Lord, who would survive?

Quia apud te propitiátio est: * et propter legem tuam sustínui te,
Dómine.

Sustínuit ánima mea in verbo ejus: * sperávit ánima mea in
Dómino.

A custódia matutína usque ad noctem: * speret Israel in Dómino.

Quia apud Dóminum misericórdia: * et copiósa apud eum
redémptio.

Et ipse rédimet Israel, * ex ómnibus iniquitátibus ejus.

Glória Patri.

Kýrie, eléison. Christe, eléison. Kýrie, eléison.

Pater noster secreto usque ad

℣. Et ne nos indúcas in tentatiónem.

℟. Sed líbera nos a malo.

℣. Sit nomen Dómini benedíctum.

℟. Ex hoc nunc et usque in saéculum.

℣. Dómine, exáudi oratiónem meam.

℟. Et clamor meus ad te véniat.

℣. Dóminus vobíscum.

℟. Et cum spíritu tuo.

Orémus.   Oratio

DEUS, qui per beátum Móysen, legíferum fámulum tuum,
tubas argénteas fíeri praecepísti, quibus, dum sacerdótes
témpore sacrifícii clángerent, sónitu dulcédinis pópulus mónitus
ad te adorándum fíeret praeparátus, et ad celebrándum convení-
ret: praesta, quaésumus; ut hoc vásculum sanctae tuae Ecclésiae
praeparátum, a Spíritu Sancto per nostrae humilitátis obséquium
sancti ✠ ficétur, ut per illíus tactum et sónitum fidéles invitén-tur
ad sanctam Ecclésiam et ad praémium supérnum. Et cum melódia
illíus áuribus insonúerit populórum, crescat in eis devótio fídei,
procul pellántur omnes insídiae inimíci, fragor grándium,
ímpetus tempestátum, temperéntur infésta tonítrua, prostérnat
aéreas potestátes déxtera tuae virtútis: ut hoc audiéntes tintinnábulum contremíscant et fúgiant ante sanctae Crucis vexíllum in
eo depíctum. Quod ipse Dóminus noster praestáre dignétur, qui

But there is forgiveness with thee, and because of thy law I trust in thee, O Lord.

Yea, in God do I trust, and my soul hopeth in His word.

From morn until night let Israel wait for the Lord;

For with the Lord there is mercy, and the plenitude of redemption is with Him.

He shall redeem Israel from all his guilt.

Glory be to the Father.

Lord, have mercy on us. Christ, have mercy on us. Lord, have mercy on us.

Our Father *inaudibly until*

℣. And lead us not into temptation.

℟. But deliver us from evil.

℣. May the name of the Lord be blessed.

℟. Henceforth and forever.

℣. O Lord, hear my prayer.

℟. And let my cry come unto thee.

℣. The Lord be with you.

℟. And with thy spirit.

Let us Pray. *Prayer*

O GOD! Thou didst command Moses thy servant and law-giver to fashion silver trumpets, whose sweet sounds should tell the people to prepare for thy worship and assemble for its celebration. So grant, we pray, that this bell destined for thy holy Church may, through our lowly ministry, be sanctified ☩ by the Holy Spirit; that its ringing will invite the faithful to the house of God and to eternal recompense. Let piety wax stronger in thy servants so often as their ears perceive the melodious peals. At its sound let evil spirits fly in terror, let thunder and lightning, hail and storm be banished, let the power of thy hand crush the powers of the air, that hearing the sounding bell they may tremble and vanish at the sign of the cross engraved thereon. This may our Lord Himself grant, Who overcoming death by

absórpta morte per patíbulum Crucis regnat in glória Dei Patris cum eódem Patre et Spíritu Sancto, per ómnia saécula saeculórum. ℟. Amen.

Nunc officians ponit incensum in thuribulum et benedicit: et primum aqua de more (pag. 8) antea benedicta aspergit circumeundo campanam, choro dicente:

Aspérges me, Dómine, hyssópo, et mundábor: lavábis me, et super nivem dealbábor.

Deinde incensat circumeundo campanam, choro dicente:

Antiphona

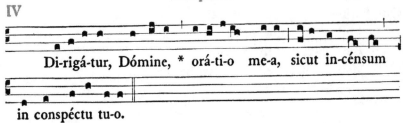

Di-rigá-tur, Dómine, * orá-ti-o me-a, sicut in-cénsum

in conspéctu tu-o.

Officians prosequitur:

Orémus.   Oratio

O MNÍPOTENS Dominátor, Christe, quo secúndum carnis assumptiónem dormiénte in navi, dum obórta tempéstas mare conturbásset, te prótinus excitáto et imperánte dissíluit: tu necessitátibus pópuli tui benígnus succúrre: tu hoc tintinnábulum Sancti Spíritus rore perfúnde: ut ante sónitum illíus semper fúgiat bonórum inimícus, invitétur ad fidem pópulus christiánus, hostílis terreátur exércitus, confortétur in Dómino per illud pópulus tuus convocátus, ac sicut Davídica cíthara delectátus désuper descéndat Spíritus Sanctus; atque ut Samuéle agnum lacténtem mactánte in holocáustum regis aetérni impérii, fragor aurárum turbam répulit adversántium: ita, dum hujus vásculi sónitus transit per núbila, Ecclésiae tuae convéntum manus consérvet angélica, fruges credéntium, mentes et córpora salvet protéctio sempitérna. Per te, Christe Jesu, qui cum Deo Patre vivis et regnas in unitáte ejúsdem Spíritus Sancti Deus, per ómnia saécula saeculórum. ℟. Amen.

℣. In honórem Sancti N. ℟. Amen.

the instrument of the cross reigneth in the glory of God the Father together with the Holy Spirit, forevermore. ℟. Amen.

The priest puts incense into the thurible, sprinkles the bell with holy water as he walks around it, while the choir sings:

Sprinkle me with hyssop, O Lord, and I shall be clean: wash me, and I shall be whiter than snow.

Then he incenses it, again walking around it, as the choir sings the antiphon:

May my prayer, O Lord, ascend as incense in thy sight.

Let us Pray.   Prayer

O CHRIST, the almighty Ruler! As thou didst once calm the stormy sea when awakened in the boat from the sleep of thy human nature, so too hasten to the necessities of thy people, and pour forth upon this bell the dew of thy Holy Spirit. Whenever it rings, may the spirit of evil depart, may the Christian people practice their faith, may Satan's power over them be stricken, and may they be strengthened in the Lord as they worship together. Let the Holy Spirit come down, as He did with joy over the playing of David's harp. And as onetime the thunder dispersed the host of foes while Samuel slew a mother-sheep as an offering to the eternal King, so when the peal of this bell penetrates the clouds, may the angelic legion guard the congress of worshippers. And let thine ever-abiding protection be salutary in soul and body to these the first-fruits among thy faithful. Through thee, Jesus Christ, Who livest and reignest with God the Father in the unity of the selfsame Holy Spirit, God, forever and ever. ℟. Amen.

℣. To the honor of Saint N. ℟. Amen.

Tum Officians producit super campanam benedictam signum crucis, et discedit cum Ministris.

Quod autem attinet ad ecclesias consecratas, in benedictione signi vel campanae curandum omnino est ut ab Episcopo vel a Sacerdote Apostolicum indultum habente servetur ritus Pontificalis Romani.

Lastly the priest signs the blest bell with the sign of the cross, and then departs with his assistants.

If this blessing is associated with a consecrated church, it is bestowed by a bishop or by a priest having apostolic indult, and the rite used is that from the Roman Pontifical.

V

BLESSINGS OF OTHER IRRATIONAL CREATURES

BENEDICTIO EQUORUM ALIORUMVE ANIMALIUM

℣. Adjutórium nostrum in nómine Dómini.
℞. Qui fecit caelum et terram.
℣. Dóminus vobíscum.
℞. Et cum spíritu tuo.

Orémus. *Oratio*

Deus, refúgium nostrum, et virtus: adésto piis Ecclésiae tuae précibus, auctor ipse pietátis, et praesta; ut, quod fidéliter pétimus, efficáciter consequámur. Per Christum Dóminum nostrum. ℞. Amen.

Orémus. *Oratio*

OMNÍPOTENS sempitérne Deus, qui gloriósum beátum Antónium, váriis tentatiónibus probátum, inter mundi hujus túrbines illaésum abíre fecísti: concéde fámulis tuis; ut et praecláro ipsíus proficiámus exémplo, et a praeséntis vitae perículis ejus méritis et intercessióne liberémur. Per Christum Dóminum nostrum. ℞.Amen.

Orémus. *Oratio*

BENE ✠DICTIÓNEM tuam, Dómine, haec animália accípiant: qua córpore salvéntur, et ab omni malo per intercessiónem beáti Antónii liberéntur. Per Christum Dóminum nostrum. ℞.Amen.

Et aspergantur aqua benedicta.

85

BLESSING OF HORSES OR OTHER ANIMALS

℣. Our help is in the name of the Lord.

℟. Who made heaven and earth.

℣. The Lord be with you.

℟. And with thy spirit.

Let us Pray. *Prayer*

O God, our refuge and our strength, give ear to the entreaties of thy Church, thou Source of mercy, and grant that what we seek with faith, we may receive in fact. Through Christ our Lord. ℟. Amen.

Let us Pray. *Prayer*

ALMIGHTY and everlasting God, Who didst assist Saint Antony to emerge unscathed from the many temptations of this world, grant thy servants to progress in virtue by his illustrious example; and by his merits and intercession, free us from the ever-present dangers of life. Through Christ our Lord. ℟. Amen.

Let us Pray. *Prayer*

LET these animals receive thy blessing, ✠ O Lord, to the benefit of their being, and by the intercession of St. Antony, deliver them from all harm. Through Christ our Lord. ℟. Amen.

They are sprinkled with holy water.

86

BENEDICTIO ANIMALIUM
gravi infirmitate laborantium

Sacerdos superpelliceo et stola violacea indutus, dicit:

℣. Adjutórium nostrum in nómine Dómini.
℟. Qui fecit caelum et terram.
℣. Dómine, non secúndum peccáta nostra fácias nobis.
℟. Neque secúndum iniquitátes nostras retríbuas nobis.
℣. Hómines et juménta salvábis, Dómine.
℟. Quemádmodum multiplicásti misericórdiam tuam, Deus.
℣. Aperis tu manum tuam.
℟. Et imples omne ánimal benedictióne.
℣. Dómine, exáudi oratiónem meam.
℟. Et clamor meus ad te véniat.
℣. Dóminus vobíscum.
℟. Et cum spíritu tuo.

Orémus. Oratio

Deus, qui labóribus hóminum étiam de mutis animálibus solátia subrogásti: súpplices te rogámus; ut, sine quibus non álitur humána condítio, nostris fácias úsibus non períre. Per Christum Dóminum nostrum. ℟. Amen.

Orémus. Oratio

MISERICÓRDIAM tuam, Dómine, súpplices exorámus: ut haec animália, quae gravi infirmitáte vexántur, in nómine tuo, atque tuae bene ✠ dictiónis virtúte sanéntur. Exstinguátur in eis omnis diabólica potéstas; et ne ultérius aegrótent, tu eis, Dómine, sis defénsio vitae et remédium sanitátis. Per Dóminum nostrum Jesum Christum, Fílium tuum: Qui tecum vivit et regnat in unitáte Spíritus Sancti Deus, per ómnia saécula saeculórum. ℟. Amen.

86

BLESSING OF SICK ANIMALS

Vested in surplice and purple stole, the priest says:

℣. Our help is in the name of the Lord.

℟. Who made heaven and earth.

℣. Deal not with us, O Lord, according to our sins.

℟. Nor take vengeance upon our transgressions.

℣. Thou, O Lord, shalt heal men and animals.

℟. For thou, O God, dost proffer fullest mercy.

℣. Thou openest thy hand.

℟. And fillest every creature with blessing.

℣. O Lord, hear my prayer.

℟. And let my cry come unto thee.

℣. The Lord be with you.

℟. And with thy spirit.

Let us Pray.   Prayer

O GOD, thou givest consolation to mankind when afflicted, and even to mute beasts. Wherefore, we suppliantly pray — let these animals not perish, for they are indispensable to our needs. Through Christ our Lord. ℟. Amen.

Let us Pray.   Prayer

THY mercy, O Lord, we humbly and perseveringly implore, that these animals afflicted with severe sickness may be cured in thy name and by the power of thy blessing ✠ . Let any effects in them of evil spirits become extinct, lest sickness afflict them again, and be thou, Lord, the guardian of their existence and the remedy to health. Through Jesus Christ, thy Son, our Lord, Who liveth and reigneth with thee in the unity of the Holy Spirit, God, for all eternity. ℟. Amen.

Orémus.

A VÉRTE, quaésumus, Dómine, a fidélibus tuis cuncta propítius flagélla: et morbórum in animália saeviéntium depélle
perníciem; ut, quos mérito plectis dévios, fóveas tua miseratióne
corréctos. Per Christum Dóminum nostrum. ℞. Amen.

Et aspergantur aqua benedicta.

87

ALIA BENEDICTIO ANIMALIUM
gravi infirmitate laborantium

℣. Adjutórium nostrum in nómine Dómini.
℞. Qui fecit caelum et terram.
℣. Dóminus vobíscum.
℞. Et cum spíritu tuo.

Orémus.

Misericórdiam tuam, Dómine, súpplices exorámus: ut haec
animália, quae gravi infirmitáte vexántur, in nómine tuo, atque
tuae bene ☩ dictiónis virtúte sanéntur. Exstinguátur in eis omnis
diabólica potéstas; et ne ultérius aegrótent, tu eis, Dómine, sis
defénsio vitae, et remédium sanitátis. Per Dóminum nostrum
Jesum Christum, Fílium tuum: Qui tecum vivit et regnat in
unitáte Spíritus Sancti Deus, per ómnia saécula saeculórum. ℞.
Amen.

Et aspergantur aqua benedicta.

88

BENEDICTIO PECORUM ET ARMENTORUM

℣. Adjutórium nostrum in nómine Dómini.
℞. Qui fecit caelum et terram.

Let us Pray.

T URN away every scourge from thy servants, we beseech thee, Lord, and drive out from these beasts the destroying sickness. For just as thou dost punish us when we deviate from thy paths, so reward us with thy mercy when we correct our evil ways. Through Christ our Lord. ℟. Amen.

They are sprinkled with holy water.

87

ANOTHER BLESSING OF SICK ANIMALS

℣. Our help is in the name of the Lord.
℟. Who made heaven and earth.
℣. The Lord be with you.
℟. And with thy spirit.

Let us Pray.

Thy mercy, O Lord, we humbly and perseveringly implore, that these animals afflicted with severe sickness may be cured in thy name and by the power of thy blessing ✠ . Let any effects in them of evil spirits become extinct, lest sickness afflict them again, and be thou, Lord, the guardian of their existence and the remedy to health. Through Jesus Christ, thy Son, our Lord, Who liveth and reigneth with thee in unity of the Holy Spirit, God, for all eternity. ℟. Amen.

They are sprinkled with holy water.

88

BLESSING OF CATTLE AND HERDS
(Cattle, sheep, goats, swine, etc.)

℣. Our help is in the name of the Lord.
℟. Who made heaven and earth.

℣. Dóminus vobíscum.

℟. Et cum spíritu tuo.

Orémus. Oratio

Dómine Deus, rex caeli et terrae, Verbum Patris, per quod ómnia facta sustentatióni nostrae trádita sunt, réspice, quaésumus, humilitátem nostram: et sicut nostris labóribus et necessitátibus subventiónem tribuísti, ita tua benigníssima miseratióne, ac caelésti benedictióne, haec pécora et arménta (hoc pecus et arméntum) bene ✠ dícere, tuéri, et custodíre, ac fámulis tuis cum temporáli provéntu grátiam perpétuam largíri dignéris; ut cum gratiárum actióne nomen sanctum tuum laudétur et glorificétur: Qui vivis et regnas cum Deo Patre in unitáte Spíritus Sancti Deus, per ómnia saécula saeculórum. ℟. Amen.

In nómine Patris, et Fílii, ✠ et Spíritus Sancti. ℟. Amen.

Et aspergantur aqua benedicta.

<h2 style="text-align:center">89</h2>

<h1 style="text-align:center">BENEDICTIO APUM</h1>

℣. Adjutórium nostrum in nómine Dómini.

℟. Qui fecit caelum et terram.

℣. Dóminus vobíscum.

℟. Et cum spíritu tuo.

Orémus. Oratio

Dómine Deus omnípotens, qui creásti caelum et terram, et ómnia animália super ea et in eis exsisténtia, ut eis uteréntur hómines; quique jussísti per minístros sacrosánctae Ecclésiae céreos ex opéribus apum edúctos in templo, dum sacrum perágitur ministérium, in quo confícitur et súmitur sacrosánctum Corpus et Sanguis Jesu Christi, Fílii tui, accéndi: descéndat tua sancta bene ✠ díctio super has apes et haec alveária; ut multíplicent, fructíficent et conservéntur ab ómnibus malis, ita ut

℣. The Lord be with you.

℟. And with thy spirit.

Let us Pray.

O Lord and God, King of heaven and earth, the Father's Word by Whom were made all creatures that sustain man! Look down, we pray, on our low estate, and as thou dost intervene in our necessities and distresses, so, too, deign to bless ✠ these cattle and flocks (this beast or herd), to guard and watch over them. But to us thy servants give everlasting grace together with creature needs, that we may praise, and glorify, and give thanks to thy holy name. Thou Who livest and reignest with God the Father in the unity of the Holy Spirit, God, forevermore. ℟. Amen.

In the name of the Father, and of the Son, ✠ and of the Holy Spirit. ℟. Amen.

They are sprinkled with holy water.

89

BLESSING OF BEES

℣. Our help is in the name of the Lord.

℟. Who made heaven and earth.

℣. The Lord be with you.

℟. And with thy spirit.

Let us pray.

O Lord God Almighty, Maker of heaven and earth! Thou didst create all living things for man's use. Moreover, thou didst order by the ministry of thy holy Church that candles made from the industry of bees shall burn during the Sacred Mystery in which we consecrate and consume the most holy Body and Blood of Jesus Christ, thy Son. Send thy holy blessing ✠ upon these bees and this beehive to make them numerous and productive, and to preserve them from harm, so that their yield of wax can

fructus ex eis proveniéntes ad laudem tuam, Fílii et Spíritus Sancti, beatissimaéque Vírginis Maríae dispenséntur. Per eúndem Christum Dóminum nostrum. ℞. Amen.

Et aspergantur aqua benedicta.

90

BENEDICTIO BOMBYCUM

℣. Adjutórium nostrum in nómine Dómini.
℞. Qui fecit caelum et terram.
℣. Dóminus vobíscum.
℞. Et cum spíritu tuo.

Orémus.   Oratio

Deus, ómnium creátor et rector, qui in animálium creatióne símilis suae speciéi propagándae virtútem contulísti, quaésumus, ut haec bómbycum sémina bene ✠ dícere, fovére ac multiplicáre tua pietáte dignéris, ut sancta altária tua, eórum opéribus adornáta, et fidéles tui eísdem fulgéntes, te, uti bonórum ómnium largitórem, toto corde gloríficent: Qui cum Unigénito tuo et Spíritu Sancto vivis et regnas in saécula saeculórum. ℞. Amen.

Et aspergantur aqua benedicta.

91

BENEDICTIO SALIS VEL AVENAE
pro animalibus

℣. Adjutórium nostrum in nómine Dómini.
℞. Qui fecit caelum et terram.
℣. Dóminus vobíscum.
℞. Et cum spíritu tuo.

be turned to thy honor, and to the honor of thy Son and Holy
Spirit, and to the veneration of the Blessed Virgin Mary. Through
the same Christ our Lord. ℟. Amen.

They are sprinkled with holy water.

90

BLESSING OF SILKWORMS

℣. Our help is in the name of the Lord.
℟. Who made heaven and earth.
℣. The Lord be with you.
℟. And with thy spirit.

Let us pray.   Prayer

O God, Maker and Director of the universe, Who in creating
living things didst endow each with the power of propagating
its own species, bless, ✠ we pray, these silkworms, foster them,
and let them multiply. May thy holy altars be adorned with the
fruit of their industry. And let thy faithful servants resplendent
in robes of silk acknowledge thee with heartfelt praise as the
Donor of every Good. Who with thy Sole-Begotten Son and the
Holy Spirit livest and reignest for all eternity. ℟. Amen.

They are sprinkled with holy water.

91

BLESSING OF SALT OR OATS
for animals

℣. Our help is in the name of the Lord.
℟. Who made heaven and earth.
℣. The Lord be with you.
℟. And with thy spirit.

Orémus.

Dómine Deus, ómnium cónditor et conservátor, cujus in manu est ánima omnis vivéntis, et spíritus univérsae carnis: exáudi, quaésumus, tuórum fidélium preces, et hanc creatúram salis (vel avénae) tua bene ✠ dictióne, tuaéque invisíbilis operatiónis virtúte perfúnde; ut animália, quae necessitátibus humánis tribúere dignátus es, cum ex eo (ea) gustáverint, ab omni morbo illaésa reddántur, et a malígni spíritus incúrsu, te protegénte, custodiántur. Per Christum Dóminum nostrum. ℞. Amen.

Et aspergatur aqua benedicta.

92

BENEDICTIO STABULI
equorum, boum aliorumve armentorum

℣. Adjutórium nostrum in nómine Dómini.
℞. Qui fecit caelum et terram.
℣. Dóminus vobíscum.
℞. Et cum spíritu tuo.

Orémus.

Dómine Deus omnípotens, qui Fílium tuum unigénitum, Redemptórem nostrum, in stábulo nasci, et inter duo animália in praesépio reclinári voluísti: béne ✠ dic, quaésumus, hoc stábulum, et defénde illud ab omni nequítia vel versútia diabólicae fraudis; ut juméntis, pecóribus, ceterísque animántibus efficiátur locus sanus, et ab omni impugnatióne secúrus. Et quóniam cognóvit bos possessórem suum, et ásinus praesépe dómini sui: misericórditer tríbue fámulis tuis, quos ad imáginem tuam creásti, paulo minus ab Angelis minuísti, et sub quorum pédibus subjecísti oves et boves univérsas, ínsuper et pécora campi; ne comparéntur juméntis insipiéntibus, et ne fiant sicut equus et mulus, quibus non est intelléctus; sed te solum Deum auctórem bonórum ómnium agnóscant, et in servítio tuo fidéles persevérent, quátenus de

Let us pray.   Prayer

O Lord God, Founder and Preserver of the universe, in Whose hand is the life and breath of every creature, hear, we beseech thee, our prayers, and bestow on this creature of salt (or oats) thy blessing ✠ and the invisible working of thy might. May the animals which thou has given for the service of men be spared from sickness when they eat thereof, and by thee be protected from the affliction of evil spirits. Through Christ our Lord. ℟. Amen.

They are sprinkled with holy water.

92

BLESSING OF A STABLE
for horses, cattle, etc.

℣. Our help is in the name of the Lord.
℟. Who made heaven and earth.
℣. The Lord be with you.
℟. And with thy spirit.

Let us pray.   Prayer

O Lord God Almighty, Who didst will that thy Sole-Begotten Son, our Lord be born in a stable, and lie in a manger between two animals, bless ✠ this stable, we pray, and guard it from the spite and deceit of the devil. Make it a safe shelter for horses, cattle, and other animals. And as the ox knows his master and the ass the manger of his lord, so grant that thy servants, who are made to thine image and closely resemble the angels, and to whom thou hast subjected all the sheep, and the oxen, and the cattle of the pastures, be not like unto senseless beasts, the horse or the mule in whom there is no understanding. But let them acknowledge thee alone as God and the Author of all good. May they faithfully persevere in thy service, show thee gratitude for

percéptis munéribus tibi grátias exhibéntes, benefícia potióra percípere mereántur. Per eúndem Christum Dóminum nostrum.
℟. Amen.

Deinde, si tunc in stabulo congregata sint animalia, addere potest
Sacerdos sequentes Orationes: **Omnípotens sempitérne Deus, qui
gloriósum,** etc., et **Benedictiónem tuam,** etc., uti supra in Benedictione
equorum aliorumve animalium, pag. 328.
Postea aspergat aqua benedicta stabulum et animalia.

93

BENEDICTIO LINTEAMINUM PRO INFIRMIS

℣. Adjutórium nostrum in nómine Dómini.
℟. Qui fecit caelum et terram.
℣. Dóminus vobíscum.
℟. Et cum spíritu tuo.

Orémus.   Oratio

Dómine Jesu Christe, qui per tactum fímbriae vestimentórum
tuórum mulíerem fluxu sánguinis laborántem, aliósque passim
infírmos sanáre dignátus es, et per sudária, et semicínctia Apóstoli tui Pauli languóres et spíritus nequam ab infírmis eádem
virtúte fugásti: praesta, quaésumus; ut qui his vestiméntis, velis,
et linteamínibus, quae in tuo nómine bene ✝ dícimus, indúti vel
opérti fúerint, sanitátem mentis et córporis percípere mereántur:
Qui vivis et regnas in saécula saeculórum. ℟. Amen.

Et aspergantur aqua benedicta.

94

BENEDICTIO LECTICAE PRO INFIRMIS

℣. Adjutórium nostrum in nómine Dómini.
℟. Qui fecit caelum et terram.

favors received, and thus merit greater benefits in future. Through the same Christ our Lord. ℟. Amen.

Then, if the animals are enclosed in the stable, the priest may add the following prayers: **Almighty and everlasting God,** etc., and **Let these animals receive thy blessing,** etc., from the blessing given above for horses or other animals, page 329.

The stable and animals are sprinkled with holy water.

93

BLESSING OF LINENS FOR THE SICK

℣. Our help is in the name of the Lord.
℟. Who made heaven and earth.
℣. The Lord be with you.
℟. And with thy spirit.

Let us pray.   *Prayer*

O Lord, Jesus Christ! By a touch of the hem of thy garment thou didst heal the woman suffering from an issue of blood, and didst restore health to divers infirm. Indeed, in thy same might thou didst dispel illness and diabolical possession from the sick who touched the handkerchief and girdle of thine Apostle Paul. Wherefore, we pray, that they who use these linens which we bless ✝ in thy name, may enjoy health of body and soul. Thou Who livest and reignest eternally. ℟. Amen.

They are sprinkled with holy water.

94

BLESSING OF A STRETCHER, OR AN AMBULANCE, OR A WHEELCHAIR

℣. Our help is in the name of the Lord.
℟. Who made heaven and earth.

℣. Dóminus vobíscum.

℞. Et cum spíritu tuo.

Orémus.   Oratio

Dómine Jesu Christe, Fili Dei vivi, dum peregrinabáris in terris, pertransíbas benefaciéndo, et sanándo omnem languórem et omnem infirmitátem in pópulis, quique hóminem paralýticum, jacéntem in lecto, ad salútem mentis et córporis restituísti; réspice, quaésumus, ad fidem et ad sensus commiseratiónis servórum tuórum, qui animáti spíritu verae caritátis, qua tu eis exémplo praeivísti, et quam in praecéptum traduxísti, vehículum hoc, ad instar léctuli artificióse éxstrui voluérunt eo fine, ut ad locum curatiónis vel aptíssime deférri possint quicúmque, aut vulnéribus sint affécti, aut quavis infirmitáte detineántur. Aegrótis ígitur, qui hoc componúntur vehículo, quod nunc in tui nóminis virtúte bene ✠ dícimus, esto, mitíssime Jesu, in itínere solátium, in perículis tutámen, in dolóribus refrigérium. Praesta, ut iídem, tuis Angelis comitántibus, ad curatiónis sedem tranquíllo cursu pervéniant, ibíque prístinam sanitátem recúperent, eáque, te miseránte, per intercessiónem sanctíssimae tuae Matris Maríae, percépta, abeúntes in domos suas, honoríficent te Deum verum: Qui cum Patre et Spíritu Sancto vivis et regnas in saécula saeculórum.

℞. Amen.

Et aspergatur aqua benedicta.

95

BENEDICTIO VINI PRO INFIRMIS

℣. Adjutórium nostrum in nómine Dómini.

℞. Qui fecit caelum et terram.

℣. Dóminus vobíscum.

℞. Et cum spíritu tuo.

℣. The Lord be with you.
℟. And with thy spirit.

Let us pray.   Prayer

O Lord, Jesus Christ, Son of the living God! In thine earthly
sojourn thou didst go about doing good, alleviating suffering
and infirmity, and restoring corporal and spiritual vigor to the
paralytic lying on his pallet. Mercifully regard, we implore, the
faith and commiseration of thy people who, animated with thine
example and precept of true charity, have constructed this
stretcher (or ambulance, or wheelchair) to bear the wounded and
infirm to the place of healing. As we bless ✠ it in thy name, let
it become, O Jesus mild, a comfort on the journey, a safeguard in
perils, a mitigation in suffering to them who will be carried
thereon. Grant that, under company of thine angels, they may
be borne in comfort to the place of cure, recovering there their
former good health. Thus favored by thy mercy and goodness
and the suffrage of Mary, thy blessed mother, let them return to
their homes praising and glorifying thee, the true God. Thou
Who livest and reignest with the Father and the Holy Spirit in
eternity. ℟. Amen.

It is sprinkled with holy water.

95

BLESSING OF WINE FOR THE SICK

℣. Our help is in the name of the Lord.
℟. Who made heaven and earth.
℣. The Lord be with you.
℟. And with thy spirit.

Orémus.

Dómine Jesu Christe, Fili Dei vivi, qui in Cana Galilaéae ex aqua vinum fecísti: bene ✠ dícere et sancti ✠ ficáre dignéris hanc creatúram vini, quam ad sustentatiónem servórum tuórum tribuísti; ut, ubicúmque fusum fúerit, vel a quólibet potátum, divína opuléntiae tuae bene ✠ dictióne repleátur.

OMNÍPOTENS sempitérne Deus, salus aetérna credéntium, exáudi nos pro fámulo tuo infírmo (fámula tua infírma, seu fámulis tuis infírmis) pro quo (qua, seu quibus) misericórdiae tuae implorámus auxílium; ut, réddita sibi sanitáte, gratiárum tibi in Ecclésia tua réferat (–ant) actiónes. Per Christum Dóminum nostrum. ℞. Amen.

Et aspergatur vinum aqua benedicta.

96

BENEDICTIO CUJUSCUMQUE MEDICINAE

℣. Adjutórium nostrum in nómine Dómini.
℞. Qui fecit caelum et terram.
℣. Dóminus vobíscum.
℞. Et cum spíritu tuo.

Orémus.

Deus, qui mirabíliter hóminem creásti, et mirabílius reformásti, qui váriis infirmitátibus, quibus detinétur humána mortálitas, multíplici remédio succúrrere dignátus es: propítius esto invocatiónibus nostris, et sanctam tuam de caelis bene ✠ dictiónem super hanc medicínam infúnde, ut ille, qui eam súmpserit (illi, qui eam súmpserint), sanitátem mentis et córporis percípere mereátur (–ántur). Per Christum Dóminum nostrum. ℞. Amen.

Et aspergatur aqua benedicta.

Let us pray. Prayer

O Lord, Jesus Christ, Son of the living God, Who in Cana of Galilee didst change water into wine, bless ✠ and sanctify ✠ this wine made by thee for man's strengthening. Let the opulence of thy divine blessing ✠ accompany it whenever it is taken as drink or poured into wounds.

ALMIGHTY and eternal God, everlasting Health of believers! Hear us for the sake of thy sick servant (handmaid, or servants) for whom we implore thy merciful assistance, that restored to health, he (she, or they) may render thee thanksgiving in thy Church. Through Christ our Lord. ℟. Amen.

It is sprinkled with holy water.

96

BLESSING OF MEDICINE

℣. Our help is in the name of the Lord.
℟. Who made heaven and earth.
℣. The Lord be with you.
℟. And with thy spirit.

Let us pray. Prayer

O God, Who hast wondrously created man and still more marvellously transformed him; Who condescendest to hasten with thy healing art to the many infirmities which beset mankind, bend a merciful ear to our entreaties, and bestow heavenly blessing ✠ on this medicine. Let him (her) who will use it regain bodily and spiritual health. Through Christ our Lord. ℟. Amen.

It is sprinkled with holy water.

97

BENEDICTIO PANIS ET PLACENTARUM

℣. Adjutórium nostrum in nómine Dómini.

℟. Qui fecit caelum et terram.

℣. Dóminus vobíscum.

℟. Et cum spíritu tuo.

Orémus. *Oratio*

Dómine Jesu Christe, panis Angelórum, panis vivus, et aetérnae vitae: bene ✠ dícere dignáre panem istum, sicut benedixísti quinque panes in desérto: ut omnes ex eo digne gustántes, inde córporis et ánimae desiderábilem percípiant sanitátem: Qui vivis et regnas in saécula saeculórum. ℟. Amen.

Et aspergatur aqua benedicta.

98

BENEDICTIO CEREVISIAE

℣. Adjutórium nostrum in nómine Dómini.

℟. Qui fecit caelum et terram.

℣. Dóminus vobíscum.

℟. Et cum spíritu tuo.

Orémus. *Oratio*

Béne ✠ dic, Dómine, creatúram istam cerevísiae, quam ex ádipe fruménti prodúcere dignátus es: ut sit remédium salutáre humáno géneri: et praesta per invocatiónem nóminis tui sancti, ut, quicúmque ex ea bíberint, sanitátem córporis, et ánimae tutélam percípiant. Per Christum Dóminum nostrum. ℟. Amen.

Et aspergatur aqua benedicta.

97

BLESSING OF BREAD AND CAKES

℣. Our help is in the name of the Lord.
℟. Who made heaven and earth.
℣. The Lord be with you.
℟. And with thy spirit.

Let us pray.   Prayer

O Lord, Jesus Christ, bread of angels, living bread unto eternal life, bless ✠ this bread as thou didst bless the five loaves in the wilderness; that all who eat it with reverence may through it attain the corporal and spiritual health they desire. Who livest and reignest eternally. ℟. Amen.

It is sprinkled with holy water.

98

BLESSING OF ALE

℣. Our help is in the name of the Lord.
℟. Who made heaven and earth.
℣. The Lord be with you.
℟. And with thy spirit.

Let us pray.   Prayer

Bless, ✠ O Lord, this creature, ale which by thy power has been produced from kernels of grain. May it be a healthful beverage to mankind, and grant that through the invoking of thy holy name all who drink thereof may find it a help in body and protection in soul. Through Christ our Lord. ℟. Amen.

It is sprinkled with holy water.

99

BENEDICTIO CASEI VEL BUTYRI

℣. Adjutórium nostrum in nómine Dómini.
℟. Qui fecit caelum et terram.
℣. Dóminus vobíscum.
℟. Et cum spíritu tuo.

    Orémus.   Oratio

Dignáre, Dómine Deus omnípotens, bene ✠ dícere, et sancti ✠ ficáre hanc creatúram cásei (vel butyri), quam ex ádipe animálium prodúcere dignátus es: ut, quicúmque ex pópulis tuis fidélibus de eo coméderint, omni benedictióne caelésti, et grátia tua saturáti, repleántur in bonis. Per Christum Dóminum nostrum.
℟. Amen.

Et aspergatur aqua benedicta.

100

BENEDICTIO LARIDI

℣. Adjutórium nostrum in nómine Dómini.
℟. Qui fecit caelum et terram.
℣. Dóminus vobíscum.
℟. Et cum spíritu tuo.

    Orémus.   Oratio

Béne ✠ dic, Dómine, creatúram istam láridi, ut sit remédium salutáre géneri humáno: et praesta per invocatiónem tui sancti nóminis; ut, quicúmque ex eo súmpserint, córporis sanitátem et ánimae tutélam percípiant. Per Christum Dóminum nostrum.
℟. Amen.

Et aspergatur aqua benedicta.

99

BLESSING OF CHEESE OR BUTTER

℣. Our help is in the name of the Lord.
℟. Who made heaven and earth.
℣. The Lord be with you.
℟. And with thy spirit.

Let us pray.   Prayer

Vouchsafe, O Lord, God Almighty to bless ✠ and sanctify ✠ this cheese (or butter) which by thy power has been formed from the fat of animals. May thy faithful people who eat it be filled with thy grace, thy blessing, and all good things. Through Christ our Lord. ℟. Amen.

It is sprinkled with holy water.

100

BLESSING OF LARD

℣. Our help is in the name of the Lord.
℟. Who made heaven and earth.
℣. The Lord be with you.
℟. And with thy spirit.

Let us pray.   Prayer

Bless, ✠ O Lord, this lard that it be healthful to mankind, and grant that in calling upon thy holy name, everyone who eats thereof may perceive a help for body and protection for soul. Through Christ our Lord. ℟. Amen.

It is sprinkled with holy water.

101

BENEDICTIO VOLUCRUM

℣. Adjutórium nostrum in nómine Dómini.
℟. Qui fecit caelum et terram.
℣. Dóminus vobíscum.
℟. Et cum spíritu tuo.

Orémus.   Oratio

Deus, univérsae cónditor natúrae, qui inter céteras diversárum creaturárum spécies, pro humáni géneris usu étiam volatílium genus ex aqua prodúcere dignátus es; de quibus Noe ex arca egrédiens holocáustum tibi plácitum óbtulit; et qui pópulo tuo ex Aegýpto edúcto per Móysen servum tuum, munda ab immúndis ségregans, ut de iis éderent, praecéptum dedísti: te súpplices rogámus, ut has mundárum ávium carnes bene ✠ dícere et sancti ✠ ficáre dignéris; ut, quicúmque ex iis coméderint, benedictiónis tuae abundántia repleántur, et ad aetérnae vitae páscua perveníre mereántur. Per Christum Dóminum nostrum.
℟. Amen.

Et aspergantur aqua benedicta.

102

BENEDICTIO UVARUM

℣. Adjutórium nostrum in nómine Dómini.
℟. Qui fecit caelum et terram.
℣. Dóminus vobíscum.
℟. Et cum spíritu tuo.

Orémus.   Oratio

Bene ✠ dic, Dómine, hos fructus novos víneae, quos tu rore caeli, et abundántia pluviárum, et témporum serenitáte atque

101

BLESSING OF FOWL-MEAT

℣. Our help is in the name of the Lord.
℟. Who made heaven and earth.
℣. The Lord be with you.
℟. And with thy spirit.

Let us pray.   Prayer

O God, Author of all nature! Among the many created species which thy bounty prompted to bestow for man's use, thou didst also preserve winged creatures from the flood. With these, Noe, in coming forth from the ark, rendered thee a pleasing burnt-offering. And in Israel's deliverance from Egypt, thou didst order through Moses, thy servant that the people should eat the birds of the air, separating the clean from the unclean. Wherefore, we suppliantly pray — do thou bless ✠ and sanctify ✠ this flesh of clean birds, so that all who eat thereof may be filled with thy bounteous blessing, and may merit to come to the feast of ever-lasting life. Through Christ our Lord. ℟. Amen.

It is sprinkled with holy water.

102

BLESSING OF GRAPES

℣. Our help is in the name of the Lord.
℟. Who made heaven and earth.
℣. The Lord be with you.
℟. And with thy spirit.

Let us pray.   Prayer

Bless, ✠ O Lord, this fruit of the vine, which thou hast deigned to bring to maturity with the aid of heavenly dew, an abundance

tranquillitáte, ad maturitátem perdúcere dignátus es, et dedísti eos ad usus nostros cum gratiárum actióne percípere in nómine Dómini nostri Jesu Christi: Qui tecum vivit et regnat in unitáte Spíritus Sancti Deus, per ómnia saécula saeculórum. ℞. Amen.

Et aspergantur aqua benedicta.

103

BENEDICTIO SEMINUM

℣. Adjutórium nostrum in nómine Dómini.
℞. Qui fecit caelum et terram.
℣. Dóminus vobíscum.
℞. Et cum spíritu tuo.

Orémus.   Oratio

Te rogámus, Dómine, ac pétimus: ut hos fructus séminum bene ✠ dícere, plácido lenis aurae afflátu fovére, rore caelésti foecundáre, et incólumes propter usum animárum et córporum ad pleníssimam maturitátem perdúcere dignéris. Per Christum Dóminum nostrum. ℞. Amen.

Et aspergantur aqua benedicta.

104

BENEDICTIO IGNIS

℣. Adjutórium nostrum in nómine Dómini.
℞. Qui fecit caelum et terram.
℣. Dóminus vobíscum.
℞. Et cum spíritu tuo.

Orémus.   Oratio

Dómine Deus, Pater omnípotens, lumen indefíciens, qui es cónditor ómnium lúminum: novum hunc ignem sanctí ✠ fica,

of rain, and favorable weather; and may we with gratitude use them in the name of Jesus Christ, our Lord, Who liveth and reigneth with thee in unity of the Holy Spirit, God, for all eternity. ℞. Amen.

They are sprinkled with holy water.

103

BLESSING OF SEED

℣. Our help is in the name of the Lord.
℞. Who made heaven and earth.
℣. The Lord be with you.
℞. And with thy spirit.

Let us pray. Prayer

We fervently entreat thee, O Lord, to bless ✠ these seeds, preserve and foster them with gentle breezes, fertilize them with heavenly dew, and deign to bring them to a full harvest for the use of soul and body. Through Christ our Lord. ℞. Amen.

They are sprinkled with holy water.

104

BLESSING OF FIRE

℣. Our help is in the name of the Lord.
℞. Who made heaven and earth.
℣. The Lord be with you.
℞. And with thy spirit.

Let us pray. Prayer

O Lord God, almighty Father, unfailing Light! Thou art the Maker of every light. Do thou sanctify ✠ this new fire, and grant

et praesta; ut ad te, qui es lumen indefíciens, puris méntibus, post hujus saéculi calíginem, perveníre valeámus. Per Christum Dóminum nostrum. ℟. Amen.

Et aspergatur aqua benedicta.

105

BENEDICTIO SUPER FRUGES ET VINEAS

℣. Adjutórium nostrum in nómine Dómini.
℟. Qui fecit caelum et terram.
℣. Dóminus vobíscum.
℟. Et cum spíritu tuo.

Orémus.   Oratio

Crámus pietátem tuam, omnípotens Deus, ut has primítias creatúrae tuae, quas áëris et plúviae temperaménto nutríre dignátus es, bene ✠ dictiónis tuae imbre perfúndas, et fructus terrae tuae usque ad maturitátem perdúcas. Tríbue quoque pópulo tuo de tuis munéribus tibi semper grátias ágere; ut a fertilitáte terrae esuriéntium ánimas bonis ómnibus affluéntibus répleas, et egénus et pauper laudent nomen glóriae tuaé. Per Christum Dóminum nostrum. ℟. Amen.

Et aspergantur aqua benedicta.

106

BENEDICTIO CAMPORUM VEL ALPIUM VEL PASCUORUM

(Approbata a S. R. C. die 1 Dec. 1886)

℣. Adjutórium nostrum in nómine Dómini.
℟. Qui fecit caelum et terram.
℣. Dóminus vobíscum.
℟. Et cum spíritu tuo.

that after the darkness of this world, we may come with pure hearts to thee Who art perpetual Light. Through Christ our Lord. ℟. Amen.

It is sprinkled with holy water.

105

BLESSING OF YOUNG CROPS AND VINEYARDS

℣. Our help is in the name of the Lord.
℟. Who made heaven and earth.
℣. The Lord be with you.
℟. And with thy spirit.

Let us pray. *Prayer*

We appeal to thy graciousness, O almighty God, that thou wouldst shower thy blessing ✠ upon these first-fruits of creation, which thou hast nurtured with favorable weather, and mayest bring them to a fine harvest. Grant also to thy people a sense of constant gratitude for thy gifts, so that the hungry may find rich nourishment in the fruits of the earth, and the needy and the poor may praise thy wondrous name. Through Christ our Lord. ℟. Amen.

They are sprinkled with holy water.

106

BLESSING OF FIELDS, OR MOUNTAIN-MEADOWS,
or Pastures
(Approved by the Congregation of Sacred Rites on Dec. 1, 1886)

℣. Our help is in the name of the Lord.
℟. Who made heaven and earth.
℣. The Lord be with you.
℟. And with thy spirit.

Orémus.

Deus, a quo omne bonum sumit inítium, et semper ad potióra progrédiens pércipit increméntum: concéde, quaésumus, supplicántibus nobis; ut quod ad laudem nóminis tui inchoáre aggrédimur, aetérno tuae sapiéntiae múnere ad términum perducátur. Per Christum Dóminum nostrum. ℞. Amen.

Orémus.

OMNÍPOTENS sempitérne Deus, qui sacerdótibus tuis prae céteris grátiam conférre dignátus es, ut quidquid in tuo nómine ab iis digne et perfécte ágitur, a te fíeri credátur: quaésumus cleméntiam tuam; ut quod modo visitatúri sumus, tu quoque vísites, et quod benedictúri sumus, tu quoque bene ✠ dícas, et ad ea quae actúri sumus, tuae poténtiae déxteram exténdas: sit ad humilitátis nostrae ingréssum, Sanctórum tuórum méritis et intercessiónibus, fuga daémonum, ac tuórum ingréssus Angelórum. Per Christum Dóminum nostrum. ℞. Amen.

Dicantur flexis genibus Litaniae Sanctorum (pag. 444), et postquam recitatus fuerit sequens

℣. Ut ánimas nostras, fratrum, propinquórum, et benefactórum nostrórum ab aetérna damnatióne erípias, te rogámus, audi nos.

Sacerdos surgens dicat:

℣. Ut hos campos (vel agros, vel has alpes, vel haec páscua, vel prata) bene ✠ dícere dignéris.

℞. Te rogámus, audi nos.

℣. Ut hos campos (vel agros, vel has alpes, vel haec páscua, vel prata) bene ✠ dícere et con ✠ serváre dignéris.

℞. Te rogámus, audi nos.

℣. Ut hos campos (vel agros, vel has alpes, vel haec páscua, vel prata) bene ✠ dícere, con ✠ serváre, et ab omni daémonum infestatióne custo ✠ díre dignéris.

℞. Te rogámus audi nos.

Let us pray.

O God, from Whom every good has its beginning, and from Whom it receives its increase, hear our prayers, we implore, that what we begin for thy honor and glory, may be brought by the gift of thine eternal wisdom to a happy ending. Through Christ our Lord. ℟. Amen.

Let us pray.

GOD of mercy and of strength, Who didst confer on thy priests above all others so great a grace, that whatever they do worthily and perfectly in thy name, is, as it were, done by thee, we beseech thy boundless goodness, that whatever we presume to visit, may be visited by thee, and whatever we presume to bless, may be blessed ✠ by thee. Stretch out thy hand of might over what we are about to do, and at our lowly coming, through the merits and prayers of thy saints, expel the devil and let thine angels preside. Through Christ our Lord. ℟. Amen.

All kneel for the Litany of the Saints (page 445); and after the verse:

℣. That thou wouldst vouchsafe to snatch from eternal damnation our souls and those of our brethren, relatives, and benefactors, we beseech thee, hear us,

The priest rises, and says:

℣. That thou wouldst vouchsafe to bless ✠ these fields (or acres, or these mountain-meadows, or pastures, or meadows).

℟. We beseech thee, hear us.

℣. That thou wouldst vouchsafe to bless ✠ and consecrate ✠ these fields (or acres, or these mountain-meadows, or pastures, or meadows).

℟. We beseech thee, hear us.

℣. That thou wouldst vouchsafe to bless, ✠ consecrate, ✠ and protect ✠ from devilish infection these fields (or acres, or these mountain-meadows, or pastures, or meadows).

℟. We beseech thee, hear us.

℣. Ut fúlgura, grándines, saevas tempestátes et nóxias aquárum inundatiónes a loco isto cleménter expéllere et effugáre dignéris.

℟. Te rogámus, audi nos.

Deinde prosequitur et absolvit Litanias: et ad finem dicit:

Pater noster secreto usque ad

℣. Et ne nos indúcas in tentatiónem.

℟. Sed líbera nos a malo.

℣. Emítte Spíritum tuum, et creabúntur.

℟. Et renovábis fáciem terrae.

℣. Dóminus dabit benignitátem.

℟. Et terra nostra dabit fructum suum.

℣. Dómine, exáudi oratiónem meam.

℟. Et clamor meus ad te véniat.

℣. Dóminus vobíscum.

℟. Et cum spíritu tuo.

Orémus.   Oratio

PIETÁTEM tuam, omnípotens Deus, humíliter implorámus, ut hos campos (vel hos agros, vel has alpes, vel haec páscua, vel prata), quos (vel quas, vel quae) áëris temperaménto nutríre dignátus es, tuae bene ✠ dictiónis imbre perfúndere dignéris, tríbuens pópulo tuo de tuis munéribus tibi semper grátias ágere, et pulsa terrae sterilitáte, esuriéntium ánimos bonis affluéntibus replére, ut egéni et páuperes laudent nomen glóriae tuae in saécula saeculórum. ℟. Amen.

Et aspergantur aqua benedicta.

107

BENEDICTIO HORREI SEU SEGETUM DEMESSARUM

℣. Adjutórium nostrum in nómine Dómini.

℟. Qui fecit caelum et terram.

℣. That thou wouldst vouchsafe mercifully to ward off and dispel from this place all lightning, hail-storm, injurious tempests, and harmful floods.

℟. We beseech thee, hear us.

Then the Litany is resumed to its completion.

Our Father inaudibly until

℣. And lead us not into temptation.

℟. But deliver us from evil.

℣. Send forth thy Spirit, and the world shall arise as new.

℟. And the countenance of the earth shall be renewed.

℣. The Lord shall give goodness.

℟. And the earth shall yield her fruit.

℣. O Lord, hear my prayer.

℟. And let my cry come unto thee.

℣. The Lord be with you.

℟. And with thy spirit.

Let us pray.   Prayer

THY kindness, O almighty God, we humbly implore, that thou wouldst shower thy blessing ✠ upon these fields (or these acres, or these mountain-meadows, or these pastures, or meadows), which thou hast nurtured with favorable weather. Grant to thy people a sense of constant gratitude for thy gifts. Destroy any infertility in the land, thus filling the hungry with an affluence of good things; so that the poor and the needy may praise thy wondrous name for all time and eternity. ℟. Amen.

They are sprinkled with holy water.

107

BLESSING OF A GRANARY
or the Harvest

℣. Our help is in the name of the Lord.

℟. Who made heaven and earth.

℣. Dóminus vobíscum.

℟. Et cum spíritu tuo.

Orémus. Oratio

Dómine Deus omnípotens, qui de rore caeli abundántiam, et de pinguédine terrae substántiam homínibus conférre non désinis: piíssimae majestáti tuae pro colléctis frúctibus grátias ágimus, tuam cleméntiam exorántes; ut has ségetes, quas de benignitáte tua suscépimus, bene ✠dícere, conserváre, et ab omni noxa deféndere dignéris: simúlque concéde; ut, quorum in bonis replésti desidérium, de tua custódia gloriéntur, misericórdias tuas sine fine colláudent, et sic tránseant per bona temporália, ut non amíttant aetérna. Per Christum Dóminum nostrum. ℟. Amen.

Et aspergantur aqua benedicta.

108

BENEDICTIO PISTRINI

℣. Adjutórium nostrum in nómine Dómini.

℟. Qui fecit caelum et terram.

℣. Dóminus vobíscum.

℟. Et cum spíritu tuo.

Orémus. Oratio

Omnípotens sempitérne Deus, qui in poenam peccáti dixísti In sudóre vultus tui vescéris pane tuo; béne ✠dic pistrínum istud quod ad teréndum fruméntum eréctum est, ut inde panis conficiátur ad nostram sustentatiónem, Angelúmque lucis ac defensiónis ei assignáre dignéris. Per Christum Dóminum nostrum ℟. Amen.

Et aspergatur aqua benedicta.

℣. The Lord be with you.
℟. And with thy spirit.

Let us pray. Prayer

O Lord, almighty God, Who dost not desist from pouring out upon men a superabundance of heavenly dew and the substance of the earth's richness, we render thanksgiving to thy most loving Majesty for all thy gifts. We continue to beseech thy clemency, that thou wouldst deign to bless, ✠ preserve, and defend from every injury this harvest. Grant, likewise, that having had our desire for earthly needs filled, we may bask under thy protection, praise thy goodness and mercy without ceasing, and make use of temporal goods in such a way as not to lose eternal goods. Through Christ our Lord. ℟. Amen.

They are sprinkled with holy water.

108

BLESSING OF A MILL

℣. Our help is in the name of the Lord.
℟. Who made heaven and earth.
℣. The Lord be with you.
℟. And with thy spirit.

Let us pray. Prayer

Almighty, everlasting God! As a punishment for sin, thou didst say: "In the sweat of thy brow thou shalt eat thy bread." Do thou bless ✠ this mill built to grind grain into flour, from which bread will be furnished for our life's sustenance. And graciously appoint an angel of light as a guard at this mill. Through Christ our Lord. ℟. Amen.

It is sprinkled with holy water.

109

BENEDICTIO PUTEI

℣. Adjutórium nostrum in nómine Dómini.

℞. Qui fecit caelum et terram.

℣. Dóminus vobíscum.

℞. Et cum spíritu tuo.

Orémus.   *Oratio*

Dómine Deus omnípotens, qui in hujus pútei altitúdinem per crepídinem fistulárum cópiam aquárum manáre jussísti: praesta: ut te juvánte atque bene ✠ dicénte per nostrae offícium functiónis, repúlsis hinc phantasmáticis collusiónibus, ac diabólicis insídiis, purificátus atque emundátus semper hic púteus persevéret. Per Christum Dóminum nostrum. ℞. Amen.

Et aspergatur aqua benedicta.

110

BENEDICTIO FONTIS

℣. Adjutórium nostrum in nómine Dómini.

℞. Qui fecit caelum et terram.

℣. Dóminus vobíscum.

℞. Et cum spíritu tuo.

Orémus.   *Oratio*

Súpplices deprecámur, Dómine, cleméntiam pietátis tuae: ut aquam fontis hujus caelésti benedictióne sanctí ✠ fices, et ad commúnem vitae usum concédas esse salúbrem; et ita omnem diabólicae tentatiónis incúrsum inde fugáre dignéris, ut quicúmque ex eo háuserint vel bíberint, vel in quibuscúmque necessáriis úsibus hausta aqua usi fúerint, totíus virtútis ac sanitátis dulcédine perfruántur, tibíque sanctificatóri et salvatóri ómnium Dómino

109

BLESSING OF A WELL

℣. Our help is in the name of the Lord.
℟. Who made heaven and earth.
℣. The Lord be with you.
℟. And with thy spirit.

Let us pray. Prayer

O Lord God Almighty, from the depths of this well thou orderest copious water to issue forth out of the pipes. Lend, therefore, thy assistance and blessing ✠ to the office which we perform, so that devilish cunning and deceit may be put to flight, and this well may remain cleansed and purified for all time. Through Christ our Lord. ℟. Amen.

It is sprinkled with holy water.

110

BLESSING OF A FOUNTAIN

℣. Our help is in the name of the Lord.
℟. Who made heaven and earth.
℣. The Lord be with you.
℟. And with thy spirit.

Let us pray. Prayer

We thy suppliants, O Lord, beseech thy loving goodness, that thou wouldst sanctify ✠ this fountain of water with a heavenly blessing, and render it conducive to common use. Do thou dispel therefrom every attack of diabolical temptation, that all who draw from it, or drink of it, or in any way use it may enjoy the full delight of its strength and healthfulness. And let them give

grátias ágere mereántur. Per Christum Dóminum nostrum. ℞.
Amen.

Et aspergatur aqua benedicta.

111

BENEDICTIO CAMPANAE
quae tamen ad usum ecclesiae vel oratorii
non inserviat

℣. Adjutórium nostrum in nómine Dómini.

℞. Qui fecit caelum et terram.

Septem Psalmi Miserére, etc., ut supra, pag. 310.

Kýrie, eléison. Christe, eléison. Kýrie, eléison.

Pater noster secreto usque ad

℣. Et ne nos indúcas in tentatiónem.

℞. Sed líbera nos a malo.

℣. Sit nomen Dómini benedíctum.

℞. Ex hoc nunc et usque in saéculum.

℣. Dómine, exáudi oratiónem meam.

℞. Et clamor meus ad te véniat.

℣. Dóminus vobíscum.

℞. Et cum spíritu tuo.

Orémus.   Oratio

Omnípotens sempitérne Deus, qui rerum ómnium cursum in mundo ineffábili sapiéntia disposuísti: praesta, quaésumus; ut hoc vásculum ad actiónum sériem indicándam destinátum, tuae bene ✠ dictiónis rore perfúndas, quo cuncta juxta órdinem fiant, et quaevis inde malígni spíritus perturbátio arceátur. Per Dóminum. ℞. Amen.

thanks to thee, the Lord, and Sanctifier, and Savior of all.
Through Christ our Lord. ℞. Amen.

It is sprinkled with holy water.

111

BLESSING OF A BELL
which is not destined to use
in a church or oratory*

℣. Our help is in the name of the Lord.
℞. Who made heaven and earth.

Then the seven psalms (page 311) are said.

Lord, have mercy on us. Christ, have mercy on us. Lord, have
mercy on us.

Our Father inaudibly until

℣. And lead us not into temptation.
℞. But deliver us from evil.
℣. May the name of the Lord be praised.
℞. Henceforth and forever.
℣. O Lord, hear my prayer.
℞. And let my cry come unto thee.
℣. The Lord be with you.
℞. And with thy spirit.

Let us pray.   Prayer

O almighty, everlasting God, thou hast ordained with indescribable wisdom the purpose of every creature on earth. Deign,
we implore, to pour out the dew of thy blessing ✠ on this bell,
destined to ring out the order of time for work and industry.
Thus may it order all things rightly, and let it ward off every
disturbance of the evil spirit. Through Christ our Lord. ℞.
Amen.

* This blessing is reserved to the Ordinary or to one delegated by him.

Nunc Officians ponit incensum in thuribulum et benedicit:. et primum aqua de more (pag. 8) antea benedicta aspergit circumeundo campanam, choro dicente:

Aspérges me, Dómine, hyssópo, et mundábor: lavábis me, et super nivem dealbábor.

Deinde incensat circumeundo campanam, choro dicente:

Dirigátur, Dómine, orátio mea: sicut incénsum in conspéctu tuo.

Tum Officians producto super campanam signo crucis, discedit cum Ministris.

112

BENEDICTIO METALLI PRO CAMPANA
dum aere conflatur

℣. Adjutórium nostrum in nómine Dómini.

℞. Qui fecit caelum et terram.

℣. Dóminus vobíscum.

℞. Et cum spíritu tuo.

Orémus.   Oratio

Dómine Deus omnípotens, qui creatúris étiam inanimátis hunc honórem tríbuis, ut ad cultum tuum destinéntur: tuam, quaésumus, bene ✠ dictiónem effúnde super hoc metállum; et praesta, ut, cum jam in rívulos ignítos prófluet, tua dirigénte déxtera et protegénte grátia, apte et conveniénter disponátur ad efformándum tintinnábulum, quo (efformánda tintinnábula, quibus) fidéles ad laudem et glóriam nóminis tui in ecclésia congregéntur. Per Christum Dóminum nostrum. ℞. Amen.

Et aspergatur aqua benedicta.

Postquam autem feliciter completum fuerit opus, Sacerdos dicit:

Psalmus 116

LAUDÁTE Dóminum, omnes gentes: * laudáte eum, omnes pópuli.

The officiant puts incense into the thurible, and blesses it. He sprinkles the bell with holy water as he walks around it. Meantime the choir says:

Sprinkle me with hyssop, O Lord, and I shall be clean: wash me, and I shall be whiter than snow.

Then he incenses it, again walking around it, as the choir says:

Let my prayer, O Lord, ascend as incense in thy sight.

Lastly he makes the sign of the cross over it, and departs with his assistants.

112

BLESSING OF THE MOLTEN METAL
for a Bell

℣. Our help is in the name of the Lord.
℟. Who made heaven and earth.
℣. The Lord be with you.
℟. And with thy spirit.

Let us pray.   Prayer

O Lord God Almighty, Who dost ennoble even inanimate creatures to the dignity of partaking in divine worship, we entreat thee to pour forth thy blessing ✠ upon this metal. And as it now issues forth a molten stream, do thou direct and guard its flow, so that it be cast into a good and artistic bell (or bells) which will summon the faithful to church to praise and glorify thy name. Through Christ our Lord. ℟. Amen.

The metal is sprinkled with holy water.
And after the casting is successfully completed, the priest says:

Psalm 116
Praise the Lord, all ye nations; praise Him, all ye peoples.

Quóniam confirmáta est super nos misericórdia ejus: * et véritas Dómini manet in aetérnum.

Glória Patri.

Postea adjungit Orationem sequentem:

Orémus. Oratio

A CTIÓNES nostras, quaésumus, Dómine, aspirándo praéveni, et adjuvándo proséquere: ut cuncta nostra orátio et operátio a te semper incípiat, et per te coepta finiátur. Per Christum Dóminum nostrum. ℟. Amen.

113

BENEDICTIO PONTIS

℣. Adjutórium nostrum in nómine Dómini.

℟. Qui fecit caelum et terram.

℣. Dóminus vobíscum.

℟. Et cum spíritu tuo.

Orémus. Oratio

Adésto, Dómine, supplicatiónibus nostris, et pontem istum, et omnes qui per eum transíbunt, bene ✠ dícere dignáre; ut inter próspera hujus mundi et advérsa tuo semper protegántur auxílio. Per Christum Dóminum nostrum. ℟. Amen.

Orémus. Oratio

E XÁUDI nos, Dómine sancte, Pater omnípotens, aetérne Deus: et míttere dignéris sanctum Angelum tuum de caelis, qui custódiat, visitet, et deféndat pontem istum, et omnes qui per eum transíbunt. Per Christum Dóminum nostrum. ℟. Amen.

Et aspergatur aqua benedicta.

For His goodness has enlivened us, and the truth of the Lord
abideth forever.
Glory be to the Father.

Lastly, he adds this prayer:

Let us pray.   Prayer

WE BESEECH thee, Lord, inspire and guide our works in
their beginning, and accompany them unto fruition, that
our every prayer and work may ever begin with thee, and through
thee be accomplished. Through Christ our Lord. ℟. Amen.

113

BLESSING OF A BRIDGE

℣. Our help is in the name of the Lord.
℟. Who made heaven and earth.
℣. The Lord be with you.
℟. And with thy spirit.

Let us pray.   Prayer

Give ear, O Lord, to our prayers, and deign to bless ✠ this
bridge and all who pass over it, that they may be assisted by thee
in every prosperity and every adversity of their earthly sojourn.
Through Christ our Lord. ℟. Amen.

Let us pray.   Prayer

HEAR us, O holy Lord, almighty Father, eternal God, and
vouchsafe to send thy holy angel from heaven to protect,
assist at, and defend this bridge and all who pass over it. Through
Christ our Lord. ℟. Amen.
It is sprinkled with holy water.

114

BENEDICTIO ARCHIVI
(Approbata a S. R. C. die 23 Julii 1924)

℣. Adjutórium nostrum in nómine Dómini.
℟. Qui fecit caelum et terram.
℣. Dóminus vobíscum.
℟. Et cum spíritu tuo.

Orémus.   Oratio

Deus, veritátis et justítiae amátor, super hoc archívum, rerum gestárum documéntis juriúmque instruméntis a témporum hominúmque injúria servándis constrúctum, bene ✠ dictiónem tuam benígnus infúnde; ut ab incéndiis aliísque perículis tutum consístat, et omnes qui huc studiórum ratióne convéniunt, veritáti et justítiae hauriéndae fidéliter incúmbant, in tuíque dilectióne profíciant. Per Christum Dóminum nostrum. ℟. Amen.

Et aspergatur aqua benedicta.

115

BENEDICTIO BIBLIOTHECAE
(Approbata a S. R. C. die 23 Julii 1924)

℣. Adjutórium nostrum in nómine Dómini.
℟. Qui fecit caelum et terram.
℣. Dóminus vobíscum.
℟. Et cum spíritu tuo.

Orémus.   Oratio

Deus, scientiárum Dóminus, bene ✠ dictiónem tuam super hanc bibliothécam benígnus infúnde; ut ipsa ab incéndiis aliísque perículis tuta consístat, et in dies congruénter augeátur, et omnes qui vel offícii vel studiórum ratióne huc convéniunt, in divinárum

114

BLESSING OF AN ARCHIVE

(Approved by the Congregation of Sacred Rites on July 23, 1924)

℣. Our help is in the name of the Lord.
℟. Who made heaven and earth.
℣. The Lord be with you.
℟. And with thy spirit.

Let us pray. *Prayer*

O God, Who lovest truth and justice, pour out thy blessing ✠ on this archive which has been constructed to preserve the documents of past events and the deeds of the judiciary from destruction by man or time. Let it safely withstand fire and every peril, so that all who come to it in quest of research may be intent on truth and justice, and may advance in love of thee. Through Christ our Lord. ℟. Amen.

It is sprinkled with holy water.

115

BLESSING OF A LIBRARY

(Approved by the Congregation of Sacred Rites on July 23, 1924)

℣. Our help is in the name of the Lord.
℟. Who made heaven and earth.
℣. The Lord be with you.
℟. And with thy spirit.

Let us pray. *Prayer*

O God, Who art the Lord of all learning, pour forth thy blessing ✠ upon this library. Let it safely withstand fire and every peril, and permit it to increase its volumes from day to day. May all who come here as officials or students make progress in knowl-

humanarúmque rerum sciéntia tuíque páriter dilectióne profíciant. Per Christum Dóminum nostrum. ℞. Amen.

Et aspergatur aqua benedicta.

116

BENEDICTIO FORNACIS CALCARIAE

℣. Adjutórium nostrum in nómine Dómini.
℞. Qui fecit caelum et terram.
℣. Dóminus vobíscum.
℞. Et cum spíritu tuo.

Orémus.   Oratio

Omnípotens aetérne Deus, a quo ómnia creáta procédunt, et qui mirábili dispositióne bonitátis tuae eis tríbuis ad usum hóminum inservíre; qui olim altáre tuum de lapídibus constrúctum calce levigáre jussísti, ut per Deuteronómium in eo scriptum tuórum servarétur memória mandatórum: te súpplices exorámus, béne ✠ dic hanc fornácem, et ab ea longe repúlsa omni versútia diabólicae fraudis, fructuósam reddas illam et aptam; ut per ignem vim virtútis suae exercéntem aptatóres hujus óperis de tua benignitáte calcem recípiant congruéntem; quibus étiam tríbue, ut in eis simul crescat tuae grátiae salutáris augméntum. Per Christum Dóminum nostrum. ℞. Amen.

Et aspergatur aqua benedicta.

117

BENEDICTIO FORNACIS FUSORIAE METALLICAE
vel coctoriae laterum et tegularum

℣. Adjutórium nostrum in nómine Dómini.
℞. Qui fecit caelum et terram.

edge of things human and divine, and increase likewise their love for thee. Through Christ our Lord. ℟. Amen.

It is sprinkled with holy water.

116

BLESSING OF A LIME-KILN

℣. Our help is in the name of the Lord.
℟. Who made heaven and earth.
℣. The Lord be with you.
℟. And with thy spirit.

Let us pray.

Prayer

O almighty, everlasting God! From thee all creatures have their origin, and by a wonderful disposition of thy goodness thou hast ordered them to serve the necessities of man. In times past thou didst prescribe that thy altar be built of stone and its surfaces be made smooth with lime, so that the words of Deuteronomy could be inscribed thereon to serve as a reminder of thy commandments. Humbly we entreat thee to bless✠ this lime-kiln. Preserve it from diabolical treachery, and render it productive and true to its purpose, so that by its fires exerting the force of their strength, the workmen may by thy bounty receive a good quality of lime. And give them, moreover, an increase of thy saving grace. Through Christ our Lord. ℟. Amen.

It is sprinkled with holy water.

117

BLESSING OF A BLAST-FURNACE
or of a Brick-Kiln

℣. Our help is in the name of the Lord.
℟. Who made heaven and earth.

℣. Dóminus vobíscum.

℟. Et cum spíritu tuo.

Orémus.   Oratio

Omnípotens aetérne Deus, a quo ómnia creáta procédunt, et qui mirábili dispositióne bonitátis tuae eis tríbuis ad usum hóminum inservíre; qui modo coércens vim flammárum tres púeros in camíno ignis illaésos custodísti, et modo illam adáugens viros illos, qui sanctos míserant in fornácem, consumpsísti: te súpplices exorámus, béne ✠ dic hunc clíbanum, et ab eo longe repúlsa omni versútia diabólicae fraudis, fructuósum reddas illum et aptum; ut per ignem vim virtútis suae exercéntem aptatóres hujus óperis metálli matériam recípiant congruéntem (vel láterum vel tegulárum cópiam recípiant congruéntem); quibus étiam tríbue, ut in eis simul crescat tuae grátiae salutáris augméntum. Per Christum Dóminum nostrum. ℟. Amen.

Et aspergatur aqua benedicta.

118

BENEDICTIO NAVIS

℣. Adjutórium nostrum in nómine Dómini.

℟. Qui fecit caelum et terram.

℣. Dóminus vobíscum.

℟. Et cum spíritu tuo.

Orémus.   Oratio

Propitiáre, Dómine, supplicatiónibus nostris, et béne✠ dic navem istam déxtera tua sancta et omnes qui in ea vehéntur, sicut dignátus es benedícere arcam Noe ambulántem in dilúvio: pórrige eis, Dómine, déxteram tuam, sicut porrexísti beáto Petro ambulánti supra mare; et mitte sanctum Angelum tuum de caelis, qui líberet, et custódiat eam semper a perículis univérsis, cum ómnibus quae in ea erunt: et fámulos tuos, repúlsis adversitátibus,

℣. The Lord be with you.
℟. And with thy spirit.

Let us pray. *Prayer*

O almighty, everlasting God! From thee all creatures have their origin, and by thy goodness thou hast wonderfully disposed them for the service of mankind. In olden times thou didst mitigate the heat of the flames to preserve the three youths in the fiery furnace, and then didst again enkindle them to destroy the men who had cast the saintly youths therein. Wherefore, we humbly entreat thee to bless ✠ this furnace. Preserve it from diabolical treachery, and render it productive and true to its purpose, so that by its fires exerting the force of their strength, the workmen may by thy bounty receive a good quality of metal (or a goodly number of brick). And give them, moreover, an increase of thy saving grace. Through Christ our Lord. ℟. Amen.

It is sprinkled with holy water.

118

BLESSING OF A SHIP

℣. Our help is in the name of the Lord.
℟. Who made heaven and earth.
℣. The Lord be with you.
℟. And with thy spirit.

Let us pray. *Prayer*

Be attentive, O Lord, to our supplications, and bless ✠ this ship and all who sail hereon, as thou wast wont to bless Noah's Ark in the Deluge. Stretch forth thy hand to them, O Lord, as thou didst reach out to Peter when he walked upon the sea. Send thy holy angel from heaven to watch over it and those on board, and keep it safe at all times from every disaster. And when threatened perils have been removed, comfort thy servants with a calm

portu semper optábili, cursúque tranquíllo tueáris, transactísque, ac recte perféctis negótiis ómnibus, iteráto témpore ad própria cum omni gáudio revocáre dignéris: Qui vivis et regnas in saécula saeculórum. ℟. Amen.

Et aspergatur aqua benedicta.

119

BENEDICTIO SOLEMNIS NAVIS PISCATORIAE
(Approbata a S. R. C. die 10 Aprilis 1912.)

℣. Adjutórium nostrum in nómine Dómini.
℟. Qui fecit caelum et terram.
℣. Dóminus vobíscum.
℟. Et cum spíritu tuo.

Antiphona

Ia3

Dó- mine. Cantor: Dóminus noster, * quam admi-rá-

bi-le est nomen tu-um in univérsa ter-ra!

Psalmus 8

Dómine, Dóminus noster, * quam admirábile est nomen tuum in univérsa terra!

Quóniam eleváta est magnificéntia tua, * super caelos.

Ex ore infántium et lacténtium perfecísti laudem propter inimícos tuos, * ut déstruas inimícum et ultórem.

Quóniam vidébo caelos tuos, ópera digitórum tuórum: * lunam et stellas, quae tu fundásti.

Quid est homo, quod memor es ejus? * aut fílius hóminis, quó niam vísitas eum?

Minuísti eum paulo minus ab Angelis, glória et honóre coronást eum: * et constituísti eum super ópera mánuum tuárum.

voyage and the desired harbor. And having successfully transacted their business, recall them again when the time comes to the happiness of country and home. Thou Who livest and reignest forevermore. ℟. **Amen.**

It is sprinkled with holy water.

119

SOLEMN BLESSING OF A FISHING-BOAT

(Approved by the Congregation of Sacred Rites on April 10, 1912)

℣. **Our help is in the name of the Lord.**
℟. **Who made heaven and earth.**
℣. **The Lord be with you.**
℟. **And with thy spirit.**
Antiphon: **O Jehovah, our Lord!**

Psalm 8

O Jehovah, our Lord! How wonderful is thy name in the whole earth.

For thy magnificence is exalted above the heavens.

From the mouths of infants and of sucklings thou hast established praise, that thou mightest destroy the foe and the scoffer.

When I behold thy heavens, the works of thy hands, the moon and the stars which thou hast made, then I must exclaim:

"What is man, that thou art mindful of him, and the children of men that thou shouldst even consider them?"

Yet thou hast made him a little less than the angels, thou hast transformed him with glory and honor, and hast made him ruler over the works of thy hands.

Omnia subjecísti sub pédibus ejus, * oves et boves univérsas: ínsuper et pécora campi.

Vólucres caeli, et pisces maris, * qui perámbulant sémitas maris.

Dómine, Dóminus noster, * quam admirábile est nomen tuum in univérsa terra!

Glória Patri.

Repetitur Antiphona:

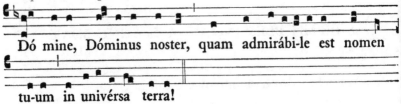

Dó mine, Dóminus noster, quam admirábi-le est nomen tu-um in univérsa terra!

℣. Dóminus vobíscum.

℟. Et cum spíritu tuo.

Orémus.   Oratio

PROPITIÁRE, Dómine, supplicatiónibus nostris, et béne ✠ dic navem istam déxtera tua sancta, et omnes, qui in ea vehéntur, sicut dignátus es benedícere arcam Noe ambulántem in dilúvio: pórrige eis, Dómine, déxteram tuam, sicut porrexísti beáto Petro ambulánti supra mare; et mitte sanctum Angelum tuum de caelis, qui líberet, et custódiat eam semper a perículis univérsis, cum ómnibus, quae in ea erunt: et fámulos tuos, repúlsis adversitátibus portu semper optábili cursúque tranquíllo tueáris, transactísque ac recte perféctis negótiis ómnibus, iteráto témpore ad própria cum omni gáudio revocáre dignéris: Qui vivis et regnas in saécula saeculórum. ℟. Amen.

℣. Dóminus vobíscum.

℟. Et cum spíritu tuo.

✠ Sequéntia sancti Evangélii secúndum Joánnem.

(Cap. 21, 1–24)

℟. Glória tibi, Dómine.

IN ILLO témpore: Manifestávit se íterum Jesus discípulis ad mare Tiberíadis. Manifestávit autem sic: Erant simul Simon

Thou hast subjected all things under his feet: sheep and oxen, moreover, the beasts of the field;

The birds of the air, and the fishes of the sea, that roam the paths of the waters.

O Jehovah, our Lord! How wonderful is thy name in the whole earth.

Glory be to the Father.

Antiphon: O Jehovah, our Lord! How wonderful is thy name in the whole earth.

℣. The Lord be with you.

℟. And with thy spirit.

Let us pray.   Prayer

GRACIOUSLY hearken to our prayers, O Lord, and with thy holy hand bless ✠ this boat and all who sail hereon, as thou didst deign to bless Noah's Ark in its course during the Deluge. Stretch forth to them, O Lord, thy right hand, as thou didst reach out to Peter when he walked upon the sea. Send thy holy angel from heaven to guard this boat and ever keep it safe from every peril, together with all on board. And when threatened dangers have been removed, comfort thy servants with a calm voyage and the desired harbor. And having successfully transacted their business, recall them again when the time comes to the happiness of country and home. Thou Who livest and reignest forevermore. ℟. Amen.

℣. The Lord be with you.

℟. And with thy spirit.

✠ Continuation of the holy Gospel according to St. John.

(John, 21, 1-24)

℟. Glory be to thee, O Lord.

AFTER this, Jesus showed Himself again to the disciples at the sea of Tiberias. And He showed Himself after this manner.

Petrus, et Thomas, qui dícitur Dídymus, et Nathánael, qui erat
a Cana Galilaéae, et fílii Zebedaéi, et álii ex discípulis ejus duo.
Dicit eis Simon Petrus: Vado piscári. Dicunt ei: Venímus et nos
tecum. Et exiérunt, et ascendérunt in navim: et illa nocte nihil
prendidérunt. Mane autem facto stetit Jesus in líttore: non tamen
cognovérunt discípuli quia Jesus est. Dixit ergo eis Jesus: Púeri,
numquid pulmentárium habétis? Respondérunt ei: Non. Dicit
eis: Míttite in déxteram navígii rete: et inveniétis. Misérunt
ergo: et jam non valébant illud tráhere prae multitúdine píscium.
Dixit ergo discípulus ille, quem diligébat Jesus, Petro: Dóminus
est. Simon Petrus cum audísset quia Dóminus est, túnica succínxit
se (erat enim nudus), et misit se in mare. Alii autem discípuli
navígio venérunt: (non enim longe erant a terra, sed quasi
cúbitis ducéntis) trahéntes rete píscium. Ut ergo descendérunt in
terram, vidérunt prunas pósitas, et piscem superpósitum, et panem. Dicit eis Jesus: Afférte de píscibus, quos prendidístis nunc.
Ascéndit Simon Petrus, et traxit rete in terram, plenum magnis
píscibus centum quinquagínta tribus. Et cum tanti essent, non
est scissum rete. Dicit eis Jesus: Veníte, prandéte. Et nemo audé-
bat discumbéntium interrogáre eum: Tu quis es? sciéntes, quia
Dóminus est. Et venit Jesus, et áccipit panem, et dat eis, et piscem
simíliter. Hoc jam tértio manifestátus est Jesus discípulis suis
cum resurrexísset a mórtuis. Cum ergo prandíssent, dicit Simóni
Petro Jesus: Simon Joánnis, díligis me plus his? Dicit ei: Etiam,
Dómine, tu scis quia amo te. Dicit ei: Pasce agnos meos. Dicit ei
íterum: Simon Joánnis, díligis me? Ait illi: Etiam, Dómine, tu
scis quia amo te. Dicit ei: Pasce agnos meos. Dicit ei tértio: Simon
Joánnis, amas me? Contristátus est Petrus, quia dixit ei tértio:

There were together Simon Peter, and Thomas, who is called Didymus, and Nathanael, who was of Cana of Galilee, and the sons of Zebedee, and two others of His disciples. Simon Peter saith to them: I go a fishing. They say to him: We also come with thee. And they went forth, and entered into the ship: and that night they caught nothing. But when the morning was come, Jesus stood on the shore: yet the disciples knew not that it was Jesus.

Jesus therefore said to them: Children, have you any meat? They answered Him: No. He saith to them: Cast the net on the right side of the ship, and you shall find. They cast therefore; and now they were not able to draw it, for the multitude of fishes. That disciple therefore whom Jesus loved, said to Peter: It is the Lord. Simon Peter, when he heard that it was the Lord, girt his coat about him (for he was naked), and cast himself into the sea. But the other disciples came in the ship (for they were not far from the land, but as it were two hundred cubits), dragging the net with fishes. As soon then as they came to land, they saw hot coals lying, and a fish laid thereon, and bread. Jesus saith to them: Bring hither of the fishes which you have now caught. Simon Peter went up, and drew the net to land, full of great fishes, one hundred and fifty-three. And although there were so many, the net was not broken. Jesus saith to them: Come, and dine. And none of them who were at meat, durst ask Him: Who art thou? knowing that it was the Lord. And Jesus cometh and taketh bread, and giveth them, and fish in like manner. This is now the third time that Jesus was manifested to His disciples, after He was risen from the dead. When therefore they had dined, Jesus saith to Simon Peter: Simon, son of John, lovest thou Me more than these? He saith to Him: Yea, Lord, thou knowest that I love thee. He saith to him: Feed my lambs. He saith to him again: Simon, son of John, lovest thou Me? He saith to Him: Yea, Lord, thou knowest that I love thee. He saith to him: Feed my lambs. He said to him the third time: Simon, son of John, lovest thou me? Peter was grieved, because he had said to him

Amas me? et dixit ei: Dómine, tu ómnia nosti: tu scis quia amo te. Dixit ei: Pasce oves meas. Amen, amen dico tibi: cum esses júnior, cingébas te, et ambulábas ubi volébas: cum autem senúeris, exténdes manus tuas, et álius te cinget, et ducet quo tu non vis. Hoc autem dixit signíficans qua morte clarificatúrus esset Deum. Et cum hoc dixísset, dicit ei: Séquere me. Convérsus Petrus vidit illum discípulum, quem diligébat Jesus, sequéntem, qui et recúbuit in coena super pectus ejus, et dixit: Dómine, quis est qui tradet te? Hunc ergo cum vidísset Petrus, dixit Jesu: Dómine, his autem quid? Dicit ei Jesus: Sic eum volo manére donec véniam, quid ad te? tu me séquere. Exiit ergo sermo iste inter fratres quia discípulus ille non móritur. Et non dixit ei Jesus: Non móritur; sed: Sic eum volo manére donec véniam, quid ad te? Hic est discípulus ille, qui testimónium pérhibet de his, et scripsit haec: et scimus, quia verum est testimónium ejus.

℞. Laus tibi, Christe.

℣. Dóminus vobíscum.

℞. Et cum spíritu tuo.

Orémus.   Oratio

DEUS, qui dívidens aquas ab árida, omnem ánimam in his vivéntem creásti, hominémque voluísti píscibus maris domínari: qui super marínos vórtices ámbulans ventis et flúctibus imperásti: Apostolorúmque rétia verbo tuo mirabíliter replésti: praesta, quaésumus, ut in navículis suis fámuli tui ab ómnibus perículis, te comitánte, liberáti, píscium multitúdinem copiósam conclúdant, ac tandem ad aetérnae felicitátis portum, méritis onústi, pervéniant. Per Christum Dóminum nostrum. ℞. Amen.

the third time: Lovest thou me? And he said to Him: Lord, thou knowest all things: thou knowest that I love thee. He said to him: Feed my sheep. Amen, Amen I say to thee, when thou wast younger, thou didst gird thyself, and didst walk where thou wouldst. But when thou shalt be old, thou shalt stretch forth thy hands, and another shall gird thee, and lead thee whither thou wouldst not. And this He said, signifying by what death he should glorify God. And when He had said this, He saith to him: Follow me. Peter turning about, saw that disciple whom Jesus loved following, who also leaned on His breast at supper, and said: Lord, who is he that shall betray thee? Him therefore when Peter had seen, he saith to Jesus: Lord, and what shall this man do? Jesus saith to him: So I will have him to remain till I come, what is it to thee? follow thou Me. This saying therefore went abroad among the brethren, that that disciple should not die. And Jesus did not say to him: He should not die; but, So I will have him to remain till I come, what is it to thee? This is that disciple who giveth testimony of these things, and hath written these things; and we know that his testimony is true.

℟. Praise be to thee, O Christ.

℣. The Lord be with you.

℟. And with thy spirit.

Let us pray. Prayer

O GOD, thou didst separate the waters from the dry land, and didst create every living thing therein; thou didst will that man rule over the fishes of the sea; wandering over its depths, thou didst command the storm and the waves; by thy word thou didst miraculously fill the nets of thine apostles! Grant likewise, we beseech thee, that thy servants, protected by thee from all dangers, may gather into their boats a good haul of fish, and come finally to the port of eternal blessedness laden with heavenly merits. Through Christ our Lord. ℟. Amen.

Orémus. Oratio

OBSECRÁMUS te, Dómine, Salvátor noster, ut famulórum tuórum labóres benedícere dignéris, quemádmodum Apóstolis tuis benedixísti, dicens: Míttite in déxteram navígii rete, et inveniétis: ut de abundántia tuae benedictiónis laeti, te Redemptórem nostrum semper exaltémus benedíctum in saécula. ℟. Amen.

RÉSPICE, Dómine, ad intercessiónem beatíssimae Vírginis Maríae, sancti Petri, ceterorúmque Apostolórum et sancti N. (Titularis navis benedicendae), ut labóres mánuum nostrárum ne despícias; sed tua sanctíssima bene ✠dictióne, a nobis cuncta peccáta repéllas, perícula submóveas, et ómnia nobis bona profutúra concédas. Per Dóminum. ℟. Amen.

Sacerdos navem aspergit aqua benedicta, dicens:

Pax et benedíctio Dei omnipoténtis, Patris, et Fílii, ✠ et Spíritus Sancti, descéndat super navem istam, et super omnes, qui in ea erunt, et máneat semper. ℟. Amen.

120

BENEDICTIO VEHICULI SEU CURRUS

℣. Adjutórium nostrum in nómine Dómini.
℟. Qui fecit caelum et terram.
℣. Dóminus vobíscum.
℟. Et cum spíritu tuo.

Orémus. Oratio

Propitiáre, Dómine Deus, supplicatiónibus nostris, et béne ✠dic currum istum déxtera tua sancta: adjúnge ad ipsum sanctos Angelos tuos, ut omnes, qui in eo vehéntur, líberent et custódiant semper a perículis univérsis: et quemádmodum viro Aethíopi super currum suum sedénti et sacra elóquia legénti, per Levítam tuum Philíppum fidem et grátiam contulísti; ita fámulis tuis

Let us pray.   *Prayer*

O LORD, our Savior, we implore thee — bless the labors of thy servants, as thou didst bless thine apostles with the words: "Cast the net on the right side of the ship, and you shall find." So that gladdened with the opulence of thy blessing, we may praise thee, our Redeemer, for all eternity. ℟. Amen.

CONSIDER, Lord, the intercession of the Blessed Virgin Mary, St. Peter, and the other apostles, as well as that of Saint N. (Patron of the boat), and despise not the work of our hands. But by thy most holy blessing,✝ keep far from us all sin, remove dangers, and give us all good things. Through our Lord. ℟. Amen.

The priest sprinkles the boat with holy water, saying:

May the peace and blessing of almighty God, Father, Son,✝ and Holy Spirit descend upon this boat and upon all who shall sail herein, and remain for all time. ℟. Amen.

120

BLESSING OF AN AUTOMOBILE OR OTHER VEHICLE

℣. Our help is in the name of the Lord.
℟. Who made heaven and earth.
℣. The Lord be with you.
℟. And with thy spirit.

Let us pray.   *Prayer*

Graciously hearken to our prayers, O Lord God, and with thy holy hand bless ✝ this vehicle. Appoint as its custodians thy holy angels, ever to guard and keep safe from all danger them that ride herein. And as by thy Levite, Philip thou didst bestow faith and grace upon the Ethiopian, seated in his carriage, and reading Holy Writ, so likewise show the way of salvation to thy servants

viam salútis osténde, qui tua grátia adjúti bonísque opéribus júgiter inténti, post omnes viae et vitae hujus varietátes, aetérna
gáudia cónsequi mereántur. Per Christum Dóminum nostrum.
℟. Amen.

Et aspergatur aqua benedicta.

121

BENEDICTIO VIAE FERREAE ET CURRUUM

℣. Adjutórium nostrum in nómine Dómini.
℟. Qui fecit caelum et terram.
℣. Dóminus vobíscum.
℟. Et cum spíritu tuo.

Orémus. Oratio

Omnípotens sempitérne Deus, qui ómnia eleménta ad tuam
glóriam, utilitatémque hóminum condidísti: dignáre, quaésumus,
hanc viam férream, ejúsque instruménta bene ✠ dícere, et benígna semper tua providéntia tuéri; ut, dum fámuli tui velóciter
próperant in via, in lege tua ambulántes, et viam mandatórum
tuórum curréntes, ad caeléstem pátriam felíciter perveníre váleant.
Per Christum Dóminum nostrum. ℟. Amen.

Orémus. Oratio

PROPITIÁRE, Dómine Deus, supplicatiónibus nostris, et
béne ✠ dic currus istos déxtera tua sancta: adjúnge ad ipsos
sanctos Angelos tuos, ut omnes, qui in eis vehéntur, líberent et
custódiant semper a perículis univérsis: et quemádmodum viro
Aethíopi super currum suum sedénti, et sacra elóquia legénti, per
Levítam tuum Philíppum fidem et grátiam contulísti; ita fámulis
tuis viam salútis osténde, qui tua grátia adjúti bonísque opéribus
júgiter inténti, post omnes viae et vitae hujus varietátes, aetérna
gáudia cónsequi mereántur. Per Christum Dóminum nostrum.
℟. Amen.

Et aspergantur via et currus aqua benedicta.

that, strengthened by thy grace and constantly intent upon good works, they may attain, after the vicissitudes of this life, the happiness of everlasting life. Through Christ our Lord. ℟. Amen.

It is sprinkled with holy water.

121

BLESSING OF A RAILWAY
and its Cars

℣. Our help is in the name of the Lord.
℟. Who made heaven and earth.
℣. The Lord be with you.
℟. And with thy spirit.

Let us pray.   Prayer

O almighty and eternal God, Who hast established every element for thy glory and man's utility, vouchsafe, we pray, to bless ✛ this railway together with its equipment, and watch over it at all times with thy benign solicitude. And let thy servants, as they are sped on the way in it, advance in thy law and thy commandments, that it may be their fortune to arrive finally at the heavenly fatherland. Through Christ our Lord. ℟. Amen.

Let us pray.   Prayer

HEARKEN graciously to our entreaties, O Lord God, and with thy holy hand bless ✛ this vehicle. Appoint as its custodians thy holy angels, ever to guard and keep safe from all danger them that ride hereon. And as by thy Levite, Philip thou didst bestow faith and grace upon the Ethiopian, seated in his carriage, and reading Holy Writ, so likewise show the way of salvation to thy servants that, strengthened by thy grace and constantly intent upon good works, they may attain, after the vicissitudes of this life, the happiness of everlasting life. Through Christ our Lord. ℟. Amen.

The tracks and cars are sprinkled with holy water.

122

BENEDICTIO SOLEMNIOR VIAE FERREAE ET CURRUUM

Clerus, vel a proximiori ecclesia, vel ab aliquo alio loco ad hoc parato, procedit usque ad stationem viae ferreae, canendo vel recitando:

Antiphona[1]

In viam pacis et prosperitátis dírigat nos omnípotens et miséricors Dóminus: et Angelus Ráphael comitétur nobíscum in via, ut cum pace, salúte, et gáudio revertámur ad própria.

Canticum Zachariae, ut supra, pag. 50.
Ibi Sacerdos delegatus, repetita Antiphona, dicit:

Kýrie, eléison. Christe, eléison. Kýrie, eléison.

Pater noster secreto usque ad

℣. Et ne nos indúcas in tentatiónem.

℟. Sed líbera nos a malo.

℣. Salvos fac servos tuos.

℟. Deus meus, sperántes in te.

℣. Mitte nobis, Dómine, auxílium de sancto.

℟. Et de Sion tuére nos.

℣. Esto nobis, Dómine, turris fortitúdinis.

℟. A fácie inimíci.

℣. Nihil profíciat inimícus in nobis.

℟. Et fílius iniquitátis non appónat nocére nobis.

℣. Benedíctus Dóminus die quotídie.

℟. Prósperum iter fáciat nobis Deus salutárium nostrórum.

℣. Vias tuas, Dómine, demónstra nobis.

℟. Et sémitas tuas édoce nos.

℣. Utinam dirigántur viae nostrae.

℟. Ad custodiéndas justificatiónes tuas.

---

[1] Ant. cum cantu, pag. 100.

122

SOLEMN BLESSING OF A RAILWAY
and its Cars*

From the nearest church or from another place previously appointed, the clergy proceed in a solemn way to the railroad station, as they chant or recite:

Antiphon: **Along ways of peace and prosperity may the almighty and merciful Lord lead us, and may the Angel Raphael accompany us on the journey. So may we in peace, health, and joy return unto our own!**

The canticle of Zachary, as above on page 51, is sung or said.
The antiphon is repeated; and at the railroad station the priest says:

Lord, have mercy on us. Christ, have mercy on us. Lord, have mercy on us.

Our Father inaudibly until

℣.**And lead us not into temptation.**
℟.**But deliver us from evil.**
℣.**Preserve thy servants.**
℟.**Who trust in thee, my God.**
℣.**Send us aid, Lord, from on high.**
℟.**And from Sion watch over us.**
℣.**Be unto us a mighty fortress.**
℟.**In the face of the enemy.**
℣.**Let the enemy be powerless against us.**
℟.**And the son of iniquity do nothing to harm us.**
℣.**May the Lord be praised at all times.**
℟.**May God, our Helper grant us a successful journey.**
℣.**Show us thy ways, O Lord.**
℟.**And conduct us along thy paths.**
℣.**Oh, that our ways be directed!**
℟.**To the keeping of thy precepts.**

---

* This blessing is reserved to the Ordinary or to one delegated by him.

℣. Erunt prava in dirécta.
℟. Et áspera in vias planas.
℣. Angelis suis Deus mandávit de te.
℟. Ut custódiant te in ómnibus viis tuis.
℣. Adjutórium nostrum in nómine Dómini.
℟. Qui fecit caelum et terram.
℣. Dómine, exáudi oratiónem meam.
℟. Et clamor meus ad te véniat.
℣. Dóminus vobíscum.
℟. Et cum spíritu tuo.

Orémus.   Oratio

O MNIPOTENS, sempitérne Deus, qui ómnia eleménta ad tuam glóriam, utilitatémque hóminum condidísti: dignáre, quaésumus, hanc viam férream, ejúsque instruménta bene ✠ dícere, et benígna semper tua providéntia tuéri; ut, dum fámuli tui velóciter próperant in via, in lege tua ambulántes, et viam mandatórum tuórum curréntes, ad caeléstem pátriam felíciter perveníre váleant. Per Christum Dóminum nostrum. ℟. Amen.

Orémus.   Oratio

P ROPITIÁRE, Dómine Deus, supplicatiónibus nostris, et béne ✠ dic currus istos déxtera tua sancta, adjúnge ad ipsos sanctos Angelos tuos, ut omnes, qui in eis vehéntur, líberent et custódiant semper a perículis univérsis; et quemádmodum viro Aethíopi super currum suum sedénti, et sacra elóquia legénti, per Levítam tuum Philíppum fidem et grátiam contulísti: ita fámulis tuis viam salútis osténde, qui tua grátia adjúti, bonísque opéribus júgiter inténti, post omnes viae et vitae hujus varietátes aetérna gáudia cónsequi mereántur. Per Christum Dóminum nostrum. ℟. Amen.

Deinde aspergit viam et currus aqua benedicta.
Post utramque Benedictionem dicitur **Te Deum,** cum Oratione **Deus** cujus misericórdiae, etc., ut supra, pag. 58.

℣. For crooked ways will be made straight.
℟. And rough ways smooth.
℣. God hath given His angels charge over thee.
℟. To guard thee in all undertakings.
℣. Our help is in the name of the Lord.
℟. Who made heaven and earth.
℣. O Lord, hear my prayer.
℟. And let my cry come unto thee.
℣. The Lord be with you.
℟. And with thy spirit.

Let us pray.   Prayer

O ALMIGHTY and eternal God, Who hast established every element for thy glory and man's utility, vouchsafe, we pray, to bless ✟ this railway together with its equipment, and watch over it at all times with thy benign solicitude. And let thy servants, as they are sped on the way in it, advance in thy law and thy commandments, that it may be their fortune to arrive finally at the heavenly fatherland. Through Christ our Lord. ℟. Amen.

Let us pray.   Prayer

HEARKEN graciously to our entreaties, O Lord God, and with thy holy hand bless ✟ these cars. Appoint as their custodians thy holy angels, ever to guard and keep safe from all danger them that ride hereon. And as by thy Levite, Philip thou didst bestow faith and grace upon the Ethiopian, seated in his carriage, and reading Holy Writ, so likewise show the way of salvation to thy servants that, strengthened by thy grace and constantly intent upon good works, they may attain, after the vicissitudes of this life, the happiness of everlasting life. Through Christ our Lord. ℟. Amen.

The tracks and cars are sprinkled with holy water. In conclusion the Te Deum, page 59, is said with the prayer: O God, Whose mercy, etc.

123

BENEDICTIO MACHINAE ITINERI AEREO DESTINATAE

(Approbata a S. R. C. die 24 Martii 1920)

℣. Adjutórium nostrum in nómine Dómini.

℟. Qui fecit caelum et terram.

℣. Bénedic, ánima mea, Dómino.

℟. Dómine, Deus meus, magnificátus es veheménter.

℣. Qui ponis nubem ascénsum tuum.

℟. Qui ámbulas super pennas ventórum.

℣. Dómine, exáudi oratiónem meam.

℟. Et clamor meus ad te véniat.

℣. Dóminus vobíscum.

℟. Et cum spíritu tuo.

Orémus. *Oratio*

Deus, qui ómnia propter temetípsum operátus es, et cuncta mundi hujus eleménta in usum humáni géneris destinásti: béne ✠ dic, quaésumus, hanc máchinam (has máchinas) itíneri aéreo deputátam (–as); ut ad laudem et glóriam nóminis tui látius propagándam, et ad res humánas prómptius expediéndas, damno quovis et perículo remóto, desérviat (–ant), et in ómnium fidélium, eándem máchinam (eásdem máchinas) adhíbéntium, ánimis caeléstia fóveat (–ant) desidéria. Per Christum Dóminum nostrum. ℟. Amen.

Orémus. *Oratio*

DEUS, qui beátae Maríae Vírginis domum per Incarnáti Verbi mystérium misericórditer consecrásti, eámque in sinu Ecclésiae tuae mirabíliter collocásti: effúnde, quaésumus, bene ✠ dictiónem tuam super hanc máchinam (has máchinas); ut, qui qui per eam (eas) itíneri aéreo sub tutéla ejúsdem beátae Vírginis se commíserint, eo quo tendunt próspere pervéniant, et incólumes ad própria revertántur. Per eúndem Christum Dóminum nostrum. ℟. Amen.

123

BLESSING OF AN AIRPLANE

(Approved by the Congregation of Sacred Rites on March 24, 1920)

℣. Our help is in the name of the Lord.

℟. Who made heaven and earth.

℣. Bless the Lord, O my soul!

℟. My Lord and my God, how wonderful are thy works!

℣. Thou traversest the clouds,

℟. And walkest on the wings of the wind.

℣. O Lord, hear my prayer.

℟. And let my cry come unto thee.

℣. The Lord be with you.

℟. And with thy spirit.

Let us pray.   Prayer

O God, Who didst create all things for thyself, and hast destined every element in the world for man's service, bless,✠ we pray, this airplane (these airplanes) Let it (them) serve in spreading the praise and glory of thee, and in expediting the affairs of men, unhindered by destruction or peril. And may it (they) foster within the souls of all who ride in it (them) a longing for heavenly things. Through Christ our Lord. ℟. Amen.

Let us pray.   Prayer

O GOD, Who didst consecrate by the mystery of the Incarnation the dwelling of the Blessed Virgin Mary, and hast miraculously transferred it to the bosom of thy Church, pour forth, we beseech thee, thy blessing✠ upon this airplane (these airplanes) May all who under the patronage of the Blessed Virgin fly in this plane (these planes) happily reach their destination, and return safely home. Through the same Christ our Lord. ℟. Amen.

Orémus. Oratio

D EUS, in te sperántium salus, fámulis tuis iter aéreum pera-géntibus ac tuam opem invocántibus, Angelum bonum de caelis cómitem benígnus adjúnge: ut ab eo custodiántur in ómni-bus viis, et ad propósitam sibi metam felíciter deducántur. Per Christum Dóminum nostrum. ℟. Amen.

Et aspergatur aqua benedicta.

124

BENEDICTIO INSTRUMENTORUM AD MONTES CONSCENDENDOS

(Approbata a Pio Papa XI die 14 Octobris 1931)

℣. Adjutórium nostrum in nómine Dómini.
℟. Qui fecit caelum et terram.
℣. Dóminus vobíscum.
℟. Et cum spíritu tuo.

Orémus. Oratio

Béne✠dic, quaésumus, Dómine, hos funes, báculos, rastros, alíaque hic praeséntia instruménta; ut quicúmque iis usi fúerint, inter árdua et montis abrúpta, inter glácies, nives et tempestátes, ab omni casu et perículo praeserventur, ad cúlmina felíciter ascéndant, et ad suos incólumes revertántur. Per Christum Dó-minum nostrum. ℟. Amen.

Orémus. Oratio

P RÓTEGE, Dómine, intercédente beáto Bernárdo quem Al-pium íncolis et viatóribus Patrónum dedísti, hos fámulos tuos: ipsísque concéde, ut, dum haec conscéndunt cúlmina, ad montem qui Christus est váleant perveníre. Per eúndem Chris-tum Dóminum nostrum. ℟. Amen.

Et aspergantur aqua benedicta.

Let us pray. *Prayer*

O GOD, the Salvation of all who trust in thee, appoint a good angel as a guardian to all thy servants who make an airplane voyage, and call upon thy help. Let him protect them along the journey, and safely conduct them to their destination. Through Christ our Lord. ℟. Amen.

It is sprinkled with holy water.

124

BLESSING OF TOOLS USED IN SCALING MOUNTAINS
(Approved by Pope Pius XI on October 14, 1931)

℣. Our help is in the name of the Lord.
℟. Who made heaven and earth.
℣. The Lord be with you.
℟. And with thy spirit.

Let us pray. *Prayer*

Bless, ✠ O Lord, we pray, these ropes, staves, mattocks, and these other tools, that all who use them in scaling the mountains' heights and precipices, in ice and snow and tempest, may be preserved from all danger and catastrophe, safely reach the summits, and return unscathed to their homes. Through Christ our Lord. ℟. Amen.

Let us pray. *Prayer*

THROUGH the intercession of Saint Bernard, whom thou hast given as patron of Alpine dwellers and travelers, protect, O Lord, these thy servants, and grant that they who climb to mountain peaks may come to the Mountain which is Christ. Through the selfsame Christ our Lord. ℟. Amen.

They are sprinkled with holy water.

125

BENEDICTIO MACHINAE AD EXTINGUENDUM INCENDIUM

(Approbata a S. R. C. die 10 Aprilis 1912)

Clerus a proximiori ecclesia, vel ab alio aliquo praeparato loco, procedit ad locum, ubi est machina benedicenda, canendo vel recitando:

Antiphona

Mansu-e-fáctus est ignis * et vim su-ae vir-tú-tis

oblí-tus est: ut fí-li- i tu- i, quos di-lexísti, Dómi-ne, ser-

véntur il- laési. Ps. Jubilá-te De-o, omnis terra, psalmum

díci-te nómini e-jus: * da-te gló-ri-am laudi ejus.

Psalmus 65

Jubiláte Deo, omnis terra, psalmum dícite nómini ejus: * date glóriam laudi ejus.

Dícite Deo: Quam terribília sunt ópera tua, Dómine! * in multitúdine virtútis tuae mentiéntur tibi inimíci tui.

Omnis terra adóret te, et psallat tibi: * psalmum dicat nómini tuo.

Veníte, et vidéte ópera Dei: * terríbilis in consíliis super fílios hóminum.

Qui convértit mare in áridam, in flúmine pertransíbunt pede: * ibi laetábimur in ipso.

Qui dominátur in virtúte sua in aetérnum, óculi ejus super gentes respíciunt: * qui exásperant non exalténtur in semetípsis.

125

BLESSING OF A FIRE-ENGINE

(Approved by the Congregation of Sacred Rites on April 10, 1912)

From the nearest church or from another place previously appointed, the clergy proceed to the fire-station, as they chant or recite:

Antiphon: Tamed was the fire's fury, and forgotten was its power and might, as thy children, beloved of thee, O Lord, were preserved intact.

Psalm 65

Exult to God, all ye on earth, sing a song to His name, let His praises resound.

Say unto God: "How wonderful are thy works, O Lord! So tremendous is thy power that even thine enemies bow down."

Let all the earth adore and sing to thee; let it sing praise to thy name.

Come hither and see the works of God, how mightily He dealeth with the sons of men.

He turneth the sea into dry land; dry-footed they passed through the river; wherefore, we will rejoice in Him.

With mighty arm He ruleth forever; His eyes behold the nations; the obstinate shall not exalt themselves.

Benedícite, gentes, Deum nostrum: * et audítam fácite vocem laudis ejus.

Qui pósuit ánimam meam ad vitam: * et non dedit in commotiónem pedes meos.

Quóniam probásti nos, Deus: * igne nos examinásti, sicut examinátur argéntum.

Induxísti nos in láqueum, posuísti tribulatiónes in dorso nostro: * imposuísti hómines super cápita nostra.

Transívimus per ignem et aquam: * et eduxísti nos in refrigérium.

Introíbo in domum tuam in holocáustis: * reddam tibi vota mea, quae distinxérunt lábia mea.

Et locútum est os meum, * in tribulatióne mea.

Holocáusta medulláta ófferam tibi cum incénso aríetum: * ófferam tibi boves cum hircis.

Veníte, audíte, et narrábo, omnes, qui timétis Deum, * quanta fecit ánimae meae.

Ad ipsum ore meo clamávi, * et exaltávi sub lingua mea.

Iniquitátem si aspéxi in corde meo, * non exáudiet Dóminus.

Proptérea exaudívit Deus, * et atténdit voci deprecatiónis meae.

Benedíctus Deus, * qui non amóvit oratiónem meam, et misericórdiam suam a me.

Glória Patri.

Repetita Antiphona, Celebrans, respondentibus circumstantibus, dicit:

Kýrie, eléison. Christe, eléison. Kýrie, eléison.

Pater noster secreto usque ad

℣. Et ne nos indúcas in tentatiónem.

℟. Sed líbera nos a malo.

℣. Salvos fac servos tuos.

℟. Deus meus, sperántes in te.

℣. Mitte eis, Dómine, auxílium de sancto.

℟. Et de Sion tuére eos.

Praise our God, ye peoples, let His praises resound.

I owe to Him my life; He doth not allow my feet to stumble.

For thou, O God, hast given us a test; thou hast purified us with fire, as silver is tried.

Thou didst let us fall into a snare; thou didst load tribulations on our backs; thou didst set strangers over our heads.

Through fire and water we had to pass; but thou hast led us out into respite.

With burnt-offerings in hand I entered thy house; I will fulfil my vows which my lips promised,

And my mouth promised when I was in trouble.

I will offer to thee holocausts full of marrow, with the smoke of burnt rams; I will offer to thee bullocks and goats.

Come hither and hear, all ye who fear God; I will narrate what good He hath done for my soul.

I cried to Him with my mouth, and I lauded Him with my tongue.

Had I desired iniquity in my heart, the Lord would not have heard me.

But God did hear me, and gave ear to my entreaties.

Blessed be God Who did not disdain my prayer, nor refuse me His mercy.

Glory be to the Father.

After repeating the antiphon, the celebrant says alternately with his assistants:

Lord, have mercy on us. Christ, have mercy on us. Lord, have mercy on us.

Our Father inaudibly until

℣. And lead us not into temptation.

℟. But deliver us from evil.

℣. Preserve thy servants.

℟. Who trust in thee, my God.

℣. Send them aid, Lord, from on high.

℟. And from Sion watch over them.

℣. Nihil profíciat inimícus in eis.

℟. Et fílius iniquitátis non appónat nocére eis.

℣. Benedícite, ignis et aestus, Dómino.

℟. Laudáte et superexaltáte eum in saécula.

℣. Benedícite, fílii hóminum, Dómino.

℟. Laudáte et superexaltáte eum in saécula.

℣. Qui líberat nos de médio ardéntis flammae.

℟. Et de médio ignis éruit nos.

℣. Confitémini Dómino, quóniam bonus.

℟. Quóniam in saéculum misericórdia ejus.

℣. Adjutórium nostrum in nómine Dómini.

℟. Qui fecit caelum et terram.

℣. Dómine, exáudi oratiónem meam.

℟. Et clamor meus ad te véniat.

℣. Dóminus vobíscum.

℟. Et cum spíritu tuo.

Orémus.   Oratio

D EUS, qui tribus púeris in fornáce Babylónis per Angelum tuum mitigásti flammas ígnium: omnes, quaésumus, pe déxteram tuam in córdibus nostris faces exstíngue vitiórum; ut ¿ temporálibus eruámur incéndiis, et ab ígnibus liberémur aetérnis Per Christum Dóminum nostrum. ℟. Amen.

Orémus.   Oratio

D EUS, cujus in mánibus nos sumus, et sermónes nostri, e omnis sapiéntia, et óperum sciéntia et disciplína: fámuli tuis opitulátor adsíste; ut, quóties instántibus incéndii periclitému angústiis, tóties suppeténtibus ingénii foveámur auxíliis. Pe Christum Dóminum nostrum. ℟. Amen.

Orémus.   Oratio

D EUS, justus hóminum gubernátor et clemens, cui tamquan Factóri suo sic omnis prómptior creatúra desérvit, ut éaden ad torméntum ímpiis exardéscat, et ad benefícium piis leni ᴧvádat: aurem tuam, quaésumus, précibus nostris benígnus ir

℣. Let the enemy be powerless against them.

℟. And the son of iniquity do nothing to harm them.

℣. Ye fire and heat, praise the Lord.

℟. Praise Him and exalt Him forever.

℣. Bless the Lord, ye sons of men.

℟. Praise Him and exalt Him forever.

℣. Who delivereth us out of the midst of flames.

℟. And leadeth us out of the midst of fire.

℣. Let us praise the Lord, for He is good.

℟. For His mercy endureth forever.

℣. Our help is in the name of the Lord.

℟. Who made heaven and earth.

℣. O Lord, hear my prayer.

℟. And let my cry come unto thee.

℣. The Lord be with you.

℟. And with thy spirit.

Let us pray. *Prayer*

O GOD, Who by thy angel didst mitigate the flames of the fire for the three youths who were cast into the furnace in Babylon, we beseech thee, extinguish in our hearts the fire of sinful inclinations, that we may be delivered both from bodily burns and from everlasting fire. Through Christ our Lord. ℟. Amen.

Let us pray. *Prayer*

O GOD, in thy hands are held all that we are and have, our speech, all wisdom, knowledge, and science. Do thou generously assist thy servants, that we may be protected in all danger of fire by the aid of every spiritual and technical force. Through Christ our Lord. ℟. Amen.

Let us pray. *Prayer*

O GOD, thou just and mild Governor of mankind, to Whom thy creature, fire is subject as to its Creator, on the one hand blazing up for the torment of the impious, on the other becoming gentle for the utility of the devout; we beseech thee to attend

ténde, et hanc máchinam compriméndis ígnibus destinátam tua muníficus bene ✝dictióne perfúnde: ut, quóties hujus éfficax instruméntum máchinae viva fide piísque cum votis fúerit advérsus éxcitas incéndii vires adhíbitum, aqua saeviéntes flammas ex eo jactáta restínguat, et igni vim totam suae virtútis erípiat, ne incéndium fidélibus in te sperántibus moléstiam áfferat, neve illis eorúmque bonis detriméntum íngerat: quátenus univérsi, ab omni formídine páriter et perículo sóspites, a suis vítiis toto corde resipíscant, ac beneficiórum tuórum mémores, sincéra mente cognóscant, tália sibi flagélla e sua quidem iniquitáte prodíre, et in tua miseratióne cessáre. Per Dóminum nostrum Jesum Christum, Fílium tuum, qui tecum vivit et regnat in unitáte Spíritus Sancti, Deus, per ómnia saécula saeculórum. ℞. Amen.

Et aspergatur aqua benedicta.

126

BENEDICTIO MACHINAE AD EXCITANDAM LUCEM ELECTRICAM

Clerus, a proximiori ecclesia vel ab aliquo alio loco ad hoc parato, procedit usque ad stationem machinae benedicendae, canendo vel recitando:

Canticum Zachariae, ut supra, pag. 50. Ibi Sacerdos delegatus intonat:

Antiphona

VI F

Lux orta est * ju-sto : rectis corde lae-tí- ti- a. Ps. Dóminus regnávit, exsúltet terra: * laeténtur ínsulae multae.

in thy benignity to our prayers, and to pour out in abundance thy blessing ✠ upon this fire-engine. So often as this equipment is employed with lively faith and devout prayers against the ravaging destruction of fire, may the stream of water which it gushes forth extinguish the fury of the flames, and divest the fire of its power, so that no injury may be suffered by the faithful who place their confidence in thee, and no damage done to their possessions. Wherefore, let all who are favored with thy protection against the fright and peril of fire turn away from sin with all their heart, and mindful of thy benefits, sincerely acknowledge that such visitations are a consequence of their sinful ways, and that they cease only by thy mercy. Through Jesus Christ, thy Son, our Lord, Who liveth and reigneth with thee in unity of the Holy Spirit, God, for all eternity. ℞. Amen.

It is sprinkled with holy water.

126

BLESSING OF AN ELECTRIC DYNAMO*

From the nearest church or from some other place previously appointed, the clergy proceed in a solemn manner to the power station, as they chant or recite:

The Canticle of Zachary, as above on page 51. Arriving at the station, the priest intones:

Antiphon: **A light riseth up for the good, and joy to the righteous of heart.**

---

* This blessing is reserved to the Ordinary or to one delegated by him.

Dóminus regnávit, exsúltet terra: * laeténtur ínsulae multae.

Nubes, et calígo in circúitu ejus: * justítia, et judícium corréctio sedis ejus.

Ignis ante ipsum praecédet, * et inflammábit in circúitu inimícos ejus.

Illuxérunt fúlgura ejus orbi terrae: * vidit, et commóta est terra.

Montes, sicut cera fluxérunt a fácie Dómini: * a fácie Dómini omnis terra.

Annuntiavérunt caeli justítiam ejus: * et vidérunt omnes pópuli glóriam ejus.

Confundántur omnes, qui adórant sculptília: * et qui gloriántur in simulácris suis.

Adoráte eum, omnes Angeli ejus: * audívit, et laetáta est Sion.

Et exsultavérunt fíliae Judae, * propter judícia tua, Dómine:

Quóniam tu Dóminus Altíssimus super omnem terram: * nimis exaltátus es super omnes deos.

Qui dilígitis Dóminum, odíte malum: * custódit Dóminus ánimas sanctórum suórum, de manu peccatóris liberábit eos.

Lux orta est justo, * et rectis corde laetítia.

Laetámini, justi, in Dómino: * et confitémini memóriae sanctificatiónis ejus.

Glória Patri.

Antiphona

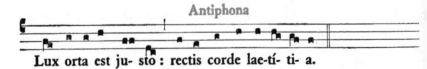

Lux orta est ju- sto : rectis corde lae-tí- ti- a.

℣. Adjutórium nostrum in nómine Dómini.

℟. Qui fecit caelum et terram.

℣. Dómine, exáudi oratiónem meam.

℟. Et clamor meus ad te véniat.

℣. Dóminus vobíscum.

℟. Et cum spíritu tuo.

Psalm 96

The Lord is King, let the earth rejoice; let the many islands be glad.

Darkness and clouds are round about Him; upon right and justice rests His throne.

Devastating fire goes before Him, and destroys His enemies round about.

His lightning illumines the world; the universe sees it and trembles.

The mountains melt like wax before the countenance of the Lord, at the presence of the Lord of the earth.

The heavens proclaim His justice; all peoples behold His majesty.

Confounded are they who worship graven things, and glory in their idols.

Adore ye Him, all His angels! Sion heareth the news with jubilation.

Because of thy judgments, O Lord, the daughters of Sion rejoice.

For thou art the Highest, and Lord over the entire earth — and exalted above all gods.

Hate evil, all ye that love the Lord; the Lord preserveth the life of His holy ones, and delivereth them from the hands of the impious.

A light riseth up for the good, and joy to the righteous of heart.

Rejoice, ye just, in the Lord, and praise ye His holy name.

Glory be to the Father.

Antiphon: A light riseth up for the good, and joy to the righteous of heart.

℣. Our help is in the name of the Lord.

℟. Who made heaven and earth.

℣. O Lord, hear my prayer.

℟. And let my cry come unto thee.

℣. The Lord be with you.

℟. And with thy spirit.

Orémus. Oratio

CONCÉDE nos fámulos tuos, quaésumus, Dómine Deus, perpétua mentis et córporis sanitáte gaudére: et gloriósa beátae Maríae semper Vírginis intercessióne, a praesénti liberári tristítia, et aetérna pérfrui laetítia. Per Christum Dóminum nostrum. ℟. Amen.

Orémus. Oratio

DÓMINE Deus omnípotens, qui es cónditor ómnium lúminum, béne ✠ dic hanc máchinam ad lumen excitándum nóviter cónditam: et praesta; ut ad te, qui es lux indefíciens, post hujus saéculi calíginem perveníre valeámus. Per Christum Dóminum nostrum. ℟. Amen.

Deinde aspergit machinam aqua benedicta.

127

BENEDICTIO OFFICINAE LIBRARIAE ET MACHINAE TYPOGRAPHICAE
(Approbata a S. R. C. die 12 Maji 1909)

Sacerdos stans ad valvas, dicit:

Actiónes nostras, quaésumus, Dómine, aspirándo praéveni, et adjuvándo proséquere: ut cuncta nostra orátio et operátio a te semper incípiat, et per te coepta finiátur. Per Christum Dóminum nostrum. ℟. Amen.

Ingrediens dicit:

℣. Pax huic dómui.

℟. Et ómnibus habitántibus in ea.

Deinde dicens Antiphonam **Aspérges me, Dómine,** etc., varias officinae partes aqua benedicta aspergit, usquedum perveniat ad aulam principalem ejusdem, ubi sistit et dicit:

℣. Adjutórium nostrum in nómine Dómini.

℟. Qui fecit caelum et terram.

Let us pray.   Prayer

G RANT to thy servants, O Lord God, we beseech thee, continual enjoyment of health in soul and body; and by the wondrous intercession of Blessed Mary ever Virgin, free us from sorrow in the present, and reward us with joy in eternity. Through Christ our Lord. R̸. Amen.

Let us pray.   Prayer

O LORD God Almighty, Creator of all light, bless ✠ this electric dynamo built for the purpose of generating light. And grant that after the darkness of this life, we may attain unto thee, Who art the unfailing Light. Through Christ our Lord. R̸. Amen.

It is sprinkled with holy water.

127

BLESSING OF A PRINTING-OFFICE AND PRINTING-PRESS
or of a Typewriter

(Approved by the Congregation of Sacred Rites on May 12, 1909)

Standing at the entrance, the priest says:

We beseech thee, Lord, inspire and guide our works in their beginning, and accompany them unto fruition, that our every prayer and work may ever begin with thee, and through thee be accomplished. Through Christ our Lord. R̸. Amen.

Entering in, he says:

V̸. Peace be unto this establishment.

R̸. And unto all who are employed herein.

Then, as he says the antiphon: Sprinkle me with hyssop, O Lord, etc., he sprinkles with holy water the various rooms of the printing-office, until he comes to the main part. Here he stops, and says:

V̸. Our help is in the name of the Lord.

R̸. Who made heaven and earth.

℣. Dóminus vobíscum.

℟. Et cum spíritu tuo.

Orémus.   Oratio

DÓMINE Jesu Christe, qui dixísti discípulis tuis: In quamcúmque domum intravéritis, salutáte eam, dicéntes: Pax
huic dómui: véniat, quaésumus, pax illa super hanc domum et
officínam ad libros impriméndos (evulgándos) praeparátam, et
super omnes degéntes in ea; et cunctos, Dómine, in ea laborántes
ab omni calamitáte ánimae et córporis erípere et liberáre dignéris;
reple scriptóres, rectóres et operários spíritu sciéntiae, consílii et
fortitúdinis, et adímple eos spíritu timóris tui, ut mandáta Ecclésiae fidéliter custodiéntes, tibi digne et próximo suo salutáriter
váleant inservíre. Béne ✠ dic ergo, bone Jesu, qui es via, véritas
et vita, hunc locum, et praesta, ut omnes illum inhabitántes, intercedénte gloriósa et immaculáta Vírgine matre tua María, ad
immarcescíbilem glóriae corónam felíciter pervéniant: Qui vivis
et regnas Deus per ómnia saécula saeculórum. ℟. Amen.

Deinde benedicit instrumenta et machinas, dicens:

Orémus.   Oratio

DÓMINE Deus, únice fons scientiárum, qui hóminum in-
génium ita illumináre dignátus es, ut nova artificiósa instruménta invenírent ad páginas typis scribéndas; béne ✠ dic,
quaésumus, has máchinas (hanc máchinam), ut per libros ad
utilitátem nostram prodeúntes nihil áliud te opitulánte discámus,
praeter sciéntiam tuam, quae vere ducit ad vitam. Per Christum
Dóminum nostrum. ℟. Amen.

Et aspergantur aqua benedicta. Finita aspersione, Sacerdos dicit:

℣. Dóminus vobíscum.

℟. Et cum spíritu tuo.

℣. The Lord be with you.

℞. And with thy spirit.

Let us pray.   Prayer

O LORD Jesus Christ, Who didst say to thine apostles: "In whatever home you enter, salute it, saying: 'Peace be unto this house,'" let this same peace, we pray, come upon this printing establishment and upon all who transact business here. Do thou, O Lord, deign to deliver from every calamity, spiritual or physical, all them that are employed herein. Fill the authors, publishers, and craftsmen with the spirit of wisdom, counsel, and fortitude, and instill in them the fear of the Lord; so that they may faithfully keep the commandments of the Church, and thus employ their vocation to thy glory and to their fellowmen's welfare. Wherefore, O benign Jesus, Who art the Way, the Truth, and the Life, bless ✠ this place, and grant, through the intercession of the glorious and immaculate Virgin Mary, thy mother, that all who are employed here may happily attain the imperishable crown of glory. Thou Who livest and reignest eternally. ℞. Amen.

Then he blesses the machines and instruments, saying:

Let us pray.   Prayer

O LORD God, thou sole Source of learning, Who hast condescended so to enlighten men's resourcefulness that they have invented new and artistic methods of printing, bless, ✠ we beseech thee, these machines (this machine). And from the books which issue forth for our enlightenment, may we learn, by thy gracious help, nothing but that knowledge which, coming from thee, leadeth truly unto life. Through Christ our Lord. ℞. Amen.

They are sprinkled with holy water. After which the priest says:

℣. The Lord be with you.

℞. And with thy spirit.

Orémus.

EXÁUDI nos, Dómine sancte, Pater omnípotens, aetérne Deus: et míttere dignéris sanctum Angelum tuum de caelis, qui custódiat, fóveat, prótegat, vísitet atque deféndat omnes in hac domo habitántes. Per Christum Dóminum nostrum. ℞. Amen.

Si benedicenda sit tantum officina libraria, omittitur secunda Oratio cum aspersione pro instrumentis et machinis. Quando autem benedicenda sint solummodo instrumenta vel machinae, praemissis versiculis: **Adjutórium nostrum,** etc., et **Dóminus vobíscum,** etc., adhibetur tantum secunda Oratio cum aspersione.

128

BENEDICTIO TELEGRAPHI

Clerus, vel a proximiori ecclesia, vel ab aliquo alio loco ad hoc parato, procedit usque ad stationem telegraphi, canendo vel recitando:

Canticum Zachariae
(Luc. 1, 68-79)

Benedíctus Dóminus, Deus Israel, * quia visitávit, et fecit redemptiónem plebis suae:

Et eréxit cornu salútis nobis: * in domo David, púeri sui.

Sicut locútus est per os sanctórum, * qui a saéculo sunt, prophetárum ejus:

Salútem ex inimícis nostris, * et de manu ómnium, qui odérunt nos:

Ad faciéndam misericórdiam cum pátribus nostris: * et memorári testaménti sui sancti.

Jusjurándum, quod jurávit ab Abraham, patrem nostrum, * datúrum se nobis:

Ut sine timóre, de manu inimicórum nostrórum liberáti, * serviámus illi.

Let us pray.   ·

HEAR us, O holy Lord, almighty Father, everlasting God, and vouchsafe to send thy holy angel from heaven to watch over, foster, protect, visit, and defend all who have business in this establishment. Through Christ our Lord. ℟. Amen.

If the printing-office alone is to be blessed, omit the second prayer, together with the sprinkling of machines and instruments. However, if only the latter are to be blessed, begin at the versicle: **Our help,** etc., then say the second prayer, and sprinkle them with holy water.

128

BLESSING OF A TELEGRAPH-INSTRUMENT*

From the nearest church or from another place previously appointed, the clergy proceed in solemn manner to the telegraph station, chanting or reciting:

Canticle of Zachary
(Luke 1, 68–79)

Blessed be the Lord God of Israel, for He hath visited and redeemed His people,

And hath raised up the Abundance of salvation for us in the lineage of David His servant.

Thus He foretold by the mouth of His holy prophets who have been from times ancient;

That we might be saved from our enemies — from the hand of all that hate us.

Now is granted the mercy promised to our fathers, remembering His holy covenant;

And the oath which He swore to Abraham our father that He would extend to us;

That we, delivered from the hand of our enemies, might serve Him without fear,

---

* This blessing is reserved to the Ordinary or to one delegated by him.

In sanctitáte, et justítia coram ipso, * ómnibus diébus nostris.

Et tu, puer, Prophéta Altíssimi vocáberis: * praeíbis enim ante fáciem Dómini paráre vias ejus:

Ad dandam sciéntiam salútis plebi ejus: * in remissiónem peccatórum eórum:

Per víscera misericórdiae Dei nostri: * in quibus visitávit nos, óriens ex alto:

Illumináre his, qui in ténebris, et in umbra mortis sedent: * ad dirigéndos pedes nostros in viam pacis.

Glória Patri.

Ibi Sacerdos delegatus intonat:

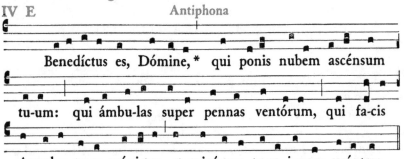

Benedíctus es, Dómine, * qui ponis nubem ascénsum tu-um: qui ámbu-las super pennas ventórum, qui fa-cis Angelos tu-os spí-ri-tus, et minístros tu-os ignem uréntem.

Postea dicitur Ps.

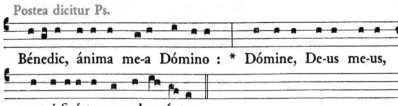

Bénedic, ánima me-a Dómino : * Dómine, De-us me-us, magni-ficá-tus es veheménter.

Psalmus 103

BÉNEDIC, ánima mea, Dómino: * Dómine, Deus meus, magnificátus es veheménter.

Confessiónem, et decórem induísti: * amíctus lúmine sicut vestiménto:

Exténdens caelum sicut pellem: * qui tegis aquis superióra ejus.

Qui ponis nubem ascénsum tuum: * qui ámbulas super pennas ventórum.

Living in holiness and righteousness before Him all our days.

And thou, child, shalt be called the prophet of the Highest, for thou shalt go before the face of the Lord to prepare His ways:

To give knowledge of salvation to His people — the remission of their sins,

Through the bounteous mercy of our God in which the Orient from on high hath visited us,

To give light to them that sit in darkness and in the shadow of death, to direct our feet into the way of peace.

Glory be to the Father.

Arriving at the station, the priest delegated for the blessing intones:

Antiphon: Blessed art thou, O Lord, Who makest the clouds thy chariot, and walkest on the wings of the winds; Who usest the winds for thy messengers, and flaming fire for thy ministers.

Psalm 103

BLESS the Lord, O my soul. My Lord and my God, how mighty is thy creation!

Thou dost clothe thyself in glory and in beauty, vested in light as with a garment.

Thou stretchest out the heavens like a tent, and coverest their heights with waters;

Who makest the clouds thy chariot, and walkest on the wings of the winds.

Qui facis Angelos tuos spíritus: * et minístros tuos ignem uréntem.

Qui fundásti terram super stabilitátem suam: * non inclinábitur in saéculum saéculi.

Abýssus, sicut vestiméntum, amíctus ejus: * super montes stabunt aquae.

Ab increpatióne tua fúgient: * a voce tonítrui tui formidábunt.

Ascéndunt montes: et descéndunt campi * in locum, quem fundásti eis.

Términum posuísti, quem non transgrediéntur: * neque converténtur operíre terram.

Qui emíttis fontes in conVállibus: * inter médium móntium pertransíbunt aquae.

Potábunt omnes béstiae agri: * exspectábunt ónagri in siti sua.

Super ea vólucres caeli habitábunt: *de médio petrárum dabunt voces.

Rigans montes de superióribus suis: * de fructu óperum tuórum satiábitur terra:

Prodúcens foenum juméntis, * et herbam servitúti hóminum:

Ut edúcas panem de terra: * et vinum laetíficet cor hóminis:

Ut exhílaret fáciem in óleo: * et panis cor hóminis confírmet.

Saturabúntur ligna campi, et cedri Líbani, quas plantávit: * illic pásseres nidificábunt.

Heródii domus dux est eórum: * montes excélsi cervis: petra refúgium herináciis.

Fecit lunam in témpora: * sol cognóvit occásum suum.

Posuísti ténebras, et facta est nox: * in ipsa pertransíbunt omnes béstiae silvae.

Cátuli leónum rugiéntes, ut rápiant, * et quaerant a Deo escam sibi.

Ortus est sol, et congregáti sunt: * et in cubílibus suis collocabúntur.

Thou usest the winds for thy messengers, and flaming fire for thy ministers.

Thou hast fastened the earth on its foundations; it shall never be shaken.

The deep like a garment was its clothing, and the waters stood high above the mountains.

At thy rebuke they dispersed, at the voice of thy thunder they fled.

The mountains rose up, and the plains sank down to the place thou didst assign.

Impassible boundaries thou didst assign to the waters, never again might they cover the earth.

In the valleys thou sentest forth springs, whose streams flowed out among the hills.

The beasts of the field drink of them; whereat wild asses quench their thirst.

Birds of heaven dwell on their banks, and from the midst of the rocks they utter their song.

Thou waterest the mountains from heavenly heights; the earth slakes its thirst from thy rain-clouds;

Bringing forth grass for cattle, and herbs for the servitors of man,

That bread might spring forth from the earth, and wine which gives cheer to man's heart;

Oil to make his face lustrous, and bread to strengthen his heart.

The trees of the field drink their fill; so, too, the cedars of Lebanon which He planted; there the birds build their nests.

The stork has his home in the heights. The high hills are a refuge for wild goats, the rock for the conies.

He hath made the moon for reckoning of seasons; the sun knoweth the hour for setting.

He calleth up darkness, and night begins, in which wild beasts of the forest roam about;

And young lions roar for their booty, and demand from God their meat.

When the sun is risen, they gather together, and rest in their dens.

Exibit homo ad opus suum: * et ad operatiónem suam usque ad vésperum.

Quam magnificáta sunt ópera tua, Dómine! * ómnia in sapiéntia fecísti: impléta est terra possessióne tua.

Hoc mare magnum, et spatiósum mánibus: * illic reptília, quorum non est númerus.

Animália pusílla cum magnis: * illic naves pertransíbunt.

Draco iste, quem formásti ad illudéndum ei: * ómnia a te exspéctant ut des illis escam in témpore.

Dante te illis, cólligent: * aperiénte te manum tuam, ómnia implebúntur bonitáte.

Averténte autem te fáciem, turbabúntur: * áuferes spíritum eórum, et defícient, et in púlverem suum reverténtur.

Emíttes spíritum tuum, et creabúntur: * et renovábis fáciem terrae.

Sit glória Dómini in saéculum: * laetábitur Dóminus in opéribus suis.

Qui réspicit terram, et facit eam trémere: * qui tangit montes, et fúmigant.

Cantábo Dómino in vita mea: * psallam Deo meo, quámdiu sum.

Jucúndum sit ei elóquium meum: * ego vero delectábor in Dómino.

Defíciant peccatóres a terra, et iníqui ita ut non sint: * bénedic, ánima mea, Dómino.

Glória Patri.

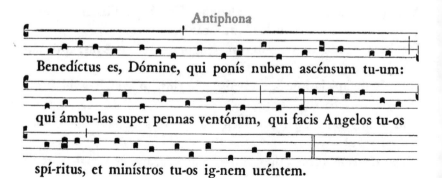

Antiphona

Benedíctus es, Dómine, qui ponís nubem ascénsum tu-um: qui ámbu-las super pennas ventórum, qui facis Angelos tu-os spí-ritus, et minístros tu-os ig-nem uréntem.

Now men go forth to their toil; their labor lasteth 'till evening.

How wonderful are thy works, O Lord! For thou hast made everything in wisdom, and the earth is filled with thy riches.

Yonder does the great sea extend wide its arms, wherein are creeping things without number,

Creatures little and great; moreover, ships sail on its waters.

Nor is there wanting the sea-monster which thou madest in mockery. They all await from thee their food in due time.

And when thou givest them food, they gather it up; thou openest thy hand, and they receive their fill.

But if thou hidest thy face, they are filled with fear; and dost thou take away their breath, so they shall fail and return to their dust.

But if thou sendest forth thy breath — then their life begins anew, and the countenance of the earth rises as new.

May the glory of the Lord endure forever; let the Lord rejoice in His works.

Doth He but look upon the earth, and it trembles; the mountains smoke at His touch.

I will sing to the Lord all my life; I will sing praise to my God while I live.

O may my praises please Him; yet will I delight in the Lord.

O that sinners would disappear from the earth, and the iniquitous be no more! Bless the Lord, O my soul!

Glory be to the Father.

Antiphon: Blessed art thou, O Lord, Who makest the clouds thy chariot, and walkest on the wings of the winds: Who usest the winds for thy messengers, and flaming fire for thy ministers.

Deinde dicit:

℣. Adjutórium nostrum in nómine Dómini.

℟. Qui fecit caelum et terram.

℣. Dóminus vobíscum.

℟. Et cum spíritu tuo.

Orémus.   Oratio

CONCÉDE nos fámulos tuos, quaésumus, Dómine Deus, perpétua mentis et córporis sanitáte gaudére: et gloriósa beátae Maríae semper Vírginis intercessióne, a praesénti liberári tristítia, et aetérna pérfrui laetítia. Per Christum Dóminum nostrum. ℟. Amen.

Orémus.   Oratio

DEUS, qui ámbulas super pennas ventórum, et facis mirabília solus: concéde, ut, cum per vim huic metállo índitam fulmíneo ictu celérius huc abséntia, et hinc álio praeséntia transmíttis; ita nos invéntis novis edócti, tua grátia opitulánte, prómptius et facílius ad te veníre valeámus. Per Christum Dóminum nostrum. ℟. Amen.

Et aspergit telegraphum aqua benedicta.

129

BENEDICTIO SEISMOGRAPHI
(Approbata a S. R. C. die 13 Febr. 1924)

℣. Adjutórium nostrum in nómine Dómini.

℟. Qui fecit caelum et terram.

℣. Dóminus vobíscum.

℟. Et cum spíritu tuo.

Orémus.   Oratio

Omnípotens sempitérne Deus, qui réspicis terram et facis eam trémere, hoc seismógraphon tua bene✠dictióne perfúnde: et

Then the priest says:

℣. Our help is in the name of the Lord.
℟. Who made heaven and earth.
℣. The Lord be with you.
℟. And with thy spirit.

Let us pray. *Prayer*

GRANT to thy servants, O Lord God, we beseech thee, continual enjoyment of health in soul and body; and by the wondrous intercession of Blessed Mary ever Virgin, free us from sorrow in the present, and reward us with joy in eternity. Through Christ our Lord. ℟. Amen.

Let us pray. *Prayer*

O GOD, thou walkest upon the wings of the wind, and thou alone workest wonders! By the power inherent in this metal, thou dost bring hither distant things quicker than lightning, and transferest present things to distant places. Therefore, grant that instructed by new inventions, we may merit, by thy bounteous grace, to come with greater certainty and facility to thee. Through Christ our Lord. ℟. Amen.

The telegraph-instrument is sprinkled with holy water.

129

BLESSING OF A SEISMOGRAPH
(Approved by the Congregation of Sacred Rites on Feb. 13, 1924)

℣. Our help is in the name of the Lord.
℟. Who made heaven and earth.
℣. The Lord be with you.
℟. And with thy spirit.

Let us pray. *Prayer*

O almighty, everlasting God, Who by glancing upon the earth dost cause it to tremble, pour out thy blessing ✠ on this seismo-

praesta; ut signa terrae treméntis in ipso congruénter adnoténtur, et ad utilitátem plebis tuae atque ad majórem tui nóminis glóriam promovéndam recte intelligántur. Per Christum Dóminum nostrum. ℟. Amen.

Virgo María dolorosíssima, esto nobis propítia et intercéde pro nobis.

Sancte Emígdi, ora pro nobis, et in nómine Jesu Christi Nazaréni defénde nos, et hoc seismógraphon ab ímpetu terraemótus.

Et aspergatur seismographon aqua benedicta.

130

BENEDICTIO AD OMNIA

Haec benedictionis formula adhiberi potest a quovis Sacerdote pro omnibus rebus, quarum specialis benedictio in hoc Rituali non habetur.

℣. Adjutórium nostrum in nómine Dómini.

℟. Qui fecit caelum et terram.

℣. Dóminus vobíscum.

℟. Et cum spíritu tuo.

Orémus.   Oratio

Deus, cujus verbo sanctificántur ómnia, bene ✠ dictiónem tuam effúnde super creatúram istam (creatúras istas): et praesta; ut, quisquis ea (eis) secúndum legem et voluntátem tuam cum gratiárum actióne usus fúerit, per invocatiónem sanctíssimi nóminis tui, córporis sanitátem, et ánimae tutélam, te auctóre, percípiat. Per Christum Dóminum nostrum. ℟. Amen.

Et aspergatur (aspergantur) aqua benedicta.

graph. And grant that the signs of the earth's tremors may be exactly recorded by it, and rightly interpreted by men to benefit thy people and to promulgate the greater glory of thy name. Through Christ our Lord. ℟. Amen.

O Virgin Mary most sorrowful, take pity on us, and pray for us!

Saint Emidius, pray for us, and in the name of Jesus Christ, the Nazarene, defend us and also this seismograph from the power of earthquakes.

It is sprinkled with holy water.

130

THE FORM OF BLESSING FOR ALL THINGS

This form may be used by any priest for the blessing of anything which has no special blessing in the Ritual.

℣. Our help is in the name of the Lord.

℟. Who made heaven and earth.

℣. The Lord be with you.

℟. And with thy spirit.

Let us pray. *Prayer*

O God, by Whose word all things are made holy, pour out thy blessing ✠ on this creature (these creatures). And grant that whosoever uses it (them) in accordance with thy will and thy law, and with a spirit of thanksgiving, may experience by thy power health in body and protection in soul, as he invokes thy most holy name. Through Christ our Lord. ℟. Amen.

It (they) is (are) sprinkled with holy water.

131

BENEDICTIO NOSOCOMIORUM ALIARUMQUE DOMORUM AEGROTIS CURANDIS

(Approbata a S. R. C. die 18 Julii 1939)

Antiphona: Omnes male habéntes Christus curávit: ipse infirmitátes nostras accépit, et aegrotatiónes nostras portávit (Matt. 8:17):

Psalmus 6

DÓMINE, ne in furóre tuo árguas me, * neque in ira tua corrípias me.

Miserére mei, Dómine: quóniam infírmus sum: * sana me, Dómine, quóniam conturbáta sunt ossa mea.

Et ánima mea turbáta est valde: * sed tu, Dómine, úsquequo?

Convértere, Dómine, et eripe ánimam meam: * salvum me fac propter misericórdiam tuam.

Quóniam non est in morte qui memor sit tui: * in inférno autem quis confitébitur tibi?

Laborávi in gémitu meo, lavábo per síngulas noctes lectum meum: * lácrimis meis stratum meum rigábo.

Turbátus est a furóre óculus meus: * inveterávi inter omnes inimícos meos.

Discédite a me omnes, qui operámini iniquitátem: * quóniam exaudívit Dóminus vocem fletus mei.

Exaudívit Dóminus deprecatiónem meam: * Dóminus oratiónem meam suscépit.

Erubéscant et conturbéntur veheménter omnes inimíci mei: * convertántur et erubéscant valde velóciter.

Glória Patri.

Repetitur Antiphona.

℣. Adjutórium nostrum in nómine Dómini.

℟. Qui fecit caelum et terram.

℣. Dóminus vobíscum.

℟. Et cum spíritu tuo.

131

BLESSING OF A HOSPITAL OR SANATORIUM
(Approved by the Congregation of Sacred Rites on July 18, 1939)

Antiphon: **All that were sick Christ healed: He took our infirmities, and bore our diseases** (Matthew 8:17).

Psalm 6

O LORD! Punish me not in thine anger; nor chastise me in thy fury.

Have pity on me, Lord, for I am weak and sick; heal me, for my bones are rotted.

And my soul is troubled exceedingly. But thou, O Lord — how long wilt thou look on?

Turn to me, Lord, and deliver my soul. Save me because of thy goodness.

For in death's realm no one is mindful of thee, and in infernal regions who shall praise thee?

I am wearied from moaning; each night I bedew my bed with weeping: my tears water my couch.

The lustre of mine eyes is become dim. I have grown old in the midst of my oppressors.

Depart from me, ye evildoers, for the Lord hath heard my piteous cry.

The Lord hath heard my supplication, the Lord hath accepted my prayer.

My foes shall be ashamed and exceedingly confused. Speedily will come their shame and consternation.

Glory be to the Father.

Repeat the Antiphon.

℣. Our help is in the name of the Lord.

℟. Who made heaven and earth.

℣. The Lord be with you.

℟. And with thy spirit.

Orémus.   Oratio

DEUS qui mirabíliter hóminem creásti, et mirabílius reformásti, atque váriis infirmitátibus, quibus humána fragílitas
detinétur, multíplici remédio succúrrere dignátus es; tuam sanctam bene✠ dictiónem super hanc domum benígnus infúnde, ut
aegrórum, huc adveniéntium, córpori et ánimae ipse medeáris,
tua eos patérna pietáte custódias, ac post vitae cursum ad gáudia
tránsferas sempitérna. Per Christum Dóminum nostrum. ℞.
Amen.

Orémus.   Oratio

DÓMINE Jesu Christe, infirmitátis nostrae solámen et salus,
qui Petri socrum et Réguli fílium a magnis fébribus liberásti, paralýticum roborásti, leprósos mundásti, Centuriónis sanásti,
mulíerem a fluxu sánguinis salvásti, ad piscínam jacéntem lán-
guidum erexísti, civitátes et castélla circúmiens omnem languórem et infirmitátem curásti: bene✠ dic, quáesumus, et sanctí✠
fica domum istam; ut omnes infírmi hic moratúri, ab omni
aegritúdine leváti, mentis et córporis sanitáte donáti, poténtiam
tuam perpétuo váleant collaudáre. Qui vivis et regnas in saécula
saeculórum. ℞. Amen.

Deinde aspergit praecipua nosocomii loca aqua benedicta et
subjungit:

℣. Osténde nobis, Dómine, misericórdiam tuam.
℞. Et salutáre tuum da nobis.
℣. Dómine, exáudi oratiónem meam.
℞. Et clamor meus ad te véniat.
℣. Dóminus vobíscum.
℞. Et cum spíritu tuo.
Orémus.   Oratio

OMNÍPOTENS sempitérne Deus, qui aegritúdines animárun
depéllis et córporum, auxílii tui super infírmos osténde vi
tútem, ut ope misericórdiae tuae ad ómnia pietátis tuae reparén
tur offícia.

Let us pray.   Prayer

O GOD, thou didst wondrously create man, and more wondrously transform him. Thou didst deign by manifold
remedies to heal the divers infirmities which beset human frailty.
Wherefore, graciously pour forth thy holy ✠ benediction upon
this hospital, that the patients may find in thee a physician of
body and soul — a kind and fatherly protector. And mayest thou
take them, following their earthly course, to the unending
blessedness of heaven. Through Christ our Lord. ℟. Amen.

Let us pray.   Prayer

O LORD, Jesus Christ, the Comfort and Deliverer in our
afflictions, thou didst dispel the heavy fever from Peter's
mother-in-law and the ruler's son, thou didst restore the paralytic,
cleanse the lepers, cure the centurion's servant; thou didst make
whole the woman troubled with an issue of blood, and didst
raise up the man lying under his infirmity at the pool of Beth-
saida; and going about the cities and towns, thou didst heal all
manner of ailments. Do thou, we beseech thee, bless ✠ and sanctify ✠ this institution, so that the sick who will be confined herein, freed from their illness and restored in body and mind, may
rightfully choose to glorify thy power forever. Thou Who livest
and reignest in eternity. ℟. Amen.

The priest sprinkles with holy water the main parts of the hospital;
then he continues:

℣. Show us, O Lord, thy mercy.

℟. And grant us thy salvation.

℣. O Lord, hear my prayer.

℟. And let my cry come unto thee.

℣. The Lord be with you.

℟. And with thy spirit.

Let us pray.   Prayer

A LMIGHTY, everlasting God, Who dispellest all corporal and
spiritual illness, manifest the power of thy help unto the
sick, that by this work of thy mercy they may be restored to the
duty of serving thee.

CONCÉDE nos fámulos tuos, quaésumus, Dómine Deus, perpétua mentis et córporis sanitáte gaudére, et, gloriósa beátae Maríae semper Vírginis intercessióne, a praesénti liberári tristítia et aetérna pérfrui laetítia.

DEUS, qui nos miro Angelórum ministério custódis et gubérnas, huic quoque dómui Angelum tuum députa custódem, qui ab ea omnes repéllat potestátes; ut aegróti in ea jacéntes ab omni formídine et perturbatióne protécti, prístinae reddántur sanitáti.

DEUS, qui ineffábili providéntia beatum Joseph sanctíssimae Genitrícis tuae Sponsum elígere dignátus es; praesta, quaésumus; ut quem protectórem venerámur in terris, intercessórem habére mereámur in caelis.

DEUS, misericordiárum Pater, per mérita et intercessiónem Sanctórum Camílli et Joánnis de Deo, quos víscera misericórdiae indútos, infirmórum adjutóres et consolatóres effecísti: aegrótis in hac domo curándis propítius adésse dignéris; ut a córporis languóribus erépti, ánimi moeróribus subleváti, ad prístinam rédeant sanitátem et débitas misericórdiae tuae gratiárum júgiter réferant actiónes. Per Christum Dóminum nostrum. ℞. Amen.

GRANT us, thy servants, O Lord God, we implore, the joy of continual health in body and mind, and by the glorious intercession of the Blessed Mary ever Virgin, free us from present sadness, and establish us in everlasting gladness.

O GOD, Who through ministering angels dost admirably watch and govern us, appoint thine angel also to guard this place, to drive away all powers of evil. May the sick herein confined be protected from fear and disquiet, and let them recover former good-health.

O GOD, Who in thine ineffable providence hast deigned to elect Saint Joseph to be the spouse of thy most holy Mo her, grant, we beseech thee, that we may deserve to have him for our intercessor in heaven, whom we venerate as our defender on earth.

O GOD, most merciful Father, Who hast raised up St. Camillus and St. John of God, men imbued with deep compassion, to be ministers and consolers to the infirm, by their merits and intercession graciously assist to recovery the sick confined in this place of healing. Deliver them from bodily ailments, and relieve them of mental terror, so that restored to former well-being, they may constantly render due gratitude to thee for thy tenderness. Through Christ our Lord. ℟. Amen.

VI

THE SEVEN PENITENTIAL PSALMS
AND LITANY OF THE SAINTS

SEPTEM PSALMI POENITENTIALES
CUM LITANIIS SANCTORUM

Pro infirmis, dum sacro liniuntur Oleo, seu pro alia necessitate dicuntur flexis genibus.

Antiphona

IV E

Ne remi-niscá- ris. Ps. Dómine, ne in furóre tu-o árgu-as

me, * neque in i-ra tu-a corrí-pi-as me. Vel: árgu-as me.

Psalmus 6

Dómine, ne in furóre tuo árguas me, * neque in ira tua corrípias
᾿me.

Miserére mei, Dómine, quóniam infírmus sum: * sana me, Dómine, quóniam conturbáta sunt ossa mea.

Et ánima mea turbáta est valde: * sed tu, Dómine, úsquequo?

Convértere, Dómine, et éripe ánimam meam: * salvum me fac
propter misericórdiam tuam.

Quóniam non est in morte qui memor sit tui: * in inférno autem
quis confitébitur tibi?

Laborávi in gémitu meo, lavábo per síngulas noctes lectum meum:
* lácrimis meis stratum meum rigábo.

Turbátus est a furóre óculus meus: * inveterávi inter omnes inimícos meos.

Discédite a me, omnes, qui operámini iniquitátem: * quóniam
exaudívit Dóminus vocem fletus mei.

Exaudívit Dóminus deprecatiónem meam, * Dóminus oratiónem
meam suscépit.

THE SEVEN PENITENTIAL PSALMS AND
LITANY OF THE SAINTS

The Seven Penitential Psalms, used during the administration of the sacrament of extreme unction and on other occasions, are said kneeling.

Antiphon: **Remember not.**

Psalm 6

O Lord! Punish me not in thine anger; nor chastise me in thy fury.

Have pity on me, Lord, for I am weak and sick; heal me, for my bones are rotted.

And my soul is troubled exceedingly. But thou, O Lord — how long wilt thou look on?

Turn to me, Lord, and deliver my soul. Save me because of thy goodness.

For in death's realm no one is mindful of thee, and in infernal regions who shall praise thee?

I am wearied from moaning; each night I bedew by bed with weeping; my tears water my couch.

The lustre of mine eyes is become dim. I have grown old in the midst of my oppressors.

Depart from me, ye evildoers, for the Lord hath heard my piteous cry.

The Lord hath heard my supplication. the Lord hath accepted my prayer.

Erubéscant, et conturbéntur veheménter omnes inimíci mei: *
convertántur et erubéscant valde velóciter.

Glória Patri.

Psalmus 31

B EÁTI, quorum remíssae sunt iniquitátes: * et quorum tecta
sunt peccáta.

Beátus vir, cui non imputávit Dóminus peccátum, * nec est in
spíritu ejus dolus.

Quóniam tácui, inveteravérunt ossa mea, * dum clamárem tota
die.

Quóniam die ac nocte graváta est super me manus tua: * convérsus sum in aerúmna mea, dum confígitur spina.

Delíctum meum cógnitum tibi feci: * et injustítiam meam non
abscóndi.

Dixi: Confitébor advérsum me injustítiam meam Dómino: * et
tu remisísti impietátem peccáti mei.

Pro hac orábit ad te omnis sanctus, * in témpore opportúno.

Verúmtamen in dilúvio aquárum multárum, * ad eum non
approximábunt.

Tu es refúgium meum a tribulatióne, quae circúmdedit me: *
exsultátio mea, erue me a circumdántibus me.

Intelléctum tibi dabo, et ínstruam te in via hac, qua gradiéris: *
firmábo super te óculos meos.

Nolíte fíeri sicut equus et mulus, * quibus non est intelléctus.

In camo et fraeno maxíllas eórum constrínge, * qui non appróxi-
mant ad te.

Multa flagélla peccatóris, * sperántem autem in Dómino misericórdia circúmdabit.

Laetámini in Dómino et exsultáte, justi, *   et gloriámini, omnes
recti corde.

Glória Patri.

My foes shall be ashamed and exceedingly confused. Speedily will come their shame and consternation.

Glory be to the Father.

Psalm 31

H APPY are they whose guilt is pardoned; whose sins are fully forgiven.

Happy is that man to whom the Lord imputes no sin, and in whose heart there is no guile!

Because I kept silence about my guilt my bones grew old; whilst I cried out all the day long.

For day and night thy hand lay heavy upon me; I tossed in my anguish, so that the thorn of sin pressed into my flesh.

But at last I acknowledged to thee my sin, and hid no longer my iniquity.

I said to myself: "I will accuse myself before the Lord of my wrongdoing:" and thou didst pardon my guilt.

Wherefore, every devout man should pray to thee while there is time.

And when the flood reaches high proportions, it shall not reach him.

For thou art my refuge in the trouble which besets me, thou art my joy. Free me from them that surround me.

I will give thee understanding, and I will instruct thee in the way thou shouldst pursue. My eyes shall counsel thee.

Be not like the horse nor the mule which have no understanding.

With bit and bridle bind fast their jaws who come not freely to thee.

The sinner requireth many scourges; but kindness envelops him who trusteth in the Lord.

Wherefore, rejoice in the Lord, ye pious ones, and be glad and exult, ye just!

Glory be to the Father.

Psalmus 37

DÓMINE, ne in furóre tuo árguas me, * neque in ira tua corrípias me.

Quóniam sagíttae tuae infíxae sunt mihi: * et confirmásti super me manum tuam.

Non est sánitas in carne mea a fácie irae tuae: * non est pax óssibus meis a fácie peccatórum meórum.

Quóniam iniquitátes meae supergréssae sunt caput meum: * et sicut onus grave gravátae sunt super me.

Putruérunt et corrúptae sunt cicatríces meae, * a fácie insipiéntiae meae.

Miser factus sum, et curvátus sum usque in finem: * tota die contristátus ingrediébar.

Quóniam lumbi mei impléti sunt illusiónibus: * et non est sánitas in carne mea.

Afflíctus sum, et humiliátus sum nimis: * rugiébam a gémitu cordis mei.

Dómine, ante te omne desidérium meum: * et gémitus meus a te non est abscónditus.

Cor meum conturbátum est, derelíquit me virtus mea: * et lumen oculórum meórum, et ipsum non est mecum.

Amíci mei, et próximi mei * advérsum me appropinquavérunt, et stetérunt.

Et qui juxta me erant, de longe stetérunt: * et vim faciébant qui quaerébant ánimam meam.

Et qui inquirébant mala mihi, locúti sunt vanitátes: * et dolos tota die meditabántur.

Ego autem tamquam surdus non audiébam: * et sicut mutus non apériens os suum.

Et factus sum sicut homo non áudiens: * et non habens in ore suo redargutiónes.

Quóniam in te, Dómine, sperávi: * tu exáudies me, Dómine, Deus meus.

Psalm 37

O LORD! Punish me not in thine anger; nor chastise me in thy fury.

For thy arrows are fastened in me, and thy hand hath laid heavy upon me.

There is no health in my flesh because of thy wrath; there is no peace in my bones because of my sins.

For my evildoing rises as a billow over my head, and weighs down my shoulders with its load.

My sores are corrupted and festering — which my folly engendered.

I am miserable and bowed down completely; I drag out my day in mourning.

My whole body burns with fever; there is no healthy spot in my flesh.

I am afflicted and humbled completely; I roared with the groaning of my heart.

My lamentation, O Lord, is apparent to thee, and my groaning is not hidden from thee.

My heart is troubled, my strength has left me, and the light of mine eyes fails me.

And when friends and relatives draw near me — suddenly they hesitate and stand still.

And they that were closest to me stand afar off; and they that seek my life use violence.

They that wish evil against me speak harmful words; and devise schemes night and day.

But I, as a deaf man, hear not; and open not my mouth, as though I were dumb.

I am become like a deaf man, with no retort in his mouth.

For thou, O Lord, art my hope; thou shalt hear me, O Lord, my God!

Quia dixi: Nequándo supergáudeant mihi inimíci mei: * et dum commovéntur pedes mei, super me magna locúti sunt.

Quóniam ego in flagélla parátus sum: * et dolor meus in conspéctu meo semper.

Quóniam iniquitátem meam annuntiábo: * et cogitábo pro peccáto meo.

Inimíci autem mei vivunt, et confirmáti sunt super me: * et multiplicáti sunt qui odérunt me iníque.

Qui retríbuunt mala pro bonis, detrahébant mihi: * quóniam sequébar bonitátem.

Ne derelínquas me, Dómine, Deus meus: * ne discésseris a me.

Inténde in adjutórium meum: * Dómine, Deus salútis meae.

Glória Patri.

Psalmus 50

MISERÉRE mei, Deus: * secúndum magnam misericórdiam tuam.

Et secúndum multitúdinem miseratiónum tuárum, * dele iniquitátem meam.

Amplius lava me ab iniquitáte mea: * et a peccáto meo munda me.

Quóniam iniquitátem meam ego cognósco: * et peccátum meum contra me est semper.

Tibi soli peccávi, et malum coram te feci: * ut justificéris in sermónibus tuis, et vincas cum judicáris.

Ecce enim in iniquitátibus concéptus sum: * et in peccátis concépit me mater mea.

Ecce enim veritátem dilexísti: * incérta et occúlta sapiéntiae tuae manifestasti mihi.

Aspérges me hyssópo, et mundábor: * lavábis me, et super nivem dealbábor.

Audítui meo dabis gáudium et laetítiam: * et exsultábunt ossa humiliáta.

Avérte fáciem tuam a peccátis meis: * et omnes iniquitátes meas dele.

Wherefore, I pray: "Let not mine enemies triumph over me — they who spoke arrogantly against me when my feet tottered slightly."

Truly I am ready for scourges; my sorrow is ever before me.

Therefore, I confess my guilt, and am concerned about my sins.

Yet mine enemies are alive and stronger than I; and multiple are they that hate me without cause.

If they return evil for good, they are intent on destroying me, for I seek after the good.

Forsake me not, O Lord, my God! Depart not from me.

Attend to my defense, O Lord — my God and my Salvation!

Glory be to the Father.

Psalm 50

BE MERCIFUL to me, O God, for great is thy goodness.

And with the fulness of thy mercy blot out my transgressions.

Wash me thoroughly from my guilt, and cleanse me from my sin.

For I am conscious of my transgressions, and my sin is ever before me.

Against thee alone have I sinned, and done what is evil in thy sight. My guilt I confess that thou mayest appear just and above reproach when thou judgest me.

Lo, iniquity was born with me! And in sin did my mother conceive me.

Surely thou lovest my sincerity; therefore, givest thou me insight to thy wisdom.

Sprinkle me with hyssop, and I shall be clean; wash me, and I shall be whiter than snow.

Let me hear joy and gladness, that the bones which thou hast humbled may rejoice.

Turn away thy face from my sins, and blot out all my wrongdoing.

Cor mundum crea in me, Deus: * et spíritum rectum ínnova in viscéribus meis.

Ne projícias me a fácie tua: * et spíritum sanctum tuum ne áuferas a me.

Redde mihi laetítiam salutáris tui: * et spíritu principáli confírma me.

Docébo iníquos vias tuas: * et ímpii ad te converténtur.

Líbera me de sanguínibus, Deus, Deus salútis meae: * et exsultábit lingua mea justítiam tuam.

Dómine, lábia mea apéries: * et os meum annuntiábit laudem tuam.

Quóniam si voluísses sacrifícium, dedíssem útique: * holocáustis non delectáberis.

Sacrifícium Deo spíritus contribulátus: * cor contrítum et humiliátum, Deus, non despícies.

Benígne fac, Dómine, in bona voluntáte tua Sion: * ut aedificéntur muri Jerúsalem.

Tunc acceptábis sacrifícium justítiae, oblatiónes, et holocáusta: * tunc impónent super altáre tuum vítulos.

Glória Patri.

Psalmus 101

DÓMINE, exáudi oratiónem meam: * et clamor meus ad te véniat.

Non avértas fáciem tuam a me: * in quacúmque die tríbulor, inclína ad me aurem tuam.

In quacúmque die invocávero te, * velóciter exáudi me.

Quia defecérunt sicut fumus dies mei: * et ossa mea sicut crémium aruérunt.

Percússus sum ut foenum, et áruit cor meum: * quia oblítus sum comédere panem meum.

A voce gémitus mei * adhaésit os meum carni meae.

Símilis factus sum pellicáno solitúdinis: * factus sum sicut nyctícorax in domicílio.

Create a clean heart in me, O God, and renew a right spirit within me.

Drive me not from thy presence, and take not from me the power of thy holy spirit.

Give me again the delight of thy grace, and uphold me with thy leading spirit.

Then will I show the godless thy ways, and sinners shall be converted to thee.

Save me from bloody violence, my Helper and my God, and my tongue shall praise thy righteousness.

O Lord, open thou my lips, and my mouth shall declare thy praise.

For hadst thou requested sacrifice, surely would I have given it. But in burnt-offerings thou hast no pleasure.

A sacrifice pleasing God is a spirit which is penitent; my heart sorrowing and humbled, O Lord, do not despise!

Deal kindly, O Lord, and graciously with Sion, and let Jerusalem arise anew.

Then shalt thou be honored with true oblations; then shall they lay young bullocks upon thine altar.

Glory be to the Father.

Psalm 101

O LORD, hear my prayer; and let my cry come unto thee.

Turn not thy face from me; in the day of my trouble bend down thine ear to me.

On the day when I cry unto thee, hear me without delay.

For my days vanish like smoke; and my bones are grown dry like firewood.

I am smitten like grass, my heart is withered, so that I forget to eat my bread.

Because of my groaning, my bones cleave to my flesh.

I am like a pelican in the wilderness; and like an owl in the dwelling.

Vigilávi, * et factus sum sicut passer solitárius in tecto.

Tota die exprobrábant mihi inimíci mei: * et qui laudábant me, advérsum me jurábant.

Quia cínerem tamquam panem manducábam, * et potum meum cum fletu miscébam.

A fácie irae et indignatiónis tuae: * quia élevans allisísti me.

Dies mei sicut umbra declinavérunt: * et ego sicut foenum árui.

Tu autem, Dómine, in aetérnum pérmanes: * et memoriále tuum in generatiónem et generatiónem.

Tu exsúrgens miseréberis Sion: * quia tempus miseréndi ejus, quia venit tempus.

Quóniam placuérunt servis tuis lápides ejus: * et terrae ejus miserebúntur.

Et timébunt gentes nomen tuum, Dómine, * et omnes reges terrae glóriam tuam.

Quia aedificávit Dóminus Sion: * et vidébitur in glória sua.

Respéxit in oratiónem humílium: * et non sprevit precem eórum.

Scribántur haec in generatióne áltera: * et pópulus, qui creábitur, laudábit Dóminum:

Quia prospéxit de excélso sancto suo: * Dóminus de caelo in terram aspéxit:

Ut audíret gémitus compeditórum: * ut sólveret fílios interemptórum:

Ut annúntient in Sion nomen Dómini: * et laudem ejus in Jerúsalem.

In conveniéndo pópulos in unum, * et reges ut sérviant Dómino.

Respóndit ei in via virtútis suae: * Paucitátem diérum meórum núntia mihi.

Ne révoces me in dimídio diérum meórum: * in generatiónem et generatiónem anni tui.

Inítio tu, Dómine, terram fundásti: * et ópera mánuum tuárum sunt caeli.

Sleep forsaketh my condition; I am become like the sparrow, lonely on the house-top.

Mine enemies rage against me, and they that formerly praised me have cursed me.

For I eat ashes like bread, and mingle my drink with tears.

Because of thine anger and indignation, thou didst whirl me up and cast me down.

My days decline like shadows, and I wither as grass.

But thou, O Lord, endurest forever, and thy renown lasteth from generation to generation.

Rise up and have mercy on Sion, for the time of grace is come; it is long here.

For the stones thereof have pleased thy servants, who feel pity even for her dust.

And then shall the heathen fear thy name, O Lord, and the kings of the earth thy glory.

For the Lord will build Sion anew, and manifest His glory.

He hath regard for the entreaties of the lowly, and ignoreth not their prayer.

Let it be recorded for future ages that the people who shall be renewed shall praise the Lord.

From His holy throne the Lord looked down; He looked from heaven on the earth,

To hear the groans of them in fetters; to set free the children of the slain;

That men might proclaim His name in Sion, and His praise in Jerusalem,

When the people assemble there, and kings to serve the Lord.

In the middle of the strength of his days he said to Him: "Reveal to me the shortness of my days;

Call me not away in the middle of my life, for thy days endure forever."

In the beginning, O Lord, thou didst establish the earth, and the heavens are the work of thy hands.

Ipsi períbunt, tu autem pérmanes: * et omnes sicut vestiméntum veteráscent.

Et sicut opertórium mutábis eos, et mutabúntur: * tu autem idem ipse es, et anni tui non defícient.

Fílii servórum tuórum habitábunt: * et semen eórum in saéculum dirigétur.

Glória Patri.

Psalmus 129

DE profúndis clamávi ad te, Dómine: * Dómine, exáudi vocem meam.

Fiant aures tuae intendéntes, * in vocem deprecatiónis meae.

Si iniquitátes observáveris, Dómine: * Dómine, quis sustinébit?

Quia apud te propitiátio est: * et propter legem tuam sustínui te, Dómine.

Sustínuit ánima mea in verbo ejus: * sperávit ánima mea in Dómino.

A custódia matutína usque ad noctem: * speret Israel in Dómino.

Quia apud Dóminum misericórdia: * et copiósa apud eum redémptio.

Et ipse rédimet Israel, * ex ómnibus iniquitátibus ejus.

Glória Patri.

Psalmus 142

DÓMINE, exáudi oratiónem meam: áuribus pércipe obsecratiónem meam in veritáte tua: * exáudi me in tua justítia.

Et non intres in judícium cum servo tuo: * quia non justificábitur in conspéctu tuo omnis vivens.

Quia persecútus est inimícus ánimam meam: * humiliávit in terra vitam meam.

Collocávit me in obscúris sicut mórtuos saéculi: * et anxiátus est super me spíritus meus, in me turbátum est cor meum.

Memor fui diérum antiquórum, meditátus sum in ómnibus opéribus tuis: * in factis mánuum tuárum meditábar.

They shall perish, but thou shalt endure; they shall grow old
    like a garment;
Like a vesture thou shalt change them, and they shall be changed.
    But thou art always the selfsame, and thy years shall not fail.
The children of thy servants shall abide, and their seed be estab-
    lished for all time.
Glory be to the Father.

Psalm 129

OUT of the depths, I cry, O Lord, to thee; Lord hearken to
    my plea!
Let thine ears be attentive to my suppliant sigh.
If thou shouldst retain man's iniquity, O Lord, who would
    survive?
But there is forgiveness with thee, and because of thy law I trust
    in thee, O Lord.
Yea, in God do I trust, and my soul hopeth in His word.
From morn until night let Israel wait for the Lord:
For with the Lord there is mercy, and the plenitude of redemp-
    tion is with Him.
He shall redeem Israel from all his guilt.
Glory be to the Father.

Psalm 142

HEAR, O Lord, my prayer, in thy fidelity give ear to my
    entreaty; in thy justice hear me!
And enter not into judgment with thy servant; for in thy sight
    no mortal is justified.
For the enemy doth strive against my soul; he hath crushed down
    my life to the ground.
He doth cast me out into darkness, among those who are long
    dead.
And fear doth grip my soul; my heart is in anguish.
Long have I reflected on days of old; I meditated on thy deeds,
    and I mused on the works of thy hands.

Memor fui diérum antiquórum, meditátus sum in ómnibus opéribus tuis: * in factis mánuum tuárum meditábar.

Expándi manus meas ad te: * ánima mea sicut terra sine aqua
tibi.

Velóciter exáudi me, Dómine: * defécit spíritus meus.

Non avértas fáciem tuam a me: * et símilis ero descendéntibus
in lacum.

Audítam fac mihi mane misericórdiam tuam: * quia in te
sperávi.

Notam fac mihi viam, in qua ámbulem: * quia ad te levávi ánimam meam.

Eripe me de inimícis meis, Dómine, ad te confúgi: * doce me
fácere voluntátem tuam, quia Deus meus es tu.

Spíritus tuus bonus dedúcet me in terram rectam: * propter
nomen tuum, Dómine, vivificábis me, in aequitáte tua.

Edúces de tribulatióne ánimam meam: * et in misericórdia tua
dispérdes inimícos meos.

Et perdes omnes, qui tríbulant ánimam meam: * quóniam ego
servus tuus sum.

Glória Patri.

In fine Psalmorum repetitur Antiphona:

Ne reminiscá-ris, Dómi-ne, de-lícta nostra, vel paréntum nostrórum: neque vindíctam su-mas de peccá-tis nostris.

LITANIAE SANCTORUM

Kýri-e, e-lé-ison.　　　Christe, e-lé-ison.　　　Kýri-e, e-lé-ison.

I extend my hands to thee; my soul thirsts for thee as parched land for rain.

Hear me speedily, Lord, for my spirit fainteth!

Turn not thy face from me, lest I be like unto them that go down into the pit.

Let me feel thy mercy in the morning, for in thee do I trust.

Reveal to me the way I must traverse; to thee do I lift up my soul.

Deliver me from my foes, O Lord, for I seek refuge with thee. Teach me to do thy will, for thou art my God.

Let thy good spirit conduct me on smooth paths, for thy name's sake uphold me, for thou art just.

Wherefore, deliver me now out of affliction, and in thy benignity destroy mine oppressors.

Destroy all them that afflict my soul, for I am thy servant.

Glory be to the Father.

At the end of the psalms, the antiphon is repeated:

Remember not, O Lord, our offenses, nor those of our parents: neither take retribution on our sins.

LITANY OF THE SAINTS

Lord, have mercy on us.

Christ, have mercy on us.

Lord, have mercy on us.

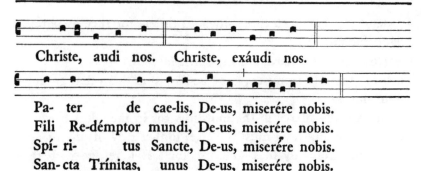

Christe, audi nos. Christe, exáudi nos.

Pa- ter   de cae-lis, De-us, miserére nobis.
Fili   Re-démptor mundi, De-us, miserére nobis.
Spí- ri-   tus Sancte, De-us, miserére nobis.
San- cta Trínitas,   unus De-us, miserére nobis.

San-cta Marí-a, o-ra pro nobis.

Sancta Dei Génitrix,	ora.	Sancte Simon,	ora.
Sancta Virgo vírginum,	ora.	Sancte Thaddaée,	ora.
Sancte Míchaël,	ora.	Sancte Matthía,	ora.
Sancte Gábriel,	ora.	Sancte Bárnaba,	ora.
Sancte Ráphaël,	ora.	Sancte Luca,	ora.
Omnes sancti Angeli et		Sancte Marce,	ora.
Archángeli,	oráte.	Omnes sancti Apóstoli	
Omnes sancti beatórum		et Evangelístae,	oráte.
Spirituum órdines,	oráte.	Omnes sancti Discípuli	
Sancte Joánnes Baptísta,	ora.	Dómini,	oráte.
Sancte Joseph,	ora.	Omnes sancti Innocéntes,	oráte.
Omnes sancti Patriárchae		Sancte Stéphane,	ora.
et Prophétae,	oráte.	Sancte Laurénti,	ora.
Sancte Petre,	ora.	Sancte Vincénti,	ora.
Sancte Paule,	ora.	Sancti Fabiáne et	
Sancte Andréa,	ora.	Sebastiáne,	oráte.
Sancte Jacóbe,	ora.	Sancti Joánnes et Paule,	oráte.
Sancte Joánnes,	ora.	Sancti Cosma et Damiáne,	
Sancte Thoma,	ora.		oráte.
Sancte Jacóbe,	ora.	Sancti Gervási et Protási,	oráte.
Sancte Philíppe,	ora.	Omnes sancti Mártyres,	oráte.
Sancte Bartholomaée,	ora.	Sancte Silvéster,	ora.
Sancte Matthaée,	ora.		

Christ, hear us.
Christ, graciously hear us.
God, the Father of heaven, have mercy on us.
God, the Son, Redeemer of the world, have mercy on us.
God, the Holy Spirit, have mercy on us.
Holy Trinity, one God, have mercy on us.

Holy Mary, pray for us,*
Holy Mother of God,
Holy Virgin of virgins,
St. Michael,
St. Gabriel,
St. Raphael,
All ye holy angels and archangels,
All ye holy orders of blessed spirits,
St. John the Baptist,
St. Joseph,
All ye holy patriarchs and prophets,
St. Peter,
St. Paul,
St. Andrew,
St. James,
St. John,
St. Thomas,
St. James,
St. Philip,

St. Bartholomew,
St. Matthew,
St. Simon,
St. Thaddeus,
St. Matthias,
St. Barnabas,
St. Luke,
St. Mark,
All ye holy apostles and evangelists,
All ye holy disciples of the Lord,
All ye holy Innocents,
St. Stephen,
St. Lawrence,
St. Vincent,
SS. Fabian and Sebastian,
SS. John and Paul,
SS. Cosmas and Damian,
SS. Gervase and Protase,
All ye holy martyrs,
St. Sylvester,

* After each invocation: "Pray for us."

Sancte Gregóri,	ora.	Omnes sancti Sacerdótes	
Sancte Ambrósi,	ora.	et Levítae,	oráte.
Sancte Augustíne,	ora.	Omnes sancti Mónachi	
Sancte Hierónyme,	ora.	et Eremítae,	oráte.
Sancte Martíne,	ora.	Sancta María Magdaléna,	ora.
Sancte Nicoláe,	ora.	Sancta Agatha,	ora.
Omnes sancti Pontífices		Sancta Lúcia,	ora.
et Confessóres,	oráte.	Sancta Agnes,	ora.
Omnes sancti Doctóres,	oráte.	Sancta Caecília,	ora.
Sancte Antóni,	ora.	Sancta Catharína,	ora.
Sancte Benedícte,	ora.	Sancta Anastásia,	ora.
Sancte Bernárde,	ora.	Omnes sanctae Vírgines	
Sancte Domínice,	ora.	et Víduae,	oráte.
Sancte Francísce,	ora.	Omnes Sancti et Sanctae Dei,	
		intercédite pro nobis.	

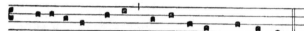

Propí-ti- us esto, parce no-bis, Dómine.
Propí-ti- us esto, ex-áu-di nos, Dómine.
Ab omni malo, lí-be- ra nos, Dómine.

Ab omni peccáto,	líbera.	Per mystérium sanctae	
Ab ira tua,	líbera.	Incarnatiónis tuae,	líbera.
A subitánea et improvísa		Per Advéntum tuum,	líbera.
morte,	líbera.	Per Nativitátem tuam,	líbera.
Ab insídiis diáboli	líbera.	Per Baptísmum et sanctum	
Ab ira, et ódio, et omni		Jejúnium tuum,	líbera.
mala voluntáte,	líbera.	Per Crucem et Passiónem	
A spíritu fornicatiónis,	líbera.	tuam,	líbera.
A fúlgure et tempestáte,	líbera.[1]	Per Mortem et sepultúram	
A flagéllo terraemótus,	líbera.	tuam,	líbera.
A peste, fame, et bello,	líbera.[2]	Per sanctam Resurrectiónem	
A morte perpétua,	líbera.	tuam,	líbera.

1. In processione ad repellendam tempestatem, bis dicitur.
2. In processione tempore mortalitatis et pestis, bis dicitur.

St. Gregory,
St. Ambrose,
St. Augustine,
St. Jerome,
St. Martin,
St. Nicholas,
All ye holy bishops and confessors,
All ye holy doctors,
St. Anthony,
St. Benedict,
St. Bernard,
St. Dominic,
St. Francis,

All ye holy priests and levites,
All ye holy monks and hermits,
St. Mary Magdalen,
St. Agatha,
St. Lucy,
St. Agnes,
St. Cecilia,
St. Catherine,
St. Anastasia,
All ye holy virgins and widows,
pray for us.
All ye holy saints of God, make intercession for us.

Be merciful, spare us, O Lord.
Be merciful, graciously hear us, O Lord.

From all evil, O Lord, deliver us.*
From all sin,
From thy wrath,
From sudden and unprovided death,
From the snares of the devil,
From anger, and hatred, and every evil will,
From the spirit of fornication,
From lightning and tempest,[1]
From the scourge of earthquakes,

From plague, famine, and war,[2]
From everlasting death,
Through the mystery of thy holy Incarnation,
Through thy coming,
Through thy Nativity,
Through thy baptism and holy fasting,
Through thy Cross and Passion,
Through thy death and burial,
Through thy holy Resurrection,

* After each invocation: "O Lord, deliver us."
1. In the procession for averting tempest, this invocation is said twice.

2. In the procession in time of death and plague, this invocation is said twice.

Per admirábilem Ascen-   Per advéntum, Spíritus
siónem tuam,   líbera.   Sancti Parácliti,   líbera.
                     In die judícii,   líbera.

Pecca-tóres, te rogámus, audi nos.

Ut nobis parcas, te rogámus, audi nos.

Ut nobis indúlgeas, te rogámus, audi nos.

Ut ad veram poeniténtiam nos perdúcere dignéris, te rogámus, audi nos.

Ut Ecclésiam tuam sanctam régere, et conserváre dignéris, te rogámus, audi nos.

Ut Domnum Apostólicum, et omnes ecclesiásticos órdines in sancta religióne conserváre dignéris, te rogámus, audi nos.

Ut inimícos sanctae Ecclésiae humiliáre dignéris, te rogámus, audi nos.

Ut régibus et princípibus christiánis pacem et veram concórdiam donáre dignéris, te rogámus, audi nos.

Ut cuncto pópulo christiáno pacem et unitátem largíri dignéris, te rogámus, audi nos.

Ut omnes errántes ad unitátem Ecclésiae revocáre, et infidéles univérsos ad Evangélii lumen perdúcere dignéris, te rogámus, audi nos.

Ut nosmetípsos in tuo sancto servítio confortáre, et conserváre dignéris, te rogamus, audi nos.

Ut mentes nostras ad caeléstia desidéria érigas, te rogámus, audi nos.

Ut ómnibus benefactóribus nosstris sempitérna bona retríbuas, te rogámus, audi nos.

Ut ánimas nostras, fratrum, propinquórum, et benefactórum nostrórum ab aetérna damnatióne erípias, te rogámus, audi nos.

Ut fructus terrae dare, et conserváre dignéris, te rogámus, audi nos.[1]

1. In processione tempore penuriae et famis, bis dicitur.

Through thine admirable Ascension,

Through the coming of the Holy Spirit, the Paraclete,

In the day of judgment,

We sinners, beseech thee, hear us.

That thou wouldst spare us, we beseech thee, hear us.*

That thou wouldst pardon us,

That thou wouldst bring us to true penance,

That thou wouldst vouchsafe to govern and preserve thy holy Church,

That thou wouldst vouchsafe to preserve our Apostolic Prelate and all orders of the Church in holy religion,

That thou wouldst vouchsafe to humble the enemies of holy Church,

That thou wouldst vouchsafe to give peace and true concord to Christian kings and princes,

That thou wouldst vouchsafe to grant peace and unity to the whole Christian world,

That thou wouldst restore to the unity of the Church all who have strayed from the truth, and lead all unbelievers to the light of the gospel,

That thou wouldst vouchsafe to confirm and preserve us in thy holy service,

That thou wouldst lift up our minds to heavenly desires,

That thou wouldst render eternal blessings to all our benefactors,

That thou wouldst deliver our souls and the souls of our brethren, relatives, and benefactors from eternal damnation,

That thou wouldst vouchsafe to give and preserve the fruits of the earth,[1]

---

* After each invocation: "We beseech thee, hear us."

1. In the procession in time of famine and want, this invocation is said twice.

Ut ómnibus fidélibus defúnctis réquiem aetérnam donáre dignéris, te rogámus, audi nos.[2]

Ut nos exaudíre dignéris, te rogámus, audi nos.

Fili Dei, te rogámus, audi nos.

2. In benedictione novae ecclesiae, surgit Sacerdos et intelligibili voce dicit, producens manu signum crucis:

Ut hanc ecclésiam, et altáre hoc, ad honórem tuum, et nomen Sancti tui N., purgáre, et bene ✠ dícere dignéris.

℟. Te rogámus, audi nos.

In reconciliatione ecclesiae violatae:

Ut hanc ecclésiam, et altáre hoc, (ac coeméterium) purgáre, et reconci ✠ liáre dignéris.

℟. Te rogámus, audi nos.

In benedictione coemeterii:

Ut hoc coemetérium purgáre, et bene ✠ dícere dignéris.

℟. Te rogámus, audi nos.

In reconciliatione coemeterii violati:

Ut hoc coemetérium recon ✠ ciliáre et sancti ✠ ficáre dignéris.

℟. Te rogámus, audi nos.

In processione ad petendam pluviam, bis dicitur:

Ut congruéntem plúviam fidélibus tuis concédere dignéris.

℟. Te rogámus, audi nos.

Ad postulandam serenitatem, bis dicitur:

Ut fidélibus tuis áëris serenitátem concédere dignéris.

℟. Te rogámus, audi nos.

Tempore mortalitatis et pestis, bis dicitur:

Ut a pestiléntiae flagéllo nos liberáre dignéris.

℟. Te rogámus, audi nos.

That thou wouldst vouchsafe to grant eternal rest to all the faithful departed,[2]	That thou wouldst vouchsafe graciously to hear us, Son of God,

2. In the blessing of a new church, the priest rises, and making the sign of the cross, says in an audible voice:

That thou wouldst vouchsafe to purify and bless ✠ this church and this altar to thy honor and to the name of thy saint, N.

℞. We beseech thee, hear us.

In the reconciliation of a profaned church:

That thou wouldst vouchsafe to purify and reconcile ✠ this church and this altar (and cemetery).

℞. We beseech thee, hear us.

In the blessing of a cemetery:

That thou wouldst vouchsafe to purify and bless ✠ this cemetery.

℞. We beseech thee, hear us.

In the reconciliation of a profaned cemetery:

That thou wouldst vouchsafe to reconcile ✠ and sanctify ✠ this cemetery.

℞. We beseech thee, hear us.

In the procession of petition for rain, the following is said twice:

That thou wouldst vouchsafe to send upon thy faithful the much needed rainfalls.

℞. We beseech thee, hear us.

In the petition for calm weather, the following is said twice:

That thou wouldst vouchsafe to send upon thy faithful calm weather.

℞. We beseech thee, hear us.

In the time of death and plague, the following is said twice:

That thou wouldst vouchsafe to deliver us from the scourge of plague.

℞. We beseech thee, hear us.

Agnus De-i, qui tollis peccá-ta mundi, parce no-bis, Dómine.

Agnus De-i, qui tollis peccá-ta mundi, exáudi nos, Dómine.

Agnus De-i, qui tollis peccá-ta mundi, mi-serére nobis.

Christe, audi nos.   Christe, exáudi nos.   Kýri-e, e-léison.

Christe, e-lé-i-son.   Kýri-e, e-lé-i-son.

Pater noster secreto usque ad

℣. Et ne nos indúcas in tentatiónem.

℟. Sed líbera nos a malo.

Psalmus 69

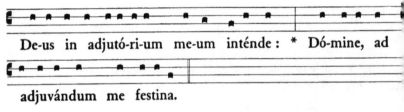

De-us in adjutó-ri-um me-um inténde :   * Dó-mine, ad

adjuvándum me festina.

Confundántur, et revereántur, * qui quaerunt ánimam meam.

Avertántur restrórsum et erubéscant, * qui volunt mihi mala.

Avertántur statim erubescéntes, * qui dicunt mihi: Euge, euge.

Exsúltent et laeténtur in te omnes qui quaerunt te, * et dicant sempér: Magnificétur Dóminus: qui díligunt salutáre tuum.

Ego vero egénus, et pauper sum: * Deus, ádjuva me.

Adjútor meus, et liberátor meus es tu: * Dómine, ne moréris.

Glória Patri.

Lamb of God, Who takest away the sins of the world, spare us, O Lord.

Lamb of God, Who takest away the sins of the world, graciously hear us, O Lord.

Lamb of God, Who takest away the sins of the world, have mercy on us.

Christ, hear us. Christ, graciously hear us.

Lord, have mercy on us.

Christ, have mercy on us.

Lord, have mercy on us.

Our Father, inaudibly until

℣. And lead us not into temptation.

℟. But deliver us from evil.

Psalm 69

Attend, O God, to my defense; make haste, O Lord, to help me.

Let them be ashamed and tremble, that seek after my life.

Let them be turned back blushing, that desire my ruin.

May confusion be their reward that say to me: " 'Tis so, 'tis so!"

But let them rejoice and be glad that seek after thee; may they that love thy grace say without ceasing: "Magnify the Lord!"

But I am poor and miserable. Help me, O God!

My helper art thou and my savior; tarry not, O Lord!

Glory be to the Father.

℣. Salvos fac servos tuos.

℟. Deus meus, sperántes in te.

℣. Esto nobis, Dómine, turris fortitúdinis.

℟. A fácie inimíci.

℣. Nihil profíciat inimícus in nobis.

℟. Et fílius iniquitátis non appónat nocére nobis.

℣. Dómine, non secúndum peccáta nostra fácias nobis.

℟. Neque secúndum iniquitátes nostras retríbuas nobis.

℣. Orémus pro Pontífice nostro N.

℟. Dóminus consérvet eum, et vivíficet eum, et beátum fáciat eum in terra, et non tradat eum in ánimam inimicórum ejus.

℣. Orémus pro benefactóribus nostris.

℟. Retribúere dignáre, Dómine, ómnibus, nobis bona faciéntibus propter nomen tuum, vitam aetérnam. Amen.

℣. Orémus pro fidélibus defúnctis.

℟. Réquiem aetérnam dona eis, Dómine, et lux perpétua lúceat eis.

℣. Requiéscant in pace.

℟. Amen.

℣. Pro frátribus nostris abséntibus.

℟. Salvos fac servos tuos, Deus meus, sperántes in te.

℣. Mitte eis, Dómine, auxílium de sancto.

℟. Et de Sion tuére eos.

℣. Dómine, exáudi oratiónem meam.

℟. Et clamor meus ad te véniat.

℣. Dóminus vobíscum.

℟. Et cum spíritu tuo.

Orémus.   Oratio

D EUS, cui próprium est miseréri semper et párcere: súscipe deprecatiónem nostram; ut nos, et omnes fámulos tuos, quos delictórum caténa constríngit, miserátio tuae pietátis cleménter absólvat.

℣. Preserve thy servants.

℟. Who trust in thee, my God.

℣. Be unto us, O Lord, a tower of strength.

℟. In the face of the enemy.

℣. Let the enemy do nothing to harm us.

℟. And the son of iniquity have no power over us.

℣. O Lord, deal not with us according to our sins.

℟. Nor take retribution on us because of our transgressions.

℣. Let us pray for our Sovereign Pontiff N.

℟. The Lord preserve him, and give him life, and make him blessed upon the earth, and deliver him not up to the will of his enemies.

℣. Let us pray for our benefactors.

℟. Vouchsafe for thy name's sake, O Lord, to reward with eternal life all them who do us good. Amen.

℣. Let us pray for the faithful departed.

℟. Eternal rest give unto them, O Lord, and let perpetual light shine upon them.

℣. May they rest in peace.

℟. Amen.

℣. For our absent brethren.

℟. Preserve thy servants who trust in thee, O my God.

℣. Send them, Lord, aid from on high.

℟. And from Sion watch over them.

℣. O Lord, hear my prayer.

℟. And let my cry come unto thee.

℣. The Lord be with you.

℟. And with thy spirit.

Let us pray.   Prayer

O God, Whose nature it is ever to show mercy and to spare, receive our petition, that we and all thy servants bound by the fetters of sin may by thy sweet forgiveness be pardoned.

E·XÁUDI, quaésumus, Dómine, súpplicum preces, et confiténtium tibi parce peccátis: ut páriter nobis indulgéntiam tríbuas benígnus, et pacem.

I NEFFÁBILEM nobis, Dómine, misericórdiam tuam cleménter osténde: ut simul nos et a peccátis ómnibus éxuas, et a poenis, quas pro his merémur, erípias.

D EUS, qui culpa offénderis, poeniténtia placáris, preces pópuli tui supplicántis propítius réspice: et flagélla tuae iracúndiae, quae pro peccátis nostris merémur, avérte.

O MNÍPOTENS sempitérne Deus, miserére fámulo tuo Pontífici nostro N., et dírige eum secúndum tuam cleméntiam in viam salútis aetérnae: ut, te donánte, tibi plácita cúpiat, et tota virtúte perfíciat.

D EUS, a quo sancta desidéria, recta consília, et justa sunt ópera, da servis tuis illam, quam mundus dare non potest, pacem: ut et corda nostra mandátis tuis dédita, et hóstium subláta formídine, témpora sint tua protectióne tranquílla.

U RE igne Sancti Spíritus renes nostros, et cor nostrum, Dómine: ut tibi casto córpore serviámus, et mundo corde placeámus.

F IDÉLIUM, Deus, ómnium cónditor et redémptor, animábus famulórum, famularúmque tuárum remissiónem cunctórum tríbue peccatórum: ut indulgéntiam, quam semper optavérunt, piis supplicatiónibus consequántur.

A CTIÓNES nostras, quaésumus, Dómine aspirándo praéveni, et adjuvándo proséquere: ut cuncta nostra orátio, et operátio a te semper incípiat, et per te coepta finiátur.

O MNÍPOTENS sempitérne Deus, qui vivórum domináris simul et mortuórum, omniúmque miseréris, quos tuos fide et ópere futúros esse praenóscis: te súpplices exorámus; ut, pro quibus effúndere preces decrévimus, quosque vel praesens saéculum

WE BESEECH thee, O Lord, hear the plea of thy suppliants, and pardon the sins of thy penitents; and deign to grant us thy tender forgiveness together with thy peace.

SHOW us, O Lord, thine unutterable mercy, that blotting out our transgressions, thou wouldst vouchsafe to snatch us from the condemnation they deserve.

O GOD, our sins offend thee, but our penance placates thine anger! Regard graciously the entreaties of thy people, and turn away the stripes which our transgressions justly deserve.

ALMIGHTY and eternal God, have mercy on thy servant N., our Sovereign Pontiff, and direct him according to thy clemency on the way to everlasting salvation, that by thy grace he may both desire the things that please thee, and strive with his whole might to execute them.

O GOD, from Whom proceed all holy desires, good counsels, and just works, give to thy servants that peace which the world cannot give; so that our hearts may be dedicated to the keeping of thy law, and the fear of our enemies being removed, we can by thy protection live our days in peace.

INFLAME, O Lord, our affections and our hearts with the fire of the Holy Spirit, that we may serve thee with chaste body, and please thee with clean heart.

O GOD, the Creator and Redeemer of all the faithful, grant to the souls of thy servants departed remission of all sins; that by our fervent prayers they may obtain the pardon they have always desired.

WE BESEECH thee, Lord, inspire and guide our works in their beginning, and accompany them unto fruition, that our every prayer and work may ever begin with thee, and through thee be accomplished.

O ALMIGHTY, everlasting God, Who hast dominion over the living and the dead, and art merciful to all whom thou foreknowest shall be thine by faith and good works; we, thy suppliants pray, that they for whom we propose to pour forth

adhuc in carne rétinet, vel futúrum jam exútos córpore suscépit, intercedéntibus ómnibus Sanctis tuis, pietátis tuae cleméntia, ómnium delictórum suórum véniam consequántur. Per Dóminum nostrum Jesum Christum Fílium tuum: Qui tecum vivit et regnat in unitáte Spíritus Sancti Deus, per ómnia saécula saeculórum. ℞. Amen.

℣. Dóminus vobíscum.

℞. Et cum spíritu tuo.

℣. Exáudi-at nos omnípotens et mi-sé-ricors Dó-minus.

℞. Amen. ℣. Et fidé-li-um ánimae per miseri-córdi-am

De-i requi-éscant in pace. ℞. Amen.

Vacante Apostolica Sede, loco invocationis Ut Domnum Apostólicum et omnes ecclesiásticos órdines, etc., dicatur: Ut omnes ecclesiásticos órdines, etc., Versus autem Orémus pro Pontífice nostro N. cum suo Responsorio, et Oratio pro eodem Pontifice omittuntur.

our petitions, whether this present world still detain them in the flesh, or the world to come hath already received their souls, may by thy benign goodness and through the intercession of thy saints, obtain pardon for all their sins. Through our Lord, Jesus Christ, thy Son, Who liveth and reigneth with thee in the unity of the Holy Spirit, God, forever and ever. ℟. Amen.

℣. The Lord be with you.

℟. And with thy spirit.

℣. May the almighty and merciful Lord graciously hear us.

℟. Amen.

℣. And may the souls of the faithful departed, through the mercy of God, rest in peace.

℟. Amen.

If the papacy is vacant, in place of the invocation That thou wouldst vouchsafe to preserve our Apostolic Prelate and all orders of the Church, etc., the invocation will be That thou wouldst vouchsafe to preserve all orders of the Church, etc. And the verse Let us pray for our Sovereign Pontiff N., together with its response and prayer, is omitted.

APPENDIX

ITINERARIUM

Clericus in ipso itineris ingressu, si solus fuerit, dicat quae sequuntur in singulari; si cum sociis, in plurali.

Antiphona: In viam pacis.

Canticum Zachariae: Benedíctus Dóminus, Deus Israel, etc., ut supra, pag. 50.

Antiphona: In viam pacis et prosperitátis dírigat nos omnípotens et miséricors Dóminus, et Angelus Ráphael comitétur nobíscum in via; ut cum pace, salúte et gáudio revertámur ad própria.

Kýrie, eléison. Christe, eléison. Kýrie, eléison.

Pater noster secreto usque ad

℣. Et ne nos indúcas in tentatiónem.

℟. Sed líbera nos a malo.

℣. Salvos fac servos tuos.

℟. Deus meus, sperántes in te.

℣. Mitte nobis, Dómine, auxílium de sancto.

℟. Et de Sion tuére nos.

℣. Esto nobis, Dómine, turris fortitúdinis.

℟. A fácie inimíci.

℣. Nihil profíciat inimícus in nobis.

℟. Et fílius iniquitátis non appónat nocére nobis.

℣. Benedíctus Dóminus die quotídie.

℟. Prósperum iter fáciat nobis Deus salutárium nostrórum.

℣. Vias tuas, Dómine, demónstra nobis.

℟. Et sémitas tuas édoce nos.

℣. Utinam dirigántur viae nostrae.

℟. Ad custodiéndas justificatiónes tuas.

℣. Erunt prava in dirécta.

℟. Et áspera in vias planas.

THE ITINERARIUM
or Invoking God's Blessing when Starting on a Journey

A cleric when starting on a journey says the following in the singular, if he is alone; if he has companions — in the plural.

Antiphon: **Along ways of peace.**

Canticle of Zachary: **Blessed be the Lord God of Israel,** etc., as above, page 51.

Antiphon: **Along ways of peace and prosperity may the almighty and merciful Lord lead us, and may the Angel Raphael accompany us on the journey. So may we in peace, health, and joy return unto our own.**

Lord, have mercy on us. Christ, have mercy on us. Lord, have mercy on us.

Our Father inaudibly until

℣. And lead us not into temptation.

℟. But deliver us from evil.

℣. Preserve thy servants.

℟. Who trust in thee, my God.

℣. Send us aid, Lord, from on high.

℟. And from Sion watch over us.

℣. Be unto us, O Lord, a mighty fortress.

℟. In the face of the enemy.

℣. Let the enemy be powerless against us.

℟. And the son of iniquity do nothing to harm us.

℣. May the Lord be praised at all times.

℟. May God, our Helper grant us a successful journey.

℣. Show us thy ways, O Lord.

℟. And conduct us along thy paths.

℣. Oh, that our ways be directed!

℟. To the keeping of thy precepts.

℣. For crooked ways will be made straight.

℟. And rough ways smooth.

℣. Angelis suis Deus mandávit de te.

℟. Ut custódiant te in ómnibus viis tuis.

℣. Dómine, exáudi oratiónem meam.

℟. Et clamor meus ad te véniat.

℣. Dóminus vobíscum.

℟. Et cum spíritu tuo.

Orémus. Oratio

DEUS, qui fílios Israel per maris médium sicco vestígio ire fecísti, quique tribus Magis iter ad te stella duce pandísti: tríbue nobis, quaésumus, iter prósperum tempúsque tranquíllum; ut, Angelo tuo sancto cómite, ad eum quo pérgimus locum, ac demum ad aetérnae salútis portum perveníre felíciter valeámus.

DEUS, qui Abraham púerum tuum, de Ur Chaldaeórum edúctum, per omnes suae peregrinatiónis vias illaésum custodísti: quaésumus, ut nos fámulos tuos custodíre dignéris: esto nobis, Dómine, in procínctu suffrágium, in via solátium, in aestu umbráculum, in plúvia et frígore teguméntum, in lassitúdine vehículum, in adversitáte praesídium, in lúbrico báculus, in naufrágio portus; ut, te duce, quo téndimus, próspere perveniámus, et demum incólumes ad própria redeámus.

ADÉSTO, quaésumus, Dómine, supplicatiónibus nostris: et viam famulórum tuórum in salútis tuae prosperitate dispóne; ut inter omnes viae et vitae hujus varietátes tuo semper protegámur auxílio.

PRAESTA, quaésumus, omnípotens Deus: ut família tua per viam salútis incédat; et, beáti Joánnis Praecursóris hortaménta sectándo, ad eum, quem praedíxit, secúra pervéniat, Dóminum nostrum Jesum Christum, Fílium tuum: Qui tecum vivit et regnat in unitáte Spíritus Sancti Deus, per ómnia saécula saeculórum. ℟. Amen.

℣. Procedámus in pace.

℟. In nómine Dómini. Amen.

℣. God hath given His angels charge over you.

℟. To guard you in all undertakings.

℣. O Lord, hear my prayer.

℟. And let my cry come unto thee.

℣. The Lord be with you.

℟. And with thy spirit.

Let us pray. *Prayer*

O GOD, Who didst lead the sons of Israel through the sea over a dry path, and didst reveal the way to the three Magi by the guidance of a star; vouchsafe to grant us a happy journey and a peaceful time, that accompanied by thy angel we may safely reach our present destination, and come finally to the haven of eternal security.

O GOD, Who didst lead thy servant, Abraham out of Ur of the Chaldeans, safeguarding him on all his wanderings — guide us thy servants, we implore thee. Be thou unto us support in battle, refuge in journeying, shade in the heat, covering in the rain and cold, a carriage in tiredness, protection in adversity, a staff in insecurity, a harbor in shipwreck; so that under thy leadership we may successfully reach our destination, and finally return safe to our homes.

GIVE ear, we pray thee, Lord, to our entreaties! And direct the steps of thy servants on the paths of righteousness, that in all the vicissitudes of the journey and of life, we may have thee as our constant protector.

GRANT, O almighty God that thy children march forth on the way of security; and heeding the exhortations of Blessed John, the Precursor, let them come safely to Him Whom John foretold, Jesus Christ, thy Son, our Lord, Who liveth and reigneth with thee in the unity of the Holy Spirit, God, forever and ever. ℟. Amen.

℣. Let us proceed in peace.

℟. In the name of the Lord. Amen.

BENEDICTIO MENSAE
Ante Prandium

Sacerdos benedicturus mensam incipit: **Benedícite,** et alii repetunt: **Benedícite.**

Deinde Sacerdos incipit Versum:

Oculi óminum, et alii prosequuntur: **In te sperant, Dómine, et tu das escam illórum in témpore opportúno. Aperis tu manum tuam, et imples omne ánimal benedictióne.**

Glória Patri. Sicut erat.

Kýrie, eléison. Christe, eléison. Kýrie, eléison.

Pater noster secreto usque ad

℣. **Et ne nos indúcas in tentatiónem.**

℟. **Sed líbera nos a malo.**

Postea Sacerdos dicit:

Orémus.   Oratio

B ÉNEDIC, ✠ **Dómine, nos, et haec tua dona, quae de tua largitáte sumus sumptúri. Per Christum Dóminum nostrum.** ℟. **Amen.**

Deinde Lector: **Jube, domne, benedícere.**

Benedictio: **Mensae caeléstis partícipes fáciat nos Rex aetérnae glóriae.** ℟. **Amen.**

POST PRANDIUM
aguntur gratiae hoc modo:

Dicto a Lectore **Tu autem, Dómine, miserére nobis.** ℟. **Deo grátias,** omnes surgunt.

Sacerdos incipit:

℣. **Confiteántur tibi, Dómine, ómnia ópera tua.**

℟. **Et Sancti tui benedícant tibi.**

Glória Patri. Sicut erat.

BLESSINGS AT MEALS
Before the Noonday Meal

The priest who is to bless the table, says: **Bless ye,** and all repeat:
Bless ye.

Then the priest begins the verse:

The eyes of all, and the others continue: **Hope in thee, O Lord,
and thou givest them food in due time. Thou openest thy hand,
and fillest every living thing with thy blessing.**

Glory be to the Father.

**Lord, have mercy on us. Christ, have mercy on us. Lord, have
mercy on us.**

Our Father, inaudibly until

$\mathbb{V}$. **And lead us not into temptation.**

$\mathbb{R}$. **But deliver us from evil.**

Then the priest says:

Let us pray.   Prayer

BLESS us, ✝O Lord, and these thy gifts which we are about
to receive from thy bounty. Through Christ our Lord. $\mathbb{R}$.
Amen.

The reader says: **Pray, father** (or **sir**) **a blessing!**

The blessing: **May the King of everlasting glory make us partakers of the heavenly banquet.** $\mathbb{R}$. **Amen.**

AFTER THE NOONDAY MEAL
the thanksgiving is rendered as follows:

The reader having said: **But thou, O Lord, have mercy on us.**
$\mathbb{R}$. **Thanks be to God,** all rise.

The priest begins:

$\mathbb{V}$. **Let all thy works bless thee, O Lord.**

$\mathbb{R}$. **And thy devout ones praise thee.**

Glory be to the Father.

Postea Sacerdos absolute dicat:

A GIMUS tibi grátias, omnípotens Deus, pro univérsis bene-
fíciis tuis: Qui vivis et regnas in saécula saeculórum. ℞.
Amen.

Deinde alternatim dicitur Ps. 50   **Miserére mei, Deus,** pag. 436.

Vel Psalmus 116

L AUDÁTE Dóminum, omnes gentes: * laudáte eum, omnes
pópuli:

Quóniam confirmáta est super nos misericórdia ejus: * et véritas
Dómini manet in aetérnum.

Glória Patri. Sicut erat.

Kýrie, eléison. Christe, eléison. Kýrie, eléison.

Sacerdos dicit   **Pater noster,** quod cum aliis secreto prosequitur
usque ad

℣. Et ne nos indúcas in tentatiónem.

℞. Sed líbera nos a malo.

℣. Dispérsit, dedit paupéribus.

℞. Justítia ejus manet in saéculum saéculi.

℣. Benedícam Dóminum in omni témpore.

℞. Semper laus ejus in ore meo.

℣. In Dómino laudábitur ánima mea.

℞. Audiant mansuéti, et laeténtur.

℣. Magnificáte Dóminum mecum.

℞. Et exaltémus nomen ejus in idípsum.

℣. Sit nomen Dómini benedíctum.

℞. Ex hoc nunc et usque in saéculum.

Deinde Sacerdos absolute dicat:

R ETRIBÚERE dignáre, Dómine, ómnibus, nobis bona faciéntibus propter nomen tuum, vitam aetérnam. ℞. Amen.

℣. Benedicámus Dómino.

℞. Deo grátias.

Then the priest says:

WE GIVE thee thanks, O almighty God, for all thy benefits: Who livest and reignest forever. ℟. Amen.

Then they alternate in saying Ps. 50 **Miserére,** page 437.

Or Psalm 116

PRAISE the Lord, all ye nations; praise Him all ye peoples.

For His goodness has enlivened us, and the truth of the Lord abideth forever.

Glory be to the Father.

Lord, have mercy on us. Christ, have mercy on us. Lord, have mercy on us.

The priest says **Our Father,** which he and the others continue inaudibly until

℣. And lead us not into temptation.

℟. But deliver us from evil.

℣. With lavish hand He giveth to the poor.

℟. His justice endureth forever.

℣. I will praise the Lord at all times.

℟. His praises shall be always in my mouth.

℣. My soul will exult in the Lord.

℟. The meek shall hear with gladness.

℣. O extol the Lord with me!

℟. And let us mightily praise Him together.

℣. Let the name of the Lord be blessed.

℟. Henceforth and forever.

Then the priest says:

VOUCHSAFE for thy name's sake, O Lord, to reward with eternal life all them who do us good. ℟. Amen.

℣. Let us bless the Lord.

℟. Thanks be to God.

℣. Fidélium ánimae per misericórdiam Dei requiéscant in pace.

℞. Amen.

Pater noster, totum secreto.

Quo finito, Sacerdos dicit:

℣. Deus det nobis suam pacem.

℞. Amen.

ANTE COENAM

Sacerdos benedicturus mensam incipit: **Benedícite,** et alii repetunt: **Benedícite.**

Deinde Sacerdos incipit Versum:

E DENT páuperes, et alii prosequuntur: Et saturabúntur, et laudábunt Dóminum, qui requírunt eum: vivent corda eórum in saéculum saéculi.

Glória Patri. Sicut erat.

Kýrie, eléison. Christe, eléison. Kýrie, eléison.

Pater noster secreto usque ad

℣. Et ne nos indúcas in tentatiónem.

℞. Sed líbera nos a malo.

     Orémus.   Oratio

B ÉNEDIC, ✠ Dómine, nos, et haec tua dona, quae de tua largitáte sumus sumptúri. Per Christum Dóminum nostrum.

℞. Amen.

℣. Jube, dome, benedícere.

Benedictio: Ad coenam vitae aetérnae perdúcat nos Rex aetérne glóriae. ℞. Amen.

℣. May the souls of the faithful departed through the mercy of God rest in peace.

℟. Amen.

Our Father, the whole inaudibly.

When finished, the priest says:

℣. May the Lord grant us His peace.

℟. Amen.

BEFORE THE EVENING MEAL

The priest who will bless the table says: **Bless ye,** and the others repeat: **Bless ye!**

Then the priest begins the verse:

THE poor shall eat, and the others continue: **and be filled, and shall praise the Lord who seek Him, and they shall live forever.**

Glory be to the Father.

Lord, have mercy on us. Christ, have mercy on us. Lord, have mercy on us.

Our Father inaudibly until

℣. And lead us not into temptation.

℟. But deliver us from evil.

Let us pray. *Prayer*

BLESS us, ✝O Lord, and these thy gifts which we are about to receive from thy bounty. Through Christ our Lord. ℟. Amen.

℣. Pray, father (or sir) a blessing!

Blessing: **May the King of everlasting glory conduct us to the supper of eternal life.** ℟. Amen.

POST COENAM

aguntur gratiae ut post Prandium, sed dicitur:

℣. Memóriam fecit mirabílium suórum miséricors et miserátor Dóminus.

℟. Escam dedit timéntibus se.

Glória Patri. Sicut erat.

B ENEDÍCTUS Deus in donis suis, et sanctus in ómnibus opéribus suis: Qui vivit et regnat in saécula saeculórum. ℟. Amen.

Deinde alternatim dicitur Ps. 116: Laudáte Dóminum, omnes gentes, et reliqua ut supra, pag. 470.

Quando semel comeditur, omnia dicuntur ut in Coena.

Praedictus modus benedicendi mensam, et agendi gratias, servatur omni tempore anni, praeterquam diebus infrascriptis, quibus Versus et Psalmi tantum variantur.

IN NATIVITATE DOMINI

usque ad Coenam Vigiliae Epiphaniae exclusive dicitur:

℣. Verbum caro factum est, allelúia.

℟. Et habitávit in nobis, allelúia.

Glória Patri. Sicut erat.

In fine dicitur:

℣. Notum fecit Dóminus, allelúia.

℟. Salutáre suum, allelúia.

Alia ut supra.

Ps. 97 Cantáte Dómino, vel Ps. 116 Laudáte Dóminum, omnes gentes, ut supra. Qui Psalmus semper ad beneplacitum dici potest etiam in aliis Solemnitatibus.

AFTER THE EVENING MEAL

Thanksgiving is rendered as at the noonday meal, except that the following is said:

℣. He hath made a memorial of His wonders, the Lord Who is kind and compassionate.

℟. He hath given food to them that fear Him.

Glory be to the Father.

B LESSED is God in His gifts, and holy in all His works. Who liveth and reigneth forever. ℟. Amen.

Then they alternate in saying Ps. 116: **Praise the Lord, all ye nations,** as above.

If only one meal is taken, the prayers are those of the evening meal. The preceding method of blessing and rendering thanks is observed at all times of the year, except the days noted below, when only the versicles and psalms differ.

ON THE NATIVITY OF OUR LORD
until supper on the Vigil of Epiphany exclusive

℣. The Word was made flesh, alleluia.

℟. And dwelt among us, alleluia.

Glory be to the Father.

At the end of the meal:

℣. The Lord hath made known, alleluia.

℟. His salvation, alleluia.

The rest as above.

Ps. 97: **Sing to the Lord,** or Ps. 116: **Praise the Lord, all ye nations,** as above. The last-named psalm may always be chosen, even on all solemn feasts.

IN EPIPHANIA
et per totam Octavam

℣. Reges Tharsis et ínsulae múnera ófferent, allelúia.
℟. Reges Arabum et Saba dona addúcent, allelúia.
Glória Patri. Sicut erat.

In fine dicitur:
Ps. 71 Deus, judícium tuum regi da, vel Ps. 116 Laudáte Dóminum, omnes gentes, ut supra.

FERIA V IN COENA DOMINI

Dicitur absolute et sine cantu:

℣. Christus factus est pro nobis oboédiens usque ad mortem.

Deinde Pater noster, totum secreto.
Quo dicto, sine pronuntiatione aliqua Sacerdos signo crucis benedicit mensam: nec dicitur Jube, domne nec Tu autem.
In fine repetitur:

℣. Christus factus est pro nobis oboédiens usque ad mortem.

Postea Ps. 50 Miserére mei, Deus, pag. 436.
Quo finito, sine Versu Glória Patri, secreto dicitur Pater noster.
Deinde Sacerdos dicit absolute Orationem.

Oratio

RESPICE, quaésumus, Dómine, super hanc famíliam tuam, pro qua Dóminus noster Jesus Christus non dubitávit mánibus tradi nocéntium, et crucis subíre torméntum.

Et non pronuntiatur Qui tecum nec Fidélium ánimae; sed secreto dicitur Pater noster, nec additur Deus det nobis suam pacem.

ON EPIPHANY

and throughout the octave

℣. The kings of Tharsis and of the islands shall offer presents, alleluia.

℟. The kings of Arabia and of Saba shall bring gifts, alleluia. Glory be to the Father.

At the end of the meal:

Ps. 71: Render thy judgment, O God, to the king, or Ps. 116: Praise the Lord, all ye nations as above.

ON MAUNDY THURSDAY

Begin at once with the following verse and without chant:

℣. Christ became obedient for our sake unto death.

Then **Our Father**, the entire prayer inaudibly.
Then without another word the priest makes the sign of the cross over the table. The reader omits **Jube** and **Tu autem**.

At the end of the meal:

℣. Christ became obedient for our sake unto death.

Then psalm 50 **Miserére**, page. 437.

After which (**Glory be to the Father** is omitted) the **Our Father** is said, the entire prayer inaudibly.

Then the priest says the following prayer:

Prayer

LOOK down, we beseech thee, O Lord, upon this thy family for whom our Lord Jesus Christ did not hesitate to be delivered into the hands of the wicked and to undergo the torment of the cross.

All else is omitted except that the **Our Father** is said, the entire prayer inaudibly.

IN PARASCEVE

Eodem modo fit sicut in Coena Domini, sed Versus dicitur ut infra:

℣. Christus factus est pro nobis oboédiens usque ad mortem, mortem autem crucis.

SABBATO SANCTO

Ad benedicendam (utramque) mensam dicitur:

℣. Benedícite.

℞. Benedícite.

℣. Véspere autem sábbati, quae lucéscit in prima sábbati, allelúia.

℞. Venit María Magdaléne, et áltera María, vidére sepúlcrum, allelúia.

Glória Patri. Sicut erat.

In fine repetitur:

℣. Véspere autem, ut supra, cum Glória Patri. Sicut erat.

Ps. 116: Laudáte Dóminum, omnes gentes cum Glória Patri, ut supra.

Kýrie, eléison. Christe eléison. Kýrie, eléison, et alia, ut supra in prima Benedictione.

IN DIE PASCHAE

et deinceps usque ad Coenam sequentis Sabbati exclusive, ad benedicendam mensam dicitur:

℣. Haec dies, quam fecit Dóminus, allelúia.

℞. Exsultémus, et laetémur in ea, allelúia.

Glória Patri. Sicut erat.

In fine repetitur: Haec dies cum Gloria Patri.

Ps. 117 Confitémini Dómino quóniam bonus, vel Ps. 116 Laudáte Dóminum, omnes gentes, ut supra.

ON GOOD FRIDAY

At the blessing of both meals all is said as on Maundy Thursday, except that the verse is:

℣. Christ became obedient for our sake unto death, even to the death of the Cross.

ON HOLY SATURDAY

At the blessing of both meals the following is said:

℣. Bless ye!

℟. Bless ye!

℣. And at the end of the sabbath, when it began to dawn towards the first day of the week, alleluia.

℟. Came Mary Magdalen and the other Mary to see the sepulchre, alleluia.

Glory be to the Father.

At the end of the meal repeat: ℣. And at the end of the sabbath, as above. End with: Glory be to the Father.

Ps. 116: Praise the Lord, all ye nations with Glory be to the Father, as above.

Lord, have mercy on us. Christ, have mercy on us. Lord, have mercy on us, and the rest as in the first blessing.

ON EASTER SUNDAY

and throughout the octave until the evening meal of the following Saturday exclusive, at the blessing of both meals the following is said:

℣. This day which the Lord hath made, alleluia.

℟. Let us rejoice and be glad thereon, alleluia.

Glory be to the Father.

At the end of the meal, repeat: This day, etc., with Glory be to the Father.

Ps. 117: Let us praise the Lord for He is good, or Ps. 116: Praise the Lord, all ye nations, as above.

IN ASCENSIONE DOMINI
usque ad Vigiliam Pentecostes exclusive

℣.Ascéndit Deus in jubilatióne, allelúia.
℞.Et Dóminus in voce tubae, allelúia.
Glória Patri. Sicut erat.

In fine dicitur:
℣.Ascéndens Christus in altum, allelúia.
℞.Captívam duxit captivitátem, allelúia.
Glória Patri. Sicut erat.

Ps. 46 Omnes gentes, pláudite mánibus vel Ps. 116 Laudáte
Dóminum, omnes gentes, ut supra.

IN PENTECOSTE
a Vigilia ejusdem inclusive, usque ad Coenam
sequentis Sabbati exclusive:

℣.Spíritus Dómini replévit orbem terrárum, allelúia.
℞.Et hoc quod cóntinet ómnia, sciéntiam habet vocis, allelúia.
Glória Patri. Sicut erat.

In fine dicitur:
℣.Repléti sunt omnes Spíritu Sancto, allelúia.
℞.Et coepérunt loqui, allelúia.
Glória Patri. Sicut erat.

Ps. 47 Magnus Dóminus vel Ps. 116 Laudáte Dóminum,
omnes gentes, ut supra.

ON ASCENSION
until the vigil of Pentecost exclusive

℣. God is ascended with jubilee, alleluia.

℟. And the Lord with the sound of trumpet, alleluia.

Glory be to the Father.

At the end of the meal:

℣. Christ ascending on high, alleluia.

℟. Hath lead captivity captive, alleluia.

Glory be to the Father.

Ps. 46: Clap your hands, all ye nations, or Ps. 116: Praise the Lord, all ye nations, as above.

ON PENTECOST
from the vigil inclusive until the evening meal of
the following Saturday exclusive

℣. The Spirit of the Lord hath filled the whole world, alleluia.

℟. And He Who sustaineth all things hath knowledge of man's prayer, alleluia.

Glory be to the Father.

At the end of the meal:

℣. All were filled with the Holy Spirit, alleluia.

℟. And they began to speak, alleluia.

Glory be to the Father.

Ps. 47: Great is the Lord or Ps. 116: Praise the Lord, all ye nations, as above.

INDEX GENERALIS ALPHABETICUS

Benedictiones Romano Pontifici Reservatae littera **R,** benedictiones autem Ordinario reservatae littera **r** notantur.

C

D

Vini pro infirmis Benedictio 342
Volucrum Benedictio 350

II

INDEX PSALMORUM NUMERICUS

INDEX HYMNORUM

491